Mark R.
Dana Paliliunas, M.S., BCBA

AIM

A Behavior Analytic Curriculum for
Social-Emotional Development in Children

Copyright © 2018 by Shawnee Scientific Press, LLC
All rights reserved.

3949 South Illinois Avenue
Carbondale, IL 62903

What the Experts are Saying

"In this curriculum, Dixon and Paliliunas weave together two practices, meditation and ACT, with a theoretical orientation, behavior analysis. The book is unique amongst curricula for children with social/emotional difficulties in that Dixon and Paliliunas build off contemporary research and practice to offer highly accessible stand-alone intervention modules, any of which can be implemented independent of the others. This book should be a "go to" for behavior therapists, teachers, and parents; for anyone who wants to help a child struggling with social or emotional difficulties."

-Cynthia M. Anderson, PhD, BCBA-D
Senior Vice President, Applied Behavior Analysis;
Director, National Autism Center May Institute

"A book that tries to integrate ABA and ACT is no mean feat. The fact that the authors are highly qualified and experienced behavior analysts is reassuring before one even opens the cover, because it is too easy to try to integrate ABA and ACT with language that belies basic behavioral principles. At the present time, there is no established scientific way to seamlessly combine ABA and ACT, either conceptually or in practice, and this may never come. But the authors of this volume have chosen to try and have, impressively, not thrown the behavioral baby out with the clinical bath water. No one book will have all the answers to this complex set of questions. But I am impressed that the authors try, while staying as close as possible to established behavioral principles and the types of interventions these suggest. This book is worth a thorough read for anyone interested in meeting the most significant behavioral and mental health challenges our children face."

-Yvonne Barnes-Holmes, PhD
Ghent University

"This timely and important book describes the integration of three effective and well-established interventions, mindfulness, acceptance and commitment therapy, and applied behavior analysis, into a coherent and unified treatment approach with children struggling to adapt and find meaning in an often chaotic and challenging world. It is a must read for any behavioral health professional wanting to help make a difference in these children's lives."

-Michael J. Dougher, Ph.D.,
President, Association for Behavior Analysis International

"This is the work schools have been waiting for. Couched in the science of behavior analysis, Dixon and Paliliunas' AIM Program integrates mindfulness and acceptance and commitment therapy to provide a cutting-edge, yet digestible curriculum to behavioral health providers, school personnel, and parents alike. The "dynamic context" sets the stage for altering the ways in which children relate to their challenging thoughts, feelings, and emotions as they navigate life, and I believe this text serves as a catalyst for service providers and parents to think flexibly about how we interact with and create nurturing, maximized learning environments for children, our future."

-Adam Hahs, PhD
Arizona State University

"Packed with creative methods for moving behavior change processes of known importance, this book gives practitioners the scientific and practical understanding needed to apply this modern form of behavior analysis to children. Wise and easy to use, it will make a difference in your practice."

- Steven C. Hayes, PhD
University of Nevada

"An incredible synthesis of the science of human behavior and mindfulness that demonstrates the substantial benefits of training children to closely attend to and cope with their own private events, and how that might lead to real and lasting change in individual lives and families. The potential of this program is limitless. This may represent the missing component of so many other approaches, such as Positive Behavioral Invention and Supports (PBIS) and character education. In fact, this program could easily replace most other attempts by helping parents, teachers, and other professional learn to enjoy challenging children for who they are and capture the joy in the now. As a resource for trainers of behavior analysts, this program gives a straightforward approach that helps behavior analysts incorporate mindfulness and ACT in a structured, scientifically-valid manner that is consistent with the foundational principles of behavior analysis. We might all look back in 20 years and agree that AIM is one of the most important works in all of child psychology and behavior analysis. This is a must read for anyone who works with children and is serious about changing lives."

-James Moore, PhD
University of Southern Mississippi

"AIM hits the mark! Dixon & Paliliunas have created an excellent blend of the most effective applications of modern behavioral science. The AIM Curriculum will help professionals accurately target childhood behavioral concerns with precision and compassion."

-Daniel J. Moran, Ph.D., BCBA-D
Past-President of ACBS

"Sadly, children face stress in multiple settings. Dixon and Paliliunas propose clinical behavior analysis as a solution. Providing numerous resources for adults who work with children in broad contexts, the AIM program includes brilliant daily lessons, individual and systems-level point tracking, and monitoring sheets. Combining acceptance, values, and behavioral activation, this book clearly presents creative techniques – laid out in modules, clear figures, and "try it" exercises. The wonderful emphasis on a functional approach to behavior and addressing context in multiple ways, such as varying support level and treatment depth, will be beneficial to teachers and clinicians alike. I highly recommend this book!"

-Amy R. Murrell, Ph.D.
University of North Texas
Co-author of The Joy of Parenting

"Dixon and Paliliunas' work represents an accessible and creative integration of three of the most transformative behavior change technologies of our time. In taking the perspective that our children's struggles are intertwined with the contexts in which they occur, this work empowers those who care for and work with children to change those contexts and, in doing so, bring meaningful change where once struggle was dominant. I strongly recommend this book to anyone interested in giving children - all children - the opportunity to truly thrive."

-Emily K. Sandoz, PhD
University of Louisiana at Lafayette

"This is an exceptional addition to the growing body of practical resources for the applied behavior analyst. Dixon and Paliliunas articulate the problems faced by children in simple, common sense terms. The AIM approach teaches three essential skills: moving on when thinking is getting in the way of acting, identifying what matters most, and behaving with respect to larger, later rewards instead of working for smaller, sooner ones. The book is filled with notes on conceptual developments that matter to the practitioner, activities, worksheets, a suggested reinforcement system, and a straightforward discussion of the way ACT more broadly, and AIM specifically, fit within competencies defined in the BACB 5th Edition Task List and the scope of practice of certified behavior analysts. Simply put: this is the book you've been waiting for."

-Thomas G. Szabo, PhD., BCBA-D
Florida Institute of Technology

"AIM is a cutting-edge system based on the best and latest of what behavioral science has to offer. The book is simple and practical for parents and professionals and will help youth develop meaningful behaviors that move them toward what they truly care about in life. AIM is an essential tool in the toolbox of any professional who wants to help young people live more effective, fulfilling lives, based on values, mindfulness, and compassion."

-Jonathan Tarbox, PhD, BCBA-D
University of Southern California

"In the aftermath of the decades long push towards self-esteem, it is wonderful to find an alternative that teaches children to pause, to hold thoughts and impulses lightly, to reflect on purpose and meaning, and to act in accord with what matters. We live in a feel goodist culture and our children need an alternative. With feet solidly on the ground in applied behavior analysis, Mark Dixon and Dana Paliliunas have crafted a book that offers a curriculum that fits the challenges of the modern classroom."

-Kelly G. Wilson, PhD
University of Mississippi

What the Implementers are Saying

"ACT helps me get past my problems and work for something that's important to me."
"Even my Grandma is using the Hexaflex now."
"Thank you so much! Tell all the staff that I said thanks for helping me learn acceptance!"
-*Anonymous students and graduates*

"One of my students returned to school after summer vacation and told me they learned something this summer: You can use ACT at home!"
-*Valerie Sprague, Teacher*

"When asked why ACT is important a student responded by saying ACT taught them to understand other people's words are just words. They don't define me."
-*Carson Bailey, Teacher*

"Our students often tell us they use mindfulness techniques to calm down when they are upset."
-*Kim Hood, Teacher*

"One of my students reflected, 'ACT helped me learn to accept the mistakes I've made and make better choices.'"
-*Jay Harvey, Teacher*

"ACT helps our children defuse from their problems and frustrations. A child was walking with me while his computer rebooted for a fourth time. He told me this walk was really helping him to defuse. He didn't remember what he was mad at anymore."
-*Christy Stanfill, Teacher*

"It is amazing to have witnessed the emotional growth of students coming to school with zero understanding of what a value is and watch them graduate a little healthier. I have seen in my students over the past six years of teaching ACT and living it every day are proof that life can be a little easier to live when we learn how to co-exist with our negative experiences."
-*MaryBeth Paul, Teacher*

"At our school, we all use Acceptance and Commitment Therapy to maintain a sense of well-being. It is not uncommon to hear students use the words 'accept and defuse' when a classmate is having trouble or see them respond with pride when they're recognized as a student. One young man reflected that he posted the Hexaflex on his refrigerator at home so he could refer to it when he wasn't at school. He added, 'This is what I live by.' Our teachers and aides also rely on ACT as they work with our most challenging students. This approach helps them remain mindful of what they are doing and why it is important. Using ACT each day is essential to everyone's success."
-*Mary Pearson, Principal*

Acknowledgements

Everyone has a few monumental days in their life that they will never forget. And for each of these special days, there are countless numbers of overlooked moments that become part of the past. As I was finalizing this book, the only thing standing between the final draft and printing was the task of writing the acknowledgments. It was on my to do list for some time, and was holding up the book, but I knew writing the acknowledgements signified the closure of this decade-long project. Because I have remained involved with many of the schools that adopted the AIM curriculum in test versions, for me the journey was still active and very much alive. How then was I supposed to put closure on something that wasn't really finished?

I know very clearly where this journey began, as it was one of those days I will never forget. And today, as I sat down to finally craft this final section of the book, something happened again, that unexpectedly put clear closure on this project. Minutes later, I rushed to my laptop computer in the middle of a cornfield and typed these words from the front seat of my car.

Today I watched a group of educators from the one of the first schools that adopted AIM being interviewed by a Social Worker and Behavior Analyst. This individual flew in from thousands of miles away to learn about AIM's radically novel approach to education. Rumors of AIM have been around for years. Some of the gossip was put out by me at various conferences, and by the increasing numbers of staff and visitors who starting raving about the curriculum. I too was part of the interview, mostly by chance timing, but I kept my mouth shut as I watched with amazement as these non-behaviorally, non-ACT educated staff talked beautifully about everything that AIM did for them and the countless numbers of kids that walked through their halls. As I sat there, all I could think about was how much the experience reminded me of watching a rock band being interviewed about their new hit album. The complexity of the responses, the collaborative culture, the true honest buy in to the approach, and the genuine love these staff had for each other, the program, and this book. These teachers and principal had become rock stars to me. They changed kids' lives for a living. They lived every page of this book every day, and understood it deeper than I could have ever hoped. Our interview, or shall I say their interview, goes on the list of the never forgotten moments in my life. The journey was now complete.

"*Yes, I can do it,*" were the first words I spoke to answer a question regarding if I could design a school for children struggling with social and emotional challenges. The truth was I had no idea if I really could *"do it."* However, as I walked through the classrooms of alternative placement sites for students with social-emotional challenges in a 100-mile radius outside of the St. Louis area, I figured I probably couldn't do any worse. Students were literally lying on desks sleeping, acting like future gang members, yelling at staff and getting absolutely nothing done. Surely, they weren't doing coursework, and sadly nothing therapeutic that helped addressed the reasons why they came into places like this to begin with. The path of a child out of their home school district is tragic. Children across the entire range of intelligence and academic performance are often removed from home schools, districts, and cooperative classrooms solely on the basis of extreme disruptive behaviors. Schools simply are not equipped to contain these types of kids. In theory, there is a genuine need for more specialized services and active treatment, something an alternative placement that is exclusively designed for this population of students could feasibly achieve. Yet when all these promises end up resulting in what I saw, I figured if all I had was a vague understanding of scientifically-based best practices I could do better. And that's about all I had, a half idea of what might work.

Six months later a visionary special education director and I got the keys to an empty grade school building and a list of about 25 students from eleven different school districts that were enrolling in yet another alternative to their home school. However, this time things were going to be different. The school was going to be based entirely on Acceptance and Commitment Therapy or ACT. Why? Because it was supposed to work for pretty much anything that negatively impacts the human condition. At least that's what the scientific literature claimed. I had dabbled a little with ACT in small experimental arrangements in my research laboratory at Southern Illinois University, created a drop-in clinic for weight loss, and even an intensive 8-week therapy program for treating disordered gambling. Surely, I could wing it again with ACT and figure out this school thing. That is what I assumed, until the first day when the kids showed up.

On that first school day, not only did 25 kids show up to my "plan" for intervention, but there was also a call from another amazing special education director that caught wind of what was going on. She asked if the approach could work within a typical K-12 district, yet isolated to three single classrooms across the age groups of elementary, middle, and high school. *"Of course it could,"* I told her. Again, I had no idea if it really could. As Carroll Byrant once said, *"No matter how many plans you make or how much in control you are, life is always winging it."*

There were a few things I actually did know would work for sure. First, the typical classroom level system needed to be destroyed. Placing a child on a multi-day punishment based system wasn't ever going to work. The generic behavior management plans of stoplights, clips, or points redeemable for nothing but social praise were also a waste of time. Anyone with even a vague awareness of contingency management could see the gaping holes of logic that these interventions contained. I also knew for sure that behavior problems had functional elements to them that were rarely addressed in intervention approaches. A child who engaged in problem behavior for attention could care less about "Fun Friday" movie time. Honestly, all that sort of goofiness made me wonder who was teaching this generation of educators. Surely, they had never stepped foot into an actual classroom to see how absurd these ideas were in practice.

Behavior management was an easy fix for every one of these classroom environments, and ACT was going to be the magic therapeutic bullet. That was the plan until I met the kids on that first day and realized they either didn't want to do ACT or the teachers didn't want to do ACT. Worse yet was when neither did. How was I going to convince both groups to get all touchy feely about their thoughts and emotions in front of each other at school? The solution came from my own kids who were around 5 years old at the time. My wife Ruth Anne and I had been tinkering around with running ACT processes on our kids for fun and had been trying to figure out a way for a kindergarten age child to become "mindful" or to "accept" that it was time for bed, step back from being worried, or to do their chores so they could do watch TV later that evening. The heavy psychological concepts of ACT needed to be stripped down to their basic elements and articulated in discrete learning trials, in language a child could understand. Watching our own kids get better with acceptance yielded hope the principles could be spun into a series of daily lessons anyone could deliver. What resulted was 180 days of ACT lessons for kids, and a book that framed these lessons within the context of autism intervention. Telling staff to "do ACT" was easy, but they needed materials that didn't exist. So, I made the curriculum. Everyone practiced, role played, and was held accountable. On day 45 of school, day 45 of the curriculum should be running. 180 days of school matched 180 days of lessons. Problem solved. Or so I thought.

Even my glorious creation had a predictable disappointing future similar to countless "intervention programs" for children. Staff could run it, put it away, and get back to school as usual for the remainder of the day. I even recall a teacher once telling her students in front of me, *"Here is Dr. Dixon. He is the one that makes us do that ACT thing."* It was a sign to me that I had successfully created the latest fad of social and emotional interventions, soon to be replaced with next year's non-empirically supported junk that sounded too good to be true.

What was missing from these 180 days of ACT lessons we made all the teachers do was a way to ensure the concepts of ACT lived throughout the entire school day and trickled into every interaction staff had with students. ACT couldn't be delivered for 20 minutes, put on the shelf, and forgotten about. Instead it needed to exist through the entire school day. As a result, classroom management systems needed to embed ACT behaviors into them, staff needed to talk proactively and reactively with the kids using ACT language, and also formal evaluations of ACT integrity needed to be conducted by school administration. In short, a culture of ACT needed to be created. And this culture was more important than just a daily ACT lesson. Tiny doses of mindfulness also helped bridge the gaps throughout the school day of low effort "breaks" to help students pause for moments to refocus on the present moment and things that were of value to them. In reality, it also gave staff a few moments to calm down from the stress of the day. Together, both groups benefited.

Only a few miles down the road additional districts wanted to jump on the AIM train as well. We had done amazing things with their students who had autism using the PEAK system, and some of these kids were getting to the point of needing more talk-based care. The newly developed complexities of language we established in these kids now seemed to have messed them up. They began to worry, get anxious, dwell on the past, and trip out on the future. Just like we all do. But the complexity of language could also bring them back to a better place. We just needed to get them to attend more to the present. To be mindful of the world around them. Mindfulness was so popping up everywhere. To us, it was already in place as an element of ACT. We launched AIM schoolwide using the RTI tier approach to thousands of kids. Less suspensions, bullying, and higher test scores. What else could a district want? Finally AIM began to trickle into individualized therapy for students who left these more isolated classrooms. Elements of AIM expanded to kids with autism as a supplement to traditional ABA therapy, an intervention to build task completion and persistence for children with ADHD, and even served as the foundations for summer camps offered to members of the Southern Illinois community. The AIM curriculum had matured, been field tested, and evolved in multiple variations in setting, population, and intensity. The time seemed right to bundle all the content that I had been sharing for years via email, Dropbox, or photocopy together into this book. And that is where Dana came onboard.

Dana had been a student of mine for about four years when I approached her about joining me on this book. She had completed her thesis two years earlier on ACT in her special education classroom when she was a teacher. Her intervention outcomes were predictably positive and fueled her drive for more ACT related research. Together we produced a handful of studies demonstrating the utility of ACT in classrooms and ABA clinics. As a teacher in her pre-graduate school life Dana had a perspective on ACT that most of my other students lacked. She got it as a Behavior Analyst AND as a teacher. She knew how to hook teachers with lessons that were instructive but also allowed for the creativity and individualization that every teacher craved. Furthermore, she understood the response-to-intervention movement and how different kids needed different levels of intervention intensity. In short, Dana knew how AIM could work and how it would work, if packaged in an easy to use format for both the Behavior Analyst and the teacher. With a few more tweaks, she knew how to also make it parent accessible. Perhaps it's best to think of me as the inventor and Dana the designer of the AIM curriculum you see in this book. Together we produced the pages of this text in a seamless arrangement that was far from organized when I handed her all my files, ideas, and photos from the field of AIM in action from the past decade.

There are so many people that deserve their own page of thanks for taking AIM from an idea, a list of ACT lessons, a constantly changing behavior point sheet, and a collection of mindfulness tips to this book. Their support built the system and their doubts pushed me to make this book even better than originally conceptualized. They include Cindy Penrod, Pam Tyler, Linda Kolwoski and Tina Dennman. Four heroes of mine that believed me when I said that AIM could work, and literally put many students' lives in my hands and told their staff to, *"listen to what Dixon is telling you to do."* If these four special education directors didn't rise up and demand more for their students than the status quo, AIM would be still just an idea of mine, that maybe was tinkered with in small scale thesis projects of my students. Instead AIM went big right away and impacted kids in areas of the country that had very few options for quality intervention. I was very lucky to work with every one of them. I doubt they would know exactly how important they were to my career and to this book. To them I owe everything. The next group of amazing professionals I owe gratitude to includes Jennifer Seachrist, Messina Langer, Laura Langley, Jennifer Freeman, Jen Weber, and Ali Underwood. Each of these talented administrators handed me the keys to the classrooms they managed and put their faith in me that I knew what I was doing. Maybe I shouldn't have been too surprised AIM did work, as it was really just the packaging of scientifically proven techniques in ways that anyone could understand. Nonetheless, these administrators embraced a vision excellence for their kids that was missing in the silly attempts of changed promised by off-the-shelf programs for social skills development. Additional thanks go out to the many teachers of the AIM curriculum. Initially this included a large number of school teachers of classrooms serving social and emotionally challenged children. However, it grew slowly to general education teachers, social workers, behavior analysts, my graduate students, and even parents of children with autism. There are so many of these implementers to thank, a finite list would surely leave someone out. As an alternative, let me say thank you to all of those persons on the front line that I have had the pleasure of getting to know and mentor over the past decade. You made this book a reality, and you made kids' lives better. The latter is perhaps the most important thing any educator or parent could hope for. I am humbled to have been even a tiny part of your careers. Last but not least, thanks are due to my daughters Monica and Mariah for practicing with me many of these ACT lessons, and to my wife and colleague Ruth Anne Rehfeldt for tolerating my excessive travel schedule as I attempted to embed AIM into location after location across the country.

Let me conclude with some advice for those seeking to improve the behavior of children with social and emotional challenges. Or in other words, all children. Language changes everything. Once we start talking we begin to interact with a psychological world that might be removed from the current time and place. Everything changes. The phenomena of behavior under the control of substitute stimulus functions of the actual stimulus objects is nothing new within the science of behavior. The problem lies in altering behavior under the control of such substitution. But this is only a problem for people who believe the three-termed contingency of antecedent-behavior-consequence is sufficient to produce results. If anyone thinks a simple differential reinforcement schedule is sufficient to change behavior of a verbally sophisticated human being, well they are a damn fool. Go flip through the pages of our most prestigious peer reviewed behavioral journals if you doubt me, and try find a robust research program that manages to alter behavior of verbally competent children in meaningful ways using direct acting contingencies. When you can't, go and examine what has been developing during the past twenty years when the participating factors of language and cognition are embedded within a traditional behavioral approach. When we start treating children with interventions that match their level of complexity, and with interventions that incorporate a comprehensive contemporary account of human behavior, we will have accomplished our AIM as caregivers.

Mark R Dixon
November 14, 2017
Carbondale, IL

TABLE OF CONTENTS

FOREWORD: AN INNOVATION IN SOCIAL AND EMOTIONAL EDUCATION 1

1. FOUNDATIONAL CONCEPTS 7
- Overview 7
- Mindfulness 9
- Acceptance and Commitment Therapy 20
- Applied Behavior Analysis 43
- Integrating Mindfulness, ACT, & Behavior Change Procedures 53
- Mindfulness, ACT, and Scope of Practice 55

2. THE AIM CURRICULUM 63
- Overview 63
- Development of Mindful Practice 66
- Therapeutic Reconditioning 68
- Functional Approach to Behavior 70
- Integrating Mindful Practice, ACT, & a Functional Approach to Behavior 72
- Complete Implementation Guide 77
- Partial Implementation Guide 114
- Potential Barriers 118
- Conclusion 120

3. MINDFULNESS ACTIVITIES 121

4. ACT DAILY LESSONS 131

5. DATA COLLECTION & PROGRESS MONITORING FORMS 239

6. ACT WORKSHEETS 269

7. FURTHER READINGS 357

Foreword:
An Innovation in Social and Emotional Education

One morning, when I was 14, I came down to breakfast to find my 8-year-old brother motionless in his seat at the kitchen counter, brow furrowed and eyes staring unblinkingly at an orange juice carton. When, after several minutes, this failed to abate, I asked him what he was doing. "Shhhh!" he admonished. "It says to, 'Concentrate.'" This gulf of communication between my brother and the good people at Tropicana® helps to illustrate the challenge of spreading of ideas. The company had developed a product that they would probably describe as tasty and nutritious, and had packaged it in a way that they presumably regarded as honest and attractive. What my brother took away from the packaging was not, however, what Tropicana had intended.

"Packaging" is at the heart of what makes the AIM Curriculum for promoting children's social and emotional well-being so appealing. Casual observers of science often focus on the process of discovery, and in particular those "Eureka!" moments in which the solutions to thorny problems become evident. There is no question that AIM is built from such discoveries. Its fundamentals trace to an extensive tradition of philosophical thought on how people make sense of their experiences, from extensive laboratory research on how people learn and think, and from extensive clinical research on some of the most intractable threats to human well-being. But this is not, I would argue, what makes AIM important. Far less appreciated than the process of discovery is the difficulty of disseminating solutions once they have been devised. If getting solutions into needy hands were simple, we would not have stories like that of Dr. John Snow.

During the Nineteenth Century, the major cities of Europe were rocked by repeated epidemics of cholera, which killed a sizeable proportion of those afflicted because no effective means of treating or preventing the disease was available. During an 1854 outbreak in London, in which an estimated 50,000 or more died, Physician John Snow used painstaking legwork to track the spread of the disease and showed, conclusively, how cholera was a consequence of poor sanitation. Yet the City of London waited until 1858 to begin construction of a modern sewage removal system, and not until 1866 was most of the city connected to it. During the intervening years, many Londoners continued to die, unnecessarily, of cholera. In such cases, what prevents a "better mousetrap" from drawing hordes of eager adopters to one's door? In his classic book Diffusion of Innovations, Everett M. Rogers showed that the wide adoption of a new technology depends on several factors that I will combine into the following brief list.

Ease of use: The innovation should require no specialized training to implement (think of the iPhone®), and be widely distributed at limited cost of time and effort. Sewers, once constructed, may be simple to use, but the expense and effort of building a city-wide sewer system in London would qualify as a counter-example of easy distribution.

Compatibility with existing beliefs and practices: The innovation must fit comfortably into how people live and how they understand the world to work. One reason why London was slow to embrace improved sanitation practices is that cholera had been previously understood as a scourge from God, sent to punish sinners who were deserving of its ravages. Sewer systems, by contrast, are an egalitarian solution driven by principles of biology rather than theology. To many of John Snow's day, then, Snow was "obviously" wrong.

Evidence of effectiveness: The innovation has got to work, and its benefits must be discernable to the untrained eye. Better sanitation definitely prevents cholera, but epidemics eventually end without intervention. By the time John Snow presented his findings to London officials, the 1854 epidemic was on the wane, so in effect there was no immediate problem to solve. An individual who adopted rigorous sanitation practices would not experience any detectable benefits. Even during an active epidemic not everyone becomes sick, so a person with good sanitation practices might never know for sure whether good health was a consequence of those practices.

In short, 1854 London was a perfect storm of impediments to dissemination, given which it may be remarkable that only a few years passed before systematic sewage removal began in the city (by comparison, 54 years elapsed between Surgeon James Lind's discovery that consuming citrus prevented and cured scurvy and the British Navy's routine stocking of citrus on long voyages).

All of which brings us back to AIM. As I have mentioned, AIM is the product of considerable innovation, but the advances of interest (mindfulness, Acceptance and Commitment Therapy, and Applied Behavior Analysis) have heretofore not been systematically applied to children's social and emotional development. Moreover, in the world of scholarly thought and research, innovation is simply the definition of what could work. What does work is that which is actually put to use on a wide scale. Just as no Londoner was saved from potential cholera exposure during the years leading up to the ultimate development of a sewer system, no child's social and emotional development can be enhanced until those in a position to work with them -- teachers, parents, and therapists, have access to the necessary innovations and understand how to implement them.

AIM was devised to reflect all three of the previously-mentioned features of successful innovations. Its foundation in scholarly literatures will be all but invisible to the typical adopter, but that is okay: What matters to a consumer is not so much why AIM works but that it does. And when I suggest that it works I mean the following.

AIM's ease of use: AIM's workbook format and daily lessons allow implementation without specialized training. Anyone who can read and follow instructions should be able to use the curriculum. The daily lessons are not time consuming and are designed to be compatible with the routines of school, home, and clinic.

AIM's compatibility with existing beliefs and practices: The workbook explains some of AIM's underlying ideas, but it does so by making common-sense connections with the reader's general knowledge. This is essential, because the scholarly literature that is AIM's inspiration is pretty technical and most non-scientists would find it all but impossible to read. To use AIM, one need not adopt a whole new theoretical perspective or master much in the way of new vocabulary.

AIM's evidence of effectiveness: The workbook defines what daily child outcomes contribute to overall well-being and explains how to monitor progress so that each child's advances can be objectively tracked. Every adopter will have a clear understanding of the benefits experienced by every child.

In conclusion, AIM is a rollout-ready solution to the often-expressed concern that today's world gives children with too little opportunity to develop the social and emotional competence that they will need for present happiness and later mastery of an adult environment. I am confident that teachers, parents, and therapists will find it a valuable support in their quest to develop well-balanced and adjusted children.

Thomas S. Critchfield, Ph.D.
Illinois State University

AIM
Accept. Identify. Move.

"'What day is it?' asked Pooh.
'It's today,' squeaked Piglet.
'My favorite day,' said Pooh."
-A.A. Milne

Chapter 1:
Foundational Concepts

Overview

Childhood is a time for carefree abandon, for fun, and for innocence to dominate every waking moment. When we were growing up our elders proclaimed to us about how these early years were supposedly the best years of our lives. Looking back, with the added baggage of adulthood, most days it seems that our caregivers were correct. How then did today's culture get to the point of needing therapeutic interventions for children? A variety of unfounded hypotheses exist ranging from increased rates of divorce, poverty, and poor education. Similar unfounded solutions abound such as the need for more intense discipline, medication, and school reform. Regardless of the guesses of cause or treatment, many of our population's youth carry considerable psychological disasters with them every day. Packed just as neatly as their backpack of books and pencils, these thoughts and experiences are carried around in their heads as they board the bus and walk into their classrooms. Thoughts also don't disappear when the dismissal bell rings. Instead they come home every night, just like that backpack, and continue to alter what is supposed to be a carefree life. However, if we look back carefully at our own childhood, perhaps it wasn't actually that carefree either.

If someone questions the need for this book, they should stroll through any school building in any city in this country for 15 minutes. Odds are they will be surprised to see a wide variety of social and emotional abnormalities exhibited by one or more students in that school's classrooms. Perhaps it is a child who refuses to line up to come in from recess, or maybe it is another who is tearing up their math worksheet. Behind these somewhat benign displays of rebellion, we may be shocked to know how these children are sleeping in a car every night, or needed to say goodbye to dad this morning as he was sent off to prison. Other children may be suffering from long-lasting emotional disorders brought on by histories of abuse, a newly acquired brain injury, or perhaps the side effect of autism and other related conditions. When these causes manifest themselves in difficulties in school, home, or both, parents and teachers look to the experts to provide a solution. Sometimes the difficulties are far greater than childhood protests of compliance. Physical aggression, verbal outbursts, bullying peers, property destruction, and suicide attempts have become unfortunately too common. Countless experts hypothesize, and countless solutions appear. It seems that every year brings a new approach to intervention, however the outcomes don't seem to match the promises that have been made.

AIM is the outcome of over a decade of implementation of three evidence-based practices of intervention for children. When fused together into a dynamic system, these three intervention elements have resulted in a very promising recipe of treatment for social and emotional problems in childhood. The first ingredient is mindfulness training. It is a technique that is hundreds of years old, that has moved from remote monasteries to corner coffee shops. The second ingredient is acceptance and commitment therapy, or ACT. ACT started in the 1990s as a treatment for substance abuse and has rapidly grown to address pretty much any abnormal condition us humans may find ourselves in. The last ingredient is applied behavior analysis, or ABA. This technological application of behaviorism approaches the world around us as the cause for our behavior, not our own internal wills or desires. As you begin a careful evaluation of each of these independent elements of AIM, you will most likely conclude that there is considerable overlap among them.

While at first glance, these approaches seem almost entirely distinct, they share common elements that all result in the same outcome: better living with adaptive, flexible behavior that leads to success in various environments. Mindfulness and parts of ACT seek to increase an individual's awareness of what is going on in the environment, right here, right now, rather than being caught up in a 'world' inside the mind. ABA and other parts of ACT seek to increase or decrease certain behaviors, making it more likely that he or she will exhibit behaviors that result in rewarding experiences in that environment. Together, these three elements help the individual be an aware, active participant in his or her own life. AIM summarizes this overlap with three overarching actions: Accept, Identify, and Move. First, the individual must learn to accept the current circumstances as they are. If life isn't going how he or she wants it to, there's no use in fixating, ruminating, or complaining about. Instead, this individual must be aware of his or her feelings about these events, and willing to accept them as they are, so that it becomes possible to let go of the immobility that is brought about by wishing things could be different, and become determined to find happiness and contentment in another way. Second, the individual must learn how to identify what is important to him or her, the qualities of life that bring meaning and fulfillment to this individual. Rather than focusing on what is wrong with life, this individual will work hard to clarify what they want their life to be about. Finally, the individual must be able to move, or to engage in whatever action is required to contact the experiences and rewards that will realize that meaningful life. Poor choices or avoidance of challenging situations no longer benefit this individual in any way, only commitment to desired outcomes will bring reward and fulfillment to the individual. Individuals must aim for the life that they want, and be resilient and persevering in this journey toward meaningful living.

Mindfulness

Everyone at some point or another has gotten caught up in the world created inside their minds, a world that is sometimes crafted through rose colored glasses, but is often constructed to look more like the worst-case scenario. A bad grade on a test at school, means failing the entire course. Late to a meeting with the boss, one is doomed to be demoted or fired. Forget to wish a friend 'Happy Birthday,' and that friendship is surely lost. People are constantly bombarded with thoughts and feelings about things occurring in their lives, and it is all too easy to get wrapped up in these thoughts, forgetting to interact with the reality of the situation. Perhaps the teacher will offer opportunities for extra credit, the boss will be understanding (or not even notice), or the friend will be forgiving after the belated birthday present arrives. As well, everyone has experienced that feeling of being on "autopilot," going through parts of the day without thinking about them or being aware of things going on. Most adults can relate to the experience of getting in their car and driving to work, and upon arrival thinking, *"How did I even get here!?"* Many children today can admit to missing an entire conversation with a sibling or parent because they were caught up getting to the next level on the newest video game. While everyone experiences this sort of mindlessness from time to time, when this becomes more of the norm than the exception, it can really limit the amount of time spent "really living" life. Because of this, practice in mindfulness has become a phenomenon in recent years. This practice helps people to let go of the stuff happening in their minds and get in touch with life going on all around them.

Overview

Scholars, spiritual leaders, and scientists have offered various definitions of **mindfulness**. The Merriam Webster dictionary defines mindfulness as, "the practice of maintaining a nonjudgmental state of heightened or complete awareness of one's thoughts, emotions, or experiences on a moment-to-moment basis." Jon Kabat-Zinn, a professor of medicine, scientist, and author, has crafted a definition that states, "Mindfulness is awareness that arises through paying attention, on purpose, in the present moment, non-judgmentally." Mainstream media has even chimed in their pop descriptions of the practice. For example, Mindful Magazine writes, "Mindfulness is the basic human ability to be fully present, aware of where we are and what we're doing, and not overly reactive or overwhelmed by what's going on around us," and *Psychology Today* calls it, "a state of active, open attention to the present." Regardless of which definition one embraces, the commonalities across all suggests that being mindful requires an *active commitment* to remaining in the *physical present*, with *non-judgmental awareness* of the events surrounding us. Although it is easy to talk about what it means to be mindful, it is a different experience learning how to live mindfully. Often times, people go about their day on autopilot, driving, walking, working, thinking about something else, whether it be something that happened the day before, the ongoing to-do list in their head, or the overwhelming number of upcoming events and activities in the coming weeks – one might say they are "mind full." The practice of mindfulness seeks to develop a person's ability to be fully engaged in the moment as it occurs.

Mind Full *or* Mindful?

The concept of mindfulness can be traced back to the word *sati* in Pali, the primary language used in Buddhist psychology over two thousand years ago, which refers to awareness, attention, and remembering. Mindfulness is one of the central concepts of the Buddhist tradition; the practice of mindfulness is developed in order to both ameliorate human suffering and aid in the path toward enlightenment. Although these practices have been prevalent in Eastern cultures for thousands of years, the western world awoke to the potential value of mindfulness-based interventions in the 1950s, when soldiers who had returned to United States after World War II reported learning about the use of these techniques, which were then utilized by researchers at the University of Massachusetts Medical Hospital to treat terminally ill patients. Later on, other scientists began to study the effects of mindfulness as a treatment, including Jon Kabat-Zinn, who is often credited with popularizing mindfulness in western society. He initiated a research program designed to treat chronically ill patients in the 1970s. This work led to the development of Mindfulness-Based Stress Reduction (MBSR) and the rise of techniques using mindfulness in the treatment of many common ailments, including anxiety, cancer, chronic pain, diabetes, depression, and more. This early research ignited the mindfulness fire that has been spreading ever since.

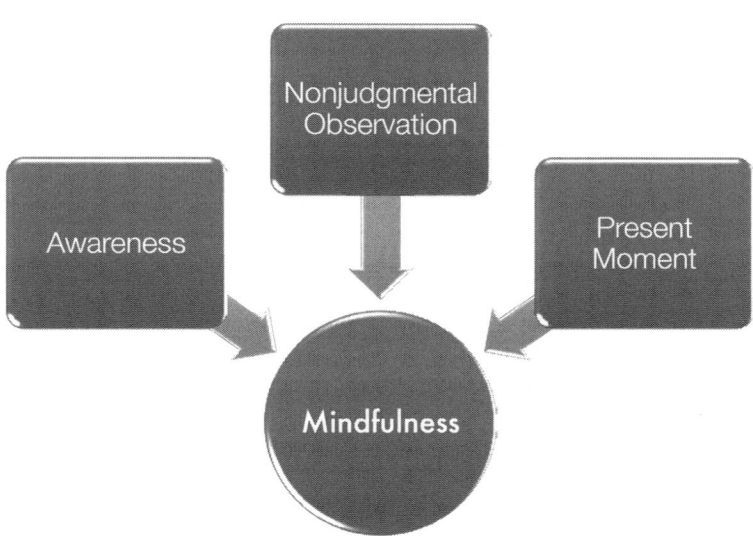

Today, mindfulness has reached the mainstream, and trickled into newly developed strip mall yoga studios across the country. In 2014, an issue of *Time Magazine* highlighted the popularity of the approach, and in 2016, that same feature was reprinted as a stand-alone special issue of *Time*. One only needs to travel to the local coffee shop or organic food store to see a multitude of events of mindfulness in their community, from mindfulness classes, to book advertisements, and live seminars. In addition to mainstream popularity, the scientific community has also chased this mindfulness craze. According to the American Mindfulness Research Association, in 1990, there were 3 peer-reviewed publications on the topic, which grew to 10 in 2000, and increase exponentially to over 600 publications in 2016. Even the federal government of the United States has created funding initiatives to further explore the utility of mindfulness in contexts as diverse as teaching preschool students to be mindful and using mindfulness as a smoking cessation treatment.

Skeptics of the mindfulness approach often note its vague independent variable, the loosely defined practices of implementation, and its wide-sweeping effects as potential confounds to its effective use and credibility. Regardless of the depth of one's belief that mindfulness can impact those who practice it, scientific research has shown that mindfulness-based interventions improve physical health, increase pre-frontal cortex activation, improve self-control, reduce immune system weakness, and improve regulation of behavior. Although the philosophical debate continues as to what mindfulness really "is", the practical utility of mindfulness-based intervention is well documented, and ripe to apply across wide ranging populations.

Approaches to Mindfulness

Mindfulness embodies many different approaches of practice, from the common view of mindfulness as meditation practice to incorporating mindfulness into everyday life. Those formal approaches to mindfulness are focused on the individual developing the awareness and ability to observe his or her inner experiences, both in terms of mind and body. Individuals may develop a strict meditation regimen, practicing for a specified length of time at a certain time every day, increasing their stamina for mindfulness over time. Certain groups with specific meditation practices may even offer week-long (or longer) meditation retreats, where individuals are taught mindfulness techniques and devote time to developing their own practice. Less formal mindfulness practices focus on developing present moment awareness and nonjudgmental observation within the context of day to day life. This way of approaching mindful practice emphasizes the individual's attention to the individual moments of the day. Rather than fostering a deeper understanding of one's self or life itself during daily activities such as washing dishes, driving to work, or eating dinner, this kind of mindful awareness cultivates present moment awareness of those moments – awareness of one's thoughts, feelings, and sensations as they are loading the dishwasher, sitting in traffic, or eating a burger. This kind of mindfulness will occur throughout the day from moment to moment, rather than during dedicated times. Whether one is practicing mindfulness through formal or informal means, the same core components remain the same. Further, these two kinds of mindful practices are not mutually exclusive; both formal and informal methods of being mindful can be incorporating into a person's daily life.

Meditative practices are often broken down into two categories: concentration meditation and mindfulness meditation. The author and clinical psychologist Christopher K. Germer speaks of an analogy for these two methods of meditating, comparing concentration to a laser light beam and mindfulness to a searchlight. Concentration meditation centers on an object of attention (anything from a burning candle to a leaf on the ground to the memory of a loved one), developing unattached, restrained, and tranquil awareness of that object. Conversely, mindfulness meditation practices bring awareness to the larger environment in which the person is in, fostering the individual's ability to discern his or her own thoughts, feelings, and sensations as they arise and as their attention shifts from one thing in the environment or in their thoughts to another over time. Again, a person can practice both methods of mindful practice on a day to day basis, in fact, the two can supplement one another, teaching the individual to direct their attention in a nonjudgmental way. Adaptations of mindfulness practice are commonplace today, making it accessible to every person, young or old, so that they can experience the benefits of mindful living.

Mindfulness in Children

Adults are not alone in their tendency to get caught up in their minds, losing touch with the present moment as it's occurring; children are just as likely to be lost in thought, contacting the world in their mind rather than the world around them, whether they are thinking about future events, things they wish they could be doing, or even just lost in imagination. Sometimes it's a lot easier to be lost in thought than dealing with the present moment, and sometimes getting lost in thought can detract from experiences in the present moment. Either way, the "noise" inside a child's mind can be psychologically dense, and if that noise dominates their behavior, it can lead to undesirable outcomes. For example, imagine a child with a difficult home life, whose father frequently calls him "stupid" or "retarded" because he has difficulty learning new material at school. Because that name-calling is related to things that happen at school, it may be difficult for the child to let go of that in his mind when he is at school. Each time he is in a certain class, he may get caught up in thoughts such as, "I'm so stupid, I'm never going to learn this," or "Dad's right, I am slow," and rather than working through difficult material, he may shut down, refuse to participate, and even act out in the classroom. If this child were able to learn how to leave that "psychological noise" outside of school, and be mindful in school, interacting with the teachers, students, and activities there that are designed to support his development without judgment, he may have an entirely different educational experience, and the ability to demonstrate resiliency when faced with negativity at home.

The idea of applying mindfulness with children was a natural extension of the initial work with adult populations, which at the beginning was focused on infusing mindfulness practices within the school day. One early demonstration of mindfulness being used in United States public schools occurred in San Francisco, where they expanded the day to include thirty minutes of meditation, and found both improved academic performance and a decrease in behavior problems. In addition, both students and teachers reported an increase in the overall well-being of students, who were feeling calmer and less angry. These kinds of outcomes are desirable in every school throughout the US and abroad. Because of this, a variety of similar programs have been documented, from training for teachers to strict meditation protocols, many of which have produced positive results for students, including greater attention and focus, empathy and compassion, emotional- and self- regulation, and increased attendance and grades.

Scientists have examined the effect of mindfulness training with various groups of children in school settings. One area of research is with children who have clinical diagnoses such as anxiety, ADHD, and autism. A recent study found that teaching a mindful meditation exercise to adolescents with high-functioning autism resulted in a decrease in the number of aggressive incidents on a daily basis, from as many as six incidents in the baseline conditions to zero at follow up. Another study, compared performance on various attention-based tasks (for example, crossword puzzles) between a group of children, including those with ADHD, exposed to mindfulness training and those in a control group experiencing standard summer school curriculum. These results demonstrated that following the training, the mindfulness group demonstrated greater performance on many of those sustained attention tasks than the control group. Research done in the school setting has revealed numerous benefits of mindfulness for students in grades K-12. One randomized control trial with first to third grade students examined an intervention incorporating sitting, movement, and body scan meditations and relaxation exercises, finding that the students who completed the program demonstrated less test anxiety and improved attention and social skills. Another study with elementary school children who were taught mindful awareness practices resulted in increases in behavioral regulation and executive function as reported by the students' parents and teachers. These are just a few of many studies which reveal the positive outcomes for children with and without disabilities who complete mindfulness-based interventions as treatment or part of a school curriculum.

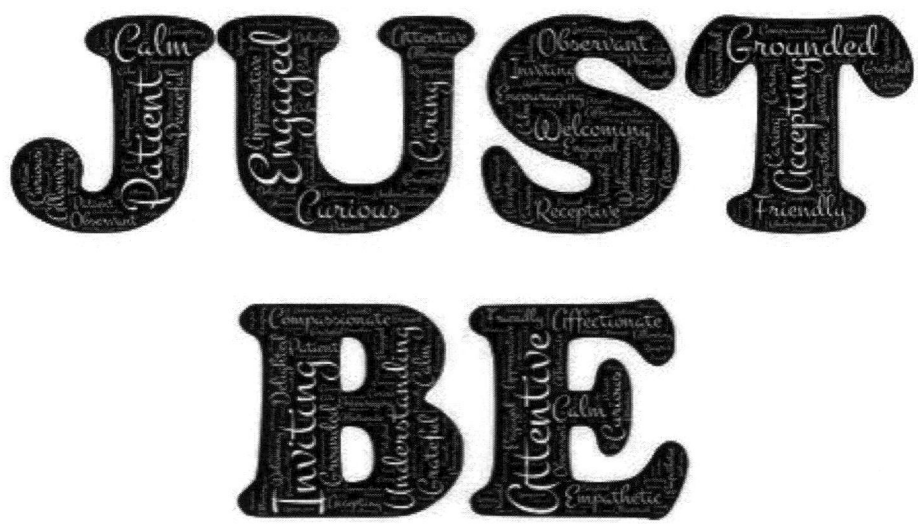

Mindfulness interventions have trickled from the school to home and clinic settings, where the general principles have remained the same, yet differed in their method of delivery. Parent-led sessions, smartphone apps, television shows, and even board games have recently emerged as the mindfulness craze continues to evolve. A quick search on Amazon.com reveals self-help guides, children's books, card games, videos, apps with titles such as "Calm," "Higher Consciousness," and "Headspace," not to mention the plethora of mindful coloring books for children, teens, and adults. All of these share a commonality: make mindfulness easy, accessible, and fun.

Although scientists have documented the positive outcomes associated with mindfulness for children, adapting these techniques and presenting them effectively to a younger population requires special attention. Many children, particularly those who could benefit most from mindfulness training, do not seem readily able to sit in one spot, engaging in intentional awareness of the moment. One of the challenges that exist for children exposed to such interventions is providing them with a reason to "buy in" to the often-difficult task of remaining in the present. Furthermore, when the present is not ideal for a child, it is understandable that they may want to let their mind drift elsewhere. The good news is, children can learn to be mindful, perhaps even more so than adults.

Given that many children who are targeted for mindfulness-based interventions are diagnosed with a learning or behavioral disability, implementers may struggle communicating the complex concepts of what it is to be mindful to a child of that capacity. Although applying mindful interventions with children may present some additional barriers, the potential outcomes of teaching the skill of being mindful, far outweighs the challenge. Not only do these interventions have immediate effects in the present, researchers have begun to discuss the potential utility of mindfulness practice as a preventative measure, and future research may likely conclude that people who develop mindfulness skills at a young age may be less likely to develop psychological health issues in the future. The incorporation of mindfulness practices into a larger framework using contemporary approaches to psychological health may provide a foundation for developing interventions that are effective for every child's well-being.

Nevertheless, figuring out how to build these skills of mindful living with children presents challenges. Parents and practitioners must learn not only the concepts of mindfulness, how to engage in mindfulness practice themselves, and how to communicate these techniques to children, they must learn how to help the child contact the positive outcomes of mindfulness. They must learn how to transform "sitting quietly in a room" into a meaningful experience of interacting with the present moment in new and exciting ways that results in some awesome outcome, such as praise for success in school, encountering more friendships, or making the winning shot during a basketball game.

There are many ways to achieve this, but it almost certainly requires two things: first, bring mindfulness to life and second, creating a connection between mindful practice and success in other areas. Mindfulness is much more than sitting still and quiet. Although meditation is one form of mindful practice, children may initially appreciate more sensory-focused mindfulness experiences, such as moving, noticing, listening, and even eating in a mindful manner.

Once a child has begun to engage in mindful behaviors and understands the effects that it has on his or her mind and body, it is time to incorporate it into everyday events. When a difficult assignment comes up, or they are focused on anger at a sibling for taking a toy, these events become opportunities to experience mindfulness in the moment, with some encourage, a child can learn to apply those same skills from mindfulness activities to challenging events in daily life. Now, the use of mindful breathing makes sense to them as a practice when feeling frustrated or distracted, instead of using an instruction to take "deep breaths" as almost a warning that if the child doesn't calm down, he or she will get into trouble! Educators and therapists can create a context for children that makes mindful behavior useful and worth the effort. They can help them to make the connection between practicing mindfulness and feeling calm, collected, and connected to the world around them.

Then it is time to help them see the long-term effects of regular mindful practice. Not only can he or she be more aware and present in the moment, the cumulative effects of doing so can lead to some pretty major changes in their lives! Perhaps he or she doesn't get as angry or overreact when things don't go their way, or the child becomes better at making free throws under pressure. Whatever the outcome, the child can make the link between it and mindful behavior. We can remind them that mindfulness helped them in an important way. And, perhaps most importantly, educators, parents, and families can praise them for practicing mindfulness, even though it can be hard or boring at times. Developing mindfulness in children draws parallels with teaching any other skill, it involves practice, prompting, and praise.

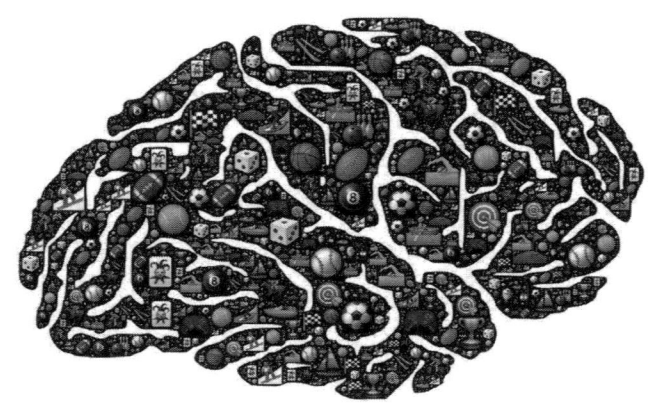

Motivation for Mindfulness

Recall Kabat-Zinn's definition, "Mindfulness is awareness that arises through paying attention, on purpose, in the present moment, non-judgmentally." When really considering each of those components and their implications, an overwhelming feeling can arise. Paying attention can be a challenge enough for most people, not to mention children who have additional challenges in this area. Add to that the qualification of "non-judgment," and the whole attempt may seem inconceivable. It's hard enough to take it easy on ourselves sometimes, but to experience thoughts and feelings without labelling them "good" or "bad," "productive" or "unhelpful," "positive" or "negative," is kind of hard to imagine. Many people, especially children, may not be able to grasp the concept of what it means, and more importantly, what it feels like, to be mindful. But, like any healthy habit, such as eating well, exercising, or getting enough sleep, the results of mindfulness practice are cumulative, and the only way to begin is to begin. Take small steps, and build the skill and the stamina needed for long-term mindful meditation practices. Just like that surprise glance looking toned in the mirror after weeks of sticking with an exercise routine, after regular practice in mindfulness, one may just find him or herself surprised at how their body feels more relaxed or how they are less reactive one day when a particularly challenging student or client tests your patience. It pays off over time. The same thing happens for children too, maybe when they notice themselves being able to remember to raise their hands before yelling out in class or taking a deep breath before an aggressive reaction to a peer's comment. These successes are the reason to commit to a daily mindfulness habit, even if it starts out small.

Adding mindfulness to the "to-do" list is not the goal. And "motivation" is not the most important thing. Action is.

The goal is to engage in a practice of mindful living that improves the everyday experience. It is to begin a habit that evolves into a way of life. If someone need to begrudgingly take a mindful minute at the beginning of the work or school day sometimes, that is OK. It is OK to feel like they want to "check-out" sometimes instead of living in the moment. Like any other thought, a mindful person would observe this feeling without judgment, and accept that it is only human to feel this way. That IS being mindful. Children are likely to report a lot of "failure" when they are first engaged in these practices, making statements such as "I didn't notice any thoughts." It is important, rather than to challenge these statements and allow them to rule the child's mind, to praise their awareness, and to foster that feeling of acceptance, and to encourage them to do try it again the next time. Like any long-term habit or lifestyle change, building mindfulness practice, for adults and children alike, requires patience, dedication, and self-compassion.

A trend may have become apparent at this point: in addition to awareness, acceptance and commitment are components of actually changing behavior. This is true in the development of mindfulness practice, as it is in many other areas of life. While developing mindfulness skills, there will be setbacks and challenges. Being open to those experiences and willing to try again the next day are the key. Life is no different. There are setbacks, challenges, barriers, and opponents that make life hard sometimes. Even the most mindful person will encounter things in his or her life that they want to change or improve. Mindful practice helps increase awareness of these desires and needs. Being accepting of these desires and needs and being capable of the commitment to choosing one's behavior can lead to those changes. Dedication to mindfulness, acceptance, and commitment can help individuals transform interactions with their own mind and the world around them. While this sounds difficult, it is something children can begin to learn from when they are very young.

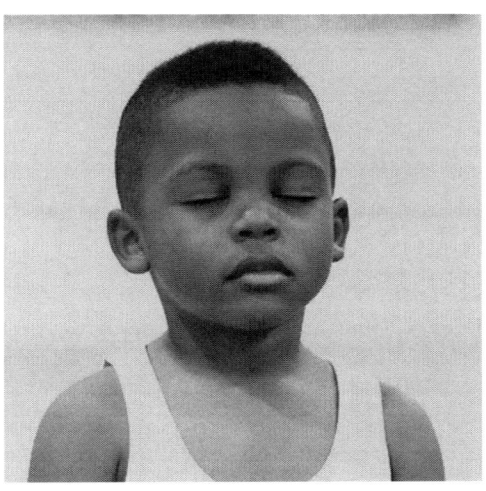

Acceptance and Commitment Therapy

People have the tendency to get trapped in their heads and miss out on life. Everyone has experienced that fallback to autopilot, that mindlessness that leads to feeling disconnected from the things going on right there in the moment. That is not the only challenge that humans who can think and act in such complex ways face. Life is hard. People frequently experience hardships, setbacks and just generally unpleasant events. People have all been in situations that brought them down or brought out the worst in themselves. Whether it is an argument with a loved one, an anxiety-provoking work environment, struggles with money, or some other distressing event, everyone has been there. Take a moment to think of one of the distressing events from personal experience. How did that moment feel? Return back to those feelings, the thoughts that ran through the mind, and what strategies were used to 'fix' it. Many will come up with the same response – they tried to fix it in some way or another. Most have tried to exert control over the situation, because they just HAD to make it better, they just HAD to be happy like everyone else, or they just HAD to stop those painful thoughts and feeling from occurring.

People have the tendency to try to fix bad situations because they are taught from the time they are young to believe that there is some destination in life that is happiness. Just as soon as a person is healthy enough, and has good enough friends and family, and a good job that pays enough money, he or she will be happy. The trouble with this view of the world is that no one will ever get there. People are never healthy or wealthy enough. As soon as they've managed to make one part of life ideal, a problem arises in another. This leads to a continuous cycle of fruitless problem solving, attempts to control the things one cannot, and a constant feeling of missing out – all of which add more feelings of distress to an already distressing situation. While this seems bleak, there is a way out. Scientists have spent years developing a technique that sidesteps that cycle of psychological distress. A way for people to live through distressing events without distress about being distressed.

Overview

Acceptance and Commitment Therapy, or ACT, originated at the University of Nevada in the late 1980s and early 1990s, as a result of work led by Dr. Steven Hayes. Dr. Hayes, a professor and psychologist, began his career researching human language and cognition, which, after grappling with his own experiences of anxiety, panic, and psychological distress, quickly expanded his knowledge of human language to the easing of human suffering. ACT rose out of a sea of countless cognitive behavior therapy interventions as an interesting alternative that focused on acceptance of one's own personal struggles, rather than the typical focus on avoidance of such struggles. For example, if a person presented with an intense fear of elevators, instead of trying to find ways to decrease the avoidance of elevators, an ACT approach would focus on developing the individual's acceptance of the distressful feelings associated with elevators, the realization that it most likely would never go away, and the resolution to find a way to live with the discomfort, while still riding elevators when needed. ACT also differs from other approaches, such as flooding, which assumes that literal exposure to an event will eliminate fear of it, and victimization, which assumes that the fear is part of who the person is, and that fear will never be surmountable.

The goal of ACT can be summarized as an individual learning to accept, or become willing to experience unpleasant feelings, without overreacting to them or trying to avoid situations that occasion them, while constantly living a life of commitment to the pursuit of valued outcomes, and to the experiences in life that are most important to them. The person no longer tries to control or eliminate those negative thoughts and feelings, or let them impede upon his or her ability to engage in the life they want. Before becoming familiar with ACT and its techniques, it is important to be aware of the theoretical basis for this approach and its relationship to a scientific understanding of human behavior.

ACT is rooted in **Relational Frame Theory (RFT)**, an empirical foundation explaining how humans learn to relate to the world around them, and its goal is to change the way we interact with our own verbal behavior, not change the content of it. What many people may not realize is that ACT is a therapeutic offshoot of this behavior analytic account of language. In order to understand how ACT works, it is important to understand the basic premises of RFT and they relate back to the therapeutic process. RFT is a psychological account of human language and cognition. Rather than analyzing the form and structure of language, as many theories of language, RFT extends upon the 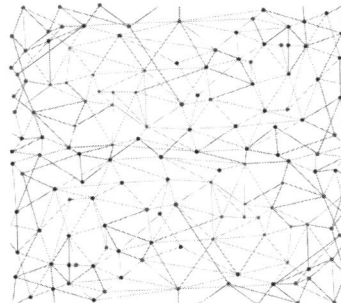 behavioral approach to understanding language (or verbal behavior), analyzing the development and use of language functionally. In other words, RFT focuses on *how* and *why* language occurs, rather than the way it looks or sounds. While RFT is thorough and complex, there are a few main concepts that are important to understand: relational framing, derived relational responding, and transformation of stimulus function.

Relational framing simply refers to the ability to respond to relations between stimuli in the environment. People learn to discriminate between the different relationships among stimuli. For example, people are able to learn that the spoken word "lemon" represents a round, yellow fruit. That's already relating two things: 1) the sound "lemon" and 2) the actual fruit. When a person first tastes a lemon, he or she experiences the sour feeling, and now can respond to seeing the fruit as well as hearing the word "lemon" by saying, thinking, or psychologically experiencing "sour." It does not stop there. He or she learns to relate this "lemon" in many different ways. They may learn that it is "more sour" than an orange, or maybe that it tastes "worse than" an apple, that it is "part of" the citrus family, or that it is "healthier than" sugar to put in tea every morning. People can relate stimuli in an infinite number of ways, along many different dimensions, such as sameness, difference, opposition, categories, perspectives, comparison, time, and so on. These relations are all connected by their shared stimuli, and are often represented in terms of 'relational networks,' or diagrams that look like word webs. A portion of the relations that people make are directly taught and reinforced, however, for most, the majority of the relations we make every day are not explicitly taught or learned, instead they are derived.

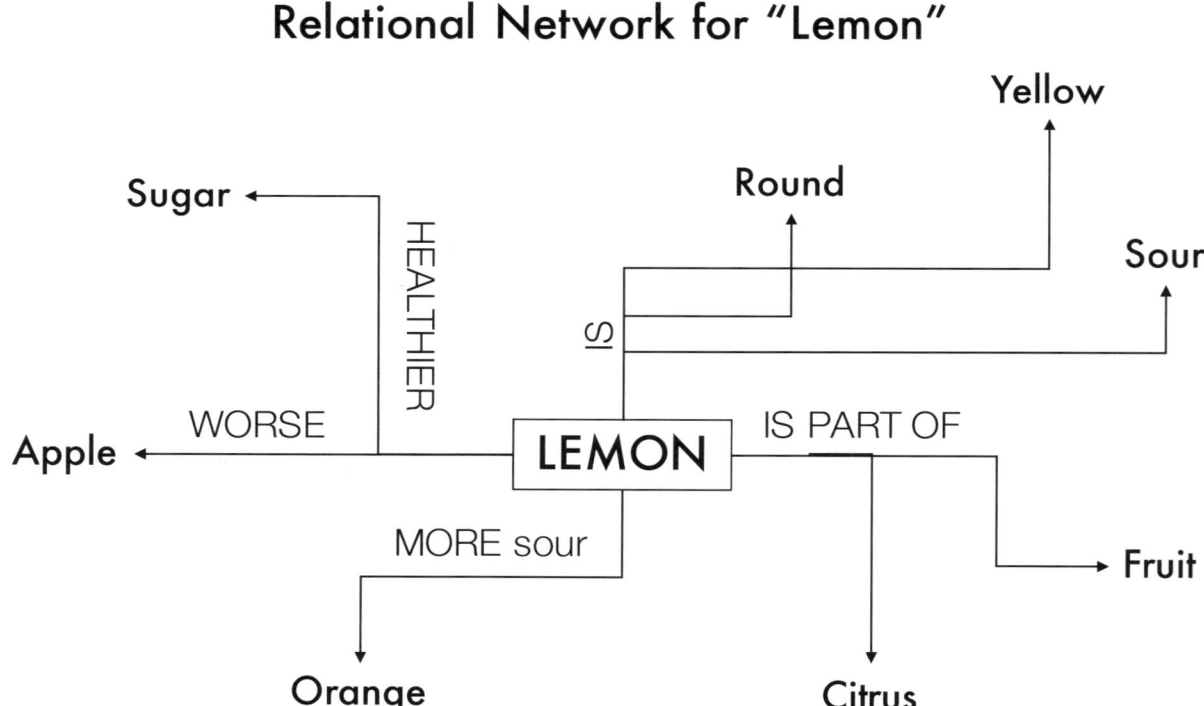

Relational Network for "Lemon"

When people engage in inferential relating without having been directly taught to do so, it is called **derived relational responding**. Individuals with more advanced language abilities are able to relate concepts together that have not been directly reinforced. They are able to get information from one experience or event, apply it to other events, and respond accordingly. For example, imagine a middle schooler who is a huge fan of *Star Wars* and starting her first year in a new school. She may feel overwhelmed and nervous about making new friends, not sure if she'll fit in at this new place. Then, she sees a girl in the back of one of her classes wearing a *Return of the Jedi* t-shirt. Instantly, she feels relief. She has a conversation starter. This is someone that could be her friend. She was able to derive, based on untrained relations, that this may be an approachable person. Most language is derived, not directly taught, and as a result, can be altered via indirect experience, which is often done by creating new relations among stimuli, for better or worse.

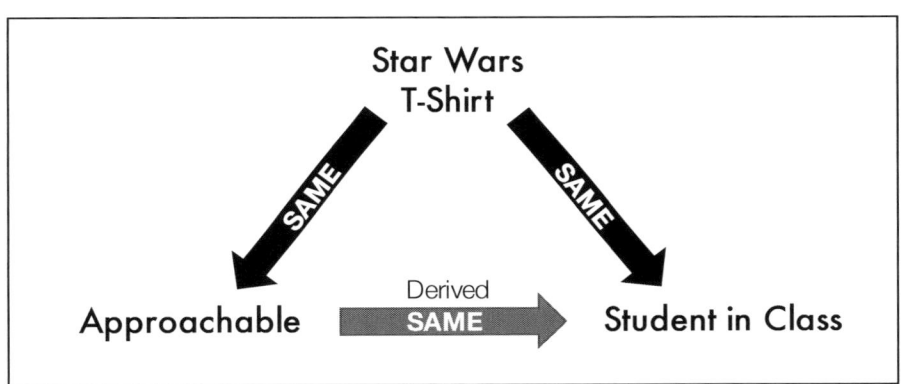

The third important concept is **transformation of stimulus function**, which is an ongoing process that occurs when people make these trained or untrained relations among stimuli. When they relate two (or more) stimuli together, the functions of one stimulus change the functions of another stimulus. For example, think back to the hardest teacher in school for the most challenging subject. For this example, imagine a math teacher. In fifth grade, a boy had this terribly challenging math teacher, Mrs. Griswold, and struggled the whole year through. The next year, he sees the name of his new math teacher, and someone tells him, *"Oh man, Mr. Burns is SO MUCH WORSE than Mrs. Griswold!"* He will walk into that math class petrified, nervous, and ready to hate that teacher and fail the class. The functions of "Mrs. Griswold" transformed the function of "Mr. Burns" with the relation "worse than." These transformations of function occur all the time, and can contribute to a lot of the psychological suffering people experience on a daily basis.

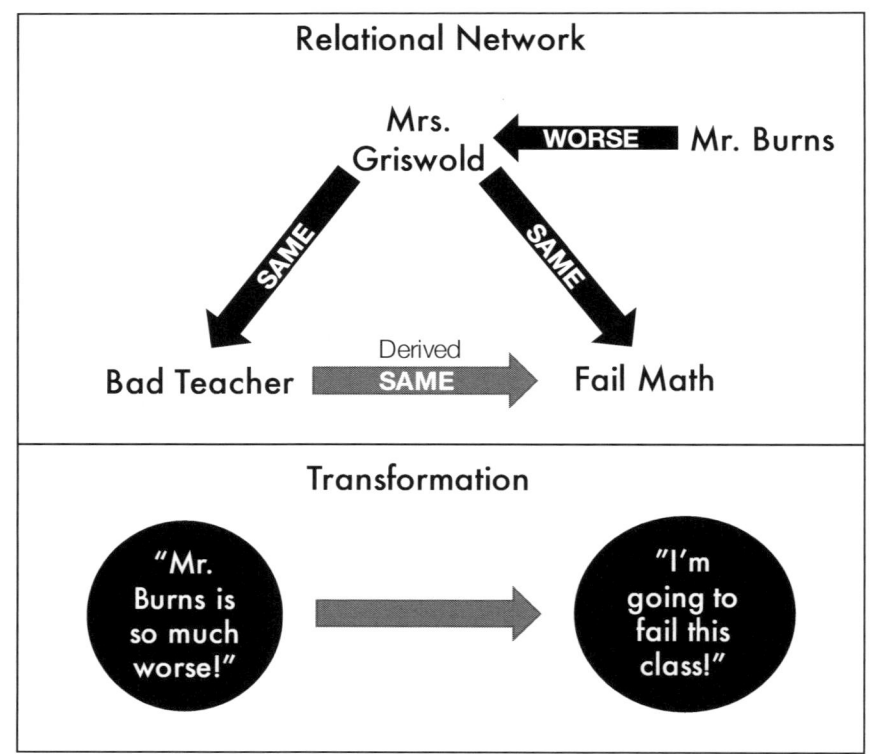

All of these language processes can occur with both arbitrary and non-arbitrary properties of stimuli. Not only can people relate stimuli based on non-arbitrary, or physical properties such as size, shape, weight, and so on, they can do so with arbitrary properties as well. For example, if someone say, an "URB" is the same as Hercules and an "ISP" is the same as an ant, and then says, "You're as strong as an URB" or "You're as strong as an ISP," you know in which case you should be flattered or embarrassed, despite those made up words having any physical relationship to strong or weak stimuli. The social, verbal community gives meaning to stimuli, and people are able to respond to them accordingly. Altogether, these processes comprise what in RFT is referred to as *arbitrarily applicable derived relational responding* – the ability to respond to relations between physical or non-physical stimulus properties, whether taught or untaught, resulting in changes in the functions (or meaning) of those stimuli.

Without a repertoire of robust complex language, talk-based interventions and therapies such as ACT would not be relevant to the individual. Further, the metaphors and experiential exercises folded into ACT would not be useful. The individual needs the ability to relate – and to develop relational networks that *create meaning* between words, events, and referents. Consider the diagram below, which breaks down a statement that may be made in the course of therapy or intervention, *"Don't be scared of dogs."* That simple phrase requires the individual be able to respond to complex relations. For example, he or she must understand that "don't be scared" refers to the opposite behavior of scared, that "scared" represents a collection of responses, both public and private, and that "dog" represents not only the image of a dog, but a set of memories related to why you are afraid of the dog.

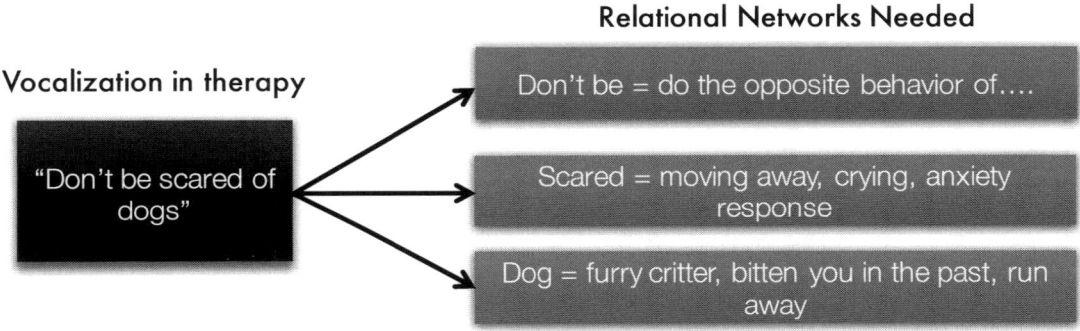

The purpose of ACT is to alter the individual's responses to frames (and their context) to produce adaptive, flexible behavior. Metaphors are an important component in ACT, and that ability to engage in more complex language is necessary, as the individual needs to be able to both understand the "point" of the metaphor, and relate it to events in their own life. The individual must be able to create relational networks that create MEANING between words, events, and their references. So, in addition to the relational networks, the individual, when presented with the statement, "Avoiding dogs is like avoiding sand in the desert," must be able to understand that "avoiding dogs" means altering their life behaviors, "is like" means that the situations are equivalent, and "avoiding sand in the desert" is something that is impossible to do. If the implementer is able to firmly establish all of the relational networks described here, and the individual is able to derive meaning among them, then the ACT metaphor become consequential. In other words, the function of the metaphor then transforms the stimulus function, meaning they reduce avoidance of dogs.

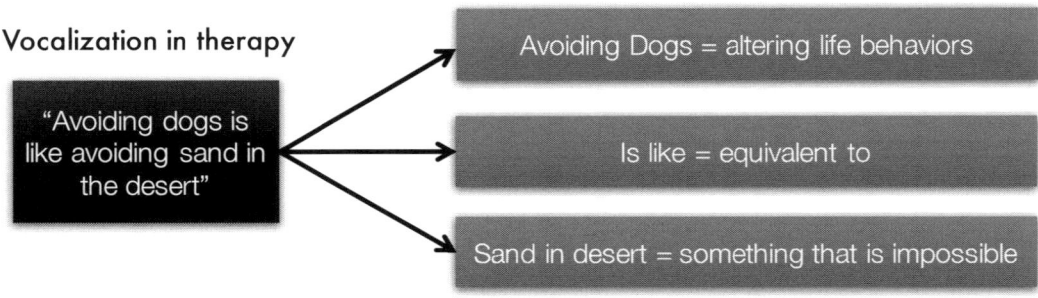

ACT, maintaining its focus on the interaction between language and suffering, incorporates traditional techniques from behavior therapy and contemporary scientific approaches to the development of mindfulness to alleviate distress and improve quality of life. The ACT approach focuses on a changing a set of behaviors, collectively referred to as **psychological inflexibility**. These behaviors include:

» Experiential avoidance, or a person's attempts to avoid or control uncomfortable or unpleasant experiences, both internal, such as thoughts or feelings, and external, such as certain events or interactions.

» Cognitive fusion, or the static belief that the content of your thoughts is literal.

» Dominance of living in the past or future, or a person being distracted by ruminating on thoughts regarding things that have happened or might happen.

» Attached to the "conceptualized self," or responding to a view of yourself as no more than a collection verbal descriptions and past behaviors.

» Lack of values clarity, or a lack of personal understanding of what matters to you and the sources of reinforcement in your own life.

» Impulsive or maladaptive behavior patterns that prohibit you from contacting your valued reinforcers.

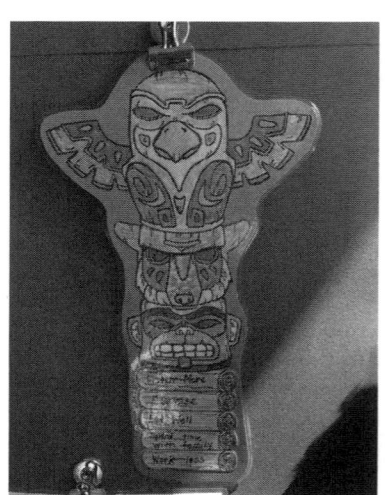

In order to reduce the problems that result from these behaviors, the ACT approach focuses on the development of what is called **psychological flexibility**, which is defined by ACT's developers as the *ability to contact the present moment more fully as a conscious human being, and to change or persist in behavior when doing so serves valued ends*. In other words, psychological flexibility refers to a person's ability to adapt his or her behavior depending on the present environment in order to more successfully obtain life's reinforcers. In order to develop this flexibility, ACT focuses on a set of behaviors, called core processes, that include: present moment awareness, acceptance, defusion, self-as-context, values, and committed actions, all of which directly target the maladaptive components of psychological inflexibility. The overarching goal of ACT can be summarized in the following question: *"In this moment, are you - not the stories you tell yourself - but you, ready to show up to what you are experiencing without defenses, move your life in a direction you value, and when you find yourself off-path, gently return to the direction you value?"*

With hundreds of international peer-reviewed scientific articles examining the effects of the therapy in application with a variety of populations, the empirical basis for ACT is well-developed. Large scale research studies have demonstrated the effectiveness of ACT in the context of general mental health, individuals with addictions, depression, psychosis, anxiety disorders, and other psychological health conditions, compared to both control groups and standard treatments. Since 2010, the U.S. Department of Health and Human Services has included ACT in its National Registry of Evidence-Based Programs and Practices due to the research supporting its efficacy, and since then, the amount of research evaluating ACT has grown considerably.

Research regarding ACT has examined both the processes through which it effects individual's behavior, as well as the effectiveness of the treatment for various populations. Dr. Hayes, and colleagues, examined the progress of ACT over time and describe the strategy used to develop an empirical basis for it. First, philosophical assumptions were clearly defined, and a basic account of complex human behavior was organized into RFT, from which a model of understanding psychological problems and intervention was developed (psychological flexibility and inflexibility). Research related to developing and testing the techniques used within the core processes has been conducted related to each part of the psychological flexibility model. For example, researchers have found that techniques related to ACT's core processes have resulted in a decrease in individuals' self-reports of psychological distress as well as willingness to engage in and persist in undesired or unpleasant tasks. Research has revealed that techniques designed to increase psychological flexibility may decrease the control of stress/unpleasant thoughts over behavior, allowing individuals to respond in more adaptive, flexible ways over in aversive situations. Other studies have found a relationship between psychological inflexibility and depression, as well as behavioral rigidity.

While the research base regarding these techniques and processes continues to accumulate, scientists have also studied the efficacy of ACT across a broad range of areas. This includes studying its effectiveness across different populations, for example chronic pain patients, individuals with diabetes, cancer patients, individuals with trichotillomania, individuals with obsessive-compulsive disorder, those who demonstrate racial prejudice, and individuals managing weight gain, among many others. This breadth of effectiveness research demonstrates the applicability of ACT across diagnoses and presenting problems. Also, ACT research has examined its effectiveness across method of delivery, including brief intervention, computer-based intervention, and self-help books. ACT research also has been completed in various settings, such as organizations, schools, communities, inpatient clinics, outpatient clinics, and workplaces. ACT research continues to venture into more challenging areas, from children with intellectual disabilities, to those with brain injuries, young children, and prisoners, as well as various societal areas such as prevention, environmental issues, and compassion. While the research regarding ACT already appears vast and provides a substantial empirical basis for its effectiveness, scientists continue to evaluate it in novel, practical contexts, focusing on long-term scientific progress and continuous development and refinement of the treatment.

ACT and Mindfulness

It may be easy to see the overlap between acceptance and mindfulness. In fact, one might consider the behavior of accepting the very means by which people are able to sustain themselves in the present moment. Recall that the main components of mindfulness include awareness of the present moment and nonjudgmental observation. Acceptance relates directly to the element of non-judgment in mindfulness, developing a sense of willingness to experience things as they occur, for better or for worse, without attempts to change them. In ACT, and in mindfulness practice, this is necessary before one is able to change his or her behavior for the better.

Put simply, ACT includes mindfulness practice by way of the development of some of its core processes, however this is only part of the story of ACT intervention. ACT combines the development of mindful behavior with traditional behavior therapy techniques such as contingency management, goal setting, and reinforcement. The six **core processes** of ACT are often presented visually in a diagram called the **hexaflex**, depicted here. Conceptually, these ACT core processes can be divided into two primary groups: the **mindful core**, focused on the reduction of language and thought interference in adaptive, flexible behavior, and the **reinforcer core**, focused on the development of those adaptive, flexible behavior patterns that result in a greater amount of reinforcement for the individual.

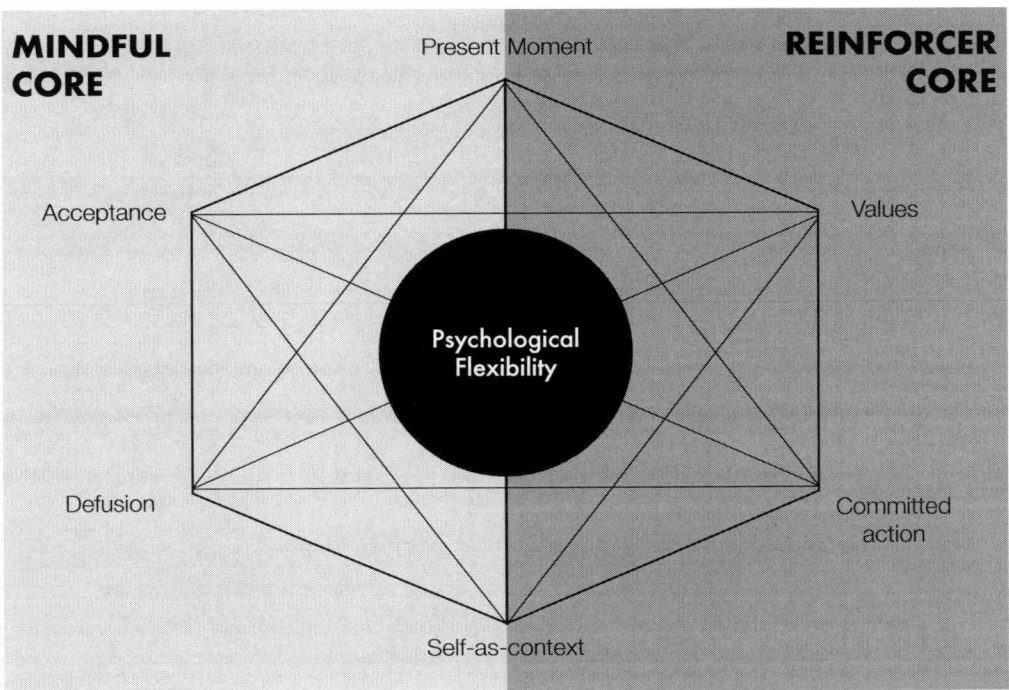

ACT Core Processes

Present Moment Awareness. This core process focuses on engaging the individual with his or her experiences with the world (the stimuli, events, and contingencies of the current environment) directly, by developing awareness of thoughts, feelings, and sensations. The aim is to help individuals live in the here and now. Present moment awareness is often targeted through traditional meditation and mindfulness activities.

When people engage in typical language processes, they may become removed from the physical stimuli in the present environment, and caught up in the relations among stimuli, opening a metaphorical rabbit hole of thoughts, feelings, sensations, and other experiences that are not necessarily occurring in the here and now. Upsetting thoughts and events do not have to be in the present physical environment to be upsetting; things that people have experienced in the past can become psychologically present at any given moment, allowing distressing reactions that can negatively affect current behavior. For example, a child at school sees a worksheet placed on his or her desk. He or she immediately becomes defiant and refuses to complete the task. To the impartial observer, that seems like a pretty simple scenario – the child is trying to get out of work, and the teacher needs to make sure he or she completes the task! However, the experience can be much more complicated for the student, who sees the worksheet, and within a few seconds engages in the following thought process: *"Oh man, I'm going to get a bad grade on this. I always get bad grades. My report card is going to be horrible again. My parents are going to be angry at me. My dad always calls me stupid when I get bad grades. He's going to call me stupid."* All of a sudden, a 'simple' worksheet has become riddled with psychological functions of disappointment, anger, embarrassment, and the anticipation of terrible events to come. Sometimes things just show up psychologically, and the approach of developing present moment awareness relies on redirection to the physical world here now, letting go of the relations to distressing events, and even becoming more observant of things in the environment that one may have missed, things that may remind one of what is important to him or her. In the development of present moment awareness, the focus is on the ability to notice when one is entangled in thoughts and feelings and to refocus on what is occurring in the present moment.

> **» Try It: Present Moment Awareness**
> Sit in a comfortable position, with your eyes closed or half closed, your spine straight, and your shoulders relaxed. Take a steady, even breath in through your nose and out through your mouth. Repeat this a few more times, until you start to notice the release of tension throughout your whole body. Now, pay attention to the feeling of the air as it moves in through your nostrils, and out past your lips. Become aware of the difference in temperature of the air on your in breath and out breath. Each time you become distracted, gently bring your attention back to your breath. After a few minutes, gently open your eyes and conclude your mindful breathing exercise.

Acceptance. Acceptance is an alternative to experiential avoidance, which involves an individual's willingness to experience external and internal experiences, both the good and the bad, fully and without judgment. Acceptance is often taught through activities that encourage the individual to engage in thoughts or activities that they might otherwise avoid, and developing the ability to tolerate both good outcomes (obtaining reinforcers) and bad outcomes (losing reinforcers).

People are almost always presented with choices regarding which behaviors they could choose to engage in at any given moment. Often times, these oppositional choices involve sooner, smaller consequences pitted against larger, later consequences. For example, when presented with a worksheet, a student may encounter the following two options: a sooner, smaller reward from escaping the task and avoiding immediate feelings of discomfort and a larger, later reward for completing the challenging task and being allowed to take a break or go to recess, not to mention the even further removed reward of doing well in school. However, as time goes on, the quick, immediate positive consequences of the escape begin to compound with aversive. An objective observer can see the long-term benefit of forgoing escape and the associated long-term aversives, but a person, especially a child, may respond impulsively to the choice that makes things better right now, despite the delayed outcomes. For many who have not learned to regulate their behavior more effectively, the impulsive choice may seem like the only choice in that moment. Take, for example, a high school student who hears someone call his or her mom a mean name; the immediate reaction may be, *"I'll feel better if I punch them,"* and follow through on that action, despite having heard about "thinking before you act," because in that moment, that initial reaction is the only option considered. A lot of the work on acceptance focuses to bring the delayed consequences into the psychological "now" in order to develop the ability to recognize that it is OK to experience "bad stuff" sometimes, and that fighting the bad stuff will not make it go away. It is important here to make the distinction between acceptance and 'giving in' to bad situations. The focus of the former is to accept one's own negative thoughts, feelings, and sensations in order to engage in behavior that produces better outcomes, whereas the latter does not work in favor of the better outcomes. Consider a child who has experienced some form of abuse, and is afraid of approaching an adult to confide in and seek help. "Giving in" to those feelings may result in the child having thoughts such as, *"This is probably my fault anyway, I better not say anything or else I could get into trouble and the abuse will happen again."* Accepting those feelings may results in the child having thoughts such as, *"I am really upset and scared that this might happen to me again if I say anything, but I will find someone safe who can help me anyway."* Developing acceptance relies upon an understanding that spending time fighting with or resisting thoughts and feelings will get in the way of moving forward in life. Furthermore, it is important to interact psychologically with those larger, later rewards in the here and now sometimes.

> ### » Try It: Acceptance and Willingness
> Grab a timer or a stopwatch and time how long you can hold your breath. Now, think about the feeling of running out of breath, the sensations you felt right before you decided to take a breath. Ask yourself, are you willing to experience that feeling just a little longer to increase your time? Could you tolerate it a bit longer for Olympic-level breath holding time? Time yourself holding your breath again, this time accepting those sensations and being willing to experience them a bit longer. Did your time change? How does this relate back to your life? What could you be a bit more willing to experience? Maybe discomfort at the gym for a longer workout or a boring movie that your partner is dying to watch? How could willingness and acceptance effect your daily experience?

Defusion. This core process, the alternative to cognitive fusion, encourages the individual to let go of the need to control or eliminate distressing thoughts or experiences by changing the way he or she interacts with them. The individual will learn to "create distance" between him or herself and the thought, lessening control of feelings over behavior.

When learning to defuse from thoughts, or step back from them and notice that they are not part of who one is, the key is the ability to discriminate between a thought and the literal world. The thoughts people have about events are not always right or true or real. However, those thoughts appear as reality. Think of the "spotlight effect," for example, the tendency for people to believe they are being noticed more than they really are. Everyone has likely been in a situation in which they spill something on their shirt, and the rest of their day is dominated by thoughts about how everyone is looking at them, 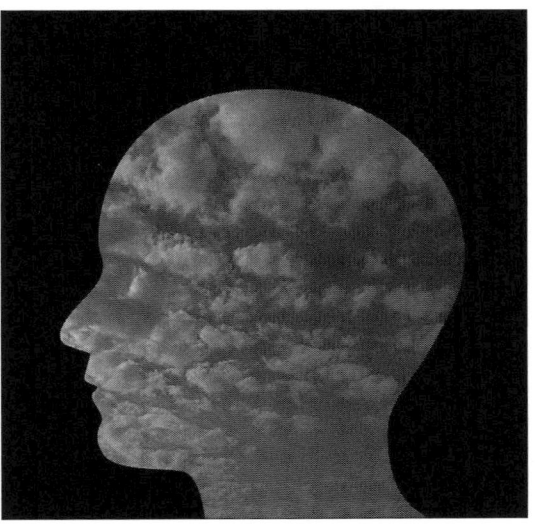 thinking they are a slob, and look terrible. Or maybe it's the day after a bad haircut. The thoughts feel so real. Defusing from thoughts, allow people to realize there is a reality separate from the thoughts, worries, and emotions which appear contained within. Activities that develop defusion attempt to create distance between the thinker and his or her thoughts. The techniques encouraging the individual to label his or her thoughts and feelings make thoughts sound silly or absurd to exaggerate the distinction between them and the literal world, and practice acceptance that all the thoughts bouncing around 'in your head' may just be noise distracting from what is really going on around in the moment. Sometimes the ability the let go of one's thoughts is important to actually engage in appropriate, adaptive behavior. Consider a child who gets caught up in the thought, *"Brian is being so unfair, it's supposed to be me who gets to play with the blocks!"* Operating on those thoughts alone, the child may end up throwing a tantrum, yelling at Brian, or knocking over his block tower. If prompted to defuse from that thought, it may prevent some of that maladaptive behavior. For example, an adult may provide a metaphor of a firecracker – writing the child's thought on the firecracker with a long, lit fuse, and talking about the choice to let the firework explode (and get in trouble) or cutting the fuse (letting go of the thought), and finding something else to do, the child may be able to re-engage in a different set of behaviors, not driven by the fixated thoughts of, *"It's unfair."* By defusing from thoughts, realizing that just because you think it, doesn't mean it is real, an individual may be better able to engage in more socially accepted and emotionally regulated behaviors.

> » Try It: Defusion
> What is one thought that comes up in your life more often than you'd like, that brings you discomfort, sadness, or pain? Perhaps you experience thoughts of incompetence like "I am not good enough," thoughts of shame like "My partner is embarrassed by me," or self-deprecating thoughts like "Why bother, I'll fail anyway." Whatever your painful thought is, I want you to give it a shape and a color. What does it look like? Now, imagine three of that thought! Imagine yourself juggling those thoughts, throwing them at a target, or bouncing them like a ball. Does that thought seem as distressing now, after seeing it in this way?

Self-as-Context. This core process develops and harnesses the individual's ability to take perspectives in order to create a distinction between one's self-as-content, or the content his or her past experiences, and self-as-context, or the stable, continuous awareness of his or her experiences, without attachment to them.

This is an abstract concept – the idea of finding the real "you" that transcends different contexts. It is hard for adults, much less children, to wrap their minds around the concept of a "real you." For a verbally sophisticated person, this concept focuses on noticing the perspective that transcends throughout life; while he or she is the person who does things, and experiences things and constantly changes, there is a part of him or her that is constant and continually experiencing the events of life. The part of the person that remembers their earliest memories as well as the most recent experience they have had. For a less verbally sophisticated individual, it is more accessible to present the idea of self-as-context as a distinction between the individual herself and his or her behavior. Just because someone has done something

"bad" doesn't make THEM "bad." It gives the individual the choice to define his or his real self as the version of him or herself that most aligns with their values, the one that engages in appropriate behaviors, and gets the things they want out of life. For a younger child, this may boil down to the question, *"Was it the real you that did that?"* or *"What would the real you do in that situation?"* By creating this distinction between the individual and his or her behavior, it makes it easier to look at oneself in the "big picture," the ability to see oneself without the labels other people have given you ("class clown," "slow kid," "jock"), without the labels one given him or herself ("stupid," "screw up," "tough guy"), and without the baggage of past behavior in order to see how they can commit to your valued life, becoming the version of "you" that they want to be what they see and what others see, as well as being comfortable enough with this stable sense of self that they are willing to accept when you change and grow or need to change and grow in order to live the life that they want to live.

> ### » Try It: Self-as-Context
> Grab a pencil and a piece of paper, divided into four sections. Draw a tree trunk and branches (with no leaves in each of the boxes). Now, finish the tree with leaves or twigs or weather elements to represent what that tree is during each of the four seasons. As well, write down what you are like during each season – how do you change throughout the year? Once you are done, look at that paper. That tree changes so much throughout the year, but it is always the same tree, standing strong. Think about yourself, are you the way you act in different ways throughout the year, or are you a stable presence, there to experience your changing ways? What is that part of your that is always there, observing and experiencing the changing "weather?"

Values. Values are intangible outcomes of purposive action that are meaningful to the individual, in contrast to specific goals or behavioral objectives. Values embody the overarching sources of reinforcement in the individual's life. Values are often targeted with activities that increase the clarity or these reinforcers, increasing their salience to the individual, therefore increasing the overall amount of reinforcement in his or her life.

The focus of values work is to move life in a direction of value and worth, or, in other words, engage in behavior that results in reinforcement or rewards. The challenge of value-based behavior relates back to the idea of smaller, sooner versus larger, later consequences; values relate to those larger, later rewards that are not necessarily always obvious to the individual in the moment. 'Values' can represent a range of things, depending on the sophistication of the individual's language development. For adults, or verbally sophisticated individuals, values are immaterial qualities or feelings that the individual wants to experience regularly in life, such as "being athletic," "feeling joyful," or being "devoted to family." For younger individuals, or individuals with less advanced language abilities, values may be more concrete, involving more tangible-based outcomes, such as "getting good grades," "having friends," or even "playing video games." As language develops, so too does the complexity of these values. The challenge with values is that the consequences can seem too far in the future, too delayed, and in conflict with more immediate reinforcers. For example, the "yumminess" of eating a big piece of cake right now may be in conflict with the desire to "be healthy," yet a pattern of cake-eating behavior will interfere with the long-term valued outcome. A lot of the work of developing values involves first clarifying what is important to the individual and then relating behavior in the here and now to those larger, later outcomes so that it is easier to interact with values in the psychological present. Consider a child who always talks about wanting her divorced parents to get back together. To help her clarify her own values, one might ask her, *"If your parents got back together, what would your life be like today?"* in order to get to the root of what it is she cares about – perhaps spending time with them or taking family trips. A person living a life driven by values, whether young or old, will constantly consider whether his or her behavior is getting what they want out of life, despite 'temptations' to engage in impulsive behavior that is detrimental to those outcomes.

> ## » Try It: Values
> Take out another piece of paper and create four columns. Remember, values are NOT goals. They are NOT objectives. They are intangible ways you want to FEEL in this life, to make your life as important and as meaningful as it can be. In the first column, fill in the following: lifestyle, relationships, wellness, spirituality, and personal growth. In the second column, rate on a scale from 0-10 how important this area of your life is to you. Then, in the third column, rate the how well you are doing on this value currently on a scale from 0-10. Finally, in the fourth column, record the "gaps" between how important the values are to you and how well you are doing with them today. Are you living your valued life in all areas?

Committed Action. Committed action refers to the development of larger and larger behavior patterns that are linked to values, or individual reinforcers. Committed action may be targeted with activities including skill acquisition, shaping, and goal setting.

Committed action keeps the individual engaged in behavior that "moves towards" values (or increases the likelihood of encountering preferred reinforcers), and maintaining that engagement after he or she 'mess up' or gets off track, rather than wallowing in the failure. Committed action involves the ability to 'pivot' one's behavior at any given moment in order to produce better outcomes, and the ability to persevere in those behaviors, even when doing so is challenging or giving up would be easier. Consider a child who values being able to play online video games with his or her friends after dinner. His or her ability to do so may be contingent upon behavior throughout the course of the day, perhaps throughout the school day, extracurricular activities, therapy sessions, and family time. Although this child may be clear that, *"I want to play my video game!"* if he or she does not have the ability to persist in behavior that will produce that outcome over the course of twelve hours (which is a long time for a child), he or she will not contact that reinforcer, and, as a result, is not more likely to 'behave' throughout the day to get it. If, however, the child learns to remain committed to this value, and respond to it throughout the day, he or she is more likely to contact this reward, and more likely to engage in appropriate behavior to do so. Again, like the concept of values itself, committed action varies greatly with the developmental level of the individual; it can be as short term as *"I am working for iPad time"* during a class period or as long term as *"I want to be a good spouse throughout my marriage."* Another important component of committed action is the ability to get back on track after making a mistake; it's easy to sit back and be stuck in what happened yesterday, but when developing commitment to values, it is important to encourage the individual to let go of past mistakes in order to engage in desired behavior now. Individuals learn that one's actions are always moving toward or away from values, as values cannot be put on "pause."

> **» Try It: Committed Action**
> Get the piece of paper from the previous values activity, and add a fifth column. Look at the values you recorded. Now, for each of those that have a significant gap, think of - Just. One. Thing. - you can do in the next week to move you toward each value, and write it in the fifth column. For example, if your value is health, perhaps commit to lifting weights twice in the next week, or signing yourself up for a 5k race. Record one actionable step you can take to move your life in the direction you want it to go. Commit to doing these behaviors in the next week. Keep this paper and revisit it in one week to check in on your commitments.

One of the most important things to remember when utilizing an ACT approach, is that the core processes that comprise both the Mindful and Reinforcer Cores, are meant to be taught and utilized in a dynamic, interactive way. ACT providers isolate those behaviors as individual components of the hexaflex to form a basis for training them to individuals, however those six core processes can be summarized simply on their own, and combined to exemplify psychological flexibility.

ACT with Children

A growing number of documented cases of ACT with children have emerged in the scientific literature, demonstrating outcomes including symptom reduction in psychological disorders, changes in problem behavior, and increase in quality of life for children with health conditions. Like ACT with adult populations, interventions designed for children focus on behavioral inflexibility that arise from language processes, which may present as psychological distress or problem behavior. Consider a child who frequently becomes disruptive, disrespectful, and noncompliant during math class, needing to be removed from the classroom in order to manage the problem behavior. This rigid refusal to complete math may arise from a series of experiences failing in math, and the attachment to the idea that he or she is terrible at math, and will be embarrassed in front of peers if forced to do math in school.

The development of mindful awareness and values-driven behavior may reshape this scenario for the child, making him or her more willing to experience failure now in order to contact success later.

Although the same basic principles of ACT apply for children, there are some accommodations that increase the likelihood of effective intervention with this group. The abstract nature of many of the metaphors used in typical ACT therapy; depending on the child's

language abilities, he or she may not be able to understand and apply the metaphors presented in treatment. In order to address this issue, implementers can make the metaphors more **concrete** and incorporate **physical activities** into a child's ACT experience. Modifications like these make ACT exercises more developmentally appropriate for children at various stages of language development. **Experiential activities** foster learning through "real life" encounters with the material, and the transformation of those events into meaningful experiences.

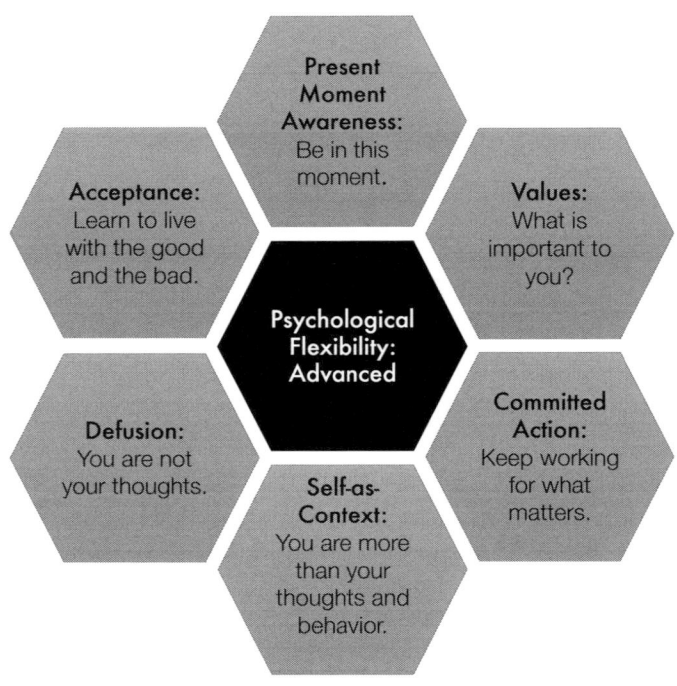

Further, it is important to "translate" ACT concepts into child-friendly language that is relatable to children at any age or developmental level, as seen in the various summaries of ACT core processes in the included figures. It is imperative that the implementer engage the child in these experiences, as they must encounter elements of the ACT model is action, not just in discussion, to facilitate behavior change. As important as it is to appropriately adapt ACT exercises to the developmental level of the child, it is equally important for the implementer to interact with the ACT core processes at his or her own level – before teaching ACT, do ACT! Throughout this curriculum the implementer must be engaged in the ACT process, practicing mindfulness and valued-based living alongside the children they work with; as the old saying goes, practice what you preach!

There are some key considerations that should be made when implementing ACT with children across the six core processes. While the basic principles of each process are the same despite the age or developmental level of the individual, different elements of each component must be made clear and explicit for children, and are summarized in the first column. In addition, the third column provides examples of developmentally appropriate language to use when targeting each core process for beginner, intermediate, and advanced ACT clients, as well as a general area to focus on developing for that group. Keep in mind that this is not an exhaustive list of language to utilize for each level, or concepts to focus on in their treatment. ACT should be individualized for each individual, in order to meet his or her specific needs.

Core Process	Considerations for Children	Example Language to Use
Present Moment Awareness	-Often predisposed to fixate on certain stimuli in the environment (even verbal stimuli) -Often daydream, think about what they are doing later, imagine, etc. -May act "lost in their head" (whether good or bad) -Teach to refocus on what is actually going on around them and disengage from unhealthy, avoidant behavior	*Beginner*: "What do you see/hear/feel right now?;" "Be here. Not there." *Focus*: Attend to stimuli in the current environment *Intermediate*: "Be aware.;" "Be here now.;" "Where are you right now?" *Focus*: Distinguish between when they are caught up in their mind and present *Advanced*: "Be in this moment.;" "Practice awareness.;" "Where is your mind now?" *Focus*: Notice when they are not present, and bring awareness back to the moment
Acceptance	-Impulsive choices may seems to be the "only" choice for behavior -Impulsive behaviors come at the cost of obtaining bigger, better things -Emphasize that everyone struggles with acceptance sometimes -Clarify different between acceptance and giving up -Provide frequent praise directly for acceptance	*Beginner*: "Be OK with things.;" "Let's move on.;" "Can you be OK with it?" *Focus*: Accept events they do not like (i.e. can't have a toy or food they want) *Intermediate*: "Be OK with the good and bad.;" "Can you accept it?" *Focus*: Accept thoughts as they are (i.e. it's ok to have good and bad thoughts) *Advanced*: "Learn to live with the good and bad.;" "Practice acceptance." *Focus*: Accepting thoughts and feelings, and continue to engage in valued behavior
Defusion	-Thoughts often become preservations and children are not always able to discriminate truth from thought -Often struggle with letting go of thoughts they have about themselves (or what they think other people think of them) -May struggle to separate events at home from events at school	*Beginner*: "Get out of your head.;" "Is it that thought real or not?" *Focus*: Notice when thoughts are not true and different from the real world *Intermediate*: "Step back from your thoughts.;" "Label your thoughts." *Focus*: Label thoughts and feelings as such (i.e. "I'm having the thought that…") *Advanced*: "You are not your thoughts.;" "Separate from your thoughts." *Focus*: Noticing thoughts or feelings controlling behavior and defuse from them
Self-as-Context	-"Self-as-Context" is an abstract concept that is difficult to understand -Emphasize "the real you" and "you are not your behavior" -Labels from themselves or others have a significant influence on children -Once they feel labeled something, they may try to avoid situations	*Beginner*: "Be the real you.;" "Is that the real you?;" "Which you is doing that?" *Focus*: Distinguish between the "real you" and "other you" *Intermediate*: "You are you, not your behavior.;" "Is that you are a label?" *Focus*: Distinguish "you" and "your behavior;" "You" are not the labels given to you *Advanced*: "You are more than your thoughts and behavior." *Focus*: Contact the perspective of transcendent self that is always present
Values	-"Value" is also an abstract concept that is difficult to understand -Often at odds with more immediate reinforcers in the environment -Make values more concrete for children (i.e. having friends, getting to do 'X') -Emphasize that they must engage in certain behaviors to get what is important	*Beginner*: "What do you want to work for?;" "What's fun?" *Focus*: Tangible objects equivalent to daily reinforcers; use term "values" *Intermediate*: "What do you like?;" What is important?;" "How can you be good?" *Focus*: Contrast smaller and larger reinforcers with delay; differentiate values/things *Advanced*: "What matters to you?;" "What do you want your life to be about?" *Focus*: Linking daily reinforcers to long-term values; increase delay to reinforcers
Committed Action	-Generally do not like to lose, and failure is a cue for more failure -Emphasize 'try and try again,' and being ready for obstacles -Encourage goal setting and breaking goals down into 'baby steps' -Need to learn to let go of past events in order to move forward	*Beginner*: "Don't give up!;" "Keep working for 'X';" "What do you need to do?" *Focus*: Engage in behaviors needed to earn reinforcers, even if they do not like it *Intermediate*: "Don't give up, even if it's hard.;" "What are the obstacles?" *Focus*: Adapt behavior to overcome challenges and obstacles *Advanced*: "Keep working for what matters.;" "Leave your mistakes behind you." *Focus*: Letting go of previous behavior so that it does not dictate future behavior

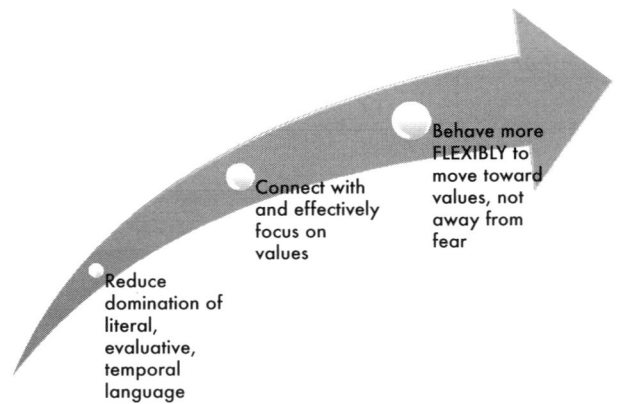

Why ACT with Children?

ACT, in addition to its large theoretical and empirical foundation, can be readily packaged to widespread use, is easy to explain to individuals of various ability levels, and is very interactive and fun to participate in! What other form of "therapy" challenges children to activities such as breath-holding contests and games of telephone in order to develop their psychological health and social well-being? ACT has demonstrated utility in both individual and group settings. Most of all, the motivation of "values" may be just what is needed to get kids to care about the fuzzy concept of "staying present." The goal of ACT with children can be summarized as reducing the dominance of language that gets in the way of living in the present moment, developing values clarity, and fostering flexible behavior related to those values. Imagine a child afraid of learning to ride a bike, an activity related to things they care about – being independent and being active. He will not try it, saying, *"I'm scared."* Applying the core processes of ACT – one may be able to respond to this child, saying, *"No you're not scared…you're James! You're just having the thought that you're scared. What does it mean to you to be able to ride the bike? Are you committed to trying even if it's a little bit scary?"* Bringing together those mindfulness and reinforce cores of the ACT hexaflex, one can help the child expand his or her world, and learn to engage in adaptive, flexible behavior, no matter what challenges they encounter. A kid's version of the ACT question can be summarized as: *"Right now, can you accept what is going on around you, commit to the things you want in your life, and try really hard to get them, no matter what?"*

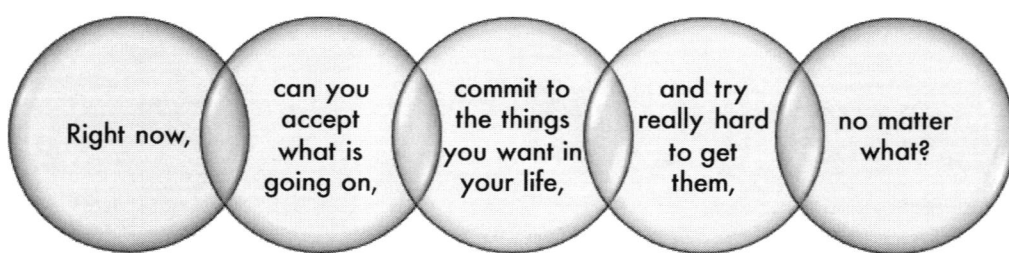

Applied Behavior Analysis

Mindfulness and ACT, two of the three elements of AIM, emphasis the language-based and psychological components of developing adaptive, flexible behavior in anyone, from child to adult. This third component, ABA, brings in principles of human behavior. The empirically forged knowledge of what makes people do what they do, and, more practically, how to get them to do the things they need to do. We are all subject to these principles, there are things in our environments that increase the likelihood that we do or do not engage in certain behaviors. Most people reliably do the dishes more often when their families thank them for doing so, or stop completely at every stop sign after getting a ticket for "rolling through" one or two. Human behavior is orderly and subject to change based on environmental variables. Because of this, scientists have learned to predict and influence what people do. Elements of this approach can be seen everywhere, from the signs reminding people to recycle their empty bottles, to advertisements that convince people to purchase another tech device they probably do not need. More directly, the effects of this approach can be seen in schools and treatment facilities, where adults and children alike are taught new skills and encouraged to behave in more prosocial ways.

Overview

Applied behavior analysis (ABA) rose from a half of a century of laboratory demonstrations that showed behavior is orderly and predictable. Change in behaviors will occur by modifying the environment. Cause is not found within the person, but rather in the surrounding contingencies for that person. John B. Watson, often cited as the father of behaviorism, proposed a form of science in the early 1900s that was purely objective and experimental, one which sought to predict and change individual's behavior. His work led to the development of behaviorism, perhaps, most famously by B.F. Skinner, who expanded the field, elaborating basic principles of human behavior by translating research done with animals into an analysis of how people behave. For decades, researchers continued to study these principles of behavior, from understanding how animals behave to applying these newly developed concepts with adults and children with disabilities and mental health conditions. While the outcomes of this research produced generally desirable outcomes, early behavior modification was scrutinized because if its use of punishment procedures, "one size fits all" approaches to rewarding desired behavior, and the emphasis on environmental control of behavior.

In the late 1980s and throughout the 1990s there was a revolution within the behavioral tradition during which a declining emphasis was placed on "rewards" for behaviors, and focused attention was placed on functional relations between the antecedents, behaviors, and consequences. The pitfalls of the behavioral approach were frequently highlighted, whereby delivering "stuff" that was assumed to be reinforcing appeared not to work as reliably as it should have. Researchers, such as Dr. Brian Iwata, began to study the functional relationship between variables in the environment and individuals' behavior. The emphasis of behavior analysis, as a result of these decades of research, is not on the topography of a behavior, meaning the way the behavior appears, but on its function, meaning the outcomes of the behavior. For example, it is not enough to know that a child engages in the behavior of biting others in order to treat it, we must know the function of that behavior – whether it results in some sort of attention, escape from an unwanted situation, or access to an object. And further, if there are other behaviors this child exhibits that result in the same function. Behavior change is still under environmental control, but to truly understand the actual contingencies by which it is sustained, strengthened, or weakened, is a pivot away from delivering Skittles for appropriate behavior toward developing individualized functional consequences evolved. Contemporary approaches have blended various ways of assessing the function of behavior in a way that takes the most effective elements of different assessments and combines them to produce a practical and effective method of assessment. The interview-informed synthesized contingency analysis (IISCA), developed by Dr. Greg Hanley, is one of these approaches. The IISCA method takes the conclusions made while interviewing the client or student and/or adults who know them well into consideration when planning to directly assess or analyze the behavior. Researchers continue to develop and refine these methods of directly assessing the function of behavior in more efficient and effective ways.

These assessments and their variations expose the relationships between events in the environment and an individual's behavior. These relationships, or functions of behavior, maintain the occurrence of the behavior. Generally, assessments reveal that a behavior is maintained by one of four primary functions of behavior: attention, escape, tangible, or sensory. Attention function behaviors are maintained by social interactions with other people in the environment from peers to adults. This may be prosocial or positive attention such as praise, conversation, or laughter. It may also be inappropriate or negative attention such as reprimands, redirection, or signs of frustration. Behaviors with an escape function are maintained by the removal or avoidance of a task or stimulus that is aversive to the individual. This could include, for example, "getting out" of completing a work demand, leaving a room, or being away from a certain person. Tangible-maintained behaviors result in the access to items of any kind, such as food, toys, or other preferred objects. Behaviors with a sensory function are maintained by some sort of physical sensation, such as lights, sounds, and tactile events. In general, behavior is maintained primarily by one of these four functions. At times, a behavior can be maintained by more than one of these functions, which is referred to as multiple control. While multiple control is possible, it is rare, and intensive assessment will often reveal a primary function for a complex behavior. When a behavior is multiply maintained by more than one function, a clinician will either design interventions for both functions or recommend determining that the behavior is not caused by a medical condition. When treating behavior that is clearly maintained by one function of behavior, two procedures are frequently used as an intervention: differential reinforcement and extinction. Differential reinforcement refers to the planned reinforcement for appropriate behaviors that result in the function rather than the inappropriate behavior. Extinction is the discontinuation or withholding of reinforcement for a previously reinforced behavior. These two procedures are typically used in tandem. For example, if a child's problem behavior is screaming when they want to stop a task and is maintained by escape, combining differential reinforcement and extinction would result in reinforcement for appropriate ways of requesting a break from the task and the withholding of the reinforcement of a break from the task when he or she screams. There are multiple variations of differential reinforcement procedures that are used depending on the nature of the problem behavior and the targeted appropriate replacement behavior.

The service of behavioral assessment, and its subsequent intervention rests upon a foundation in which a small number of controlling variables are responsible for essentially all behaviors that we as humans engage in. Regardless if it is self-injury, verbal aggression, excessive shopping, overeating, or problem gambling, the causes for these vastly different maladaptive behaviors remain rather similar. Historically, the concept of functional accounts of behavior originated with Dr. Brian Iwata, who's research developed the functional analysis, a scientific approach to determining the relationships between stimuli and responses that maintain the occurrence of a behavior, and has evolved from the standardized 4-condition arrangement to include variations such as brief and trial-based analysis. A number of procedural deviations have also occurred which many have considered to ease the efforts of the original approach, but have been noted to have some shortcomings in terms of accurate predicting of true function.

These procedures are very effective and hundreds of published studies emerged. Exponentially more clinical cases improved with the functional approach to understanding behavior. However, the challenge that remained was once people started talking with complexity, the immediate antecedent-behavior-consequence relationships appeared unable to accurately predict existing behaviors. Language seemed to change things.

Once a person is able to derive relations and respond relationally, these relations can begin to affect behavior in the bigger picture, and the functions of the stimuli involved in the relations are transformed, resulting in both positive and negative outcomes for the individual. On one hand, an individual with these relational abilities can interact more meaningfully with the world around him or her, noticing relationships among events, making inferences, problem solving in difficult situations, developing a cohesive, detailed understanding of the world. On the other hand, these same language processes, when undesired derivations occur or unpleasant functions are transformed, can lead to rigid patterns of behavior, worries, anxieties, phobias, and psychological suffering. The difficult part of all this is, one cannot have one side of the "language coin" without the other; people cannot encourage the development of advanced language abilities that result in logical and thoughtful behavior without also allowing for the potential development of worry and fear. And perhaps, although this is a challenge, it is not a problem. If educators and therapists foster the development of psychological flexibility and adaptive behavior, they can maximize individual's potential to flourish in his or her environment and minimize the negative impact of psychological distress on his or her quality of life.

There is no greater challenge for many traditionally trained behavior analysts, behavior interventionists, or behavioral psychologists than attempting to link the seemingly cognitive blur of ACT processes into a Skinnerian account of behavior. The traditional account is one in which an antecedent or "trigger" sets the occasion for a behavior to occur, and once it does, if followed by something that is deemed positive by the person may increase the probability of the behavior occurring in the future. This **A-B-C model** has served the field of behavior science for well over seventy years. However, challenges arise when the behavior of the person in question is mediated by verbal events that may transcend the simple "trigger" that is attempting to occasion behavior.

ABA with Children

ABA was utilized in the education and treatment of children, starting nearly from its inception. Behavior analysis focuses on the principles that explain how learning takes place, and its application to children is clear. Children, those with and without learning challenges, have a lot to learn in terms of academic and social behavior. ABA techniques are frequently used by parents, teachers, therapists to improve a children's behavior and teach them new skills. ABA is implemented as an individualized therapy for children with autism and other disabilities. As well, techniques developed to understand why problem behaviors occur and how to treat them are frequently used in schools.

Functional behavior assessment involves three general approaches that each seek to gain a better understanding of why people do the things they do. *Interviews or questionnaires*, which provide a standardized and often quantifiable report of an individual's behavior are often quick to administer and have some demonstrated reliability, however they emphasize constructs explaining how or why behaviors occurs, and tend to be a poor predictor of actual behavior, with generally weak correlations with data from actual behavioral events. *Direct observation*, another assessment method, involves an observer recording behavioral events as they occur, which, again, are relatively easy to complete, and capture the natural context, allowing the assessor to identify correlational antecedents and consequences. Despite these benefits, direct observation can be time consuming, require substatial effort and resources from staff, and data can only be analyzed following the observation. Finally, *experimental analyses* directly manipulate environmental variables in a contrived context, demonstrating the cause and effect of behavior called 'experimental control.' Although these analyses provide scientific rigor in assessment procedures, they can be risky depending on the nature of the behavior, are time consuming, require significant training for implementers, and involve a complex analysis of data. Often, this level of assessment is unnecessary for the majority of standard functional behavior assessments.

Once a behavior function has been identified, informed treatment approaches can be crafted to not only suppress the challenging behavior, but also increase an **alternative positive or proactive** behavior. The four common **functions of behavior** are attention, escape, tangible, and sensory. *Attention* includes things that results in a social interaction, such as eye contact, conversation, laughter, and even reprimands. *Escape* includes the removal of an item, task, person, or any stimulus that the person finds unpleasant or aversive.

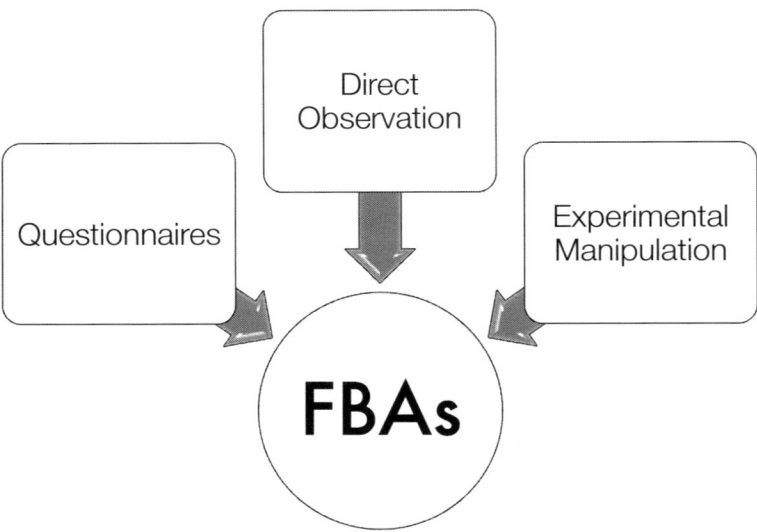

Tangible refers to obtaining physical items, some examples of which may include food, toys, and electronics. Finally, *sensory* refers to some quality of the event that provides some physical stimulation, such as lights, sounds, sensations, or tastes. Interventions are often designed to reduce the problem behavior, and replace it with an alternative appropriate behavior that obtains the same function, require less effort than the problem behavior, and is socially acceptable. For example, a student who often acts out to escape difficult tasks at school, may be taught an alternative behavior of requesting help or a break when he or she feels frustrated with the task.

One of the greatest challenges within the functional assessment and intervention enterprise is identifying distant or private contingencies that impact the A-B-C relationship. For example, if someone notices that Ronny displays aggression most likely on Mondays, towards different children in the classroom, but the selection of victim appears random, and no antecedent can be identified, he may be inclined to conclude it is Monday that Ronny is most upset about. However, after further investigation he discovers that Ronny's dad drinks heavily on Sundays and only during Chicago Cubs baseball games, and then hits Ronny, will he clue into the complex relational arrangement of stimuli that reveals only peers wearing Chicago Cubs t-shirts are victims of his aggression on Monday mornings. In short, the t-shirts are evoking private functions of his dad, and perhaps negative self-rules of *"fight back"* or *"no one is going to hit me so I will fight back,"* which can be escaped from by engaging in aggressive behaviors in the classroom. In another scenario, if someone observes that Alice has a tendency to ask to go to the nurse at the same time of day, right before gym class, it is an easy to assume that Alice is being "lazy" or trying to get out of hard work, therefore should contact disciplinary action for trying to out of P.E. However, if she further assesses the situation, she may learn that two students who Alice experienced a bullying issue with two years ago are in that class, and she believes that if they see her struggle during gym class, she will be bullied again, so it is "safer" for her to avoid going altogether.

An understanding of how these private events, prior experiences, and self-rules interact allow us to more completely analyze the causes of challenging behavior for many of the children educators and therapists work with. It should not be assumed that there is always such a higher-level reason for challenging behavior for every child examined. In fact, for those children that lack higher level cognitive skills, their behavior will most likely be simply under the control of the antecedent right there in the immediate environment. However, those children who think about the past, or fixate on a constructed future that has not yet happened, are probably interacting behaviorally with private events which need analysis to evaluate the relative contributions of such to their eventually emitted behavior.

The challenge here lies in the difficult nature of tracing these private events back to their source. For example, how, through the use of evidence-based techniques, can the distant, verbal events that influence a child's behavior be understood? Traditional behavior analytic methods of behavior assessment may be insufficient for revealing the relationship among private events, problem behavior, and the current environment. The inclusion of techniques such as ACT helps to understand how verbal events can come to be related to, and even transform the function of stimuli in the present context.

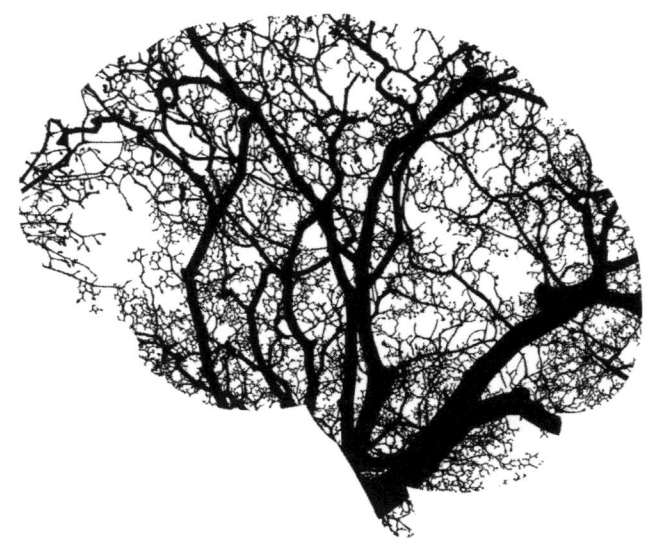

Contingency Management

Given the challenges children today face, the needs they have extend beyond academic instruction and learning supports. The unpleasant experiences and challenges children face outside of school or therapy trickle into these settings. Not literally in most instances, but rather psychologically as private covert behavior that is recalled from home is interacted with throughout many aspects of any given school day. The reverse is also true, in which the consequences of being bullied at school do not end when the dismissal bell rings. Instead that victim heads home only to carry the weight of that incident into the house and most likely taint the experiences that remain as the day comes to a close. It is foolish to think that at any given time a child will simply attune to the current environment, notice the antecedents, emit the correct behavior, and acquire the delightful consequences programmed for their success. Instead, another layer of our awareness, and their action, needs to be analyzed and then targeted for intervention. By layering ACT upon the typical contingency arrangements utilized for the child, one may better understand and overcome the challenges impeding optimal success.

Managing contingencies sounds like a task for someone with a business degree. If nothing else it sounds quite impersonal. However, contingency management is really nothing more than identifying the stuff that is motivating to the child and the conditions under which behavior is most likely to occur. These sorts of motivations are referred to as the reinforcers they want to work for. Often times errors are made when people assume what the reinforcers are for a given child – even their own. Luckily there are many ways to evaluate the potential reinforcers that might drive a child to greater levels of achievement. If thinking broadly about the concept of reinforcers as not only things but also ways to live, the ACT component of *values* appears closely aligned.

Within a school environment, **contingency management** may take a variety of forms. One of the most common is the classroom treasure box or fun Friday activity in which the children will work for extended periods of time, maybe days or weeks, in order to gain access to stuff that the teacher deemed to be reinforcing. The funny thing that happens, however, is that many times what the teacher thinks the children want and what the students actually want are different. If a peer in class calls Peter a loser and his mom a pig, and the only thing dangling over Peter's "turn the other cheek" behavior is a movie at the end of the week, it is no surprise that he may forgo positive behavior and physically or verbally attack that peer. As the reinforcing value of making that other child suffer is most likely greater than whatever value the movie Peter didn't even want to see might have had. Compound that with a long delay in time to gain access to the movie, versus the immediate positive feeling that attacking the peer will yield, and none of us should be surprised as to why Peter is going to miss out on his "Fun Friday." Furthermore, when Peter finds sitting in the office at lunch recess to be reinforcing because he is overweight and does not like going outside, the contingency management problem is exponentially compounded.

For too many years, teachers have grabbed onto a one-size-fits-all approach to managing the contingencies of behavior for their classroom of students. The stoplight system of green equals good, yellow is a warning, and red means the student is in trouble is just too simplistic to control challenging behavior for many students. Endless variations of this approach to behavior management have been developed such as behavior rainbows (various colors are better/worse behavior levels), bees in a hive (farther from the hive the worse your behavior is), or the French Fry board (in which each child has their own supersize fry container affixed to the bulletin board adorned with 5 close pins that resemble fries). Emit a bad behavior and lose a fry. There is nothing worse than a bad day on top of an empty fry container. What is even worse, however, is when a teacher encounters a student who does not respond to her "system" in the classroom, that student is targeted for transition to a more restrictive class or school environment. Many change of placements would be unnecessary if teachers had the opportunity to receive better training to understand and navigate the individual nature of contingency management and how it links back to a functional account of the child's behavior.

Building an effective contingency management system takes careful planning. The teacher needs to understand how to evaluate preference, include functional reinforcers, and link access to such items and activities to both classroom rule adherence, and therapeutic behavior change goals. If done correctly, and the reinforcers found within are more powerful (or equally functional) to those sustaining the problem behaviors, important gains can be made for the students. The funny thing is that a lot of money is not necessary to build this type of system, because most of the reinforcers are things that do not cost a dime. Instead, they are the non-tangibles that sustain challenging behavior that should be included. Examples include teacher attention, peer attention, escaping from an assignment, taking a break, listening to music, opting out of a class for a day, or taking a 5-minute nap. While these may sound like radically inappropriate "treasures" to place inside of that dysfunctional treasure box, the real question is that if these consequences are being contacted for inappropriate behaviors right now, are they not the exact behavior consequences that the children want? When one uncomfortably comes to the conclusion that these might be the reinforcers, the only way to combat their tendency to produce challenging behavior is to control their delivery for positive behaviors instead. While, these are not the only reinforcers to be included in the classroom system, they most certainly need to be considered when creating function-based interventions.

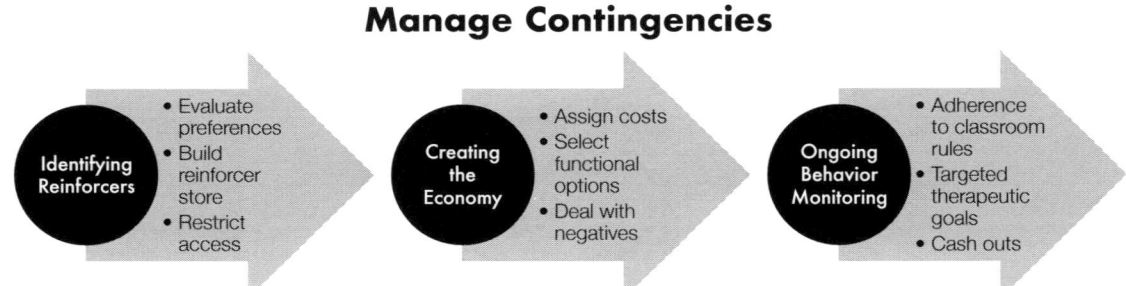

Managing contingencies in a child's home or when receiving therapy at home or in a clinic follows the same basic premises as doing so in the school setting. Similar to the predicament that many teachers encounter, parent and therapists may face some social stigma for building in functional reinforcers that are not typically associated with rewards for good behavior. In the home or private setting, it is equally important to evaluate the child's preferences for reinforcers, which may include commons rewards such as watching television, but may also involve activities such as skipping a family game night every so often, getting to play Candyland (even though the child seems too old for it now), or getting to sleep in and go to school late one morning. Again, one of the keys to designing these contingencies is to restrict access to these reinforcers so that the child encounters them if, and only if, they engage in the targeted appropriate behaviors. So, this means that if sleeping in is a reinforcer, someone is there to wake the child up every morning until he or she earns it!

In any setting, if the development of positive behavior is the goal, then the teacher or therapist must develop a system of reinforcement that is based on function. Beyond identifying effective reinforcers, the implementer must create an exchange system, that standardizes the procedures for earning reinforcement. Clear expectations and strict adherence to point systems and schedules for obtaining earned reinforcers, as well as the programmed consequences when inappropriate behavior does occur, create a system that sets the child up for success. Finally, once a **function-based system** is established, the implementer must continuously monitor the child's progress, in terms for his or her behavior, therapeutic goals, and frequency and functions of his or her chosen reinforcers. How do you do, as the implementer, manage all of this? Create a systematic procedure that does all of this and incorporate ACT intervention along the way.

Integrating Mindfulness, ACT, and Behavior Change Procedures

The Dynamic Context

Rather than providing solely a set of "strategies" for a child to use when he or she is in a difficult situation, ACT seeks to alter the context in which a behavior occurs, the child's relationship to verbal behavior about the event (what they think or what others say), and reinforce a set of flexible, adaptive behaviors that lead to preferred outcomes. The ultimate goal is to increase the likelihood of the child responding to the contingencies that you have arranged or that exist naturally in the environment that reinforce appropriate behaviors. To do so, the child must learn to discriminate when his or her thoughts or feelings related to the event are impeding his or her access to reinforcement and to learn to make choices that increase access to reinforcement, even when those preferred outcomes are delayed or less salient in the moment.

For example, consider the scenarios below, two alternate contexts in which a child is given an assignment to complete. In the first non-ACT context, he or she refused to complete the worksheet, and missed out on the opportunity for recess, a larger-later reinforcer. He or she is responding to the smaller-sooner reward of getting out of that aversive task, possibly saddled with thoughts like, *"I suck at this, I won't do it,"* or *"There's no way you can make me do this!"* In the second ACT context, the child is able to complete the assignment and get to recess, because he or she is responding to that larger-later reward of recess, rather than opportunity to escape the task. With ACT, perhaps the student has thoughts like, *"Man, I hate this, but I'll do it because I'm so excited for that kickball rematch later!"* ACT becomes the bridge of time to tolerate the delay. It brings the future rewards psychologically here right now. It helps the child respond flexibly to this less than ideal situation. The difference between ACT and non-ACT contexts lies primarily in the individual's interactions with verbal stimuli. In the non-ACT context, that child is interacting with the immediate contingencies, without responding to the delayed negative consequence of losing recess. In the ACT context, however, the child is responding to both immediate and delayed consequences with both preferred and non-preferred outcomes, but all of those events are related to the antecedent event and interacted with in the psychological present, the child is able to "experience" those consequences verbally before ever contacting them.

By incorporating processes from the mindful and reinforcer cores, the child will, on the one hand, relate the smaller-sooner reinforce of avoid an aversive task to the delay negative consequence of losing recess, and interact with those contingencies psychologically in the moment. On the other hand, the larger-later reinforcer of going to recess will become more salient to the student, who is now more likely to engage in behavior related to that reinforcer. Behaviors related to acceptance, defusion, values, and committed action are all likely to interact in this scenario (within the grey ACT context box in the following diagram) to produce adaptive, desired behavior, whereas the absence of these behaviors in the non-ACT context (within the white box in the diagram) favor the emission of maladaptive, inappropriate behavior. The emphasis here is altering the **context** in which the individual is responding, both via language processes.

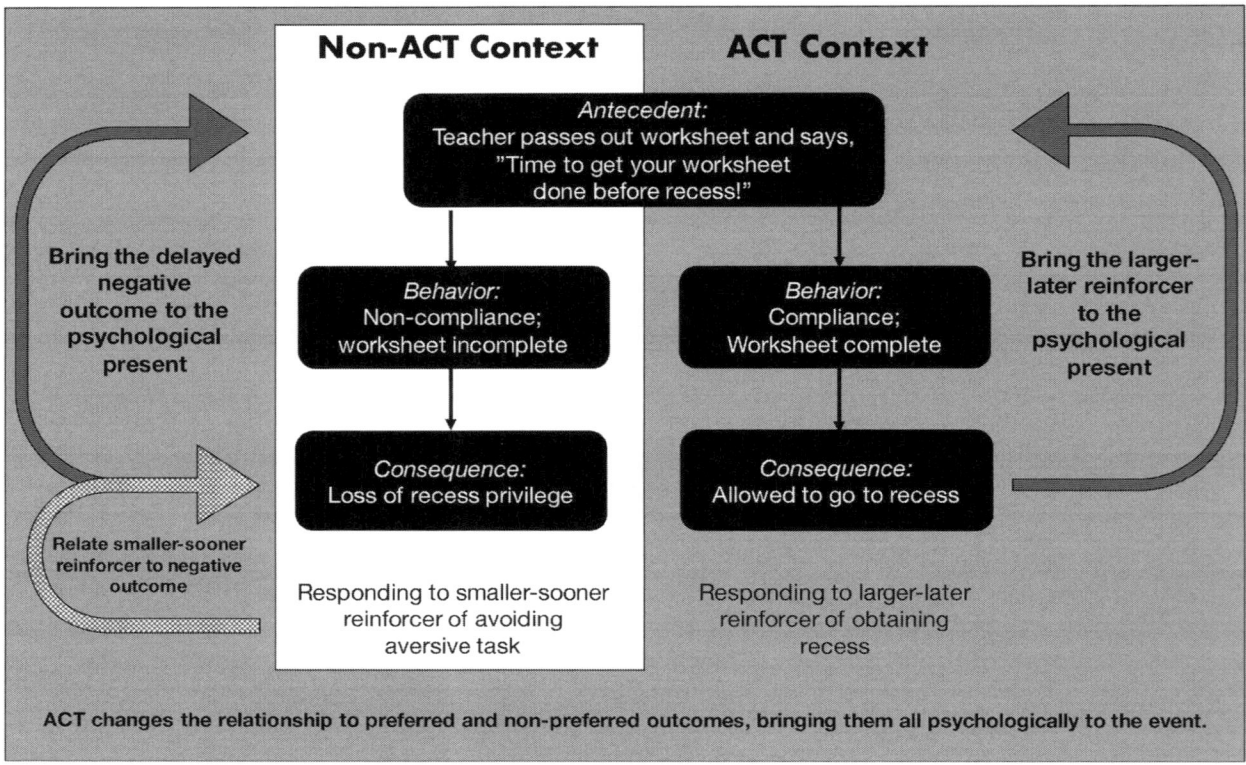

Imagine another scenario in which another child begs and pleads with her parents to allow her to take piano lessons. They agree, and the child begins to learn to play the instrument, and enjoys it very much! After several months of lessons, she learns that all of the piano students must play in a recital in a few weeks. This child is afraid of performing or speaking in public, and immediately insists that she will not partake in the recital, only to learn that participation is a requirement of continued lessons. In the non-ACT context, this child may respond to the smaller-sooner reinforcer of avoiding participation in the recital, while losing her opportunity to play piano. Given the ACT context, however, she may learn to respond to the larger-later reinforcer of continued experience playing piano and taking lessons, and overcome her fear of performing for an audience in order to access this preferred outcome.

Mindfulness, ACT, and Scope of Practice

Interdisciplinary teams work together to manage children's behaviors and support their social-emotional development. Each member of that team provides a particular expertise and set of professional practices to support the child. Each professional involved in managing behavior must be aware of and adhere to his or her own professional code and defined scope of practice. Individuals working in schools and clinical settings need to consider their own professional boundaries when deciding to implement ACT with their students or clients. Furthermore, those persons not appropriately and sufficiently trained in applied behavior analysis must use caution in conducting functional behavioral assessments, writing treatment plans, and interpreting data suggesting treatment gains. Some professional standards have been reviewed and are outlined with some considerations when selecting the intervention and target behaviors for change. It is imperative that implementers review their own professional standards before beginning any intervention or treatment with a student or client.

Educators

Educators, who are held responsible for both academic and social-emotional growth for their students, follow learning standards, which are precise, outlined descriptions of what students should know and skills they should be able to perform throughout their education. They are learning or educational objectives. While there are both state-level and national-level standards for academic content, there are also social-emotional learning standards. All fifty states have adopted social-emotional learning standards for early education/preschool students. Increasingly, states are adopting such standards for elementary and high school students. The Collaborate for Academic, Social, and Emotional Learning (CASEL) is a group that works with school districts to develop social emotional learning standards for students at all levels of education. CASEL has identified five core competencies related to social-emotional development, including self-management, self-awareness, social awareness, relationship skills, and responsible decision making. While not every school or district will utilize these exact standards for social-emotional development, they are broad categories that should be applicable to most other guidelines. These core competencies have clear relationships to ACT in several different ways.

Core Competency	Description in the CASEL Framework & ACT Connection
Self-Management	*The ability to successfully regulate one's emotions, thoughts, and behaviors in different situations.* • The "Mindful Core" focuses on the development of regulating emotions and thoughts, responding to the present environment, and the "Reinforcer Core" emphasizes engaging in behaviors that increase access to reinforcement.
Self-Awareness	*The ability to accurately recognize one's own emotions and thoughts and how these influence behavior.* • Multiple core processes develop the ability to engage in self-awareness. Present moment awareness and self-as-context teach the individual observe his or her own thoughts and emotions, while both defusion and acceptance emphasize the relationship between thoughts, emotions, and behavior.
Social Awareness	*The ability to take the perspective of and empathize with others, including those from diverse backgrounds and cultures.* • Again, the "Mindful Core" encourages the ability to observe and evaluate one's own behavior in relationship to others. As well, the ACT model incorporates activities that develop perspective-taking skills, so that the individual can relate to both his or herself and others.
Relationship Skills	*The ability to establish and maintain healthy and rewarding relationships with diverse individuals and groups.* • While ACT does not explicitly teach relationship skills, if an individual's values are related to interpersonal relationships, he or she will identify the behaviors needed to develop and maintain those relationships.
Responsible Decision Making	*The ability to make constructive choices about personal behavior and social interactions based on ethical standards, safety concerns, and social norms.* • The "Mindful Core" develops awareness of environmental conditions and private thoughts and feelings, and how these effect the individual's behaviors. The "Reinforcer Core" emphasizes how choices effect the individual and his or her values.

Related Service Providers

According to the Individuals with Disabilities Education Act (IDEA), a piece of legislation in the U.S. that ensure individualized and appropriate education for students with disabilities, it is required that related services that ensure the student advances toward their annual goals. Some examples of common related services are speech and language pathology, physical therapy, occupational therapy, social, mobility services, and health-related services. Like educators, professionals who provide related services will have their own standards or professional guidelines/codes that dictate their professional scope of practice. These providers should consult these guidelines before determining if incorporating ACT-related intervention is appropriate for their role on the child's educational team. For example, speech pathologists may consult the American Speech-

Language-Hearing Association (ASHA) for practice guidelines, and social workers may consult the National Association of Social Workers (NASW) for information on the scope of practice. Below are some examples of behaviors, disorders, and conditions that may be most appropriate for an educator or related service provider, as well as some questions that may help determine which services may be most appropriate.

Student Behaviors

Related Service Providers	Educator
Audiology, Speech Impediments, Fine motor skills, Neglect, Anxiety, Medical Needs	Bullying, Taking Items, Disrespect, Talking Out, Work Refusal, Inattention, Lying, Inappropriate Language, Tardiness
Help student benefit from special education services; address specific skill areas	Visible, measureable, & countable; may interfere with classroom learning
<u>Are any of these manifesting in behavior in class that impede learning?</u> Yes -> Redefine and treat the outcome behaviors No -> Ensure appropriate care by trained professional.	<u>Are these symptoms of an actual clinical disorder that requires additional treatment?</u> Yes -> Refer for appropriate care by trained professional No -> treat using ACT and ABC analyses

Behavior Analysts

Behavior analysts, in order to be responsible practitioners, must abide by certain constraints that are outlined by established ethical codes and clinical guidelines, which dictate what practices fall within the behavior analytic scope of services. When considering the inclusion of ACT-based approaches to behavioral intervention, it is critical that the behavior analyst remain in compliance with these standards and expectations, and ensure that their application of ACT is consistent with them. The behavior analyst must also keep in mind the various practice acts in place within their state or territory of practicing, and how such acts often dictate what professions can offer and/or seek financial reimbursement for specific services. The Behavior Analyst Certification Board (BACB), has developed both an ethical code and clinic guidelines which are applicable to the majority of professionals in this field. A review of the *Professional and Ethical Compliance Code for Behavior Analysts,* revealed two components of the code that are of particular importance in regard to ACT. The first is the requirement of conceptual consistency (4.01), which states that "behavior analysts design behavior-change programs that are conceptually consistent with behavior analytic principles." While mainstream explanations of mindfulness may not seem readily applicable to scrutiny in terms of behavior analytic principles, however, ACT itself is developed from a foundation of a behavior-analytic theory of human language, consistent with such principles. Traditional behavior assessment methods may be insufficient when treating individuals with sophisticated verbal behavior, therefore, in order to provide a conceptually-sound intervention for this population, the behavior analyst must incorporate advances in the understanding of human behavior, related to derived responding, rule-governed behavior, and antecedent interventions that impact the ABC relationship, all of which are included in the theoretical foundation of ACT, and its empirical basis. The second is the requirement to describe conditions for behavior-change program success (4.06), which states that, "behavior analysts describe to the client the environmental conditions that are necessary for the behavior-change program to be effective." In order to do so, the behavior analyst must describe behavior change in terms of measurable behavior outcomes. While ACT does target private events and covert self-rules as part of the therapeutic process, the effectiveness of this intervention, when implemented by a behavior analyst, must be evaluated in terms of its effect on quantifiable, observable events, such as changes in target behaviors. As a result of this ethical guideline, it is important that if a behavior analyst is referred a case in which the treatment goals are not directly measurable or are based on constructs, he or she must either reformulate the treatment into a behavioral conceptualization or refer the case to another professional. The behavior analyst must also keep in mind that just because ACT can be traced back to behavior analytic principles as its theoretical foundation, it does not mean that any behavior analyst could or should implement ACT. Instead, it is critical to make sure that before implementing procedures that appear new or beyond what was covered in formal educational coursework, that the behavior analyst seeks to obtain the appropriate and relevant training and supervision in this content area.

In addition to an ethical guideline, the BACB provides a guide to the knowledge and skills that serve as the foundation for the board-certified behavior analysts, called the *Task List*, which can provide a framework to assess the conceptual consistency of an intervention with behavior analytic principles. A review of the *BCBA/BCaBA Task List (5th ed.)*, revealed a number of items that directly relate to the implementation of ACT as a behavior intervention, which are outlined in the following table in addition to their specific relationship to ACT intervention. It should be noted, however, that while ACT is conceptually consistent with behavior analytic principles, it is not directly applicable to every content item on the *Task List*, and should only be utilized for appropriate clients.

Content Item	Description on BACB/BCaBA Task List (5th ed.) & ACT Connection
F-3	*Identify and prioritize socially significant behavior-change goals* • The ACT focus is entirely rooted in selecting pragmatic goals for the client; all behaviors targeted for intervention directly relate to the client's natural environment, and therapeutic goals must relate to adaptive, flexible behaviors.
G-1	*Use positive and negative reinforcement procedures to strengthen behavior* • The "Reinforcer Core" of the ACT model emphasizes contingency management, and incorporates reinforcement procedures to strengthen adaptive, flexible behaviors.
G-2	*Use interventions based on motivating operations and discriminative stimuli* • ACT intervention conditions natural environmental stimuli as motivating operations evoking adaptive, flexible behavior, and reduces the influence of delayed reinforcement on current behavior, increasing the saliency of discriminative stimuli for delayed reinforcers and their potency.
G-6	*Use instructions and rules* • ACT addresses problem behavior that is the result of rule-governed behavior that maintains maladaptive and inflexible behavior. As well, ACT will develop instructions and rules that occasion the occurrence of adaptive, flexible behavior.
G-10.	*Teach simple and conditional discriminations.* • Both the "Mindful Core" and "Reinforcer Core" require instruction in simple and conditional discriminations. For example, the client must learn to discriminate between stimuli present in the environment and those in their verbal behavior, as well as the distinction between "literal" and "nonliteral" thoughts. As well, the client must discriminate between behavior related to values and behavior that is not related to values.
G-19	*Use contingency contracting* • The "Reinforcer Core" relies on both therapist and client input in the development of contingency contracts related to the client's valued behavior and therapeutic goals. These contracts will be monitored by both the therapist and the client to evaluate therapeutic outcomes.
G-20	*Use self-management strategies.* • As part of the "Mindful Core," clients will learn to monitor their own behavior in order to learn when to implement therapeutic techniques (i.e. defusion); he or she will need to discriminate between behavior that is "mindful" and behavior that is not, and respond accordingly. As part of the "Reinforcer Core," clients will learn to monitor their own behavior related to valued outcomes, and implement self-management strategies in order to increase adaptive, flexible behavior, and evaluate their own progress.
G-22	*Use procedures to promote maintenance.* • Although ACT exercises may occur in analog settings, transfer to the natural environment is a key component of ACT. The overarching therapeutic goal of ACT is the development of an operant that includes adaptive, flexible behavior, which is mediated by both natural environmental contingencies and the clients' verbal behavior.

Mental Health Practitioners

Mental health practitioners who work in various fields such as clinical psychology, clinical child psychology, school psychology, and counseling, and in various locations such as schools, hospitals, and community organizations/clinics, may specialize in providing services to children with a large variety of disorders and disabilities. These professionals may treat biological problems, emotional or developmental problems, mental disorders, substance abuse, cognitive deficits, and trauma-related issues, among many others. Within the field of mental health services, there are many specialties and corresponding governing agencies that dictate the scope of practice for those professionals. The American Psychological Association (APA) and American Counseling Association (ACA), for example, provide guidelines for practice for psychologists and counselors, respectively. Keep in mind that although a person may hold a license in psychology, social work, or education as a teacher, this does not make them an expert in behavior management. Additional training, coursework, supervision, and/or credentialing may be necessary before having the relevant skills to conduct a behavioral assessment or design a functionally appropriate treatment plan.

There are many symptoms that children present with that all professionals will be potentially asked to provide input on or treatment for. It is critical that each professional practice within his or her scope of professional boundaries and experience. Many states provide explicit regulations on who can treat who and for what. A professional must make sure that they stay within their scope of practice, as well as their own abilities. There are two main categories of issues that a child may be thought of as ripe for ACT intervention. They include clinical diagnoses and behavioral manifestations. Overlap between these two categories of symptoms is common, however the implementer will need to evaluate the presenting problems for the child and determine if he or she believes they are comfortable with the potential depth of your intervention. If a child has a clinical diagnosis of reactive attachment disorder, it may be very difficult to build a reinforcer store that will override such psychological distress. However, if a label of anxiety is being used to describe a child that simply does not want to talk in front of the class, it may be possible that escape maintained consequences with a changing criterion intervention is sufficient. Understand this is a bidirectional challenge, as a highly trained clinical psychologist may have very limited abilities to reduce challenging behavior, and an over-tendency to diagnose a common behavior problem. In the case of any doubt, consult other professionals to ensure that the implementer is operating within his or her limits of their role as a professional.

Below are some examples of behaviors, disorders, and conditions that may be most appropriate for a behavior analyst or another service provider, as well as some questions that may help determine which services may be most appropriate.

Childhood Symptoms

Clinical Psychologist Licensed Therapist Social Worker	Behavior Analyst
Substance Use, Anxiety, Fearful, Depression, Sexual Abuse, ADHD	Bullying, Avoidance, Self-Injury, Property Destruction, Work Refusal, No Friends, Verbal Aggression, Throwing Items, Spitting
Unseen, diagnoses, & not measurable	Visible, measureable, & countable
<u>Are these convenient ways of labeling actual behavior?</u> Yes → Redefine and treat the outcome behaviors No → Ensure appropriate care by trained professional.	<u>Are these simplistic ways of labeling actual clinical disorders?</u> Yes → Refer for appropriate care by clinically trained professional No → treat using ACT and ABC analyses

Professional Boundaries of Competence

Although the use of ACT, behavior analytic, or any other treatments may fall within an implementers' professional scope in terms of the nature of the problem behavior and their setting, it is also imperative that each professional act within his or her own professional competence. The *Professional and Ethical Compliance Code for Behavior Analysts* sets clear expectations regarding competency for behavior analysts, stating that all behavior analysts must provide services, teach, and conduct research only in the confines of their own competency, and before engaging in a new endeavor, he or she must obtain sufficient training, supervision, or consultation on the subject matter (1.02). While a behavior analyst may have a conceptual understanding of an intervention such as ACT, it is imperative that he or she obtain the necessary training to be able to implement it correctly. These same considerations apply each to profession to which ACT may be a useful intervention technique, from teachers to psychologists. Although this book is designed to provide a curriculum and the foundation of knowledge to implement it, each professional should examine his or her own competence and seek out additional training as needed.

Chapter 2:
The AIM Curriculum

Overview

Accept, identify and move. Together these three words provide a powerful directive towards positive behavior change. But even more important is how these three words instruct us how to live a more value-driven life. Accepting everything that comes our way in life is difficult and many people will see it as a sign of weakness, of wallowing, or of giving up. Accepting however is nothing like this. True acceptance requires us to realize that what has already happened, has happened. We cannot think our way out of changing the past. We cannot disengage or distract ourselves from the non-preferred, difficult, or tragic things that have been part of our life. And, we cannot pretend the future is already here and somehow practice how we are going to overcome the challenges that it brings. It is at these exact moments in life, when we find ourselves about to jump into the struggle to control things we never will, that we need to identify what matters most. The choice is simple. Stay and fight things we will never be able to change, or move beyond the entanglement these thoughts bring. When we can identify our own psychological drifts backwards or leaps forward in time towards events that are not here yet, it is critical that we notice those thoughts and move past them. And when we really move, and not just say we are going to move, we begin to contact the positive consequences of doing so. These are real

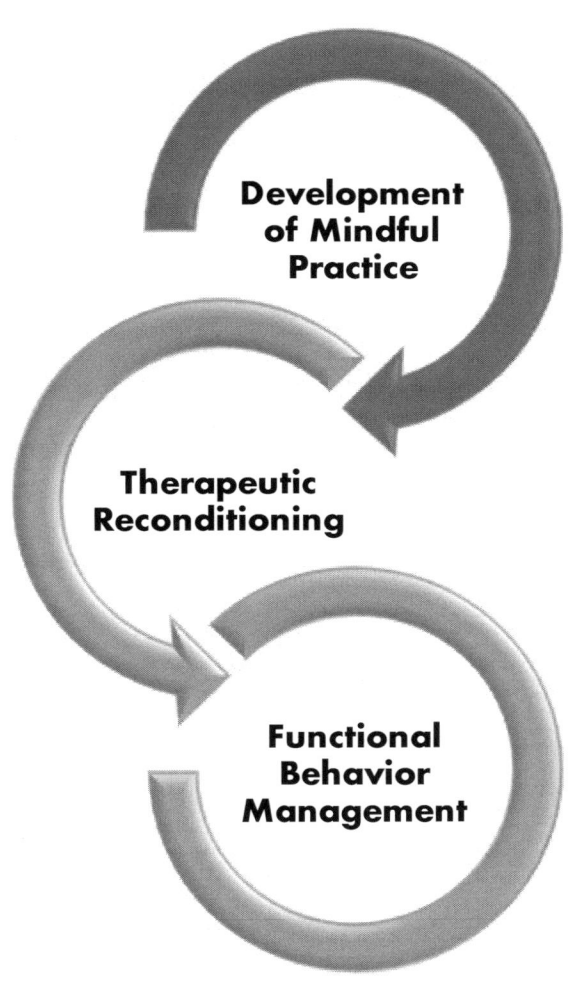

63

consequences, which produce real change and motivation to keep accepting, and moving towards what we want our lives to be about.

AIM as the acronym for accept, identify, and move serves as the general philosophy towards a value driven life. If we can accept both the wonderful and the terrible that is the natural course of everyone's life, identify what really matters to us and what we want our life to be about, and move towards these goals and values, we might just make it. Such a lofty philosophy is put forward in a structured and organized curriculum that many people will be able to successfully implement by following along with this text.

AIM, was designed to introduce the rather complex concepts of mindfulness, ACT, and ABA into the lives of children in fun and accessible way across a variety of settings. AIM was also crafted so that the entire curriculum or elements of it could be implemented with minimal background training in the complexities of the philosophies behind the practices. AIM incorporates mindfulness practice, therapeutic intervention, and functional behavior assessment. Combining these three elements allows for a targeting of the variables that maintain maladaptive behavior, the way the environment is either increasing or decreasing the likelihood of adaptive, flexible behaviors, which can alter the effects of contexts in which the child interacts with both his or her thoughts and the contingencies he or she encounters. AIM was designed and refined throughout years of implementing these practices with children in various schools and treatment centers. As parents began to see the success of AIM within the day environment, they became curious about how to implement the program at home. Slight variations in the original approach were made, and home-based elements are now included in the program. Even further additions to AIM were made to allow for self-monitoring and management so that graduates could maintain a mindful approach to as they moved into adulthood.

For about 10 years now AIM has been operating in many settings to serve both as the testing ground for the concepts and techniques contained within this book, and also to concurrently serve as the active treatment approach for referred children who are affected with social and emotional challenges.   What started out as an individual child intervention based on the science of behavior, evolved into a classroom management approach, and finally into a school district-wide philosophy. Once surrounding school systems caught on to the successes that occurred in the original district, others wanted to get on board with the program. AIM began as a consultative model devoid of standardized curriculum, forms or data collection materials, and slowly was packaged into the content of this book because of the need to replicate the procedures across additional districts that wanted to go online. In the recent years, summer camps, after school social groups, and parent led homework activities all fractioned off from the original AIM model.

This current text collects all the elements of the full AIM approach, and supplements it with creative ways of delivering the curriculum across many different settings, and at different levels or intensities of implementation. Furthermore, this book presents relevant issues specific to different types of implementers of the program. Commentary for parents, teachers, behavior analysts, and other care professionals are provided throughout. Some readers may find themselves diving into the entire AIM program, while others may begin only with the ACT or mindfulness lessons. Parents may opt out of the contingency management approach and focus solely on introducing mindfulness into the life of their child. As a total packaged intervention AIM can yield powerful outcomes, yet even the isolated elements, all rooted in extensive scientific research findings, have the power to change the behavior of a child.

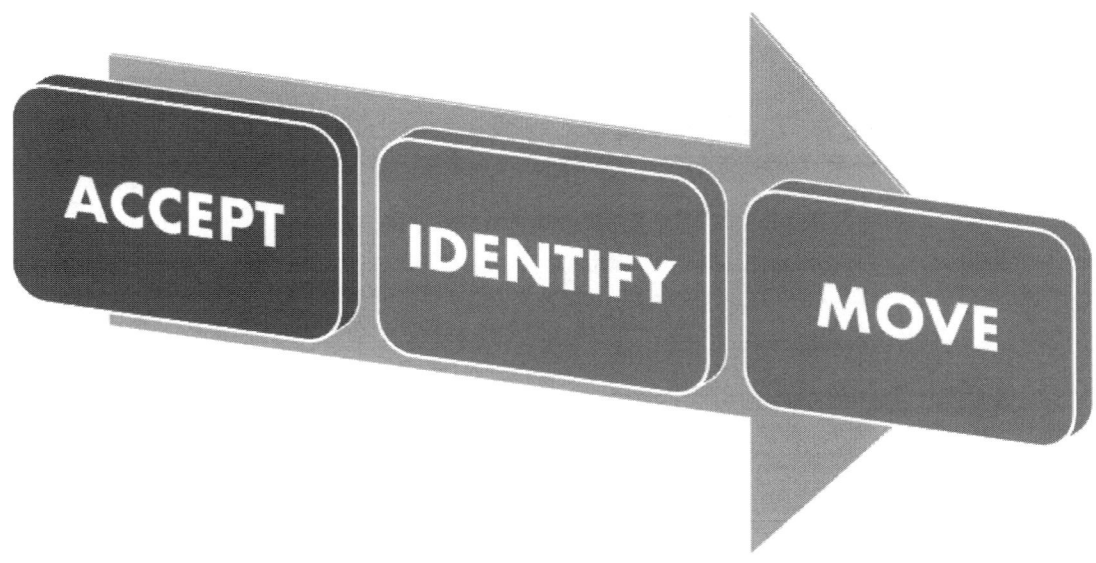

1: Development of Mindful Practice

Mindfulness is a process towards an idealized outcome. A person will never become completely mindful across their entire life, but can be better able to detect when they begin to drift from the present moment into entangled thoughts of the past or future. In the context of AIM, the mindfulness agenda is simply to get the child to notice their mind, understand how their mind pulls them away from the present, and how the drifting into thoughts can lead to missing out on what they value in life. The concept of mindfulness will be different for a 5-year-old and a 17-year-old. And what is "valued" in life for a 5-year-old is going to be much different than a 17-year-old. However, the means by which you help either child to discover awareness of the present moment will remain the same. Parents, educators and behavior analysts will all struggle with delivery of mindfulness guidance at first. It seems quite foreign of a concept to pop up at the dinner table, on the playground, or in math class. However, shockingly kids really dig it. And after you step back from the mystical connotations that seem to be surrounding the concept of mindfulness, it will become very easy to pull off. All you are really doing is providing verbal instructions to the child for them to become aware of the present environmental events and stimuli that are occurring at this exact moment in time. The events may be within their own body – like their breath, the weight of their hands, how their feet feel inside their shoes. Or, the events may be outside their body – like the sound of rain, noticing the light of a sunset, or the feeling of the wind blowing against their face. Your instructions will be simple statements regarding how the child can notice these events and stimuli. By the refocus of attention to these internal or external stimuli of the present, they are concurrently losing focus on other self-generated rules and substituted stimulus functions that involve distance places, times, or people. Hence, their minds are returning to the present.

AIM provides mindfulness intervention in two different ways. First, there is a list of 75 different mindfulness moment activities that can be delivered to the child at various times throughout the day. This is not an exhaustive list of how to teach mindfulness, but rather a collection of some of the easiest ways to get kids to buy into the idea of noticing their mind. Implementers of AIM will quickly be able to run these examples, and should continue onward creating and seeking out additional techniques on their own. Phone apps, videos, music CDs, and toys can all be added to the current list of mindfulness activities. Second, the mindfulness core of ACT provides a variety of possibilities of experiential lessons that can be delivered in an organized fashion to the child. The latter mindfulness intervention is more detailed, experiential, and time consuming than the first. The former should be considered fast, brief, and fun ways to take the mindfulness approach in isolation into the life of the child, while the latter is a deeper therapeutic approach toward lasting change by intertwining mindfulness and the motivation to become mindful in the first place.

Mindful Awareness	Mindlessness
NOTICING... ▶ The beauty of the sunset ▶ The light transitioning to dark ▶ The temperature dropping as the sun goes down ▶ The illuminating of the clouds behind the sun ▶ The reflection of the sun in the water disappearing as it sets ▶ The sounds of nighttime animals beginning ▶ The stillness of the water against the setting sun in motion ▶ Right here, right now	WORRYING... ▶ About the tasks yet to accomplish today ▶ About the argument with a friend earlier ▶ About the traffic on the drive home after sunset ▶ About playing catch up at work tomorrow ▶ About which bills are due this week and not having enough money ▶ About finding the time to exercise tomorrow ▶ About how you never take enough time to stop and enjoy the sunsets over the water ▶ Past or future events

Left margin: Responding to present stimulus conditions

Right margin: Responding to distant substituted stimulus functions

2: Therapeutic Reconditioning

"Therapy" can be an intimidating idea for someone not explicitly trained as a counselor or therapist. A common definition of therapy is "treatment, especially of bodily, mental, or behavioral disorder." Treatment is what educators, therapists, and other professionals provide on a daily basis. In the context of AIM, the emphasis is not on "therapy" in terms of the typical connotation of the psychotherapeutic approach, but on reconditioning the child's behavior, both explicitly in terms of the instruction and indirectly by way of behavior management techniques. For educators and teachers, the emphasis will remain on observable, measurable behavior. This approach to ACT emphasizes the specific training and instructional approaches that increase the skills necessary to engage in psychologically flexible behaviors, such as increasing the saliency of discriminative stimuli (events in the environment) for delayed reinforcers and their potency, increasing verbal behavior that regulates appropriate behavior and decreasing that which results in inappropriate behavior, teaching self-monitoring and self-awareness skills, and promoting contact with reinforcement for appropriate behaviors. In addition to a therapeutic stance involving open awareness of both the implementer's and child's thoughts and behaviors, the implementer also acts as the "manager of contingencies," ensuring that reinforcers are contacted for adaptive behavior, and not otherwise.

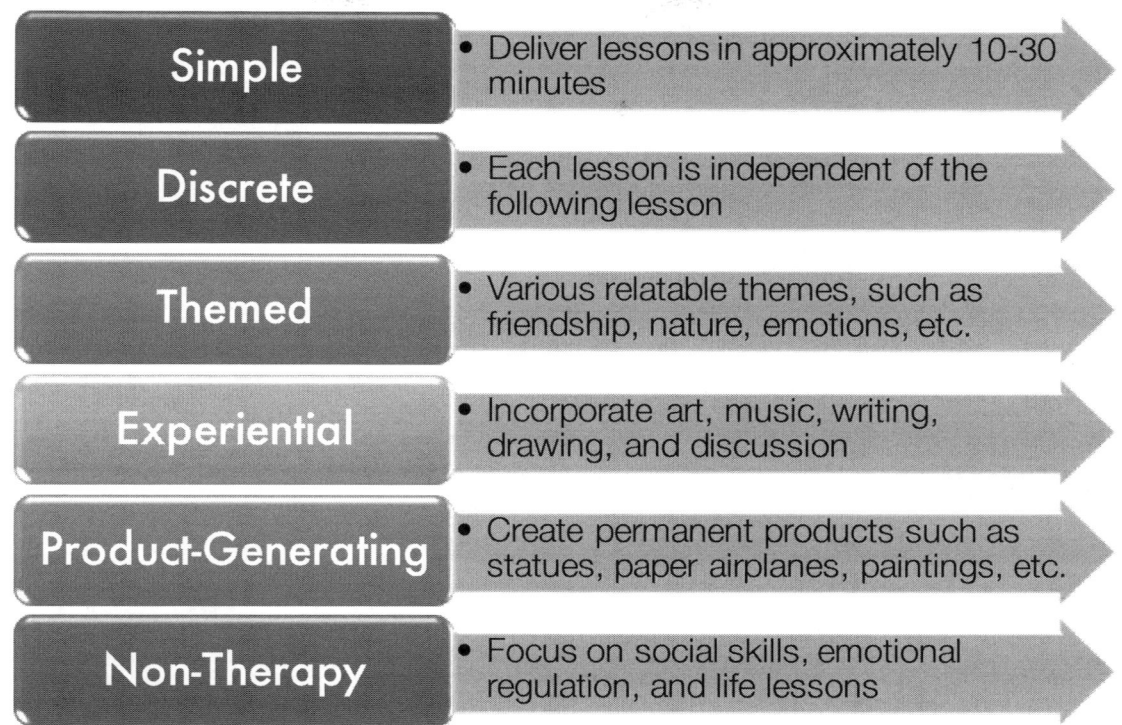

AIM provides a curriculum to deliver ACT in a 3-tier system. Each tier provides a different level of support and depth into the ACT core processes, from brief, preventative supplements to more intensive, personal exercises. While ACT is targeted specifically in the curriculum, it is incorporated into the contingency management plan, with ACT check-ins on a regular basis, and ACT embedded into responses to negative behaviors. The AIM delivery method for ACT to be implemented with children is unique from the traditional methods of providing therapy in other contexts, in a format that is accessible and easy to deliver in an intervention with a younger population rather than a talk therapy only environment. The key characteristics of the ACT curriculum are its simple format of brief, intensive lessons related to psychological flexibility, discrete arrangement of activities that are complete and do not rely on having participated in previous exercises, themed modules that that are relatable to children of various ages, focus on hands-on experiential activities, the creation of various products that are tangible reminders of ACT metaphors, and an emphasis on social-emotional skill development. These characteristics are woven into each component of the AIM curriculum, creating a consistent, cohesive therapeutic experience that stresses skill acquisition and behavior change.

3: Functional Approach to Behavior

A functional approach to behavior assessment looks at the relationship between environmental triggers, the individual's behavior/responses, and the events that follow the behavior to understand what is causing the behavior and what is maintaining its occurrence. Analyzing behavior in this way reduces the causes of behavior to one of the four primary functions of behavior (attention, escape, tangibles, sensory). If the assessor correctly identifies the function of an individual's behavior, the treatment developed will likely be successful; if not, the treatment will be ineffective or may increase the occurrence of the inappropriate behavior.

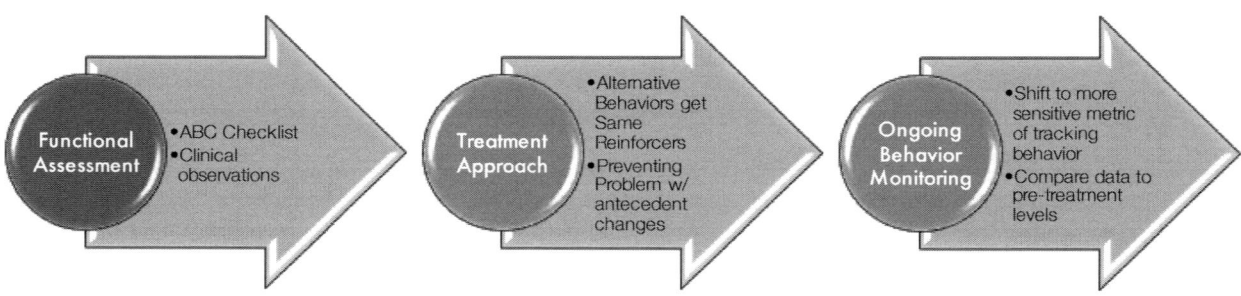

The functional treatment approach incorporates reliance on data collection and both preventative and reactive measures focused on environmental, verbal, and situational stimuli to reduce the likelihood of maladaptive behaviors occurring.

Data collection involves standardized means of monitoring the occurrence of target maladaptive behaviors, which can be collected through formal records, within the moment by the person working with the individual, as well as by the child himself in a self-monitoring format. Preventative strategies should be incorporated to reduce the likelihood of the problem behavior occurring in the first place; the implementer should consider how the physical environment is arranged, the form of the verbal behavior used to communicate to the individual, as well as situation-relevant variables such as tasks and activities. All of the preceding variables should be designed to minimize the "value" of the maladaptive behavior in the setting. Reactive strategies should be incorporated to respond to the occurrence of problem behavior, as well as reduce the likelihood of it occurring again in the future. Again, these strategies should incorporate variables related to the physical environment, language used in communication, and the current situation so that access to functional reinforcers when maladaptive behavior occurs is minimized or eliminated and access to those same reinforcers are maximized when adaptive behavior occurs.

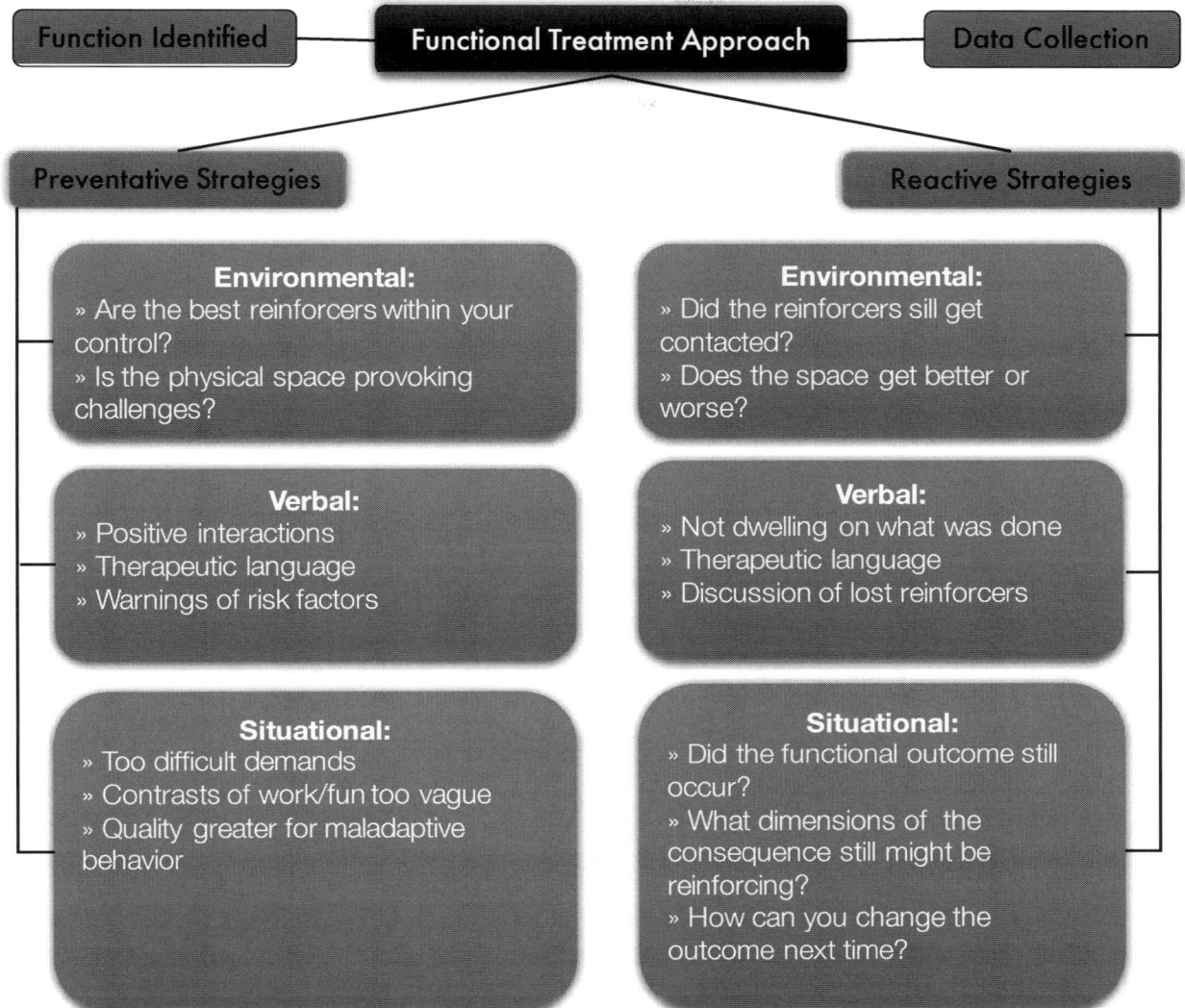

The ACT approach should be built in throughout this A-B-C conceptualization, and incorporated in each part of the treatment process. The typical flow of behavior across time consists of an antecedent that sets the occasion for the person to emit a certain behavior that is then followed by a consequence. When such consequences yield "reinforcers," behaviors in the future are more likely to occur in the presence of such antecedent triggers. While it is possible to respond to behavior in terms of the observable events only, the AIM program incorporates verbal behavior and thoughts into behavior management practices using mindfulness and acceptance based processes. Mindfulness, ACT, and functional behavior management have individual components within the AIM curriculum, however they work together in a dynamic way to facilitate lasting positive behavior change for children.

Integrating Mindful Practice, ACT, and a Functional Approach to Behavior

Each unit within this behavioral event can be addressed within the ACT approach, resulting in both proactive and reactive adult responses that are consistent with mindfulness- and values-based techniques. Awareness improves the adult's observation of the antecedent event, setting the stage for the adult to be aware of current environmental conditions and child behavior, and understanding of how the child failed to maintain flexibility. When the behavior occurs, the adult can communicate to the child using ACT language, again increasing the salience of ACT processes for the child. Finally, following the behavior, the adult can treat the student for more flexibility of responding moving forward, evaluating both the child's and adult's behavior in terms of the ACT processes.

The Flow of the Behavioral Event

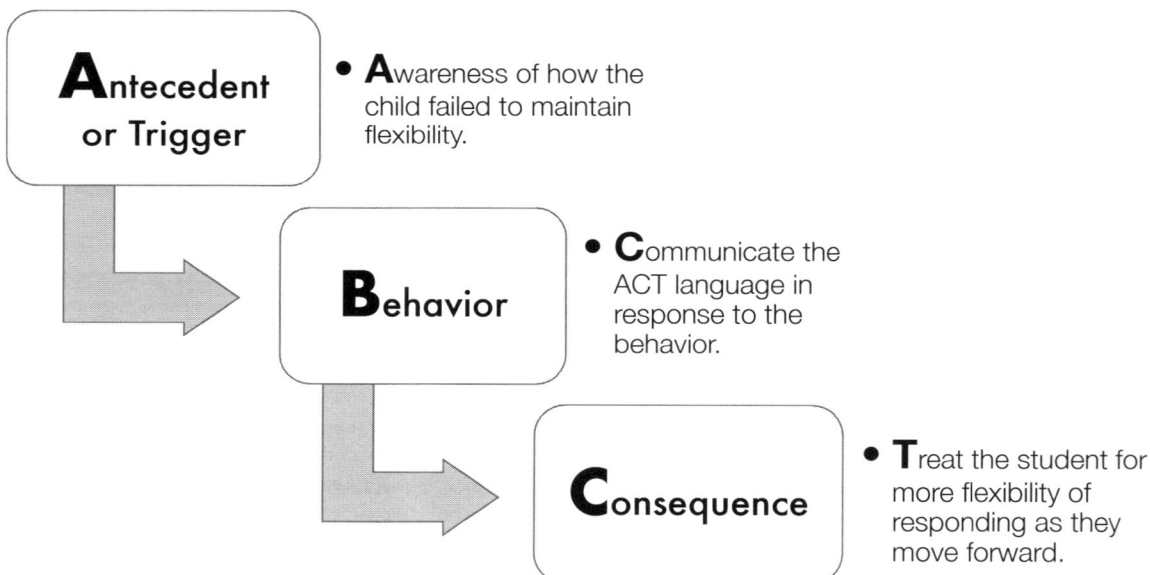

When practicing awareness of the behavioral event, the goal is to utilize one's own awareness in order to develop the child's and help him or her become aware of the ACT processes that interact with his or her behavior. Then, specific ACT-based language related to the behavioral event can be used to discuss the event with the child, as it is occurring. Finally, when resolving the event with the child, focus on how you can build his or her skills with parts of the mindful core, reinforcer core, or both, increasing the child's capacity to manage any situation mindfully in the future.

Where ACT helps enhance the typical ABC contingency is by using the challenging behavioral episode as both a feedback and teaching opportunity for the child. For example, if a child is presented a low-preferred task, like sorting their laundry, and it results in the verbal refusal of, *"No way, I hate you,"* and the consequence of avoiding the task for a few moments as the parent yells at them, the ACT reaction here is to identify what exactly went wrong when the task was presented. In this case it is possible that the child failed to keep in mind that even though the task of sorting laundry is really boring, completing it allows for them to get closer to leisure time later in the evening. Here the present moment the child was not flexible with their thoughts of, *"I hate laundry"* or, *"I don't want to work anymore today,"* and allowed them to dominate influence on the antecedent, *"Sort your laundry before you go outside."* Reminding the child of this fusion to thoughts and lack of acceptance is important. Yet, just as important is the parent's communication of this observation to the child in a non-threatening and non-judgmental way. There is a huge difference between the parent saying, *"You need to work when I tell you to,"* and, *"I know you hate laundry but getting it done gets you closer to being able to watch a movie later."* Additional comments such as, *"I know it's really hard to accept stuff you don't like"* or reminding them of the delayed consequences of these actions, can also be helpful to minimize a similar reaction to the laundry task in the future. If there are any sorts of good behaviors that accompanied the laundry revolt, make sure to capitalize on them and provide appropriate positive attention to these events. For example, in the middle of the laundry revolt, the parent noticed that the child let the dog outside to use the bathroom. While this is not an overwhelmingly positive behavior, make sure to reinforce this tiny display of attending to the present moment, and how it might be wise to attend to other such present moment events (like laundry tasks) in the future. Comments such as, *"Although screaming at me is really not that cool, I did appreciate how you let Fido outside in the middle of your fit. See even when you think you are totally fused to your thoughts, you noticed an event in the present. This is awesome, and if you did it more with more things, I have a funny feeling you could get to the goal of watching the movie before it is too late and you need to go to bed."*

This combination of responding functionally to a child's behavior and infusing ACT language into the behavioral event is a cornerstone of the AIM approach. While it is too great a task to provide instructions for incorporating ACT-related communication into every behavioral event, the examples throughout this text should provide enough exemplars to use with various clients or students. As well, a table is provided that provides lists of generally ACT-consistent responses to each of the six core processes. As the implementer, it is in the best interest to become well-acquainted with the verbiage typically included in ACT exercises, as well as the metaphors frequently used. During each behavioral event, focus on understanding the immediate consequences maintaining the behavior (such as escaping a task) as well as the role of language in the child's responses (such as being unwilling to accept the possibility of feeling embarrassed if they cannot complete the task). Once fluency in this functional approach to problem behavior is developed, the role of contingency management becomes evident.

Contingency Management. The overall goal of contingency management is that problem behavior fails to gain access to the once-desired consequences and positive behavior must be able to gain access to functionally-equal consequences (attention, escape, tangibles, or sensory). As well, the implementer must consider how delays to reinforcement and the probability of obtaining reinforcers may negatively impact programming for behavior change.

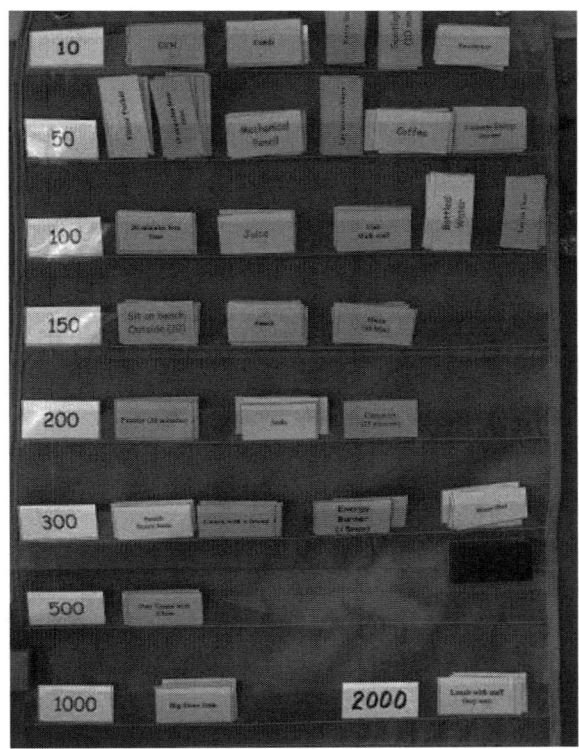

The AIM curriculum incorporates contingency management primarily through a point system, which provides a mechanism for reinforcement delivery, which can range from a simple statement of "I am working for..." to complex, ongoing point management, and provides points for ACT-related behaviors. The images included represent various methods of arranging point systems, from simple to complex; methods for developing and implementing a contingency management system will be provided later in the text.

Contingency management will be most effective when certain technical considerations are made prior to implementation. Reinforcers should be completely individualized to the child; "one size fits all" will not work for most challenging behaviors. Just like each child has a unique history, the most effective reinforcers for that child will be distinct as well. In addition, the delivery of the contingency should be as immediate as possible. First, if a token or point system is used, the faster the point or token is delivered to the individual following the appropriate behavior, the better. Second, the shorter the duration of time between the occurrence of the appropriate behavior and access to the actual reinforcer, the better. While the delivery of effective reinforcers is particularly important, ensuring that access to the reinforcers is controlled by the implementer is also crucial. In order for access to reinforcement to be 'contingent upon' appropriate behavior, access should be restricted in the event of any inappropriate behavior. Initially, setting a "small" or easy to accomplish contingency can help to increase the likelihood of the child earning the reinforcer, for example, earning a toy for a minute after completing one task. Over time, this can be extended so that the child completes a larger number of tasks before earning access to the back-up reinforcer. One way to extend this is by increasing the number of

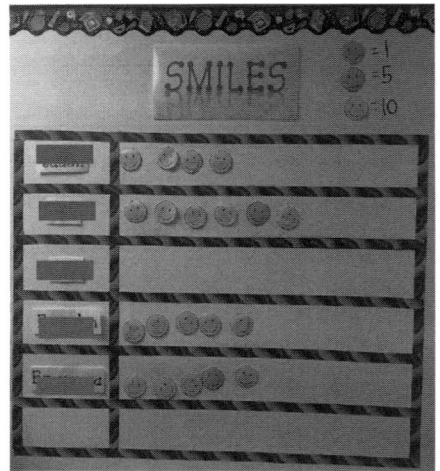 points or tokens needed to earn the reinforcer over time. For more advanced learners, goal setting can be a helpful way to engage the child in the process of learning to extend his or her tolerance for temporally extended rewards. For both more simple and complex contingency management systems, the implementer must not "stretch out" the contingency "too thin" so that there is too much demand for appropriate behavior for a smaller reinforcer. This type of arrangement would likely result in the child continuing to engage in maladaptive behavior. Establishing clear expectations or rules for how the contingency management system works can eliminate ambiguity and ensure consistent application of the system. AIM incorporates these considerations, in a way that is likely to be more effective than other packaged interventions that rely on arbitrary contingencies, unequal intervals of time for reinforcer delivery, or caregiver whims as to when points or tokens are to be delivered.

AIM embraces a child-centered stance that is driven by individual performance. The use of individualized, functional reinforcers promotes optimal behavior change. This may involve providing specific reinforcers for different children, and/or making a variety of function-based reinforcers readily available to at any given time. Moving away from generic 'prizes,' toward individualized reinforcers that match the function for the inappropriate behavior will yield lasting results. The AIM curriculum focus is on increasing alternative adaptive behaviors that result in the same consequences as the maladaptive behaviors that are targeted for reduction. Teaching a child to request or "buy" a break with points results in far more adaptive, flexible behavior than arranging an environment in which refusing to work or falling asleep is more effective for the child in obtaining a break from demands. Adults engage in these alternative behaviors all the time, such as excusing oneself to the bathroom when a meeting gets heated at work rather than arguing or yelling at their colleagues, and it is important to teach children how to regulate their behaviors in a similar way that fits within the parameters of their present culture

Complete Implementation Guide

The AIM Program includes the synthesis of multiple behavior analytic techniques to promote positive behavior in children. This system involves five main components:

1» *Mindful Practices:* Practicing mindfulness can occur in almost any setting with very little preparation, materials, or effort. Seventy-five different mindfulness moments are provided that should be implemented when possible throughout the child's day.

2» *Daily ACT Lessons:* One hundred seventy-five days of ACT experiential activities are included within this program. Each day, the child will reflect on an ACT core process and engage with the implementer in one or more experiential activities designed to increase their understanding of ACT concepts and apply this understanding to their own thoughts, feelings, and behavior.

3» *AIM Point System:* Tools for managing a point system are provided with the program, including planning matrices for token economies and point tracking forms for various settings (including home, school, and therapy).

4» *Functional Reinforcement:* Built within the AIM Point System matrices and forms, are opportunities to plan for a variety of different reinforcement schedules, cash-out systems, and data collection regarding functional reinforcers.

5» *Ongoing Progress Monitoring:* Continuous data collection is important for evaluating the effectiveness of a child's intervention plan. Included within the program are ACT-incorporated ABC data collection forms, point tracking forms, a weekly ACT report, a self-monitoring form, a point exchange log, tools for assessing implementation fidelity, a measure of psychological flexibility as reported by both children and their caregivers, and a rubric for quantitatively assessing a child's ACT work.

AIM Program Function-Based Intervention

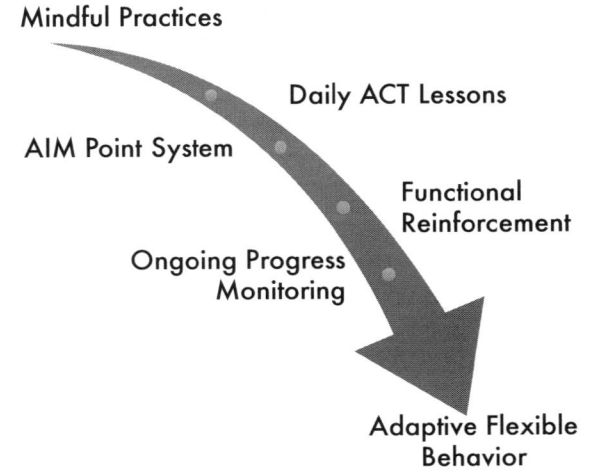

1» Mindful Practices

Ideally, these mindful moments should fill gaps of time between activates, transitions to other environments, before going to bed at night, right after recess, or prior to a difficult task being presented. There is no specific dose of mindfulness moments required, but rather an approach should be taken to integrate mindfulness throughout the day in a multitude of ways. Each of the seventy-five provided mindful moments serve as a creative example of how to capture mindfulness from everyday tasks. They are exemplars which will teach the child not only how to be mindful when guided through one of these 75 experiences, but also how to engage in mindful practices themselves as that child encounters the world each and every day. The list of activities provided in the text provide short descriptions of brief, simple activities to complete with the children. Implementers are encouraged to modify these activities for time or developmental level. The activities are divided into three components: Mind, Body, and Interaction. The "Mind" activities focus on mindful awareness of thoughts; the "Body" activities focus on mindful awareness of one's body; and the "Interaction" activities focus on developing mindfulness through quick, experiential events.

> » *Mindful Moments: Mind.* This set of twenty-five activities focuses on the relationship between the child's thoughts and the present moment. These activities will prompt the students to mindfully notice their thoughts and feelings in the moment, and practice the skill of letting go of those thoughts and feelings to attend to the present moment.
> » *Mindful Moments: Body.* This set of twenty-five activities focuses on the child's awareness of his or her own body in the moment. These activities will prompt the students to engage in some bodily action and notice the physical sensations they experience, as well as how these may or may not interact with their behavior.
> » *Mindful Moments: Interaction.* This set of twenty-five activities focuses on incorporating mindfulness of both mind and body through a series of interactive exercises that involved interacting with materials, sensory experiences, and/or other people to develop the ability to be present in the moment.

Present moment awareness is incorporated throughout the various ACT lessons in the text, however practicing the challenging components of non-judgmental observation and acceptance of difficult or painful thoughts or feelings that are included in mindfulness practices require frequent, targeted practice which can be done at any time or day or any location. These activities relate to the "mindfulness" method of meditation.

AIM also provides an avenue to incorporate more formal, concentration meditation practice. Provided are four scripts for brief, guided meditations to be used at different parts of the day. Implementers may choose to incorporate one or more of these scripts on a routine basis, completing the same meditation at a certain time each day in order to develop meditative skills and build the child's stamina for meditation. Although scripts are provided for these activities, implementers may choose to follow these scripts loosely, modifying them for time or developmental level, as well as simply to encourage more variation during meditation. It may benefit the child to begin with shorter one- to three-minute meditation sessions, and slowly extend the length of these sessions over time, until they are able to engage in meditation for ten, fifteen, or even thirty minutes. Using the formats of the scripts included, implementers may also write individualized scripts that may benefit their clients or students in unique ways. For example, if a child engages in challenging before following lunch each day, it may be beneficial to develop a mindfulness script to use at the end of lunchtime. The following four themes for guided meditations are provided due to their universal nature and easily-relatable content for various populations and settings.

» *Morning Gratitude Meditation.* This meditation guide encourages the child to engage in gratitude at the beginning of each day, integrating mindful breathing and intentional statements of appreciation. This practice may orient the child to their values at the beginning of the day and help to identify particular reinforcers that may be effective throughout that day.

» *Daily Focused Attention Meditation.* This scripted meditation emphasizes mindful breathing and the child's attention to the present moment without distraction from ongoing thoughts and feelings. In this meditation, they are encouraged to "Notice and Let Go" when thoughts or feelings enter their awareness. They meditation may help to build "momentum" for present moment awareness and decrease the effect of previous events on the child's subsequent behavior.

» *Relaxation Meditation.* This guided meditation is intended to be used following activities that may have energized the child, before engaging in a task that requires additional focus and stillness. Throughout this meditation, they will bring awareness to part of their bodies and intentionally relax them, letting go of their tension and stress. This may be most beneficial after lunch, recess, exercise, or other physical activities.

» *End of Day Meditation.* This brief scripted meditation focuses on the release of troublesome thoughts or feelings about the day that may lead to challenges after school, therapy, or before bedtime. During this meditation, the child is encouraged to defuse from and let go of thoughts and feelings, bringing awareness to the stillness in their minds and the calmness in their bodies.

2 » Daily ACT Lessons

Included are examples of the structure and format of the daily ACT lessons included in the AIM curriculum. The one hundred seventy-five daily ACT lessons, found in the next section of the text, are divided into 5-day modules and grouped by a theme, which is outlined in the 'Module Description' section at the beginning of each module. Subsequently, a brief 'Preparation Notes' section is provided, which provides ideas to consider when planning for completing the activities with a child or children, potential modifications for individualizing the curriculum, as well as discussion of challenging topics or concepts from within the activities. Next, the 'Modules Materials List,' outlines the materials that will be needed for each experiential activity for each day, separated by what will be needed for the Tier 2 and 3 activities. In the example below the section for Day 1, Tier 2 is visible. The material needed for this activity is "WS D1T2," which stands for Worksheet Day 1, Tier 2. Some ACT lessons are accompanied by a worksheet that aids in the completion of the activity. These worksheets can be found within this text following the ACT curriculum. These worksheets should be saved, and, when appropriate, evaluated using the ACT-focused rubric, so that the implementers have opportunities to monitor a child's progress with the ACT material. Finally, a 'Module Journal Prompt' is provided, which is an optional supplement can be used with older children to facilitate their reflection on the concepts and ideas explored that week. Alternatively, the implementer can utilize the prompt as an additional source for discussion.

Module 1: Introduction to the Hexaflex

Module Description:
This introductory week is designed to present the concepts of the Hexaflex to the child.

Preparation Notes:
When preparing daily activities, consider if whole group or small group arrangements would work best for your children, and plan your materials accordingly.

Materials List:

Tier	Day 1	Day 2	Day 3	Day 4	Day 5
2	»WS D1T2	»Paper »Pen/Pencils	»Balloons »Paper	None	»Tape
3	None	»3 different sounding bells, noisemakers, or chimes	»Balloons »Paper	None	»Tape

Journal Prompt:
What are the struggles you experience in your mind? How do they get in the things matter most to you in life?

Overview of the module theme and considerations for implementers related to the content or activities for the module, or curriculum in general.

Materials required for each experiential activity, reported by tier, including associated worksheets (located in the Appendix).

An optional journal prompt is included each module; these can be completed in writing, or used as additional discussion starters.

AIM Tier System

Tier 1
- Minimal to no challenging behaviors.
- Designed as a preventative support as well as a mindful supplement to social and life skills development.

Tier 2
- Occasional, but infrequent, low- to medium- intensity challenging behaviors
- School examples: teasing or work refusal
- Home examples: disrespect or refusing to follow directions

Tier 3
- Frequent and/or high-intensity challenging behaviors
- School examples: aggression toward peers or teachers or property destruction
- Home examples: verbal or physical aggression toward family or elopement

The AIM program utilizes a tiered approach to provide appropriate intervention based on the needs of the child, and the amount of time and resources available to the implementer. Within each "day" of intervention, the three tiers are related in terms of topic, core process, and experiential activities. For the majority of the groups of Tier 1-3 activities, a child could complete each of the activities as a set or the individual tasks on their own, as they are independent of one another. For some, however, the Tier 3 activity builds upon the Tier 2 activity, so the child would need to complete the second activity before the third. In a school setting, it may be appropriate to utilize Tier 1 as a universal or school-wide support, Tier 2 as a classroom-wide activity, and Tier 3 as a small-group activity for students with a higher level of need for behavioral support. In a therapeutic clinical setting or in a home setting, the three tiers may be competed throughout the course of a day or a therapy session. Alternatively, the three activities may be divided among several days or therapy sessions. The implementer will need to evaluate the needs of the child he or she is working with, as well as the format of service delivery to determine the most appropriate approach to ACT delivery across the three tiers. Again, in a school setting, one module may be completed in a week, whereas in therapeutic contexts a module may be completed over the course of several weeks or a month.

In the figure below, the layout and content for one day of ACT activities is outlined. The label identifying the number of the ACT day is located in the upper left-hand corner. In the columns to the right of the number, are the lesson's title, and its focus ACT core processes. Immediately below this heading row is the tiered content.

» Tier 1: The content located in this section is designed to serve as a preventative support and supplement to social-emotional development. The content here should be shared with the child and used as prompt for discussion, when appropriate.

» Tier 2: Tier 2 is divided into two sections: first, the discussion, a narrative to be used to facilitate a meaningful discussion with the child (remember, it is important that the implementer engages actively in both discussion and activities); second, the experiential activity, which describes how to set up, explain, and complete the activity. Activities in this tier will typically be less structured, and focused on teaching ACT concepts and developing metaphors.

» Tier 3: Tier 3 is also divided into the two sections: discussion and experiential activity. The activities at Tier 3 differ from Tier 2 in that they are generally more personal, and require that the child relates the ACT metaphor and/or activity to their own life/lives, often focusing specifically on problem behavior.

The tiered activities are designed to coordinate with one another, and the concepts introduced in Tier 2 are further developed during Tier 3. In most cases, Tier 2 can stand alone as an activity, whereas Tier 3 requires the completion of the Tier 2 discussion and/or experiential activity. Tiers with an associated worksheet are marked with a "»" symbol for reference.

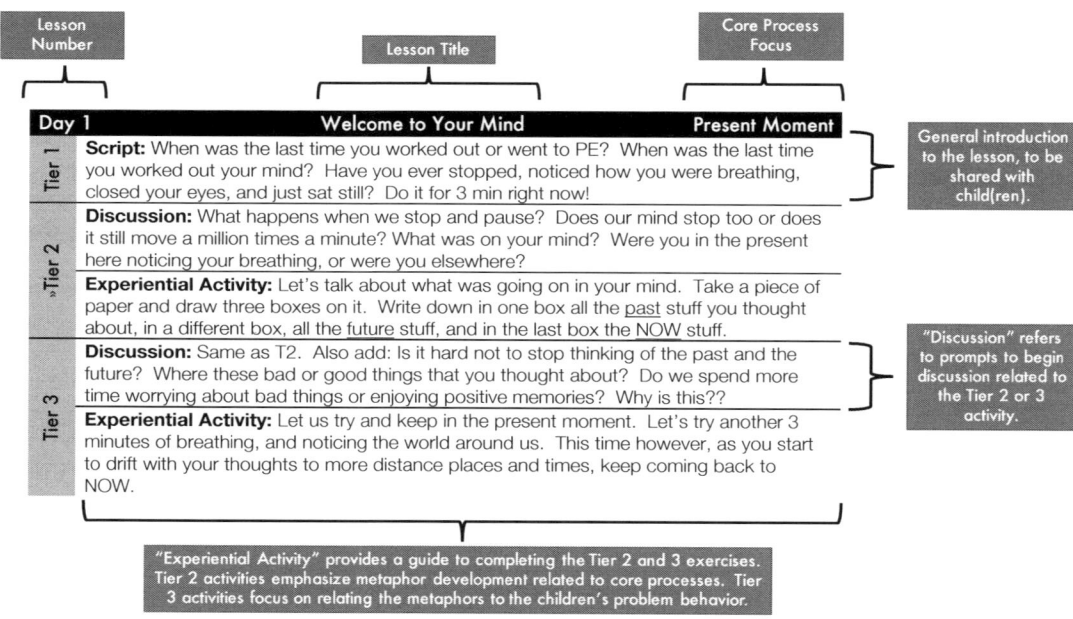

The ACT lessons are designed to be used with school-aged children across a wide range of ages. However, implementers may find that as they are planning for implementing the lessons with your child/student/client, that some of the lessons may not be completely applicable to his or her developmental level. In this case, the implementer can modify certain elements of the curriculum to "skew" the activity for a slightly more advanced or novice learner. As the implementer, critically analyze the activity, and accommodate the participant's needs without eschewing the overall metaphor or point of the activity. There are several simple ways to modify the lessons to suit their needs, including, some of which are exemplified in the example below:

» Read the scripted sections, narrative prompts, and exercise directions, and modify the complexity or the content of the language to fit the developmental level of the child. For example, if a word is too complex, change it to a less advanced synonym. Or, if the examples provided within the text are not compatible with the treatment environment, change them.

» Review the experiential activities in order to determine if they are feasible for the child participating in the curriculum. If the activity is not appropriate, be creative with ways to modify it to maintain its message and engage the child. Simple changes can occur, such as turning a writing activity into a drawing or discussion-based activity. When possible, reformatting the activity into a game-like exercise for a larger number of participants or a child that is difficult to hook into new and different activities may help. Finally, if it is difficult to obtain all of the necessary materials to complete an activity, or to monitor all of the participants sufficiently to do so, consider presenting the activity as a model, so that the child can see it live, but it eliminates some of the procedural difficulties.

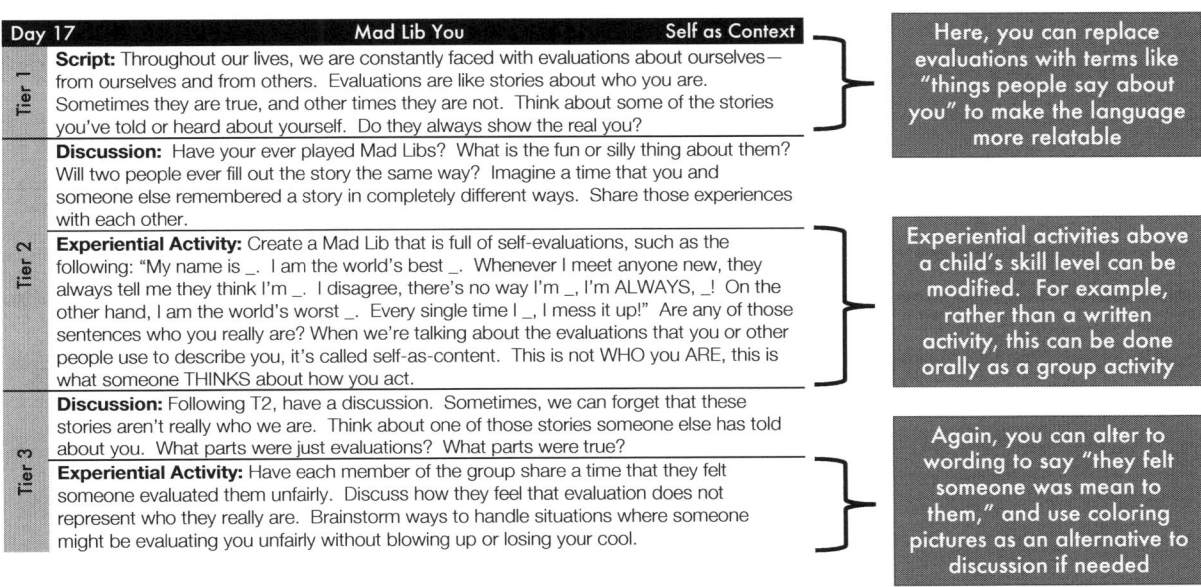

Intervening with ACT. Although AIM is designed to provide both a general framework for intervention as well as specific ACT activities to complete with children at set periods of the day, ACT language should be incorporated into many interactions throughout the school day, therapy session, or other service delivery, particularly during times of challenging behaviors or psychological inflexibility. The "ACT Interaction" is integral in the translation of ACT skills learned during intervention times to the rest of the day or session, and the opportunity to provide reinforcement to children for engaging in "ACT-consistent" behavior. In the school setting, all adults within the system (teachers, paraprofessionals, and administrators) should all be familiar with ACT and how to incorporate specific ACT language into interactions with students. Similarly, in the clinic or home setting, all therapists and family members should be able to incorporate these principles into communication and provide a consistent "ACT front" throughout the child's day. ACT can be built into the behavioral event, at each state – from antecedents, to behavior emission, and consequences delivered by focusing on the following model: *Awareness, Communicate, Treat.*

Implementers should practice *Awareness* throughout the time spent interacting with the child by being very observant of the child's behavior and noticing when a child is struggling with behaving in a psychologically flexible way. Notice if child appears to be choosing non-values or having difficulty with acceptance of unpleasant consequences. When aware of the child's behavior and surrounding environmental events, the implementer may be better able to identify potential antecedents of problem behavior, and either able to prevent or ameliorate subsequent challenging situations.

The implementer must also *Communicate* to the child during a challenging behavioral event using ACT-consistent language. The old adage "practice what you preach" is radically important here. The implementer *must* model ACT language and thought processes in the moment, bringing the skills the child has learned from the ACT lessons into the present environment, where they are directly applicable to his or her life and exhibited challenging behavior. ACT language can be incorporated into communication with the child in both proactive and reactive ways. If the child is demonstrating psychological inflexibility, the implementer can challenge these behaviors directly, in reaction to the rigidity, and redirecting back to ACT core processes. For example, the implementer may prompt the child acting aggressively by saying, *"Let's get back to the present moment,"* or, *"Did this get you closer to your values?"* As well, the implementer can proactively prompt the child to engage in psychologically flexible behavior prior to a challenging behavior occurring. For example, if the implementer has noticed that the child has been choosing non-values and seems to be losing commitment to, when a possible antecedent to problem behavior occurs, he or she may prompt the child by saying, *"Let's commit to doing better from this point forward,"* or *"Can you tell me what your values are today?"* to direct the child to be more adaptive and flexible before the inappropriate behavior occurs. Both proactive and reactive ACT language should be built into the natural communication flow with the child.

Finally, the implementer must *Treat* using the ACT approach. Here there must be an incorporation of ACT concepts into the behavioral event. Here, the implementer should encourage the child to utilize the strategies learned from prior ACT lessons in the moment *and* provide reinforcement when the child begins to engage in any adaptive, flexible behaviors. For example, if the child is having difficulty remaining in the present moment, continuing to be aggressive and talking about something that happened before school or the therapy session, after communicating to the child using ACT-friendly language, the implementer should help the child focus on a present moment awareness activity, acknowledging the current environment and stepping away from the distractions in their mind.

Awareness	Communicate	Treat
• Not present in current moment • Fused to thoughts • Choosing non-values • Losing commitment • Wrong self • Difficulty with acceptance	**Reactive ACT** • Let's get back in the present • It's ok that did not work out. We need to accept it. • Is this the real you that is here right now? • Did this get you closer to your values? **Proactive ACT** • Can you tell me what your values are today? • Stop, pause, and come back to the present. • Let's commit to doing better from this point forward • I like the real you I see right now	• Acknowledge current environment • Stepping back from current verbalizations • Reminding of prior stated values • Encouraging commitment • Refocus to self-as-context • Acceptance of the entire event (good/bad)

Using "ACT Phrases to Go." Communicating with ACT language in both proactive and reactive ways to each of the six core processes can be a challenge. It requires both the awareness of the child's current behavioral functions and psychological flexibility, as well as fluency of "speaking in ACT." Included in the curriculum is a set of possible responses in each of the six areas for reference, and individualize to each client or student in each unique behavioral event. Remember, although certain phrases and key words are important in developing the child's flexible responding, reliance on stock phrases, may result in the child responding to the disingenuous application of ACT to his or her situation.

AIM: ACT Phrases to Go

Acceptance:	Defusion:
(P) Accepting that you had to do work now was awesome. I know it can be hard to do sometimes.	(P) Letting go of that thought was rough to do. Good job remembering what's really important.
(P) I see you are accepting that's time for work.	(P) You let go of your disappointment and did not lose points. Way to go!
(P) I see you accepted that free time is over.	(P) Great job not responding to those comments/thoughts. Good defusion!
(P) I know you want me to help you now, so thanks for accepting I will be there soon.	(N) You don't need to be fused to that thought now. We have other things to do.
(N) You have to accept that everything is not going to be perfect. And that's ok.	(N) Are you letting those thoughts control you? Why don't you defuse them?
(N) I know you really wanted X to happen. Accepting we have to do work is part of the day.	(N) Cut the fuse off this mess, and let's get back to earning points.
(N) Your points are not high enough to buy X. Let's buy something else and accept it's a bummer. Let's get ready for next time.	

Self-as-Context:	Values:
(P) I like how are being the real (STUDENT NAME) right now!	(P) I really like the way you are doing X. You must be working towards getting stuff you value from the store later today.
(P) I noticed that you seem ok right now being who you really are.	(P) You are letting me know you value (learning/friendship/graduation/etc.) by doing (work/participating, etc.).
(P) I like how you put that mess in the back of your mind for now, and are focused on right now.	(P) You are getting really close to getting your X. Keep chasing those values.
(N) Are you acting like the real you right now or is this behavior just the thoughts you have?	(N) (Remember) what you are working for?
(N) Are these thoughts just what other people say, or is this TRUE?	(N) Do you value buying (bad behavior point removal), or buying (stuff in the store)?
(N) Are these thoughts descriptions or evaluations?	(N) You told me earlier that you wanted to buy X. Have you changed your values now that you are doing (bad behavior) instead?
(N) Where is the real (STUDENT NAME) right now?	

Present Moment:	Committed Action:
(P) I really like how you are staying in the present now and not letting other stuff bug you.	(P) You are doing a great job staying committed to your values. It's hard sometimes but you are keeping on track.
(P) I like how you are focusing on X. You are in the present moment! Way to go.	(P) You are not letting of anything get in your way of completing your work today. Awesome! Stay committed!
(P) Way to block out those distractions right now. Hold on to the present.	(P) I love how you came back and did X after you fell off the path towards your values.
(N) Worrying about the future or what you think is happening is not part of the present.	(N) I think you wanted to buy X later at cash out. Are you moving towards or away from the thing you value? Let's get back on track!
(N) That's all fine I guess, but I am staying in the present. Are you?	(N) Doing X is not being committed to your values. Those are still your values, right?
(N) Are you right here right now, or have you drifted into the past to worry about x?	(N) Can you jump over this mess and stay committed to your value?

3 » AIM Point System

Careful monitoring of behavior using point sheets to deliver and remove points contingent upon the child's behavior is an important component of the AIM system. In order to help standardize this process, AIM includes multiple variations of point sheets to be used in various settings. In general, these point sheets break a time period (a day, a therapy session) into smaller components. For each time block, the child has the opportunity to earn and lose points for social and ACT-related behaviors; each block includes the gain or loss of 0, 5, or 10 points in each category. A brief description of behavior related to each point delineation is provided on the point sheet. As well, there is a space to record the behaviors for which the child earned or lost points. On some point sheets, there is a space to record the possible function of this behavior based on observation (attention (A), escape (E), tangible (T), or sensory (S)). It is imperative that the student earn or lose points at the end of each time interval. Another section provides a summary of points earned during the allotted time periods, and the amount of point spent at the reinforcer store. These calculations result in a summary total for the end of that time period. Finally, a third section provides a space to record examples of behaviors related to each component of the hexaflex the child demonstrated that day or session. Collectively, these point sheets allow for continuous behavior monitoring, frequent opportunities for reinforcement and feedback, and built-in data collection. Blank versions of all point sheet are provided within the text.

AIM Point Calculator A: Classroom Behavior. This point sheet provides space to break the school day into subjects or class periods, depending on the student's schedule. Unique features of this point sheet include AM and PM cash outs for the point store and both student and teacher examples of ACT behaviors in the reflection. The Bank Balance for the beginning of the day is recorded in the top row. When monitoring point balance, at the end of the morning periods, the implementer would sum the total points earned and subtract the total points lost for a morning sub-total. Then, the number of points spent in the reinforcer store is subtracting, to provide a morning total. Finally, the function of the reinforcer purchased in the store is recorded by circling attention (A), escape (E), tangible (T), or sensory (S). This process is repeated for the afternoon periods, and an end of the day total is calculated. Both the implementer and the student can provide examples of ACT related behavior; it is up to the discretion of the teacher to determine whether or not they can provide the same examples or if novel examples are required. A school-based point sheet should follow the student throughout the day, completed by the relevant teacher or paraprofessional at the end of each time interval. An example of a completed AIM Point Calculator A is provided for review.

AIM Point Calculator A

Name: James Date: 8/8/17 Starting Points: 175

Time Period	Classroom Behavior Points			ACT Behavior Points				
	Points Earned	Points Lost	Target Positive Behaviors	Points Earned	Points Lost	Challenging Behaviors	Function
1	0 5 (10)	(0) 5 10	Completed routine	0 (5) 10	(0) 5 10		A E T S
2	0 (5) 10	(0) 5 10		0 (5) 10	(0) 5 10	Refused work	A (E) T S
3	(0) 5 10	(0) 5 10		(0) 5 10	0 5 (10)	Avoidance	A (E) T S
4	0 (5) 10	0 5 (10)		0 (5) 10	(0) 5 10	Tore paper 2x	A (E) T S
Lunch	0 (5) 10	(0) 5 10		0 5 (10)	(0) 5 10		A E T S
5	0 5 (10)	(0) 5 10	Followed directions	0 (5) 10	(0) 5 10		A E T S
6	0 5 (10)	0 (5) 10		0 (5) 10	0 5 (10)	Fused to schedule	A (E) T S
7	0 5 (10)	(0) 5 10	Helped peer with HW	0 5 (10)	(0) 5 10		A E T S
8	0 5 (10)	(0) 5 10		0 5 (10)	(0) 5 10		A E T S
TOTAL:	POSSIBLE = 360				EARNED = 110			

10 pts for >1 instances of appropriate/targeted positive behavior OR violations of rules/negative behavior
5 pts for 1 instance of appropriate/targeted positive behavior OR violation of rules/negative behavior
0 pts for 0 instances of appropriate/targeted positive behavior OR violations of rules/negative behavior

	Bank Balance:	175
AM	Earned Points:	+ 25
	Lost Points:	− 30
	Sub-Total:	= 170
	Cash Out:	− 50
	Total:	= 120
	Purchase Function:	A (E) T S
PM	Earned Points:	+ 85
	Lost Points:	− 15
	Sub-Total:	= 190
	Cash Out:	− 50
	Total:	= 140
	Purchase Function:	(A) E T S

	ACT Reflection
Student Ex.	Present Moment: Completed morning routine without distractions
	Acceptance: Finished work after I was angry
	Defusion: Let go of schedule to help my friend with homework
	Self-as-Context: Acted like a helper
	Committed Action: Followed directions after lunchtime
	Values: Helped a friend: friendship value
Teacher Ex.	Present Moment: Follow direction when others weren't
	Acceptance:
	Defusion: Let go of "I won't do it."
	Self-as-Context:
	Committed Action: Completed morning routine so fast!
	Values:

Notes:

End of Day Balance:  140

AIM Point Calculator B: Therapy Session Behavior. This point sheet provides the ability for a therapist to complete a point sheet during one therapy session. This format is unique because it is designed to be isolated for a single session. There is no carry over of points from session to session. Because of this one-session boundary, there are some differences regarding the store and cash-out procedures. At the top of point sheet is a space to record the reinforcer menu for that session. First, a point range for low, medium, and high cost reinforcers. Then, the potential reinforcers at each level can be listed. This provides the therapist an opportunity to vary reinforcers for each session dependent upon the child's preference. Then, there is a space to record expected and target behaviors for both session and ACT behaviors, and the same earn/loss metric for time intervals within the session, which may be time or activity-based. The cash out section on this point sheet only contains the points lost subtracted from the points earned during this single session, and a space to record the reinforcer(s) selected at cash-out, as well as function.

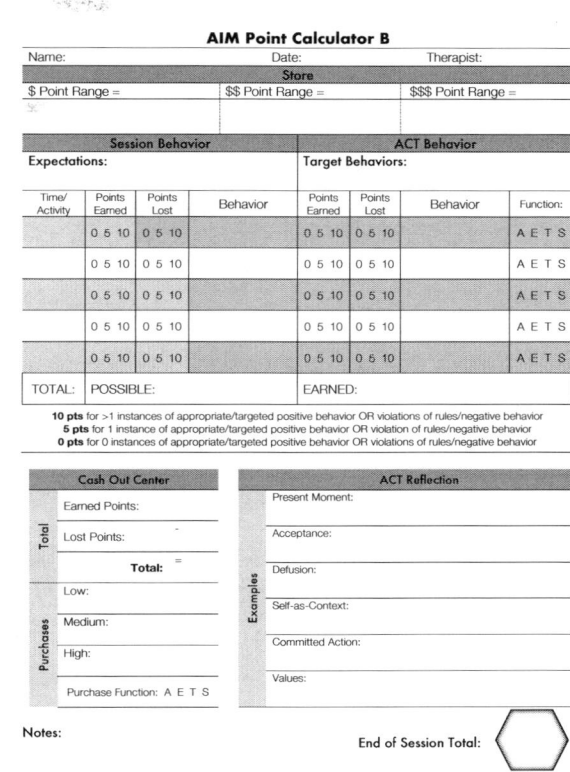

AIM Point Calculator C: Daily Therapy Behavior. This point sheet allows for tracking behavior throughout multiple therapy sessions during a day, including or excluding time between sessions. If a child has multiple therapy sessions, or carries a point sheet from one location to another, this point sheet may be most appropriate. All calculations for this type of point sheet are completed in the same fashion as Point Calculator A, and the language on this point sheet remains general enough to be used by multiple implementers throughout the day. Again, like the classroom behavior calculator, this point sheet is designed to be carried over multiple days with a continuing balance.

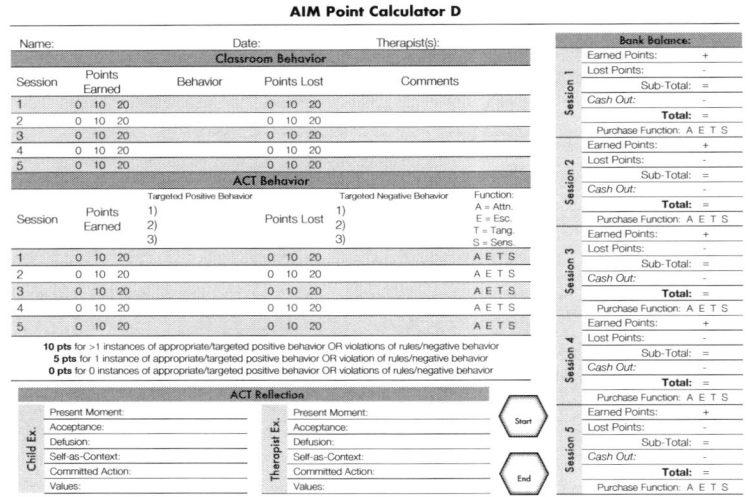

AIM Point Calculator D: Weekly Behavior. This point sheet is designed to be used over the period of one week, with spaces to record points for up to five different sessions. Instead of breaking the point sheet down into time periods per session, points are awarded or removed at the end of each session, so the increments for points in the format are 0, 10, or 20 points earned or lost. The Bank Balance for the weekly format provides a space to calculate points earned and lost within a session, a sub-total, and the cost of reinforcers purchased that session, as well as their associated function. This weekly point sheet is cumulative, so the previous session total acts as the balance for the following session. There is a space to record both the starting and ending balance for the week, as well as a weekly ACT reflection with space for both the child and therapist to record examples of psychologically flexible behavior among the six core processes. It is recommended that this point sheet only be used with children whose age and/or developmental level make it appropriate to evaluate behavior only at the end of a session, rather than during multiple intervals throughout the day.

AIM Point Calculator E: At-Home Behavior. This point sheet is designed for use in the home setting, completed by one or more of the child's family members. This point sheet is nearly identical to AIM Point Calculator B, and is designed to be used within the confines of one day, with no carryover of point balance. Because it is not intended to be completed by professionals, there is no space to record the possible function of challenging behaviors. This point sheet may be particularly useful to use from the time the child returns from school until bed time, or throughout the day on weekends. Family members should be trained on how to use this point sheet appropriately, as well as provided frequent feedback regarding implementation.

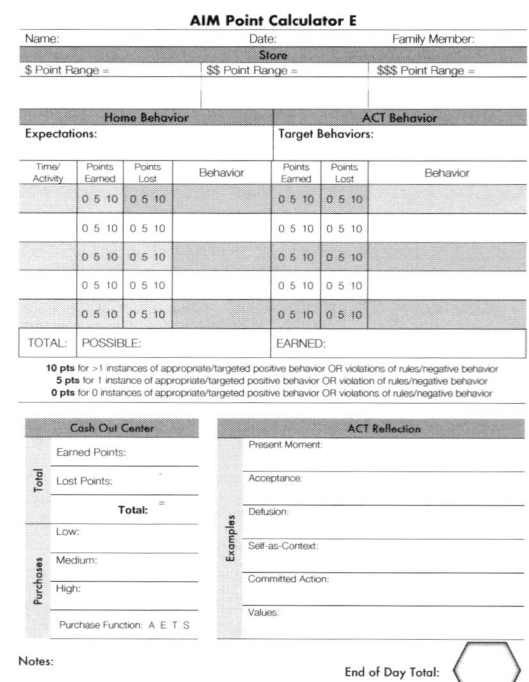

AIM: My ACT Monitor: ACT Self-Management. This form is designed for a child to use him or herself in order to monitor ACT behavior regarding each of the six core processes that comprise the hexaflex. Only children who are the appropriate age and/or developmental level to be able to independently track their own behavior should be asked to use the ACT Monitor. Doing so may help the child develop self-management strategies as well as improved awareness of his or her own behavior. The form includes a key that represents each component of the hexaflex as well as a code for examples of inflexible behavior. Each day, the child is asked to keep a running tally of ACT behavior by recording the letter code for present moment awareness, acceptance, defusion, self-as-context, values, committed action, or inflexibility each time he or she engaged in behavior related to one of those categories. At the end of the week, the child can count the total number of instances of each category of behavior, as well as a sum total of flexible moments (those components of the ACT hexaflex), in order to compare it to the previous week's total. This form might also be used strictly for feedback purposes. However, it is recommended that the implementer create some form of contingency management for the totals. The child may set a weekly goal, and receive a reinforcer for meeting or exceeding that goal, or aim to beat the previous week's total by a certain amount to earn a reward. A completed example of the ACT Monitor is provided for review.

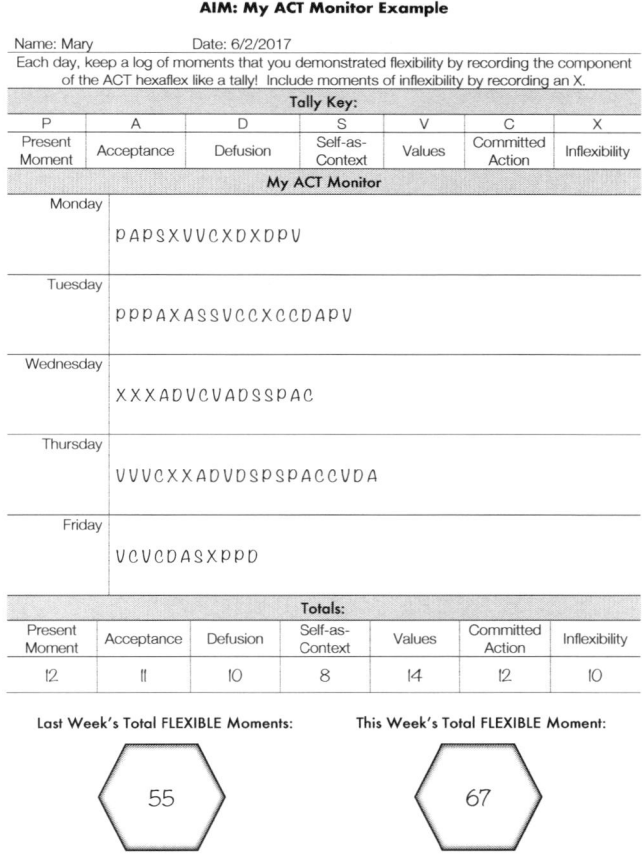

4 » Functional Reinforcement

Once a consistent point system is arranged, appropriate functional reinforcement must be designed to ensure that the children are accessing timely, meaningful reinforcement for appropriate behavior. Maintaining a system of functional reinforcement involves the design and maintenance of a "store" at which the children can use earned points to purchase functional reinforcers. The challenge of a reinforcer store is in creating a system that is as dynamic as the behavior we aim to shape in the child. The main components of such a system, and how to create a sustainable structure, is outlined below.

Incentives and Motivational Strategies. When developing a behavior management system, the implementer must not only set clear expectations for the child, he or she must include incentives and motivational strategies in order to facilitate behavior change. When developing this system, there are several important factors to consider including:

» *Acknowledging appropriate behavior:* How will appropriate behaviors be targeted? Assign points or some other symbolic reward when the child engages in appropriate behavior. The AIM system utilizes points, which are a form of currency in the system, but any other type of symbolic "money" can be included, for instance, younger children may prefer the use of tokens or stickers over less tangible points. Once a "currency" is chosen, determine how much appropriate behavior will "earn," and delineate time- or activity-based segments for point delivery.

» *Acknowledging inappropriate behavior:* In addition to providing points for targeted appropriate behavior, implementers may consider assigning an amount of points lost for engaging in inappropriate behavior and/or violating school, home, or therapy rules and expectations. Similar to the earning of points, loss of points will occur at regularly scheduled intervals throughout the school day, calendar day, or session, depending on the setting for the intervention.

» *Point Exchanges:* The child will earn and lose points throughout the day, which will be exchanged or "cashed in" for access to reinforcers at pre-determined times. The number of exchanges or cash outs in a time interval should be developmentally appropriate. For example, younger children will require more frequent cash outs for smaller reinforcers, yet older children will need fewer exchanges for larger.

» *Available Reinforcers:* When determining the reinforcers available to the child, it is important to ensure that there are a number of options available related to each for the four common functions of behavior at various "prices." Lower cost items should be functional, however less desirable than higher cost items, therefore increasing the value of earning a large number of points, while ensuring access to reinforcement for any amount of appropriate behavior.

Relationship between Mindfulness and Point Systems. It may seem counterintuitive to some to provide points for ACT-related behavior. However, implementers have to link points and consequences for engaging in ACT-related behavior. When a child completes a non-preferred work task, reinforce him or her for task completion, however, also link that behavior pattern to the students' values. Explicitly state (and reinforce) that completing the worksheet is moving that student closer to his or her value of getting extra recess (feeling like part of the school community) at the end of the day. Here, the trick is to reinforce the behavior with social praise, and also bring the delayed reinforcer of recess into the psychological present for that child. Put more simply, the phrase "going to recess" is related to or functionally similar to the actual recess, and as a result, some reinforcement for hearing the word "recess" and imagining the event may occur even before the event itself. It brings what is happening "later" into choice-making "now." In addition, discussion about "accepting" the boring work reinforces self-management strategies that the child used to deal with the non-preferred task long enough to earn recess, rather than becoming non-compliant and escaping the task by putting his or her head down on the desk. The goal is to link the concepts in ACT to the child's behavior in real life, and to reward him or her when the concepts and their behavior aligns. In doing so, there is an increase the likelihood of the child engaging in the appropriate and ACT-related behaviors, and use of ACT-based language to talk about their own behavior.

Removing Points for Inappropriate Behavior. Some implementers may be concerned with removing points or allowing a child to have a negative point value during a given day. Initially, AIM was crafted as an intervention that did not included loss of points/point removal at any point in time. The idea that "once points have been earned, they cannot be taken away," is attractive, and seems fair to the children participating in the program. However, this system is not always the most effective or reflective of the natural environment. For example, adults earn money (points) for going to work (engaging in appropriate behavior). Once that money is earned, it cannot be taken away, until that same adult gets a parking ticket and has to pay a fine using her hard-earned money (lose points). Embedding contingencies as similar to the natural environment as possible will increase the likelihood that the appropriate behavior will generalize to other situations.

Over the years, it became clear that the children participating always seemed to find a "loophole" in the system. For example, consider a child who frequently sleeps throughout the day, but is awake and participatory just after lunch each day to earn enough points to play with the iPad at the end of the day. Or, another child who quietly refused work during math class only. Yet another child breaks a window and tries to stab a teacher with a pencil in a matter of five minutes, but behaves appropriately throughout the rest of the day. Earning zero points during one time interval may not always be the "fair" response, especially if the latter child has enough points earned or saved that he can still buy his preferred item in from the store at the end of the day. In this scenario, dangerous or severe problem behaviors my still be followed by reinforcement, which is contra to the goal of the point system. Just as AIM establishes contingencies for appropriate behavior, contingencies for inappropriate behavior must be included in the intervention to produce the highly preferred and significant outcomes sought after.

Dynamics of the Reinforcer Store. The first step in creating a system of reinforcement is to determine the frequency of exchanges, appropriate price points, and available reinforcers. Refer to the example AIM Point System Matrix, a tool developed to aid in the design of function-based systems of reinforcement. A blank version of this matrix is included in the text. This tool outlines the following components.

» <u>Frequency of Cash Outs</u>: It is necessary to provide opportunities for "cashing out" or exchanging points for reinforcers on a regular basis, that is amenable to the developmental level of the child. In a school setting, students in lower grade levels will generally require more exchanges than those in upper grades, however, this is not a hard and fast rule, as some older children will require more frequent cash outs. This depends on the child's ability to tolerate delays to reinforcement. Avoided in the development of this system is a situation in which inappropriate behavior gets more access to timely, high preferences reinforcers than appropriate behavior. Implementers need to ensure access to high quality reinforcement at reasonable time intervals. It is preferable that these time intervals fit into the daily schedule, however it may be important to adjust the current routine to create a cash out schedule that works. In an individual setting, this part of planning can be completely tailored to the needs of the student or client.

» <u>Price Points:</u> It is equally important to create reasonable price points in the store the correspond the available points throughout the day or session. The implementer will want to avoid setting costs that are so low that children who engage in inappropriate behavior can access high-quality reinforcers, yet so high that the children who engage low levels inappropriate behavior cannot access any reinforcement. The intentional design of point prices can become more fluid for older, more advanced children. In other words, it is important for younger, less advanced children to participate in a store that is highly controlled, with the minimum price for some items as low as five or ten points, but the maximum price would require earning 90 percent or more of possible points for five or ten consecutive days. However, older, more advanced children may be able to tolerate fewer restrictions, so high-cost items that require more "saving" are appropriate. The implementer needs to use professional knowledge of the child involved and clinical judgment to determine the appropriate ratios for the situation. It is also important to track the point data as a check and balance on this system. For example, if a child consistently earns only 20 percent of points per day, the implementer must consider what is the metric of this success or failure. For example, the system designed may have "set the bar" too high, the child may need to do some additional ACT and skill instruction, or the implementer need to re-evaluate the items in the store.

AIM Point System Matrix Example

Use this grid to develop rules for point exchange and cash outs.

Age	Exchange	Price Points	Positives	Negatives
5-8	3 times per day	*Minimum Price:* 5 pts *Maximum Price:* No more than 5 days at 90% total points possible	4 per function	5 total
9-12	2 times per day	*Minimum Price:* 10 pts *Maximum Price:* No more than 10 days at 90% total points possible	6 per function	7 total
13-15	1-2 times per day	*Minimum Price:* 10 pts *Maximum Price:* No delay/cost restrictions	8 per function	7 total

Use this grid to ensure that functional reinforcers are available at various price points.

Function	Low Cost	Medium Cost	High Cost
Attention	Switch seats Line leader Work with partner	Sit with friend at lunch 5-minutes 1:1 staff time Teacher's helper	Tell joke to class 15-minute 1:1 staff time Lunch with teacher
Escape	Skip a problem 3-minute break Teacher does a problem	Skip an assignment 5-minute break Take a walk	Homework pass 10-minute break Visit another teacher
Tangible	Candy Snacks Trinkets	Soda Juice iPad Time	Computer Time Toys Lunch
Sensory	Shoes off Sensory toy Sit on bean bag	Art box Extra PE time Music time	Extra recess Sensory room Movie time
Notes:			

» <u>Selecting Reinforcers:</u> Once the implementer has established a cash out and point distribution policy, it is time to select reinforcers to include in the store. There are two main details to remember when selecting reinforcers: 1) Make sure there are reinforcers available across the four functions (attention, escape, tangible, and sensory), and 2) Make sure there are reinforcers available at every price point (high, medium, and low). The goal is to ensure that there are valuable reinforcers available to each child, as well as provide appropriate amounts of reinforcement for children who demonstrate lower levels of appropriate behavior as well as high levels of appropriate behavior. Remember, the goal is to reinforce ALL appropriate behavior, which does not require the complete absence of all inappropriate behavior. Notice the table in the Point System Matrix that will help to ensure that both of these criteria are met. Choosing various reinforcers is another important task in this process. This endeavor does not need to be radically expensive or a one-time project. Functional reinforcers are often inexpensive or free, and implementers are encouraged to regularly update the items available in the store. Choosing reinforcers is an opportunity to get creative in brainstorming ideas of what the clients or students may be interested in, as well as an opportunity to seek their input. Asking the child to provide input on selection of reinforcers is an excellent way to ensure that they are interested in the items available as well as obtain "buy in" for the system in general. It is also not necessary to provide entirely different items at each price level, as it is possible to scale time or quality of the reinforcer according to price. For example, lower points for smaller amounts of time (e.g. 2 minutes of tablet time) and higher points for more of the same reinforcer (e.g. 15 minutes of tablet time). Or, vary the quality, such as a less expensive experience (e.g. tablet with educational applications only), and a more expensive version of that experience (e.g. tablet with awesome games). Included is an example "Point Store Menu" to provide some ideas for beginning the design of a system. Implementers may choose to have a written or picture-based menu, depending upon the age and developmental level of your clients or students. Remember, the goal is to transform what is gained with problem behavior into a reinforcer for appropriate behavior. For example, rather than being sent to the office as a disciplinary measure, a child should earn an office visit for appropriate behavior. Rather than a class clown getting laughs for inappropriate behavior, the child earns time to be a "standup comedian" in the classroom.

» <u>Sales, Specials, and Inflation:</u> Like any shopping experience, creating variation using promotions is a way to maintain the children's interest in the reinforcer store. The implementer may consider setting up weekly sales, during which some items in the store are available for a reduced price for a restricted amount of time. Or, specials such as "buy one get one half off," or "buy one get one free" can stir up the children's excitement for certain items. Providing options for group reinforcers is another option. For example, include a "class game time" option that a student can buy for 250 points, but each student who joins in the game must also pay 50 points to participate. Again, this is another avenue for the implementer to use some creativity to maintain the children's enthusiasm and interest for the reinforcer store. Another important variable to consider is the cost of items over time. Ideally, students will receive fewer points at the beginning of the year/AIM experience, and over time, as adaptive, flexible behavior increases, earn more and more points. As a result, inflation of points becomes necessary. Implementers may choose to set a lower cost for items in the beginning, but increase the value as children earn more points. Remember, the goal is to provide meaningful, affordable reinforcement to increase appropriate behavior, NOT to dangle a "carrot" of reinforcement that the child cannot access.

AIM Example Point Menu

Low Cost	Medium Cost	High Cost
10 Points: *Gum *Small candy *Extra straw *Send text message	**150 Points:** *Sit on bench outside *Snack *Music/Phone (15 min)	**500 Points:** *Play game with class *Help out in office *30 minutes of movie time
50 Points: *Mechanical pencil *10 minute in-class break *Lay across chairs *Skip journal for the day	**200 Points:** *25 minutes free computer time *25 minutes of puzzle *Soda *No homework pass	**1000 Points:** *Select item to purchase from a local store (under $5)
100 Points: *Juice *Bottle water *Sitting/laying on floor *20 minutes of free time *10-minute visit with staff	**300 Points:** *Extra visit to store *Wear a hat *15 minute energy burner *Lunch with a friend	**2000 Points:** *Lunch buy out *Individual Movie

Stay Tuned for Daily and Weekly Specials!

» <u>Response Cost</u>: Another component of the reinforcement system is the loss of points for certain behaviors. While children will lose points on their point sheets for individuals inappropriate behaviors, certain "high frequency" classroom or therapy behaviors will be "fined" within the point store. For example, swearing may cost the child 15 points as a fine, and throwing an item in the classroom may cost 50 points. While it is important to have appropriate responses costs for individual behaviors, the "costs" for bad should not be bigger than the "costs" for good; again, the goal is for everyone to be able

AIM Example Point Loss Matrix

Use this grid to develop rules for loss of points contingent on certain behaviors.

Response	Cost
Swearing at adult or peer	10
Disrespectful statements to adult or peer	15
Disruptive action	20
Refusal to complete a task	20
Ignoring a direction	20
Destruction of materials	40
Verbal threats to adult or peer	50
Physical aggression (pushing, hitting, or kicking)	100
Elopement (leaving the designated area)	100

Notes:

to afford to purchase reinforcers, but fines for inappropriate behavior should make it far more difficult to access those items that are the most highly preferred. In addition, do not forget that students also lose points on their point sheets for certain inappropriate behaviors, so while the goal is to establish costs for inappropriate behavior, it is not to create double or triple fines when combined with the point sheet metric. A form for outlining response costs as a model for implementers to follow is provided. The response costs included should be appropriate to the common behavior problems in the environment and the point ratios designed in the reinforcer store.

» <u>Managing the Point Bank:</u> Another important component of the reinforcer store is managing the bank of points that the child has. This is useful for both data collection purposes and for tracking which reinforcers are most valuable to the child. Keeping the child's current point totals posted visibly somewhere in the classroom, office, or home as a visual reminder of their current point status is recommended. As well, use logs of point exchanges (both five and seven day versions), that allow the implementer to keep track of the child's starting balance, earned and possible points, items purchased with prices, as the primary function of those purchases. Then, they are able to determine both the ending balance for that time period, as well as a weekly points percentage by dividing the total number of points earned by the total possible points for that time period. This information is useful for data monitoring purposes; if a child's behavior is improving, the percent of possible points earned should increase over time.

AIM Weekly Point Exchange Log (5 Days)

Name: Dates:

Day	Starting Balance	Earned Points	Possible Points	Items Purchased	Purchase Price	Primary Function
MONDAY						A E T S
TUESDAY						A E T S
WEDNESDAY						A E T S
THURSDAY						A E T S
FRIDAY						A E T S
Weekly Total:				Weekly Points Percentage:		

Responding to Negative/Inappropriate Behaviors. As outlined, inappropriate behavior should be fined and charted on the child's point sheet. This is the designed consequence for these behaviors. The implementer must be aware that once a consequence/fine has been delivered, that negative behavior event is over. If a problem behavior occurs during time interval one, once that interval is over, the child has a "fresh start." If his or her behavior during time interval two is highly appropriate, he or she should be praised, given points, and provided reinforcement appropriately. It can be difficult as the implementer not to bring up previous events as way to temper the experience of the current appropriate behavior, but you must learn to leave the past in the past. Immediate consequences for these behaviors are most important, and increasing appropriate behavior is the primary goal. The language used around negative behavior is important. For example, if a child is being disrespectful and refusing to complete a task, the implementer, rather than reprimanding that behavior, may choose to ask, *"Did you want to buy a break now instead of saving for that item you want in the point store later?"* Ideally, the cost of an inappropriate behavior in (i.e. 100 points for refusing to complete a task) will cost more than the reinforcer for appropriate behavior (i.e. 50 points for a 15-minute break). It is the implementer's responsibility to help the child make these connections, and learn to pick their battles. The child will contact reinforcement and responses costs; therefore, it is not necessary to frequently reprimand and correct inappropriate behavior. It will all be reflected on the point sheet.

Organizing the Physical Space. Part of the goal of AIM is to infuse the ACT and contingency management components into the everyday conversation and experience in the child's environment. While it is important to consistently discuss these topics, it is equally necessary to include them in the physical environment. Posting point totals is one method of providing a visual reminder of the point system, as is posting the reinforcer menu and other components of the store. The reason for doing so is twofold. First, visuals around the environment serve as reminders or cues to consider them when making choices. Second, publically posting points and progress create a social contingency for engaging in appropriate behavior. In the natural environment, having others be aware of your behavior and its outcomes is one of the reasons people engage in appropriate behavior. The target is to create the same environment, where individual children cannot "hide" from the point system. In addition to visually including the contingency management system, it is critical to post ACT-related items throughout the space. A hexaflex should be readily present in any environment where it matters: in the classroom, in the therapy office, in the child's home at various locations. As well, completed ACT lessons should be posted and referred to when they are relevant to the child's behavior, both as a proactive and reactive strategy. Values and committed action should also be highlighted around the physical space. Children's values, long-term goals, and short-term goals should be visible throughout the location. From simple written statements such as, *"I am working for..."* to more complex collages of things that represent the child's chosen values, anyone who enters the environment should be able to discern the values and committed actions of those involved.

A checklist of the components needed to design and implement the AIM program ACT lessons and point system is included. Utilize this checklist to aid in planning the individualized AIM program. Keep in mind that the implementer may need to adjust or alter each of the components throughout the time they spend implementing the AIM program. The specifications of each component should always reflect the current abilities and needs of the child they are working with.

AIM Program Design Checklist		
Component	✓	Notes
Daily ACT Lessons		
Schedule		
# of Lessons/Week		
Tier Divisions Outlined		
Implementers Selected		
Groups Created (if needed)		
ACT Communication Planned		
Point System & Reinforcement		
Point Calculator Selected		
Time Intervals Selected		
Implementers Selected		
Self-Management Considered		
Reinforcer Store Organized		
Frequency of Cash Outs Detemined		
Price Points Outlined		
Reinforcers Selected		
Reinforcer Menu Created		
Variability Established (ie Sales)		
Response Cost Outlined		
Bank Management Planned		
Physical Space		
Points Posted		
Menu / Store Info Posted		
Hexaflex Posted		
Lessons Posted		
Values/Actions Posted		

Additional Notes:

5 » Ongoing Progress Monitoring

Data collection and continuous progress monitoring are a cornerstone of any behavior analytic intervention, and AIM is not different. AIM includes several methods of collecting data regarding child behavior, evaluation of ACT performance, and assessment of appropriate implementation of the curriculum. Before beginning any components of this curriculum, it is important to establish data collection methods and plans for ongoing progress monitoring.

Daily Data Collection Methods. In order to determine the effectiveness of the invention for a particular child and modify it to meet the child's needs, data regarding challenging behavior frequency and function must be continually collected. AIM suggests three methods of data collection for

Levels of Data Analysis
- Percentage of points earned per week
- Number of ABC data sheets
- Types of behaviors that occur
- Percentage of different antecedents and functions across problem behaviors

these purposes, however the inclusion of additional data regularly collected at each setting are recommended. Data should be analyzed in several different ways, specifically: the percentage of points earned by the child each week, the number of behavioral events that were recorded, the types of behaviors that occurred, and the various antecedents and consequences that most often occurred with problem behaviors. Included in the curriculum are three data collection tools that provide all of the necessary information for data analysis.

» *AIM Point Calculator Data.* Regardless of the AIM Point Calculator form used with a client or student, the implementer can complete the AIM Weekly Point Exchange Log, which provides a summary of the number of points earned and total possible points earned per day or session. By calculating the total earned and possible points for the week, dividing the earned by the possible points, and multiplying by 100, the implementer can determine the weekly point percentage for that child.

$$\left(\frac{EarnedPoints}{PossiblePoints}\right) * 100 = WeeklyPointAverage$$

If it is preferred to manage data monitoring using technology, implementers can create a spreadsheet that calculates the weekly point average, using the following sample spread sheet as a guide. First, create four columns labelled 1) "Week of," 2) "Earned Points," 3) "Possible Points," and 4) "Weekly Point Average." Then, after completing the Weekly Point

Exchange Log, enter the date (i.e. Cell A2), total earned points (i.e. Cell B2), and total possible points (i.e. Cell C2). Then, calculate the weekly point average by selecting the appropriate cell (i.e. Cell D2), entering the formula "=B2/C2," selected the "Number" icon in the Home toolbar, and setting the cell contents to percent. In the example below, the child's weekly point average is demonstrating an overall increasing trend, suggesting that the intervention is currently effective. Creating a graph of this data is recommended when included in progress reports or evaluations. Most spreadsheet applications provide tutorials for creating various line graphs to represent this data.

	A	B	C	D
1	Week of	Earned Points	Possible Points	Weekly Point Average
2	8/6/17	515	1800	29%
3	8/13/17	530	1800	29%
4	8/20/17	440	1800	24%
5	8/27/17	600	1800	33%
6	9/3/17	745	1440	52%
7	9/10/17	800	1800	44%
8	9/17/17	860	1800	48%
9	9/24/17	1050	1800	58%
10	10/1/17	1500	1800	83%
11	10/8/17	1375	1800	76%

» *AIM ABC Record Log.* This data collection form is intended to be completed each time the child engages in a problem behavior event. A completed example of this log is provided for review. First, basic information, including an ID number for the event, data, time, setting, and observer initials is recorded. Then, the observed antecedent, behavior, and consequence is recorded (or multiple, if needed). The approximate duration and subjective intensity of the behavior event are noted in the next column. Finally, the possible function and elements of psychological inflexibility apparent to the observer are recorded. Finally, a space to record narrative notes regarding the event is provided.

AIM ABC Record Log   **Name:**

ID #: 12	Antecedent:	Behavior:	Consequence:	Duration:	Possible Function:
Date: 3/4	☑ Present task ☐ Asked to wait ☐ End activity ☐ Activity Denied ☐ Item Denied ☐ Transition ☐ Alone ☐ Item Removed ☐ Loud setting ☐ Given attention ☐ Other:	☐ Refusal ☐ Physical aggression ☑ Verbal aggression ☐ Self-Injury ☐ Elopement ☐ Disruption ☐ Other:	☐ Verbal redirect ☐ Physical prompt ☐ Ignored ☐ Continue task ☐ Verbal reprimand ☐ Removed from activity/location ☑ Alternative task ☐ Time out ☐ Other:	☐ <1 m ☐ 1-5 m ☑ 5-15 m ☐ 15-30 m ☐ .5-1 h ☐ 1-2 h ☐ 2+ h Intensity: ☐ Low ☑ Medium ☐ High	☐ Attention ☑ Escape ☐ Tangible ☐ Sensory ☐ Unclear Possible Inflexibility: ☐ Lack of contact with moment ☑ Experiential avoidance ☐ Fusion ☐ View self-as-content ☐ Unclear values ☐ Inaction/Impulsive action ☐ Unclear
Time: 1:33p						
Setting: RmIO						
Initials: MP						

Notes: Math class: subtraction assignment presented. Allowed to complete a review worksheet instead.

This data can be analyzed in a number of ways. One possibility is to create a scatterplot of the occurrence of behavior events based on time in order to reveal patterns in the time of day or certain activities that a behavior occurs during. As well, frequency of various antecedents, behaviors, and consequences can be analyzed. To do so, the implementer would sum the number of times each of the possible events occurred over a series of behavioral incidents. For example, in a spreadsheet, it is possible to record the frequency of each antecedent event by creating a column for the event ID number, and each of the possible antecedents. Then, for each behavior event, record a "1" in the relevant cell for each time that antecedent was observed (for example, ID #12, a "1" is entered into Cell B3 for "Present Task"), and a "0" if the antecedent was not observed (as in Cells C3-I3 in the example). Once all of this data is inputted, the sum for each antecedent can be calculated by entering creating and selecting a cell for the total number (i.e. Cell B14), entering the formula =SUM(B3:B12) [the cells that include data for 'Present Task'], and pressing enter. In this example, the antecedent "Present Task" was observed on 6 instances, "End Activity" on 1 instance, "Activity Denied" on 2 instances, and "Item Denied" on 1 instance. Again, it is possible to create a bar graph summarizing this data, which is a feature in most spreadsheet applications. This process can be repeated with each of the remaining variables recorded on the Record Log (e.g. Behavior, Consequence, Function). Simply replace the column headings with the appropriate terms and enter the corresponding data. This data can help reveal patterns in the environmental events that occasion and maintain a behavior, as well as it's possible function. In addition, the frequency of events can be monitored with this method.

	A	B	C	D	E	F	G	H	I
1					Antecedents				
2	ID#	Present Task	Asked to wait	End activity	Activity Denied	Item Denied	Transition	Alone	Item Removed
3	12	1	0	0	0	0	0	0	0
4	13	1	0	0	0	0	0	0	0
5	14	0	0	1	0	0	0	0	0
6	15	0	0	0	1	0	0	0	0
7	16	1	0	0	0	0	0	0	0
8	17	1	0	0	0	0	0	0	0
9	18	0	0	0	1	0	0	0	0
10	19	1	0	0	0	0	0	0	0
11	20	0	0	0	0	1	0	0	0
12	21	1	0	0	0	0	0	0	0
13		Present Task	Asked to wait	End activity	Activity Denied	Item Denied	Transition	Alone	Item Removed
14	TOTAL:	6	0	1	2	1	0	0	0
15									

» *AIM ACT Record Log.* The AIM ABC Record Log has a "partner" form that summarizes the ACT interaction during the behavioral event. Copying these two forms back-to-back is recommended so that the corresponding forms for each event can be completed and housed together. A completed example of this form is provided for review. Again, basic information, including an ID number for the event, data, time, setting, and observer initials is recorded. Then, the implementer's observation of elements of psychological inflexibility are recorded under "Awareness." Next, representative statements of the methods the implementer used to communicate to the child using ACT-language are recorded. Finally, representative statements of the treatment technique(s) utilized by the implementer during and after the behavior event are marked in the final column. Lastly, a location for narrative or anecdotal notes is provided. This form can be used to track two variables. First, it can monitor the frequency of each component, in the same manner as the ABC Record Log (and recorded and/or graphed on a spreadsheet in a similar way). Second, it can be used as a reference to evaluate if the implementer is selecting communication and treatment language and actions that correspond to the likely function of the child's behavior.

AIM ACT Record Log   Name:

ID #: 12	Awareness:	Communicate:	Treat:
Date: 3/4/17 Time: 1:33pm Setting: Rm10 Initials: MP	☐ Not in the current moment ☐ Fused to thoughts ☐ Chasing non-values ☑ Losing commitment ☐ Wrong self ☑ Difficulty with acceptance	☐ Let's get back in the present moment. ☐ It's ok that did not work out. We need to accept things, even stuff we don't like. ☐ Is this the real you that is here right now? ☑ Did this get your closer to your values? ☐ Tell me what your values are today. ☐ Stop, pause, and come back to the present. ☑ Let's commit to doing better moving forward. ☐ I like the real you I see right now.	☐ Acknowledge current environment ☑ Stepping back from current verbalizations ☐ Reminding of stated values ☐ Encouraging commitment ☐ Refocus to self-as context ☑ Acceptance of the entire event

Notes:

ACT Assessments. In addition to collecting data on the child's daily behavior, regular assessment of their performance on ACT activities and evaluations of psychological flexibility are required. These assessments provide ways to monitor the child's progress in terms of understanding and applying ACT concepts in quantitative and qualitative ways, as well as methods to track the child's reports of flexibility over time. Included are three methods of evaluated ACT-related behavior and performance.

» *ACT Quantitative Analysis Scale (AQAS).* The AQAS is a rubric that can be applied to a child's performance on ACT Daily Lessons. This rubric can be used to assess the experiential activities included in the curriculum, in terms of precision, scope, and depth of the responses. If the activity was discussion-based, the child's comments during conversation can be evaluated; likewise, written or otherwise creative responses can be evaluated using the rubric. In each of the three sub-scoring categories, the child can score a 0, 1, 2, or 3. These scores are summed to provide a total score on the assessment (out of a possible maximum score of 9). Scores on this measure can be tracked over time as an indication of the child's ability to interact with ACT concepts and metaphors. A completed example of the AQAS is provided for review.

AIM: ACT Quantitative Analysis Scale (AQAS)

Name: Sam   Date: 5/4/17

Use the rubric below to rate the individual's responses to ACT lesson experiential activities, both written and verbal. Sum the scores for precision, scope, and depth to obtain a total score.

Score	Precision	Scope	Depth
0	Not applicable/no answer	Not applicable/no answer	Not applicable/no answer
1	Answer is broad and generic, could apply in many settings, not just the current setting/question	Answer applies to the current activity/discussion ONLY	Gave minimal details/elaborations OR gave details/elaborations that did not satisfy requirements of current activity
2	Answer is logically sound and meets requirement of the activity, but is broad ✓	Applies to the current activity; with the help of researcher/therapist can be elaborated to fit other scenarios	Gave enough detail/elaboration for the researcher to understand, but not enough to fully complete the activity
3	Answer is detailed and concise, meets requirement of activity, and fully answers the question	Response fulfills requirement of the current activity and translates easily into novel areas which are related to the original prompt/question ✓	Gave elaboration/details which were fully understood by the researcher and fulfilled the requirements of the activity ✓
Sub-scores:	2	3	3
Total Score:		8	

Developed by Kelsey Kryszak, MS, BCBA, Jordan Belisle, MS, BCBA, and Dr. Mark R. Dixon, BCBA-D (2017)

» *AIM Weekly ACT Report.* This assessment tool provides a qualitative record of a child's understanding of ACT concepts and the number and quality of examples of ACT-related behavior. Once a week, with the support of the implementer, the child and the adult will provide examples of instances of behavior that occurred throughout the week that exemplify qualities of each core process in the ACT hexaflex (present, moment, acceptance, defusion, self-as-context, committed action, and values). Finally, the child should choose the moment from the week that best represents his or her best "ACT Moment of the Week," and draw a picture or write a short story describing the event. These can be collected in a portfolio or journal demonstrating the child's development throughout a period of time, such as a school year.

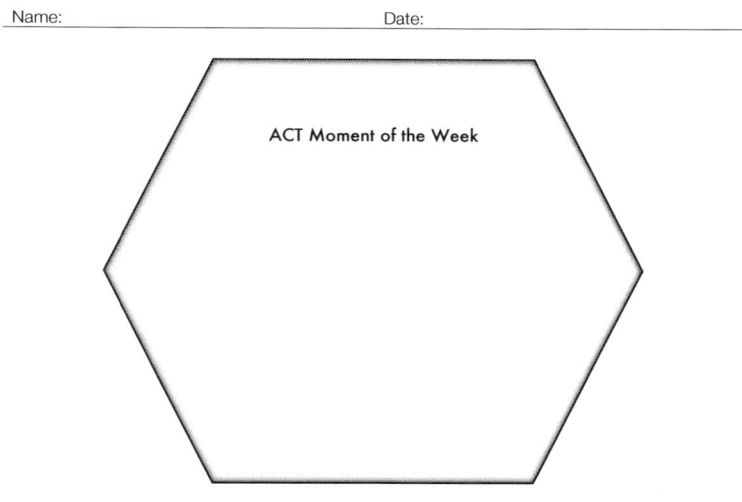

» *Child Psychological Flexibility Questionnaire (CPFQ).* The AIM curriculum includes an assessment of a child's level of psychological flexibility in two different questionnaire forms. The first is a self-report measure (CPFQ-Child Report) completed by the child, either independently or with the support of an adult if necessary, depending on the child's level of development. The second is a caregiver-report measure (CPFQ-Caregiver Report) that is completed by a service provider, parent, or other adults who is familiar with the child. These two questionnaires are matched item by item; the child version includes age-appropriate language, while the adult version assesses the same behaviors with more detailed, sophisticated language. Any child participating in the AIM curriculum should be able to complete the self-report measure, whether they read it themselves or have it read to them by an adult. The child measure includes a graphic scale to provide a visual aid in selecting abstract responses such as *"never," "sometimes,"* or *"all the time,"* which is presented below. Both the CPFQ-Child and Caregiver reports provide a total score that indicates psychological flexibility, as well as individual subscales for each component of the ACT hexaflex. This helps to provide an overall report of the child's behavior, as well as a way to help identify specific ACT targets for the child. Each questionnaire includes a guide for scoring as well as a score report form that summarizes responses. The CPFQ can be administered at regular intervals during treatment to the child, a caregiver, or both to determine changes in accounts of the child's engagement in mindful, adaptive behavior as a measure of progress and growth.

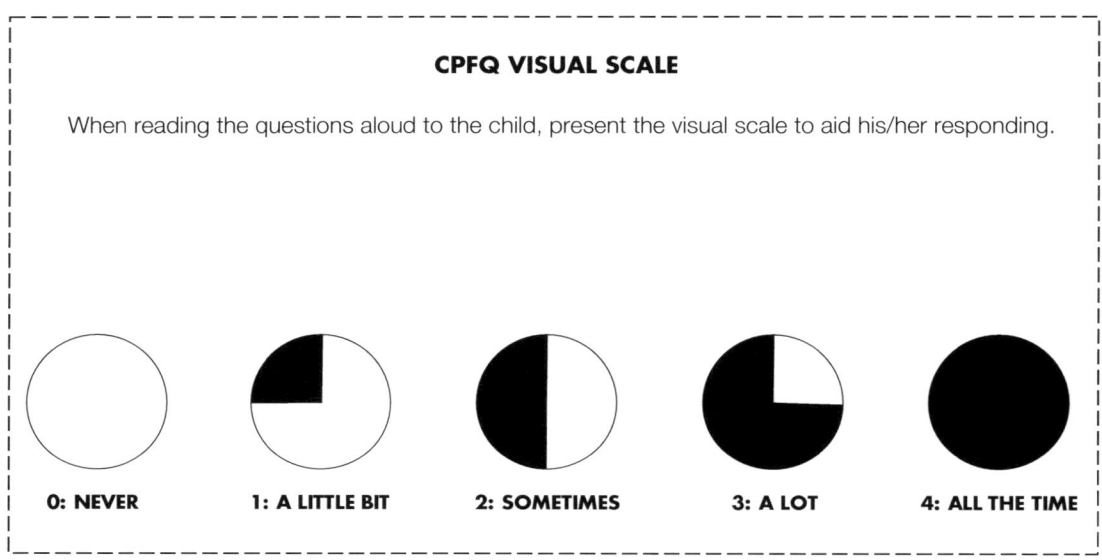

!"*Other Measures of Mindfulness and Flexibility.* Researchers have developed empirically validated self-report measures of mindfulness and psychological flexibility specifically for children. The Avoidance & Fusion Questionnaire for Youth (AFQ-Y; Greco, Murrell, & Coyne, 2005) measures fusion, avoidance, and inaction to provide a quantitative report of the child's psychological inflexibility based on 17 items within the questionnaire. The Children's Acceptance and Mindfulness Measure (CAMM; Greco, Smith, & Baer, 2009), is a 10-item measure of the child's reports of acceptance and mindfulness. Both of these measures are available online from various sources, for no or minimal costs. Administering these assessments at regular intervals (i.e. 3 or 6 months) provides a measure of changes in these core components of ACT over time.

Training and Evaluation. While this text is meant to provide the foundational knowledge and directions for implementation of the AIM program, it is not meant to replace all training in behavior analytic technologies, mindfulness practice, and the application of ACT procedures. It is recommended that implementers of this curriculum seek further professional development and technical skill development in two primary ways: continuing education and mindfulness practice.

» *Continuing Education.* Behavior analysts, educators, and most other professionals in human service professions are encouraged and required to engage in continuing education activities following completion of their degree, certification, and/or licensure. This is to ensure that the professionals maintain their skills and remain up-to-date on the newest developments in the field. Research on the topic of continuing education opportunities related to ABA, ACT, and mindfulness will reveal numerous options for university coursework, workshops, multi-day training, and webinars designed to enhance professional's skills in these areas. Implementers of this program should seek out and obtain additional training on each component of the AIM program. This is needed not only to improve the implementer's skill set, but to better prepare him or her to train other therapists, educators, and families to implement ACT and contingency management procedures.

» *Incorporating Mindfulness and Acceptance with Staff.* In addition to receiving formal training in ABA, ACT, and mindfulness approaches, it is recommended that implementers of the AIM curriculum engage in ACT and mindfulness practices themselves. Practice in these skill sets will deepen the implementer's understanding of these topics. Further, those who practice mindfulness are better able to teach and encourage mindful, flexible behavior to children. Research has indicated that engaging in mindfulness practice or receiving ACT training can not only benefit professionals by decreasing stress in the workplace, but can help improve their performance as well. The best implementers of the AIM curriculum will be mindful and psychologically flexible. Various measures are available to assess adults in these areas; it is

recommended that all implementers of this curriculum complete these assessments, and if they demonstrate high levels of psychological inflexibility themselves, seek out ACT services of their own.

Implementation Fidelity. **Implementation fidelity** refers to the degree to which an intervention is delivered as it was designed or intended. It is incredibly important; without measures of fidelity, it is not possible to know if the intervention is responsible for changes in behavior. Conversely, if behavior change does not occur, it is necessary to ensure that the treatment is being implemented accurately and completely before making changes it. The AIM program provides two measures of implementation fidelity: the *ACT Evaluator* and *ACT Treatment Fidelity Checklist*.

» The *ACT Evaluator.* This rubric is a tool to assess an implementer's awareness of opportunities to deliver ACT, ability to communicate in a way consistent with the ACT model, and infusion of ACT in treatment. The Evaluator tool has both a 5-day and 7-day version, each of which provide a rating (on a scale from one [never] to five [always]) in each of the previously listed areas for each day of the week, which can be calculated in terms of percentage for easy data monitoring. In addition, there is an opportunity for the evaluator to provide descriptive feedback, both positive and constructive, to the implementer. This evaluator tool can be used on a weekly basis or for a week at set intervals to monitor implementer's incorporation of ACT into daily interactions with clients or students.

AIM: ACT Evaluator (5 Day)

Individual Name: James   Week of: 1/4/2017

Day of Week	Awareness Individual was aware of opportunities to deliver ACT.	Communicate Verbal responses to child problem behavior were consistent with the ACT model.	Treat ACT language was delivered to increase probability of psychological flexibility in the future.
Monday	1 2 3 4 **5**	1 2 3 **4** 5	1 2 3 **4** 5
Tuesday	1 2 3 **4** 5	1 2 3 4 **5**	1 2 3 4 **5**
Wednesday	1 2 **3** 4 5	1 2 3 4 **5**	1 2 **3** 4 5
Thursday	1 2 3 4 **5**	1 2 3 **4** 5	1 2 3 **4** 5
Friday	1 2 3 4 **5**	1 2 3 4 **5**	1 2 3 4 **5**

Total Score: ____ / ____ (max) = ____ %   Scale: 1 = never..........5 = always

Exceptional Moment of the Week:	When Max was having a behavior crisis on Tuesday, you were able to help him return to the moment and refocus on values!
Teachable Moment of the Week:	On Wednesday, you seemed a bit distracted and missed a couple of opportunities to deliver ACT in the afternoon.

ACT Treatment Fidelity Checklist. This checklist is a tool to assess the implementation of the AIM program system. It can be used to evaluate the system in a classroom setting, as well as a clinic-based or home-based program (or any location in which the AIM program is implemented). The checklist can be completed at any set period of time (e.g. weekly or monthly) to ensure maintenance of the AIM program components, from the physical arrangement of the intervention area to implementation of the ACT and contingency management portions of the program. Each of twelve areas are rated 'Absent,' 'Needs improvement,' 'Acceptable,' or 'Not observed. Based on those ratings, an overall appraisal rating of 'Needs Improvement,' 'Average,' 'Above Average,' or 'Excellent' is selected. Finally, there is a space for the observer to provide comments or feedback to the implementer. Clear expectations for each of the twelve areas evaluated are provided as well. For example, Item 10, "Adult use of ACT language," a rating of 'Absent' refers to no use of ACT language, a rating of 'Needs Improvement' refers to inconsistent use of ACT language, and a rating of 'Acceptable' refers to consistent use of ACT language.

AIM: ACT Treatment Fidelity Checklist

Location: Residence Date of Evaluation: 3/10/17
Implementer: Brooke Observer: Luke

Treatment Component	Absent	Needs Improvement	Acceptable	Not Observed	Comments
1. Visible hexaflex in the room			X		
2. Completed ACT experiential activities displayed in room			X		
3. Completion of ACT lesson each day			X		
4. Earned points displayed in room			X		
5. Points delivered on schedule		X			
6. Variety of items in store across behavior functions			X		
7. Store items for sale across range of values			X		
8. Cashing out occurs at pre-set intervals		X			
9. Using ACT during crisis/problem behavior episodes			X		
10. Adult use of ACT language		X			
11. Organization of ACT materials			X		
12. Data management system updated regularly			X		

Overall Appraisal Rating (circle one): Needs Improvement **(Average)** Above Average Excellent

Partial Implementation Guide

Although implementing the entire AIM program is required to maximize the benefits of the intervention for children, it is possible to incorporate parts of the curriculum into the daily instructional or therapy routine to focus on one part of the three-component system: mindfulness practice, acceptance and commitment lessons, or a functional approach to behavior.

Bringing Mindfulness into the Child's Life

If the emphasis of the intervention is on developing the child or children's mindfulness skills, and ability to attend to the present moment, professionals may choose to implement the mindfulness and meditation practices independently of the remainder of the AIM curriculum. The mindfulness activities and meditations are designed to be implemented flexibly. They are generally brief, require few materials, and are easily incorporated into existing daily routines. When implementing these exercises separately, no modifications are required, although some limitations do arise. First, the child or children will not be aware of the context of mindfulness. There activities are experience-based, and do not provide educational opportunities to teach them about the foundations of mindfulness and acceptance. As well, there is no longer a designed system to provide reinforcement for applying those mindfulness skills outside of the activities without a specific contingency-based behavior management system. The following are considerations to make when implementing the mindfulness activities separately from the rest of the AIM program:

» *Developing a Schedule:* These exercises may be completed on a regular routine basis, or on an "as-needed" basis at the discretion of the implementer. However, it should be noted that to build mindfulness skills, frequent, dedicated practice is necessary.

» *Selecting Participants:* Implementers must decide if the mindfulness activities will be done with all clients and/or students, or with a select few, and attend to the need to modify activities for the individual- or group-format of their practice.

» *Assessing Mindful Progress:* Without a formal data collection system, it may be difficult to determine if the use of mindfulness activities is having a quantifiable, objective positive effect on the child or children's behavior. It is recommended that some form of data collection be developed to monitor progress.

» *Generalizing Mindfulness Skills:* Without a predetermined system of reinforcement for engaging in mindful behavior, implementers will want to develop a plan to encourage the generalization of mindful practice outside of the designated activities and into the child or children's everyday lives.

Implementing ACT Lessons

If the emphasis the intervention for the clients or students is the social-emotional component without specific targets for behavior change, professionals may implement the ACT Daily Lessons as a standalone intervention. These lessons are designed to teach children skills related to each of the six core processes of the hexaflex: present moment awareness, acceptance, defusion, self-as-context, values, and committed action. As children encounter these lessons, they will practice psychological flexibility and connect these processes and concepts back to their own lives. When implementing the ACT lessons in isolation, no additional materials are required and no modifications must be made to the curriculum. The following are considerations to make when implementing the ACT lessons separately from the rest of the AIM program:

» *Developing a Schedule:* Just as a schedule of implementation is necessary when implementing the entire curriculum, the ACT lessons will require a daily or weekly schedule for how frequently lessons will be completed.

» *Including the Tier System:* The focus of the three tiers built into the ACT lessons still apply when isolating this component. It is up to the implementer to decide whether to divide children into groups who receive individualized ACT instruction, or if the entire group or individual child will complete activities from all three tiers.

» *Assessing ACT Progress:* Without data collection from all three components of the AIM curriculum, the implementer will need to determine the best way to monitor the child's performance related to ACT. This may include the AQAS rubric, ACT-specific questionnaires, and Weekly ACT Report, but it is also possible to include data collection related to student behavior (i.e. office referrals or descriptive data) to evaluate the impact on their behavior outside of the lessons.

» *Incorporating ACT throughout the Day:* While the entire curriculum is designed to build a cohesive way of talking about and addressing child behavior, when completing ACT lessons separately, it will be important for the implementers to determine a method for building in ACT concepts and practicing behaving flexibly in the natural environment. This may involve informal conversations using the *Awareness, Communicate, Treat* approach, or more formal inclusion of ACT during behavioral events that is evaluated using the tools provided in this text. Remember, it is important to bring ACT "to life" for children outside of the specific lessons to bring about meaningful behavior change.

Functional Approach to Behavior

If the goal of intervention for the included clients or students is to produce behavior change for specific target behaviors or to generally increase appropriate behavior in the school or therapy setting, then it is possible to implement only the functional reinforcement components of the AIM curriculum with the children. These strategies are designed using ABA techniques that seek to reinforce appropriate, desired behaviors. Implementing this AIM component may be the most challenging, as it removes the therapeutic elements from the system and requires some modifications to the intervention elements. As well the complexity of the system and the difficulty maintaining control of reinforcers in various settings can be difficult. The following are considerations to make when implementing functional reinforcement separately from the rest of the AIM program:

» *Designing a Point System:* The Point Calculators described in the Complete Implementation Guide may not apply if ACT instruction is not provided with the functional approach to behavior management. Included in the text is an example calculator that removes the ACT elements (Point Calculator F); depending on the setting, additional modifications may be needed. In this arrangement, points will not be earned or lost for "ACT" behaviors, and children will reflect on "successes" and "challenges" rather than examples of their psychological flexibility.

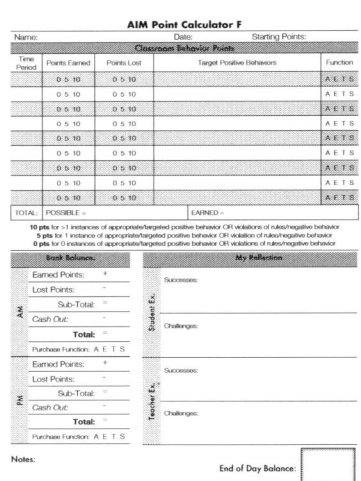

» *Dynamics of the Point Store:* Implementers of the functional reinforcement system in isolation will design and execute the point store in the same way as those incorporating ACT and mindfulness into the intervention. Appropriate reinforcers, variability, frequency of cash outs, and all other components of the point store must be included.

» *Data Collection and Monitoring:* Keeping a log of weekly points and ABC data collection will be the key to monitoring this component of the AIM program. All of the procedures for calculating and tracking student progress will be the same when using partial implementation of the curriculum.

» *Responding to Negative Behavior:* As outlined in the Complete Implementation, a problem behavior occurs during time interval one, once that interval is over, the child has a "fresh start." The language used should remain similar to the complete system, although the incorporation of ACT elements will be absent in this approach. Implementers should remain calm while providing consequences for inappropriate behavior.

Advantages and Disadvantages of Partial Implementation

Component	Advantages	Disadvantages	Settings	Scale of Ease
Mindfulness Practice	» Can be incorporated throughout school or therapy » Is fast and easy to implement » Mindfulness can standalone as a skill that has positive effects	» Progress monitoring and data collection are limited. » Children do not contact reinforcement for engaging in appropriate and/or mindful behaviors. » Transfer of mindfulness skills to everyday life is more of a challenge	Home	4/4
			Group Therapy	4/4
			School/Classroom	3/4
			One-on-One Instruction	4/4
ACT Lessons	» Can be completed within specific intervention groups or classes » Targets the development of psychological flexibility » Focuses on social-emotional skills	» Progress monitoring and data collection are limited. » Children do not contact reinforcement for engaging in appropriate and/or mindful behaviors. » Transfer of ACT skills to everyday life is more of a challenge	Home	2/4
			Group Therapy	4/4
			School/Classroom	4/4
			One-on-One Instruction	3/4
Functional Behavior Approach	» Effective for increasing appropriate behavior in various settings » Can be modified for many situations and individualized for specific children	» Does not address the social-emotional or language deficits exhibited by many children » Does not provide a therapeutic way to communicate with children during behavioral events. » Generalization of behavior changes to other environments is less likely	Home	1/4
			Group Therapy	2/4
			School/Classroom	3/4
			One-on-One Instruction	2/4

Potential Barriers

It is naïve to believe that a simple read of this book and a brief training to all parties involved in the intervention process, will be sufficient to bring about magical amounts of positive change. The real challenge begins once the seeds this book provides have been planted. It will require a significant amount of commitment from the implementers to:

»**The new role of "delivering therapy:"** In many environments, such as schools, clinics, or homes, it is not traditionally the role of teachers, paraprofessionals, behavior analysts, families and others to provide these therapeutic interventions. However, ACT and behavior management approaches need to be applied consistently across contexts to have their maximum impact.

»**The ACT language:** Much of the language of ACT is contra to the typical way people discuss feelings and emotions. For example, if someone were sad about a friend moving away, it would be common to respond in a way such as, *"Don't be sad! You'll keep in touch and make new friends!"* With the ACT approach, the script is flipped. One might say something like, *"It is OK to feel sad! Are you willing to accept those feelings? What can do you do to continue your commitment to having good friendships?"* The only way to become fluent in "ACT language" is to practice it regularly, and in relationship to one's own life.

»**The emphasis on positive when people mostly react to negatives in their regular lives:** Again, the intuitive respond to many situations is to react with attempts to fix or control the situation, or struggle against it. Implementers must pivot toward a focus on letting go of those tendencies and seeking positive outcomes in every scenario.

»**The added work required to pull this off:** ACT will not always be the easiest or quickest way to respond to challenging behavior. Running ACT lessons, discussing a behavior event in terms of ACT processes, completing point sheets on regular intervals, designing and maintaining a reinforcer store will not be easy. However, once a system is developed and clients or students begin to experience the outcomes, it will be worth the effort.

»**The pushback from the kids:** *"It's stupid."* It will be heard at all grade levels and ages. But success also comes at all these same grades and ages. The factor that determines success, is not delivering the program, or the specific make-up of the class, group, or individual child. Instead it is the honest buy in from the people delivering the intervention.

Show Up - For Real

In this book, most of the tasks that are required for implementation involve techniques that some readers will be unfamiliar with or cause uncomfortable feelings. You are going to talk about being lonely or anxious with a child who is supposed to see you as an authority figure. You are supposed to be the adult who has your life together, not someone struggling with the same mess in your head that this child has. However, some honest and appropriate disclosure is exactly what is needed in order to make AIM work. You have to show up to every one of the mindfulness and ACT sessions just as open and willing to participate as the child you are treating. Of course, you need to use some discretion and not disclose your most inappropriate thoughts or actions, but you sure can share moments of your life and thoughts that fit within the context of the lessons you are delivering. When you do show up this way, the child will begin to understand that the struggles that they have are really no different. Of course. the actual events and actual thoughts will be different between the two of you, however it is critical to provide the child an insight into the uncomfortable reality that everyone struggles.

When you only go through the motions of the tasks needed to complete AIM, and keep yourself at a distance, you will weaken the outcomes of this curriculum. During years of pilot testing and examining the differences between successful and unsuccessful users it became clear that one thing alone made all the difference – the implementer. Even at an early age children can detect how much we care about a topic, and the excitement in our voice. Stand in front of these children and read the ACT lessons word for word, and AIM will crumble right in front of you. Yet, if you use these lessons as the general theme, and you bring them to life with your own experiences, ideas, crafts, videos, music, stories, books, or games the child will want to get involved along with you. Finally, take the blame yourself if things are not working. It will be easy to explain away your failures with the child by saying things like *"he or she is too X to understand"*. Replace X with "young", "old", "busy", "complicated", "behaviorally challenged", "low functioning", or "high functioning". All these excuses have been said before by implementers that never showed up to fully deliver the curriculum with an open and complete level of commitment.

Conclusion

Decades have passed since there has been a radically different approach to fostering the social and emotional well-being in children. The punitive directive of punishing inappropriate behaviors was replaced with the more "contemporary" approach of reinforcing the positive. In isolation, this philosophy will work fine for the majority of children that probably can navigate the world successfully within the general rules of good behavior established within their culture. However, these rather simplistic interventions have failed when attempted with our most fragile children who struggle with significant social and emotional distress. A number of commercially available visually appealing repackaging of the same approaches are readily available for purchase through many major therapy or educational resource stores. However, these "one-size-fits-all" scripted interventions often have a similar sub-optimal outcomes due to limited depth of theoretical conceptualizations and weak empirical support. The types of children who respond to most simplistic behavioral and social-emotional interventions will continue to succeed regardless of the program. And the same children who always struggle to achieve success and are bogged down with psychological problems will continue to need more help. AIM is the first curriculum that integrates the behavioral, social-emotional, and psychological needs of children using entirely evidence-based theories and techniques. The AIM approach may not provide a "one-size-fits-all" answer to challenging behavior, but it does provide a framework that can be fit to the needs of any child.

AIM provides tools for creating immense behavioral changes in children. For the first time, a curriculum integrating what have been very divergent literatures on mindfulness and behavior analysis, and articulates the common ground between these two areas under the auspice of ACT. The connections between the two approaches have always been there, and some of those clinicians practicing ACT have been aware of the synergy for years. Yet, many others on both ends of the spectrum have never truly understood the connections between these concepts. AIM takes on the challenge of addressing the dynamic nature of child behavior in the context of previous experiences and current environment. If we succeed in this endeavor, we can have a life-altering impact on our clients, students, and our own children. Because changing the lives of children struggling with how to live with their emotions should be one of the most important aims in our professional careers.

Chapter 3:
Mindfulness Activities

Mindful Moments: MIND

1	Ask the child(ren) to sit in front of a blank TV or computer screen. As they engage in mindful breathing, prompt them to imagine the thoughts or feelings that pass through their minds on the TV screen, watching them play out.
2	Instruct the child(ren) to lay down on the ground looking up. As they breathe steadily, ask them to imagine their thoughts floating past their heads, as if they are birds flying by in the sky.
3	Direct the child(ren) to imagine a volume button on their hand. Ask them to sit and attend to their thoughts. Every few seconds, tell them to increase or decrease the volume of their thoughts, noticing how that changes their reactions to them.
4	Ask each child to write his or her name down on a piece of paper. Holding the paper in front of their face, prompt them to notice what thoughts, feelings, and sensations arise as they look at their name.
5	Take the child(ren) outside, and ask them to look up at clouds. Prompt them to notice one thought/feeling they have been experiencing a lot that day, and assign it to one of the clouds, then breathe mindfully, watching as the cloud passes by.
6	Ask each child to think of one thought they frequently have. Then, have them write it on a piece of paper, but backwards and try to read it aloud. Does the thought have the same effect on them emotionally when it is backward?
7	Present a rose (or an image of one) to the child(ren). Prompt them to consider the beauty of the rose as well as the pain of the prick of the thorn. Discuss how thoughts and feelings can have the same "double edge" effect.
8	Play a song with lyrics in a language none of the children understand. Ask them to notice if they have any emotional reactions without knowing what the singer is saying, and discuss how language and sounds can have many different meanings.
9	Ask each child to draw a cell phone on a piece of paper. Then, as they mindfully breathe, noticing the conversation happening within their own mind, record the thoughts they have on the phone as text messages. Do they need to respond?
10	Bring in a wind chime (or play the sounds of one) for the child(ren). Ask them to predict the next exact time of the tone – when with the chimes meet again? It is too hard to do! Discuss how it is equally hard to predict what they will think!
11	Give each student a real (or paper) flower. As they breathe mindfully, ask them to remove a petal from the flower each time they notice a new thought, and drop the petal to the ground each time they let that thought pass. How quickly does it go?
12	Provide each child with a wand to blow bubbles. Ask them to blow bubbles, and then try to put a thought or feeling they experience "inside" each bubble before they all pop.

Mindful Moments: MIND

13	Play the credits of a movie for the child(ren). Ask them, instead of reading the names and titles on the screen, the replace those with the thoughts, feelings, and sensations they experience while they are playing.
14	Discuss the difficulty of living when thoughts and feelings seem confusing or controlling. Tell them a story, and ask them questions about it. Then repeat with a different story, only ask them to cover their ears. Did they understand?
15	Give each child a stack of "thank you" cards. Tell them to be mindful of their thoughts, and as they occur, write a "thank you" to their mind for that thought. When they have filled up their cards, discuss what it felt like to do so.
16	Ask the child(ren) to close their eyes and breathe mindfully. Prompt them to imagine a bicycle wheel spinning if front of their eyes. Then, as thoughts arise, attach them to one of the spokes, noticing how they blend together over time.
17	Give each child a stack of playing cards, and ask them to close their eyes while attempting to build a house of cards structure, relying on their feeling and imagination to complete the task.
18	Present a clock with both second and minute hands to the child(ren). Challenge them to observe the clock carefully, and attempt to notice the thought they are having every five seconds, watching the clock and counting the seconds between.
19	Direct the child(ren) to sit as perfectly still as possible for three to five minutes, attempting not to move, twitch, or blink, taking notice of both their thoughts and feelings during this time.
20	Give each child a small cup of water, an empty cup, and an eye dropper. Set a timer for five minutes. Direct the child(ren) to use the dropper to move one drop of water to the empty cup for each thought noticed. How much water is transferred?
21	Remind the child(ren) of the classic "counting sheep" strategy to help people fall asleep at night. Then, rather than counting the sheep, ask them to assign a thought they have to each sheep as it passes through their imagination.
22	Ask the child(ren) to create a series of "fortunes" that they might find in a fortune cookie related to their mindfulness of thoughts. Then, take turns pulling fortunes and relating them to their lives.
23	Ask the child(ren) to assign a thought they have frequently, good or bad, to each item of clothing they are wearing. Then discuss why they assigned each thought to each article of clothing.
24	Prompt the child(ren) to think of five people close to them. Then, try to put into words what they believe each person thinks of them, being mindful of how that makes them feel and why they choose those statements.
25	Set a timer for three minutes, asking the child(ren) to write down each thought they have during that time. Then, prompt them to assign a flavor to each thought, what would they taste like, and why?

Mindful Moments: BODY

1	Give each child a ribbon or other small object, and ask them to hold it in front of their face. As they breathe, prompt them to practice awareness of how the ribbon moves in sync with their breathing.
2	Put a few drops of water on each child's forehead, knee, or palm, and ask them to close their eyes and be mindful of how the liquid moves along their skin. What path does it take? How does it feel?
3	Prompt the students to close their eyes and hum one of their favorite songs. As they hum, direct their attention to the feeling they experience in the lips, on their teeth, on their tongue, and around their mouth. How does it feel?
4	Engage the child(ren) in a simple muscle relaxation activity. Prompt them to notice where there is tension in their body, then gently squeeze and relax those muscle groups, releasing the tension from their body.
5	Engage the child(ren) in a "Reverse Race." Rather than winning by being the first to the finish line, challenge the students to take such slow, measured steps while being mindful of their movements. Last one to the finish line wins!
6	Ask the child(ren) to sit crossed-legged on the floor on lay down on their backs with their eyes closed. Direct them to take even, steady breaths, inhaling through their nose and exhaling through their nose. Notice how the air feels as it moves.
7	Place a fan in front of the child(ren), letting the air blow towards them. Prompt them to close their eyes, feeling the air move along their skin, being mindful of how their skin reacts to the fan and the air's motion along their skin.
8	Give each child something heavy that they can hold in one or two hands (i.e. a weighted ball or bag of flour). Direct them to hold the item out in front of themselves for as long as they comfortably can, noticing the weight on their arms.
9	Engage the child(ren) in mindfully making isolated body movements. For example, prompt them to try to move one eyebrow or just one of their toes at a time, noticing how challenging it is and how the rest of their body reacts.
10	Bring the child(ren) outside for a mindful walk. As they are walking around outside, encourage them to be aware of how their body moves as they walk, how it feels to step on the ground, and all of the sights and sounds around them.
11	Create an area with open space, and engage the child(ren) in mindful stretching. Encourage them to breathe in before a stretch, and exhale as they stretch their arms, legs, etc., noticing how each body part feels as it moves.
12	Ask each child to take their shoes off, and walk on various surfaces (i.e. tile, wood, concrete, fabric, etc.). As they take steps, notice not only how the surface feels on their skin, but how their feet feel from the heel to the toe as they step.

Mindful Moments: BODY

13	Give each child a partner, and ask them to stand at various distances from one another (i.e. up close, back to back, a yard away), and notice how the sensations in their bodies change when they are closer to and farther from another person.
14	Give each child a blanket or towel and direct them to roll themselves up "like a burrito," snugly. As they are in the roll, prompt them to close their eyes and breathe, noticing how they feel with the pressure around the body.
15	Obtain a piece of each for each child completing the activity. Ask each child to place their hand palm up, and place a piece of ice on it. Direct them to mindfully observe how the ice melts and how it feels in their hand.
16	Play different kinds of music to the child(ren). Without dancing, ask them to be mindful of how each kind of music makes them feel within their bodies. Does their heartrate change or do their toes want to start tapping?
17	Teach the child(ren) some simple yoga poses, and challenge them to create their own sequence of yoga movements, noting what thoughts and feelings led them to put those movements in a certain order.
18	Ask each child to lay down on the floor and simply "be" for five to ten minutes, with only the direction to stay awake. After the activity, discuss what it is like to do nothing for that period of time and how it affected their body.
19	Engage the child(ren) in a brainstorming activity, asking them to try to consider what their body feels like when they are asleep, and generate a list of ways to describe what sleeping feels like. How can they recall this when they are awake?
20	Take the child(ren) outside on a sunny day. While outside, prompt them to sit or lay down and engage in mindful breathing, noticing the way the sun feels at it touches their skin and warms them from the outside in.
21	Direct each child to attempt to do a handstand (with or without support). Prompt them to be aware of what it feels like to be upside down. Can they feel their blood moving differently? Has their breathing changed?
22	Give each child a comb or brush, and ask them to brush their hair. What does it feel like? Can they feel the bristles moving through their hair? If they reach a tangle, how does it feel?
23	First, ask the child(ren) to stand up as straight as they possibly can, noticing the way their spine feels as they lengthen it. Then, ask them to hunch their backs as much as they can, noticing the change in the feeling.
24	Take the children on a brief jog or run around the area. Ask them to job mindfully, noticing how their breathing changes and their heartrate fluctuates as they move. Then, stop jogging and notice how these return to normal.
25	Ask the child(ren) to talk in strange voices (like cartoon characters, with accents, etc.). As they do, ask them to consider what they must do with their mouths, tongues, throats, and stomachs in order to produce those various sounds.

Mindful Moments: INTERACTION

1	Give each child a piece of chocolate or another food that melts. Tell them to place the food on their tongue, and just notice how it melts, and how it feels inside of their mouth. How is this experience different from simply eating it?
2	Give each child a "pile" of shaving cream, and prompt them to use their fingers to paint with it. As they are painting, notice how the shaving cream moves, how it conforms to the shapes they want it to be.
3	Fill a glass of water to the very top for each child participating. With their face just above the glass, direct them to speak in various tones and volumes, watching how their voice ripples on the waves of the glass of water.
4	Ask each child to use an ink pad to stamp their fingerprint onto a piece of paper. Using a copier, enlarge these fingerprints, and give the child(ren) an opportunity to trace their fingerprint like a maze.
5	Provide each child with nail polish, and provide time to paint their nails mindfully. As they paint, prompt them to attend to the details, to notice the challenge of keeping polish off their skin, and how it changes as it dries.
6	After giving each child a piece of gum, allow them a few moments to chew it and try to blow bubbles. As they do, prompt them to be mindful of how the gum changes as it grows and what happens when it pops.
7	Engage the child(ren) in a game of mindful jump rope. First, have them jump normally, and count how many times they can jump. Then, jump mindfully, aware of the motion of the rope and the child's body, and see how the number grows.
8	Try to have a conversation over the noise of a hair dryer. Discuss how difficult it is to clearly understand one another over the sound. Relate this idea to the difficulty of thinking clearly when there is a lot of "noise" in your head.
9	On a rainy day, make everything quiet in the room, and engage the child(ren) in mindful breathing as they listen to rain (or the sound of rain on a sound machine). Prompt them to notice the sound of each drop as it lands on the ground.
10	Play a game of telephone with the child(ren), but make it a "mindful" game. Encourage the children to listen to the "phone message" as mindfully as possible, increasing the likelihood that it is translated correctly.
11	Provide each child a cup of hot chocolate, or another beverage that must be consumed slowly. Prompt the child(ren) to drink the beverage mindfully, noticing the taste and the feeling of it as it moves through their mouth.
12	Give each child an egg. Prompt them to try to crack the egg with one hand. If you squeeze it tight it can't break. Is the egg hard or soft? How does this relate back to our thoughts? Are they always what they seem?

	Mindful Moments: INTERACTION
13	Obtain a ball and play a game of catch with the group. Direct the child(ren) to pass the ball around randomly, and each time the ball is tossed to them say the thought they are having at that very moment before throwing it to the next person.
14	Engage the child(ren) in a trust fall activity. In pairs, practice a trust fall. Prompt the children to be aware of how their body feels as they fall and are caught as well as the thoughts they have before, during, and after the activity.
15	Ask each child to turn around and/or close their eyes, then play a video for them. Then, ask them to try to draw the scene with as much detail as possible, simply using their observations from sound to guide them.
16	Give each child a book, and challenge them to walk with the book balanced on their heads. Prompt them to be mindful during the experience, noticing way their body moves to balance the book, as well as the thoughts they have while doing so.
17	Place various items in paper bags. Direct the child(ren) to closed their eyes, and mindfully feel the items within each bag, attempting to guess what each item is. Discuss how their body is able to transmit those messages from hands to brain.
18	Find an instructional video of Thai Chi for children. Play the video, encourage the child(ren) to participate in the video, engaging in slow, focused movements while practicing steady, deep breathing.
19	Give each child a spin top, and ask them to make it spin for as long as they can. Prompt them to watch the top mindfully, noticing each revolution it makes before it falls down, and how its rate changes over time.
20	Place a clear cup of water in front of the child(ren). Place a couple of drops of food coloring in the water, and prompt them to watch it as it disperses throughout the cup. How long does it take to diffuse?
21	Bring in one or more snow globes and share them with the child(ren). Allow them to shake the globe, and observe it mindfully as the snow or glitter settles, noticing how it moves through the liquid and lands on the bottom.
22	Direct the child(ren) to breathe at different rates (i.e. breathe fast, breathe slow, breathe to a rhythm, etc.). As they are doing so, take note of how their thoughts direct their breathing as well as how the rest of their body responds to the changes.
23	Give each child a cotton ball, and ask them to make the cotton ball move across a table in a perfectly straight line. Prompt them to notice the concentration and control that it requires in order to do so.
24	Give each child a partner, and a blank sheet of a paper. Ask one partner to draw or write something on the piece of paper with just the tip of their finger, and the other partner to try to guess what it is. Then, have the partners switch roles.
25	Ask the child(ren) to develop their own mindfulness activity, and provide a rationale for why it fosters mindfulness. Have them teach the activity to someone else and prompt them through engaging in mindfulness.

Brief Guided Daily Meditations

Morning Gratitude Meditation	"Good morning. Let us begin this day with a moment of gratitude. Begin by sitting in a comfortable position. Sit in a chair or on the floor with your legs crossed. Feel your body against the chair or the floor. Notice the air passing in through your nose and out through your mouth as gently and steadily breath. Take the next few moments to simply be aware of these breaths. [Wait 1 minute.] On your next in breath, think of something you are grateful for this day. You may be grateful for the sunrise this morning, an event upcoming today, the opportunity to be with a friend today, or anything else you appreciate today. On your next out breath, release all of your gratitude for this day out into the world. Let your joy and thankfulness out into the world. For the next several breaths breath in something you are grateful for and release your gratitude back into the world. [Wait 1 minute.] Return your attention to this moment, and feel ready to begin your day."
Daily Focused Attention Meditation	"Find a comfortable position to sit in, with your feet flat on the floor, your spine straight, your shoulders relaxed, and your face looking straight ahead. Gently relax your eyes, so that they are closed or half-closed. Notice how your body feels in your chair, the temperature in the room, and noises quietly in the background. Now, bring your attention to your breath. Bring all of your attention to your breathing. Take gentle, steady, regular breaths. Take the next few moments just to breathe. [*Wait 30 seconds*.] Feel the air and is enters through your nose, and as it leaves your mouth. Notice how cold it is as you breathe in and how warm as you breathe out. Notice your thoughts as they come and go. If you find yourself becoming attached to a thought, simply notice it, and let it go. Each time a thought catches you, simply 'Notice and Let Go.' Take the next several moments to attend to your breathing, noticing and letting go of your thoughts. [*Wait 3 minutes*.] Bring your attention back to this moment, noticing the room around you again, slowly opening your eyes. Be ready to focus your attention throughout this day."

Brief Guided Daily Meditations

Relaxation Meditation	"After an activity, perhaps exercising, eating, or working, you may notice your body holding some tension, feeling tight or stiff, and your mind holding on to thoughts about what happened before or what is happening next. Take a moment now to notice any feelings of tension, tightness, or stiffness in your body. Where are those feelings? Now, sit or lay in a comfortable position, maintaining your awareness of how your body feels. Bring your attention to your feet, noticing any tension, squeezing those muscles, and then completing relaxing that part of your body. As you do so, take even, steady breaths. Move your attention to your legs, noticing any tension, squeezing those muscles, and then completing relaxing that part of your body. Continue to breathe. Now, bring attention to your stomach and back, noticing any tension, squeezing those muscles, and then completing relaxing that part of your body. Maintain your breaths. Move your attention to your arms, noticing any tension, squeezing those muscles, and then completing relaxing that part of your body. Do not forget to breathe. Finally, bring your awareness to your whole body, and take three deep breaths, releasing any remaining tightness or stiffness as you do. Lay for a moment, with your body completely relaxed. Now, you are ready to continue your day, relaxed and mindful of your body."
End of Day Meditation	"Your day today is coming to an end. Let us take a few moments to be mindful of your thoughts, feelings, and sensations after a full day. As you sit in a comfortable condition, gently breathe in and out. Attend to your breath, keeping your body relaxed. Each time you notice a thought or feeling, imagine that it floats from your mind out into a star in front of you, getting higher and higher in the sky until you can no longer see that thought or feeling. Keep your breathing steady, as you slowly and carefully watch all of your thoughts and feelings move up into the starry sky. [*Wait 3-5 minutes.*] Notice the feeling of stillness within you, now that you have released all of your thoughts and feelings."

Chapter 4:
Daily ACT Lessons

Module 1: Introduction to the Hexaflex

Module Description:
This introductory week is designed to present the concepts of the Hexaflex to the child.

Preparation Notes:
When preparing daily activities, consider if whole group or small group arrangements would work best for your children, and plan your materials accordingly.

Materials List:

Tier	Day 1	Day 2	Day 3	Day 4	Day 5
2	»WS D1T2	»Paper »Pen/Pencils	»Balloons »Paper	None	»Tape
3	None	»3 different sounding bells, noisemakers, or chimes	»Balloons »Paper	None	»Tape

Journal Prompt:
What are the struggles you experience in your mind? How do they get in the way of things that matter most to you in life?

Day 1	Welcome to Your Mind	Present Moment

Tier 1
Script: When was the last time you worked out or went to PE? When was the last time you worked out your mind? Have you ever stopped, noticed how you were breathing, closed your eyes, and just sat still? Do it for 3 min right now!

»Tier 2
Discussion: What happens when we stop and pause? Does our mind stop too or does it still move a million times a minute? What was on your mind? Were you in the present here noticing your breathing, or were you elsewhere?

Experiential Activity: Let's talk about what was going on in your mind. Take a piece of paper and draw three boxes on it. Write down in one box all the <u>past</u> stuff you thought about, in a different box, all the <u>future</u> stuff, and in the last box the <u>NOW</u> stuff.

Tier 3
Discussion: Same as T2. Also add: Is it hard not to stop thinking of the past and the future? Were these bad or good things that you thought about? Do we spend more time worrying about bad things or enjoying positive memories? Why is this?

Experiential Activity: Let us try and keep in the present moment. Let's try another 3 minutes of breathing, and noticing the world around us. This time however, as you start to drift with your thoughts to more distance places and times, keep coming back to NOW.

Day 2		Saying Yes	Acceptance

Tier 1 — Script: Every day we encounter fun stuff and bad stuff. We have good thoughts about cool things, and not so good thoughts about not so cool things. Like tests, and homework, and summer being over. We can't change any of it. Say YES! The good and the bad make up life. The best part is, no test, no homework, and no school year lasts forever. Fun is always coming back.

Tier 2 — Discussion: What are some thoughts that you have which are awesome? Some thoughts that you wish could be true and real right now? How much time do you think about these thoughts? What is a thought or worry you have that you wish you could press the delete button and make go away? Do you ever spend time trying to get that "delete" button to come true?

Experiential Activity: Write down the lyrics to a song that you hated at first but it became cool or better over time. Then describe what changed to make it better. Could your thoughts, the ones you want to delete, be like this song? You just change how you react.

Tier 3 — Discussion: How can something that sounds like noise at first, become beautiful over time? What is a song you first hated that became cool after a while? What made it cool? If the noise was always the same, did you begin to "hear" it differently?

Experiential Activity: Locate three different types of bells, chimes, or noisemakers. Have three children each take only one of these bells. The first child should ring their bell whenever they have a good thought, the next whenever a bad, and the last a neutral.

Day 3		Cutting the String	Defusion

Tier 1 — Script: It is hard to let go of things that we like, and even the things we don't like. Sometimes we carry a lot of thoughts in our mind, and every day there are just more and more being added. When was the last time you just let go? When was the last time you cut the string? Imagine you are holding a big helium balloon. Instead of letting go, stop and cut the string. Watch the balloon float away. Watch that balloon of all those thoughts float far up into the sky.

Tier 2 — Discussion: What is a thought you would put in this balloon and let go? If you could put the thoughts of someone you love in this balloon, what would those thoughts be? Why would you want to let these thoughts go?

Experiential Activity: Pass out a balloon to each child. Have them roll up a piece of paper with a thought they want to let go, and put it inside the flat balloon. Blow it up, and toss the balloon away. Discuss if the thought is gone – or maybe just a little less powerful.

Tier 3 — Discussion: What is a thought you would put in this balloon and let go? If you could put the thoughts of someone you love in this balloon, what would those thoughts be? Why would you want to let these thoughts go?

Experiential Activity: Follow T2, and include passing the balloon to another person in the class. Ask that other person to call it by the name of their pet (or a pet they know of). Pass this "pet" back to the original person. Notice how this thought stuffed inside a balloon with a pet name becomes a bit less troublesome.

Day 4		Flat Tire	Committed Action
Tier 1	**Script:** Have you ever had a flat tire? Maybe on your bike, or when you were riding in a car? A flat tire can cause us to think the whole world has come to an end. Yet, flat tires always get fixed and we keep moving forward. We all get flat tires now and then.		
Tier 2	**Discussion:** When did a flat tire mess up your life? Is there a "flat tire" kind of thing (not a real tire) that sometimes knocks you off your path or slows you down? What is it? What type of "air" can you use to inflate that "tire"?		
	Experiential Activity: Spend some time looking for videos online of people that can change a flat tire really fast. How can they do it this quickly? Maybe being ready for, and practicing with flat tires keeps us driving forward.		
Tier 3	**Discussion:** When did a flat tire mess up your life? Is there a "flat tire" kind of thing (not a real tire) that sometimes knocks you off your path or slows you down? What is it? What type of "air" can you use to inflate that "tire"?		
	Experiential Activity: Spend some time looking for videos online of people that can change a flat tire really fast. How can they do it this quickly? Maybe being ready for, and practicing with flat tires keeps us driving forward.		

Day 5		The Long Jump	Values
Tier 1	**Script:** How far can you jump? If you try really hard can you jump farther than anyone else? What about when you are not paying any attention to your jump? Do you do better or worse? To jump far, you have to know what you are jumping to.		
Tier 2	**Discussion:** When you really want something, you often have to work for it. The stuff you can just reach easily does not seem to have as much value as the things that take time and effort to acquire. When in the past month did you want something really bad that you had to jump far to try and get?		
	Experiential Activity: Place a piece of tape on the floor and note it as the "start line." Make a number of other tape lines at various distances from the start line. Label these other lines as targeted values that a person might have. Jump from the start to the value.		
Tier 3	**Discussion:** When you really want something, you often have to work for it. The stuff you can just reach easily does not seem to have as much value as the things that take time and effort to acquire. When in the past month did you want something really bad that you had to jump far to try and get?		
	Experiential Activity: Follow T2 and include additional tasks of jumping towards other people's values. Why don't we care as much about some of these jumps? Do they care about ours? Have individual people discuss why they selected certain values and how they plan on jumping farther towards them in the future.		

Module 2: All About You

Module Description:
During this week, children will learn how they can relate different parts of the Hexaflex to their own lives.

Preparation Notes:
Some of the activities this week include children creating materials to hang in the classroom or keep in their desks as a reminder or cue to reference their acceptance and values based strategies; if possible, it may be beneficial to laminate or reinforce these items so they last.

Materials List:

Tier	Day 6	Day 7	Day 8	Day 9	Day 10
2	»WS D6T2 »Pencil/Crayons	None	»Bubbles	»Paper »Crayons/Markers	None
3	»WS D6T3 »Pencil/Crayons	»Paper »Pencil/Crayons	»Bubbles	»Large Paper	»Index Card »Crayons/Markers

Journal Prompt:
Who are you? What are the experiences, thoughts, feelings, and sensations (good AND bad) that you feel show the real you? What are the things in your life that guide you?

Day 6	Chameleon	Self-As-Context

Tier 1

Script: Have you ever seen a chameleon? It changes color to fit in with its surroundings, its environment. Even though the chameleon changes all the time, no matter what color it is or what situation it is in, it is always the same animal. Think about how, like the chameleon, you change, but always remain the same you.

»Tier 2

Discussion: Just like the chameleon, you change how you act in different situations. Think of a few places in your life. How do you think and act in the environments? What parts of you are always the same no matter where you are?

Experiential Activity: Provide each person with a piece of paper divided into four sections. Have them label each section with a different part of their life. Write or draw how they are different in each situation. Then, in the center, have them draw a large circle in the center, and tell them to, "Draw or write the part of you that is always there, no matter where you are."

»Tier 3

Discussion: Follow T2, and include a discussion of the following questions, "Do you ever hide that real you when you feel sad, angry, or upset? Do you ever try to hide your own pain by changing your behavior or acting differently than who you are? Does this ever get you into trouble in your life?"

Experiential Activity: Have each person create a "T-Chart" on a piece of paper (or the back of the T2 activity) with the two columns: "How I Hide Myself" and "The Real Me." In the first column, draw or write ways in which each person changes how they act to protect themselves. In the second column, draw or write things that describe who they really are. Ask which person they want people to see.

| Day 7 | You've Got a Friend...In You | Acceptance |

Tier 1 — Script: Think of a time that a friend of yours made a mistake. Remember how you handled the situation. Were you kind to them, telling them that it is OK to make mistakes and that you still care about them? Now think of a time you messed up, and what you thought to yourself. Were you as kind to yourself as you were to your friend?

Tier 2 — Discussion: If a friend were feeling down because they had a problem, what kinds of things would you say to them to help them feel better? Sometimes, when we have our own problems, we are not as kind to ourselves; we might think "You're so dumb" or "You always mess everything up." Don't you deserve to be as good a friend to yourself as you are to other people? It's OK to be kind to yourself!

Experiential Activity: Draw two thought bubbles on the board or a large piece of paper. Brainstorm things you would say to a friend to help them get through a hard situation. In the other, brainstorm things you could say to yourself when you have a problem that show caring, not blaming.

Tier 3 — Discussion: What are some qualities of friendship that show how two people care about each other, accept each other for who they are (both good and bad), and support each other when they need it?

Experiential Activity: Ask each person to draw a picture of a time that he or she messed up, got in trouble, or did something they regret. Below the picture, write some of the thoughts they had after, for example "It was all my fault." Above it, write some of the thoughts you could say to yourself as a supportive friend, accepting yourself for the good and bad, for example, "I did my best."

| Day 8 | Thought Bubbles | Defusion |

Tier 1 — Script: Have you ever seen an illustration of a person with a thought bubble coming out of their head, showing you what, in that moment, they are thinking? And just like a bubble, a thought comes, floats by for a while, and, then, POP, it's gone! Today, try to notice how your thoughts come into you mind and then they are gone!

Tier 2 — Discussion: Sometimes we all get caught up in our thoughts and they feel so important. When these thoughts are good they can distract us, and when they are bad, they can make us feel pain. But, our thoughts don't last forever, they come and go all day long! Give examples of thoughts everyone has had today that have come and gone, "Pop!"

Experiential Activity: Have all of the group members lay on the ground, taking slow, deep breaths. Blow a constant stream of bubbles over their heads. Tell them to pick a bubble, imagine a thought they are having inside of it, watching it float past and then pop. After one pops, notice a new bubble-and a new thought-and pay attention to how it just floats by and then it is gone!

Tier 3 — Discussion: Follow T2, and say, have you ever tried to hold on to a thought? Sometimes when we have painful thoughts we let them bring us down, almost like we are trying to carry them around. Think of a painful thought you've tried to carry with you. If our thoughts come and go like bubbles, can we hang on to them, or do we let them go?

Experiential Activity: Blow additional bubbles in front of the group members. Have them each choose a bubble, imagine a sad or painful thought inside of it, then try to grab it, to keep it with them. When each bubble pops, discuss how that is like a thought passing by instead of sticking around.

| Day 9 | My Totem | Values |

Tier 1
Script: In some Native American cultures, a totem is used as an important tribal or family emblem. Totems with animals on them represent teachers or guides that you connect to in a meaningful way and symbolizes the way you want to live your life. Think about an animal that represents something you care a lot about, something you value.

Tier 2
Discussion: In our lives, we all have something. Something that we want our life to be about. When something is very important to us, we can call it a value. Ask everyone to think of something that they value, and decide what animal represents that value. Share the responses with one another.

Experiential Activity: Have each person draw a picture of the animal that he or she has chosen and describe how that animal presents something that is important in their lives.

Tier 3
Discussion: Sometimes when we have a lot going on in our lives, we can have a hard time figuring out or remembering what it is that we care about. We might be confused and start living a life that doesn't fit in with our values. This is why some people use totem poles as a reminder of those values.

Experiential Activity: Have each person share a way in which he or she has acted that doesn't line up with his or her values. Together, develop a list of ways that you can get back on track after losing sight of your value. Hang this list on the wall, and use all of the different animals the group drew in order to make a totem pole as a reminder of values. Hang it somewhere in the room that each person can turn to when they feel lost.

| Day 10 | My Mantra | Present Moment |

Tier 1
Script: A mantra is a strategy you can use when you are practicing being mindful. It is a phrase that you can silently repeat as you take deep breaths in and out, noticing each breath and letting your thoughts pass as your repeat your mantra to yourself. Spend the next minute just breathing, repeating a phrase to yourself as you inhale and exhale.

Tier 2
Discussion: A mantra isn't usually a random phrase that we repeat in our minds while we practice mindful breathing. A mantra usually has some meaning or importance to us. For example, it could be something like, "I am peaceful." Or "Let it go." Brainstorm together a few mantras that could be used when breathing mindfully.

Experiential Activity: After each person has chosen a mantra that is meaningful to him or her, practice mindful breathing again for 3-5 minutes, encouraging each person to repeat that mantra in their mind, as they let their thoughts pass, evenly breathing in and out.

Tier 3
Discussion: Mantras can be useful when you are feeling upset in some way and feel a need to calm down. Think of things that often make you feel upset and maybe "lose your cool." You can develop your own mantra that helps you manage those feelings. For example, if you get really tense when you are angry, your mantra could be, "Breath in peace, breath out anger."

Experiential Activity: Take an index card and create a mantra for yourself, writing it down and decorating the card. Your mantra should be meaningful to you, but short and easy to remember, such as "Let it go." Have each person carry that card with them all day, reminding them how they can use it with breathing to come back to the present moment.

Module 3: The Climb

Module Description:

Children will learn that being present in your life and focusing on your values will help you live the life you want, but it won't always be easy!

Preparation Notes:

Each week, Tiers 2 and 3 include both a foundation for discussion and an activity. Make sure to review the discussion prompt ahead of time, and use it as a guide, not a script.

Materials List:

Tier	Day 11	Day 12	Day 13	Day 14	Day 15
2	»Construction Paper »Tape	None	»One large rock »Crayons	»Paper »Watercolors/Paintbrushes	»WS D15T2
3	None	»WS D12T3	»Small rocks/pebbles	»Paper »Paint/Paintbrushes	»WS D15T3 »Crayons/Pencils

Journal Prompt:

What are the obstacles you face in your life, and how can you rely on acceptance and values practices to help you overcome them?

Day 11	Life Ladder	Committed Action

Tier 1 — Script: Life can be like a climb toward your values, and you can set goals along the way to help you reach them. Each rung on the ladder can represent one of your goals in life. Imagine climbing this ladder. Each movement you make to reach the next rung, or the next goal, is a committed action in moving you toward your value.

Tier 2 — Discussion: Revisit your values. Choose one value that means a lot to you. What does it take to make your life move toward that value? Can you sit around and wait for it, or do you need to be active and work to make your life meaningful to you? What are some examples of goals you can set to help you climb toward your values?

Experiential Activity: Each person will create a ladder out of construction paper. At the top of the ladder, write one of your values. On each rung of the ladder, write a different goal or action that will help move you to that value.

Tier 3 — Discussion: Have you ever climbed a ladder? Is it easy or hard? Sometimes, you might feel like you've lost your balance, or your arms and legs are getting tired, and you don't want to go on. Moving up that ladder toward your goals can be the same way, it can be hard to always work toward your goals. What are some ways that you've struggled keeping focus on your goals and values?

Experiential Activity: Along one side of the ladder, write down obstacles that might get in your way or lead you away from your values. Along the other side, write down how you can remind yourself to keep climbing the ladder, meeting your goals, and moving toward what you value.

| Day 12 | Centered Chaos | Present Moment |

Tier 1 — Script: Sometimes when we think of being mindful we think of sitting in a calm, quiet room with no distractions, but that's not always how life is! Sometimes you are in a big crowd or a loud place and may feel the need to slow down and find your way back to the present moment. Today, no matter how busy your classroom or hallway might be, try to focus on the present moment.

Tier 2 — Discussion: We often practice being mindful in quiet, calm places, but sometimes when we need it the most, we are in a loud, crazy, noisy place! Where might you go that you would benefit from being in the present moment, but it might not be so easy?

Experiential Activity: Create a distracting environment by putting on TV shows, movies, music, or having lots of people around. Practice mindfulness, even just taking a few deep breaths, and center yourself in the present moment, despite all the distractions. Close your eyes, feel your body in the chair on the floor you are sitting on, and become aware of your breath, letting the thoughts and noise come and go from your awareness.

Tier 3 — Discussion: Not only do we need to learn to be present when the world around us is chaotic, but we need to learn how to recognize when we need to practice mindfulness when the world inside our heads feel chaotic too. Have you ever felt like there was so much going on in your mind that it seemed too loud to deal with?

Experiential Activity: Draw a picture of inside your mind, with all of the thoughts, feelings, and ideas you have moving around, causing chaos. Sit on the floor, close your eyes, and imagine your mind in that way. Watch how those thoughts move around, interact with one another, and then see them all leave your mind, one by one. Once all of those thoughts have gone, sit quietly, practicing deep breathing, feeling the calm.

| Day 13 | As Solid as a Rock | Self-as-Context |

Tier 1 — Script: Remember that part of yourself that's always there, no matter where you are, what you're doing, or what you're thinking. That's called your self-as-context. As you go throughout your day, notice that part of yourself that is unchanging, while your experiences change.

Tier 2 — Discussion: Imagine a rock sitting near a pond. Through the seasons, the appearance of the rock may change…it could be covered in mud, moss, or snow. But underneath it all, the rock remains the same. How do you change throughout the day, week, month, or year?

Experiential Activity: Put a large stone at the front of the room. Ask the group members to list words that represent how they might feel before a big test, writing on a rock with a crayon. Then, wipe the words off of the rock. Repeat with different situations. No matter how the words change, how does the rock remain the same?

Tier 3 — Discussion: Sometimes, we forget that the things people say about us do not define who we are. What are some things people have said about you that make you feel sad or mad? Although we may feel emotional when people say those things, we should always remember that the words will fade away and we will remain the same.

Experiential Activity: Give each group member a small stone or pebble. Ask them to write words that other people have used to describe them on the rocks using crayons. Tell the participants to keep the rock in their pocket or backpack for a week and see what happens to the words. Do they fade away?

| Day 14 | A Picture of Struggle | Acceptance |

Tier 1
Script: The thoughts and feelings we have throughout each day help us form the painting of our lives. All of our experiences, good and bad, add to that painting. Today, try to allow yourself to the good and the bad, and to imagine how all of your thoughts and feelings add color to your life.

Tier 2
Discussion: Identify a thought, feeling, or experience that you struggle with or against often in your life. Maybe it's a feeling about yourself, something another person said about you, or a negative experience you encountered. What colors would represent those events?

Experiential Activity: Using a piece of paper and a set of watercolor paints, paint an image of what that struggle looks like. Take note of how your struggle appears in your art. How does this struggle make your life harder? Is it darker or harsher? Would your art actually be better without those colors?

Tier 3
Discussion: When we try to push away the things we struggle with, could it make us miss out on some of the best parts of your life? Imagine painting a picture of something you love-it could be a favorite food, your home, someone you care about. Without all of the colors, bright and dull, would the picture be as beautiful?

Experiential Activity: Tell each group member to paint a picture of something colorful, but inform them that they can't use half of the colors in the palate. Is it hard to do? Could it be better to have a life full of colors, even if some of them represent things that are hard for you?

| Day 15 | Prioritization Station | Values |

Tier 1
Script: Once you've started to realize your values, those things in life you care about, it can feel overwhelming! How can you move toward all of those things at one time? Today, let's think about which of those values matter the most to you and try to focus on those.

Tier 2
Discussion: It can be helpful, not only to remember those things that you value, but to realize which are most important to you. Why do you think it is important to have your values ranked in a special order? That's called prioritizing.

Experiential Activity: Gather everyone participating in the activity to the center of the room. Present two possible values to the group, indicating that they need to choose which one is MORE important to them, and go to one side of the room or the other to show which they choose. Repeat this activity with a variety of different values that may be appropriate to the group, and in a variety of different combinations.

Tier 3
Discussion: Following T2, have a discussion. Which values were the most important to you? Which ones did you choose least often? It's OK to have a lot of things that you care about, but sometimes you will have to make choices about the things that matter most to you in your life.

Experiential Activity: Have each person cut a piece of paper into a triangle. Using pencil or marker, have them write the things they value the most at the very top of the triangle, and fill in the bottom of the triangle with things that they care about, but aren't their top priority.

Module 4: Accepting the Good and the Bad

Module Description:
This week, children will explore the good and bad thoughts they experience, and how to live with all of their thoughts and feelings.

Preparation Notes:
Some daily activities require the internet or other sources of technology to discover appropriate music, videos, etc. to use. Search for these ahead of time to increase the "flow" of the activities!

Materials List:

Tier	Day 16	Day 17	Day 18	Day 19	Day 20
2	»Paper/Pencils	»WS D17T2 »Pencils	»Permanent marker »Balloon	»WS D19T2/3 »Paper »Crayons/Markers	»Song to play
3	»Paper »Pen and Pencil	»None	»Permanent marker »Paper towel	»WS D19T2/3 »Crayons/Markers	»None

Journal Prompt:
What are some of the good and bad thoughts your experience ALL THE TIME? Would your life be as full if you didn't experience all of them? What can you do to take the power away from these thoughts when they start to overwhelm you?

Day 16	Magic Eraser	Defusion

Tier 1
Script: When you have thoughts, are they permanent or temporary? Does a thought that you have need to stay that way forever, or can it change over time? Close your eyes and imagine something you used to hate (maybe a food, or a game, or something else) that you like today. It's just fine to change over time!

Tier 2
Discussion: Think about your math class. Does your teacher tell you to use a pencil? Why? They do that because, just because you've written something down, it doesn't mean it's permanent. Your thoughts are no different. It's like your brain writes thoughts in pencil!

Experiential Activity: Pass out a piece of paper to each person. Tell them, using a pencil, to write down a painful thought they used to have. Now, erase the parts of that thought have changed over time and write in what you think today! Next time you have a painful thought just remind yourself "This is just in pencil!"

Tier 3
Discussion: We all have certain thoughts or feelings that really bother us, some that won't seem to go away. It might seem like they are written in pen or marker, and we can't change them. But the truth is, we get to choose whether we pick up a pencil or a pen, we can choose to look at our thoughts as permanent or changing.

Experiential Activity: Give each person a piece of paper and a pen. Ask each person to make a list of 3-5 painful thoughts that feel like they are permanent. Then, pass out pencils, and challenge each member of the group to re-write those thoughts in different ways, changing each one into something they can live with.

| Day 17 | Mad Lib You | Self-as-Context |

Tier 1

Script: Throughout our lives, we are constantly faced with evaluations about ourselves—from ourselves and from others. Evaluations are like stories about who you are. Sometimes they are true, and other times they are not. Think about some of the stories you've told or heard about yourself. Do they always show the real you?

Tier 2

Discussion: Have your ever played Mad Libs? What is the fun or silly thing about them? Will two people ever fill out the story the same way? Imagine a time that you and someone else remembered a story in completely different ways. Share those experiences with each other.

Experiential Activity: Create a Mad Lib that is full of self-evaluations, such as the following: "My name is _. I am the world's best _. Whenever I meet anyone new, they always tell me they think I'm _. I disagree, there's no way I'm _, I'm ALWAYS, _! On the other hand, I am the world's worst _. Every single time I _, I mess it up!" Are any of those sentences who you really are? When we're talking about the evaluations that you or other people use to describe you, it's called self-as-content. This is not WHO you ARE, this is what someone THINKS about how you act.

Tier 3

Discussion: Following T2, have a discussion. Sometimes, we can forget that these stories aren't really who we are. Think about one of those stories someone else has told about you. What parts were just evaluations? What parts were true?

Experiential Activity: Have each member of the group share a time that they felt someone evaluated them unfairly. Discuss how they feel that evaluation does not represent who they really are. Brainstorm ways to handle situations where someone might be evaluating you unfairly without blowing up or losing your cool.

| Day 18 | Permanence | Acceptance |

Tier 1

Script: Sometimes the harder you try to make those bad thoughts or feelings we all have sometimes go away, the worse off you are! Think of one word that really has a negative effect on you, one word that makes you angry or embarrassed. How would it be different if you were able to accept that thought or feeling?

Tier 2

Discussion: What does it mean to be accepting of a thought or feeling? Does it mean you accept that it's true OR does it mean that you accept that you have a thought or feeling, without giving it power over you? Maybe if we left painful thoughts alone, they would still be there, but they might not make us feel so bad.

Experiential Activity: Get ready for a game of balloon volleyball. As a group, come up with a bad thought that everyone tries to avoid. Write it on the balloon with permanent marker. Present two choices: 1) Try to get the word off the balloon-and maybe pop it! Or, 2) To leave the word on the balloon and play the game anyway. Is it still fun?

Tier 3

Discussion: When we let ourselves live with our sad or painful thoughts, we get the chance to see that they aren't really permanent. If we just left them alone, we might see how they slowly fade away over time. We're not stuck with them!

Experiential Activity: Take a permanent marker and write a painful word on the back of everyone's hand, just big enough to see. Having it right there on your body must not feel good. How can we make this go away, and FAST? Take a wet paper towel or a hand wipe and try to scrub it away. You scrub and scrub, but there it remains, except now you feel worse! Your hand is red, sore, and you could've removed a whole layer of skin! How does something similar to this happen when you try to scrub those thoughts from your brain? What if you let it be, left it on your hand until it fades away with a couple days worth of hand washes and showers?

Day 19	No Mud, No Lotus	Committed Action

Tier 1 — Script: Imagine a shallow, murky, muddy pond. You really want to swim in the pond, but the mud is just too gross. This dirty pond is the home of a beautiful flower called a lotus. This flower begins to grow at the bottom of muddy ponds like this. It slowly works its way through all the mud, and finally breaks through the water to the surface. When you have a struggle today, think of how you are like a lotus flower blooming.

Tier 2 — Discussion: Sometimes in life, we all go through hard times, like the muddy, murky water that a lotus flower must go through. But, if you keep your values in mind and remain committed to achieve your goals, you will make it through the muddy times and reach the light.

Experiential Activity: Draw or color a picture of a lotus emerging from the muddy water. Above the lotus, write or draw a representation of the value you experienced because you were willing to go through the hard times.

Tier 3 — Discussion: Following T2, talk more about what kinds of "mud" everyone experiences when they are moving toward their values, trying to achieve their goals. What are obstacles in your life?

Experiential Activity: Take out each member's picture of a lotus flower. Ask the participants to add to this drawing. In the water, have them write or draw some of the obstacles or difficult times they have encountered.

Day 20	Eyes Closed, Feelings Open	Present Moment

Tier 1 — Script: When you slow down and really start to pay attention to way your body feels in each and every moment, you might be surprised at how much emotion your feel in a short period of time. Pause for the next three minutes. Notice how many different emotions come to mind.

Tier 2 — Discussion: Music is one way that humans share their emotional experience. What are some songs that make you feel happy, sad, maybe even angry? Do you ever stop everything you're doing just to notice the emotions you feel while you listen to a song? Music can help you get "in tune" with how your body feels when you experience different emotions.

Experiential Activity: Play a piece of music with a lot of variation (such as a classical piece of music). Have everyone in the room close their eyes, listening to the music closely. When the music makes them feel happy, have them raise their left hand, when they feel sad raise their right hand, and raise both hands when they feel some combination. After listening to the song, have a discussion about how much their feelings changed throughout the course of a song.

Tier 3 — Discussion: We can feel our emotions come and go when we pay attention to our bodies. Have each person describe how their body feels when they are angry or upset. How do they tend to act when their bodies feel that way? What if we stopped to notice those emotions, rather than acting on them?

Experiential Activity: Practice breathing mindfully as a group for five minutes. Ask all of the participants to sit, with their eyes closed, and be open to the feelings in their bodies. As they breathe, prompt them to notice those sensations as they come, and feel the tension release in their bodies as they exhale.

Module 5: The Give and Take

Module Description:
The children will explore how they contribute to their own experience and how their experience affects them.

Preparation Notes:
Self-as-context can be a difficult concept to understand and develop, for adults and children! If your children are struggling with this idea, focus on the distinction between "who you are" and "your thoughts and behavior" for now. This concept will be revisited on a regular basis.

Materials List:

Tier	Day 21	Day 22	Day 23	Day 24	Day 25
2	»WS D21T2/3 »Tape »Sticky notes	»WS D22T2 »Pencil/Markers	»Spoon »Plastic egg	»Yarn »Index cards	»Balls
3	»WS D21T2/3	»Paper »Pencil/Markers	»Spoon »Plastic egg	»WS D24T3	None

Journal Prompt:
Are you an active part of your life experience or are you passively experiencing life? Do the things you do, say, and think effect how you feel, or is all of that out of your control?

Day 21	Sticking to Your Values	Values

Tier 1

Script: We all probably have multiple things that we value, maybe doing well in school, spending family time, being a good athlete. Sometimes we're better at sticking to some of our values more than the others. Think about the things that you value, which ones do you stick to and which ones have you let slide?

Tier 2

Discussion: Who has more than one thing that is important to them, more than one value? That's OK! It can be hard to make choices that move you in the direction of all of your values, so it's important to realize which values you are sticking to and which you haven't been doing a great job of following. Why does this matter?

Experiential Activity: Place a long piece of tape vertically on the wall per person and give them 5 of 2 different color sticky notes. On each set, have them write values. Ask them to show how important each value is by sticking it along the tape (the bottom is not important and the top is the most important). Repeat with the other set, but this time, place the notes to show how good you are at sticking to this value. Now, the bottom is 'never follow this value' and the top is 'always follow this value.'

Tier 3

Discussion: Look at where your sticky notes are. Do the notes with the same values match up along the line of tape? Or do you have values that are important to you that you haven't been very good at sticking to? Why do you think that is? How can you do a better job of sticking to that value?

Experiential Activity: For each sticky note that is stuck near "Never follow this value," decide on a way to move toward that value that each person can do today or this week so that sticky note can move up toward "Always follow this value."

| Day 22 | Writer, Producer, Director! | Self-as-Context |

Tier 1 — Script: We have already learned about the self-as-content, those parts of you that are based on what you and others say or think. Today, we're going to focus on the self-as-process. This is the part of you that is always there observing what is happening, noticing your thoughts, feelings, and actions as they occur.

Tier 2 — Discussion: Have you ever stopped to notice yourself noticing something? Have you ever stopped and thought, "Who is that thinking this thought? Or saying these words?" It's almost as if you are watching the movie of your own life. Except you get to write, produce, and direct that movie!

Tier 2 — Experiential Activity: Provide each person with a three panel "storyboard" for a scene from the movie of their life to draw pictures, thought bubbles, speech bubbles, etc. You are the writer, procedure, director of this movie-you get to tell the story however you want!

Tier 3 — Discussion: Think about that scene from your movie. Who was there recording all of this as it happened? Who took notice of the details, attached meaning to the words people said, decided how it was going to play out?

Tier 3 — Experiential Activity: Draw a scene from your life movie that shows you acting badly or getting into trouble. Were you there recording this as it happened? Could you have change the script or the actions in that scene if you were?

| Day 23 | Mind In Balance | Present Moment |

Tier 1 — Script: Often in life you are faced with a challenge that you need to work with others in a team in order to overcome. Mindfulness can help support groups in working together, just as it can help an individual person get through a difficult moment. How can you work with your peers to support mindfulness?

Tier 2 — Discussion: What do you think practicing mindfulness in a group would be like? What would be the challenges of doing so? What would be the benefits-how could it help the group out?

Tier 2 — Experiential Activity: Find something that requires a lot of balance and concentration to perform, such as passing a spoon with an egg on it. Stand in a straight line, everyone facing the same direction. The first person starts the activity, taking the object to balance, turning face the person behind him or her, and passing them the object. Then the next person turns and passes, repeating until the last person has the item. If the object falls or spills, or someone in the group disrupts the mindful atmosphere, start the activity over.

Tier 3 — Discussion: Discuss how mindfulness helped the group succeed. What kinds of behavior from the other members of the group made it more difficult to be mindful and complete the task? Have you ever been the person in a group trying to distract everyone from the present moment?

Tier 3 — Experiential Activity: Complete the activity again, except with someone who has been instructed to try to disrupt the group's mindful behavior. Encourage the group to stay focused on the present moment, letting the distractions pass them by. Can we stay mindful even with disruptions in our own lives?

| Day 24 | Word Web | Defusion |

Tier 1
Script: Words, thoughts, feelings, and actions can be connected in ways we never even realize! Sometimes the ways we relate words together makes sense to use, but other times we make relationships between words that don't make sense or even make our lives seem harder!

Tier 2
Discussion: Words and language are all interconnected, but it is through our own experiences that we give meaning to those words and the way they relate to one another. How could this be a challenge in your life? How could this be a benefit?

Experiential Activity: Stand in a circle with each person holding a card with something different written on it. Get a ball of yarn, and have the first person hold on to the end, say what is written on his or her card, and toss the ball to someone else. That person should say his or her word, explain how it relates to the previous word, and toss it to the next person. Continue until everyone has had at least one chance to relate their card to another.

Tier 3
Discussion: Think of two words or ideas that are connected in a way that makes you feel bad or upset. Maybe you have related "math" and "dumb" together so whenever you go to math you think about being dumb. Is all of that real, or is it just something your mind has made up?

Experiential Activity: Have each participant think of two words or ideas that they have related together that sometimes causes them pain or sadness. How does this "mind meld" interfere with your valued life? Are those two ideas really connected in that way?

| Day 25 | Tonglen Toss | Acceptance |

Tier 1
Script: Tonglen is a kind of meditation used by Tibetan Buddhists. It means giving and receiving. When you practice this kind of meditation, you are opening yourself to the struggles, the pain in the world and sending out your positive energy, caring, and compassion back to the world when you breathe in and out.

Tier 2
Discussion: The Tonglen meditation helps people open themselves up to others, make connections with others, and realize the good and bad in life. Can you open yourself up to feeling others' struggle and giving them compassion?

Experiential Activity: With a partner, find a ball, and stand a few feet apart. The partner holding the ball will share an emotion they are struggling with and toss the ball to their partner to "accept" the suffering as he or she breathes in. As the partner exhales, they toss the ball back, sending their compassion back with it. Take turns in this activity until both partners feel open to the other's pain and supported by his or her community.

Tier 3
Discussion: The Tonglen meditation can help you feel balanced and content with the world, knowing you are giving and receiving caring and kindness every day. How can this improve your life?

Experiential Activity: Practice Tonglen meditation for five minutes. Each time you breathe in, imagine yourself opening up to the struggles, the pain in the world. Each time you breathe out, imagine sending out your positive energy, caring, and compassion back to the world.

Module 6: One Thing at a Time

Module Description:
Life can be overwhelming at times, but this week children will learn to tackle their life experiences and challenges one step at a time.

Preparation Notes:
When arranging the environment for a guided meditation, consider how to increase the likelihood of children's mindful participation. You may choose to space the children out throughout the room, dim the lights, play soft music, or incorporate whatever ideas you have.

Materials List:

Tier	Day 26	Day 27	Day 28	Day 29	Day 30
2	None	»Sticky notes »Pen/Pencil	»Paper »Markers/ Crayons	»WS D29T2 »Markers/ Crayons	»Paper »Markers/ Crayons
3	»WS D26T3 »Markers/ Crayons	»WS D27T3 »Pen/Pencil	»Paper »Markers/ Crayons	»Paper »Art Supplies	»WS T30T3 »Markers/ Crayons

Journal Prompt:
When do you feel overwhelmed, like life (or one part of your life) is just too much for you to handle? How can you break things down so you can commit to the challenge?

Day 26 — Walking to Cloud Mine — Values

Tier 1

Script: Have you ever heard the phrase, "Keep your eyes on the prize?" Think for a moment about what that means. It means to keep focused on the thing that is important to you, your value. No matter what happens today, always remind yourself to keep your eyes on that value that you're moving toward.

Tier 2

Discussion: Have you ever been in the car, noticing a cloud in the distance? As you watch that cloud, the car might move toward it, getting closer and closer, but you'll never reach it. How is that similar to your value?

Experiential Activity: Guided Meditation: Begin by finding a comfortable position with your spine straight and shoulders relaxed. Take three breaths. Close your eyes and picture yourself at the beginning of a long, straight path through a park. In the distance, notice a fluffy white cloud above. You can see it just clearly enough to see it is in the shape of something you value. Start walking toward it. You will never reach the cloud, but you will get closer, becoming clearer to you as you approach. Every step you take is a decision toward that value. When you are ready, slowly bring yourself back to the present. Remember, you can look for that cloud in the distance to guide your way.

»Tier 3

Discussion: What does that value in the sky look like for you? When you close your eyes what do you see? Sometimes that picture might be fuzzy or unclear, but that's OK, just keep moving toward it and it will become clearer.

Experiential Activity: Have the group members each divide a piece of paper in half. On one side, draw what their "value cloud" looks like on a crisp, sunny, clear day. On the other, draw what it might look like when it's foggy and the cloud is less clear.

| Day 27 | Just One Thing | Committed Action |

Tier 1

Script: Think of all the different things that you value. When you do so, it may feel overwhelming-all those actions and goals you need to work on in order to move toward those values. However, you don't have to do it all at once. Today, think of just one thing you can do to move toward a value.

Tier 2

Discussion: Sometimes it can feel overwhelming when you think of all the committed actions you will need to live your valued life. Sometimes it is easier to take things one day at a time, to focus on just one thing you can do in a day to move you toward your values. It can be something big or small, it doesn't matter. It is a choice you have made to be committed to your own happiness. Have you ever felt stressed out by all this?

Experiential Activity: Today, take a sticky note and write down just one thing you will do today to move you toward your values. At the bottom, put two checkboxes labelled "Yes" and "No." Keep that sticky note in your pocket today. Before you go to bed tonight, take a look at the note. Did you achieve your goal for the day? Check yes or check no. If you checked yes, take a moment to be proud of your committed action. Either way, tomorrow will be a new day, and you will have a new opportunity to do just one thing.

Tier 3

Discussion: Following T2 on the next day, discuss whether or not each group member was able to accomplish their one committed action for the day before. Can it help to plan things out step by step?

Experiential Activity: On a piece of paper, have the group members each plan out one committed action they can take per day for a week. Make sure each day the action is attainable and moves toward a value.

| Day 28 | Concentration | Present Moment |

Tier 1

Script: Is your mind ever moving so quickly that you can't focus on just one thing? Sometimes we need to slow down, stop, and take notice of just one thing. That way your life doesn't just pass you by-you are there to experience every moment of it!

Tier 2

Discussion: Have you ever walked past a store or house or any other building a million times, and one day you were actually paying attention and you noticed something entirely new about that building? When we stop to really see what is in front of us, we may experience things we missed out on in the past.

Experiential Activity: Choose an object and place it in front of you. Spend three to five minutes observing an object while you practice taking steady, deep breaths. Notice all of the detail of the object. Then draw that picture as clearly as possible with it out of sight. When you're done, compare the real object to your drawing. How clearly did you remember the object?

Tier 3

Discussion: We can be focused inside of our mind as well as outside of it. Not only can you examine something in front of you, you can examine an image of something you have in your mind. You can study your memories, thoughts, and feelings just like you can an object.

Experiential Activity: Ask the group members to close their eyes. Tell them to imagine something they really love; it can be a family member, a prized possession, a place, or anything else. Notice all of the details of what they see in their mind, slowly taking deep breaths. Now, draw that object as clearly as possible. Did you notice anything new about that object or memory that you love?

| Day 29 | From Miserable to Magical | Defusion |

Tier 1
Script: Have you ever been in a situation where you or someone else was really sad or mad, and then all of a sudden, something makes them start laughing? Suddenly all of those sad or angry thoughts are different, they are funny or silly or just not as serious. Our thoughts and feelings can change at the drop of a hat!

Tier 2
Discussion: Who doesn't like when someone calls them "stupid" or says that something they do is "stupid?" Raise your hand if you've ever had the thought, "I am stupid." Share with one another the kinds of feelings that come up when you look at the word on the page. A lot of those feelings may not be very good, but remember, we can change the way we relate to words, how we feel when we see they can change.

Experiential Activity: Give each person a piece of paper with the word "stupid" printed on in in a large, plain font. Ask each member of the group to take out markers or crayons or paints, and turn that word "stupid" into a picture of a unicorn. What feelings come up when you look at that word now? Always remember, a word is only a word.

Tier 3
Discussion: What is another word that causes you a lot of pain when you see it or think it? Have each person share a word that is hard for them to hear. Can we transform these words too?

Experiential Activity: Have each person write their personal miserable word on a piece of paper in large, plain writing. Then have them use art materials to turn that word into something they love (maybe an animal or a game or a toy). Does that word hurt so much to look at now, or does it make you feel something different?

| Day 30 | Eye, Observing | Self-as-Context |

Tier 1
Script: Remember that observing self-as-context you that is ever present in your life, the you who has been watching during every moment you have experienced? As you go about your day today, try to stop three times and notice that "you" that is there observing everything happening around and inside you.

Tier 2
Discussion: Many cultures think of the eye as the "gateway" into who you are. Why do you think that is? Could it be related to that idea of self-as-context? What do your eyes do? What would your life be like if you didn't have eyes?

Experiential Activity: Draw an eye that represents this version of you that is more than your body, your experiences, and your thoughts. Draw an eye that sees all, every moment, every experience, every tear, every image you come across in your life.

Tier 3
Discussion: Sometimes we don't see so well. Sometimes we might have blurry vision that makes us see events different than we occur. Think of practicing mindfulness like putting on a pair of glasses. When we stop to notice things going on as they occur, how is that like improving our vision?

Experiential Activity: Think of a difficult event in life. Draw what you first thought it looked like, before you had your mindfulness glasses on. Now, draw it with your mindfulness specs on. How is what really happened different from what you thought before?

Module 7: Willingness

Module Description:
This week, children will focus on willingness, learning how to accept, not struggle with, their feelings, and explore areas in life they may still be unwilling to experience.

Preparation Notes:
For some children, mindfulness activities that involve sitting still and quiet can be a challenge. All activities that involve silent meditation or mindful breathing exercises can be adjusted in length to accommodate your children's needs. Build up their stamina over time!

Materials List:

Tier	Day 31	Day 32	Day 33	Day 34	Day 35
2	»Healthy snack	»Paper »Tape	»WS D33T2 »Pen/Pencil	None	None
3	»WS D31T3 »Crayons/Markers	»Streamer »Marker	None	None	»WS D35T3 »Markers/Crayons

Journal Prompt:
What is willingness? How do BOTH willingness and unwillingness effect you in your daily life?

Day 31	Are You Willing to Enjoy It?	Acceptance

Tier 1 — Script: Take a moment to reflect on the idea of willingness, being open to experience, difficult thoughts, feelings, or events in order to live a more valued life. Throughout your day, take note of if you are willing or if you are fighting against these challenges.

Tier 2 — Discussion: What does it mean to practice willingness in our lives? What does it look like when you are being willing or unwilling? It's time for a snack. Wouldn't you LOVE an ooey gooey warm chocolate chip cookie with a nice cold glass of milk? Don't you wish you could have that? Instead, today we'll be having [a healthy, but tasty food] for snack.

Tier 2 — Experiential Activity: Give each person half of a healthy snack, and time to eat. Then, pose some questions. Did they enjoy the snack? Were they too busy thinking about a cookie and feeling upset? Maybe, instead of focusing on how much we wish things were different, we could accept that this is the snack and be willing to enjoy it. Next, while eating, focus on the great qualities of this snack, along with how good you feel because it is healthy. Did you enjoy the snack more this time, accepting it? When have you missed out on something good because you were too busy being upset it was not as planned?

»Tier 3 — Discussion: There are times in all of our lives when we have missed out on an experience because we were too busy thinking about something we think would be better than what we have. Can you think of examples of this in your own lives?

»Tier 3 — Experiential Activity: Give each group member a piece of paper and on one side, have them draw how they looked when they were unwilling to accept a situation, maybe sad, upset, missing out on some fun. Then, on the other side, draw what they would have looked like if they were willing to accept the situation and make the best of it.

| Day 32 | The Finish Line | Committed Action |

Tier 1 — Script: We've all started to identify what our values are, and ways that we can be committed to moving toward those values in our lives, each and every day. This means that sometimes we have to be willing to go through the difficult times, the obstacles, that stand in our way. Life can feel like a long race; what is in the way of you getting to the finish line?

Tier 2 — Discussion: A lot of the obstacles we face are inside ourselves. They are the thoughts and feelings we experience that can feel like they get in our way, like "I'm not good enough" and "I can't." What thoughts get in the way of your committed action? If we think of life like a long race, and we were more willing to live with these thoughts, wouldn't it be easier to get to the finish line?

Experiential Activity: Have each member of the group write their thought on a piece of paper and hold it up in front of their face. If we tried to run a race like this, how would it go? Tape the paper to each child's shirt and have them run in a race. Did those thoughts get in your way when you took them with you? Were you thinking about them as you ran?

Tier 3 — Discussion: Sometimes we also have obstacles that are outside of us, things in our environment that get in our way. Do you ever try to fight against those setbacks, or do you accept them and move on?

Experiential Activity: Get out a long streamer, and using a marker, write down the barriers the group members encounter. Set up that streamer at the finish line. Run another race, this time, being committed to running toward values, without focusing on those barriers. At the end, the group will break through those barriers, but they never had to fight against them.

| Day 33 | You Are Not the Thinker | Self-as-Context |

Tier 1 — Script: Kamand Kojouri, an author and poet, once said, "You are not who you think. You're not even the thinker. You are the one conscious of the thought." Think about how this idea relates to you as self-as-content ("who you think"), self-as-process ("the thinker"), and self-as-context ("the one conscious of the thought").

Tier 2 — Discussion: Remember yourself as self-as-context, the part of you that is aware of all of the thoughts and feelings that you have. That part of you has a choice: you can fight all of the thoughts that don't want and struggle with them, or you can be willing to experience them, noticing them, and letting them go. Which choice do you want to make?

Experiential Activity: Give each person a piece of paper with three concentric circles drawn on it. In the outside ring, write or draw examples of thoughts/feelings you have had. In the middle ring, write things that you experience yourself doing, such as "I notice…," I feel….", and "I think…." Finally, in the inner circle, draw a representation of who you really are.

Tier 3 — Discussion: When you are aware of 'you' as self-as-context, it's almost like you can watch yourself and your thoughts. Has there ever been a time when you noticed yourself fighting your feelings and thoughts, but continued to do it anyway? How could your life be better if you chose not to struggle like that?

Experiential Activity: Visualization activity: Close your eyes. Picture a time in your life when you remember struggling against your thoughts. See yourself, notice what you are doing and what you are thinking. Now, imagine yourself being willing to have those thoughts without fighting them. How are things different? Be proud of yourself for being able to notice those thoughts and feelings without them bringing you down.

| Day 34 | Simply Grateful | Present Moment |

Tier 1 — Script: People are often so caught up in their schedule, to-do list, or activities that they forget to appreciate the little things in their lives. Do you ever feel like you're taking things for granted?

Tier 2 — Discussion: Have you ever rushed out of the house, on your way to school or practice or the movies, and forgot to tell your parent that you love them or thank them for making you dinner? Can you think of any other moment when you were caught in the moment and missed out? Could you be more willing to stop, slow down, and appreciate those little things?

Experiential Activity: Take a few minutes to slow down, and express your gratitude while practicing mindfulness of breath. Breathe in, feeling the air flow in through your nostrils. Breathe out, letting the air out through your mouth and think of something in your life you are grateful for.

Tier 3 — Discussion: We've all experienced times when we felt a lot of anxiety, butterflies in our stomachs, thoughts that just won't go away. One way to deal with these feelings of anxiety is to interrupt them with gratitude. In those moments that you feel lost in your feelings, what can you stop and be grateful for?

Experiential Activity: Think about a situation where you feel a lot of anxious or nervous feelings. Imagine yourself there. Notice all of the thoughts, feelings, and sensations that come up in your body. Now, think about something, in that moment you can be grateful for. How are those thoughts, feelings, and sensations different now?

| Day 35 | Along the Road | Defusion |

Tier 1 — Script: The thoughts and feelings we experience are like signs or billboards that we pass along the road of life. Some are good, some bad. When you focus on them too much it can be dangerous, but if you refuse to look at them, we can miss out on the signs that are there to guide your way. Today, notice those signs, but then let them pass.

Tier 2 — Discussion: Just like a sign or billboard, a thought comes and goes. Sometimes the billboard is advertising something you like, other times the billboard is something you hate. You never have to choose just one billboard to watch. Are you willing to look at all those signs?

Experiential Activity: Guided meditation: Close your eyes. Imagine you are sitting in the back seat of a car, with your seat leaned back, and the window wide open. As the car goes, you see a billboard coming. As it approaches, you see your most current thought written on the board. Imagine how the board looks, the font, the pictures. Just as you have a clear view, the car passes it and you see another in the distance. Watch these signs for a while. When you are ready, slowly open your eyes, and come back to this moment.

Tier 3 — Discussion: Do you find that there are some thoughts you keep getting stuck on, those that you can't let pass you by? What are those thoughts? How can you learn to let them go?

Experiential Activity: Make a billboard for that one thought you have a hard time letting go. Make that billboard a work of art. Transform that painful or stressful thought into something you're willing to look at. Take a few moments to look at it. Now that it's easier to watch this thought, is it easier to let it go?

Module 8: Exploring Mindfulness

Module Description:
This week the children will participate in a series of hands-on activities to practice mindfulness.

Preparation Notes:
Several activities this week use materials that may not be in an everyday classroom. Take a look ahead of time, and if you cannot find the same materials, be creative and find a substitute!

Materials List:

Tier	Day 36	Day 37	Day 38	Day 39	Day 40
2	»Music »Paper/Pencil	»Cups »Water »Ping Pong balls	»Popsicle sticks »Cup »Marker	None	»WS D40T2 »Pencils/Crayons
3	»Music	»WS D37T3 »Pen/Pencil	»WS D38T3 »Pencil	»WS D39T3 »Pen/Pencil	»Paper »Markers/Crayons

Journal Prompt:
What does it FEEL like when you are practicing acceptance or mindfulness? What does it feel like in your body, in your thoughts, and in your emotions?

Day 36	Feel the Beat	Present Moment

Tier 1
Script: Do you ever stop to listen to the sounds around you, whether it's conversation, background noise, music, or something else? As you go about your day today, be mindful of the noises, voices, and sounds all around you.

Discussion: Has anyone ever stopped just to listen to a song and notice the movement of the song? How it ebbs and flows, goes softer and louder, faster and slower? If you pay attention, you can see how the music moves, almost like a heartbeat.

Tier 2
Experiential Activity: Create a long piece of paper (either take pieces of paper and tape/staple them together or get rolls of receipt paper) for each person. Pick up a pencil and play clips of music from a few different genres of music, perhaps classical, rap, rock and roll, and country. During each clip, pick up a pencil and try to track the way the music moves on your paper, creating a line on the paper that represents the "heartbeat" of the song. How is the heartbeat different for each piece of music?

Tier 3
Discussion: It's fun to record the heartbeat of the music on paper, but you can stop and feel the beat inside of you, if you're willing to slow down, clear your mind, and really hear the music. When might it be helpful in your life to stop and listen?

Experiential Activity: Have the group select a sound to listen to. Play the song, encouraging each member to practice mindfulness, being aware of the movement of the song and how it affects them.

| Day 37 | Sink or Swim | Acceptance |

Tier 1

Script: We all face challenges or situations that we do not want to face, that we wish would just go away. Sometimes we can get so focused on what we cannot change that we miss out on something good in the here and now. Today, challenge yourself to let go of something you cannot change and appreciate this day.

Discussion: What are some experiences in your lives that you have missed out on because you were focused on something else-something in the past or future that you cannot control?

Tier 2

Experiential Activity: Give each person a ping pong ball and a cup of water, about half full. Tell them, without using any tools, it is their job to make the ball sink and stay underwater. Meanwhile, there will be a party at the other end of the room with a movie or snacks. As soon as they are able to make the ball stay until the water, they can come join the party. Let everyone try to get the ball to sink. Why can't they get the ball to sink? What are they missing out on? Imagine that ping pong ball is really a painful thought or experience you're trying to push down deep inside you so it won't bother you. Can you do it and still live your life? Or will it just keep popping back up to the surface? What if you let it float and all went to the party anyway?

Discussion: What are some things that you can do to help let go of the painful thoughts or feelings that get in the way of you living your life?

Tier 3

Experiential Activity: As a group, brainstorm strategies for accepting painful experiences; create an "Acceptance Toolbox" for the members of the group to keep.

| Day 38 | Playing the Odds | Defusion |

Tier 1

Script: Our language is a crazy thing – we are able to make connections between all sorts of different events, feelings, and thoughts. Today, pay attention to the things you relate together in your mind…when you each lunch, does it bring up a particular memory? Does a game in PE remind you of a certain feeling?

Discussion: Our ability to relate different thoughts and ideas together is amazing! It gives us the ability to be creative and use our imaginations! If you open yourself up to all the connections you can make in the world, you can have a richer and more diverse experience with the world!

Tier 2

Experiential Activity: Get a package of popsicle sticks, a large cup, and a marker. Take one popsicle stick and come up with one negative thing to write on it. Place it in the cup. What are the odds of pulling out that one thought? 100%! Have one child pull it out and say it aloud. He or she must come up with another word somehow related to that word. Write that word on a new stick and put both back. What are the odds of pulling out the original stick now? Only 50%. Repeat this process, with the odds of pulling out the negative thought diminishing. Talk about how our language works the same way, every time we relate two new words, we expand the way we think, the way we react, and how we experience the world.

Tier 3

Discussion: The way we relate words and feelings together can make life more interesting and exciting, but it can also make life feel harder sometimes. What kinds of thoughts and feelings go together that might make your life harder sometimes?

Experiential Activity: Have each child make a chart with one painful thought they experience and all the thoughts and feelings that they relate to it. Then expand the chart, including things to relate to that word that can make it a little less difficult to deal with.

Day 39	Opposites	Self-as-Context

Tier 1
Script: We use words to describe ourselves all the time…smart, silly, dumb, etc. Are these words who we really are or just words describing some things that we do?

Tier 2
Discussion: Sometimes the words we use to describe ourselves are accurate, but other times, they are not. Have you ever called yourself beautiful? How about ugly? How can we use these opposite words to describe the same person?!

Experiential Activity: Have a discussion, starting with a series of polls. Raise your hand if you are smart. Raise your hand if you are clumsy. Raise your hand if you are gullible. Raise your hand if you are brave. (Continue with as many adjectives as you like). Are each of those things always true, or do they change sometimes? Are these evaluations WHO you are or just behaviors you exhibit?

Tier 3
Discussion: So, we know that sometimes we use opposite words to describe ourselves…but now let's think about which ones are always true. What are opposite words you have used to describe yourself (or someone else!) in your lifetime?

Experiential Activity: Create a two-column table on a piece of paper, that has sets of antonyms listed on either side (for example, clever/gullible, smart/dumb, fast/slow, considerate/rude, etc.). Identify times when you acted each way. We use words like these to describe ourselves, but are they always the truth?

Day 40	Who CARE-acters?	Values

Tier 1
Script: Everyone has certain people, fiction or nonfiction, who they look up to for some reason or another. That reason might be that they represent something that you value. Think of some character that you admire – why do you think that is?

Tier 2
Discussion: Everyone has a favorite hero and a villain from a book or movie that they like! Who is your favorite hero character? And what villain do you think is the most interesting? How do these characters relate back to your values, and what characteristics do you want to show the world in your actions?

Experiential Activity: Take a piece of paper and divide it in half. On the top of one side, write down what you think your favorite hero values. Below it, draw a picture of that hero doing something that makes you think that is his or her value. Do the same on the other side of your paper, except this time with the villain. Which character has values closer to your own, and why?

Tier 3
Discussion: It can help us to keep our values in mind by having some representation of them. What kinds of characteristics would represent the things you value? What would that look like in how the person looks, acts, and thinks?

Experiential Activity: Each child will design his or her own values superhero, a character that represents the things that they care about the most in the world. Have each child share with the group why this character represents their values.

Module 9: Full Circle

Module Description:
This week children will start to pull together the parts of the hexaflex and be introduced to how they interact with one another in real life.

Preparation Notes:
This week, the children learn the distinction between accepting and giving up. This is an important idea! Be sure they are clear on this difference before moving on. Spend more time discussing the difference and providing examples of acceptance/giving up if needed.

Materials List:

Tier	Day 41	Day 42	Day 43	Day 44	Day 45
2	»Whiteboard/ chalkboard	»WS D42T2/3 »Pen/Pencil	»Chalk	»Whiteboard/ chalkboard	None
3	»WS D41T3 »Crayons	»WS D42T2/3 »Pen/Pencil	»Chalk	»Whiteboard/ chalkboard	»Paper/Pencil

Journal Prompt:
What is the difference between accepting and giving up? How would either of those behaviors affect you and your values? How can you learn to accept your challenges without giving up?

Day 41 — Accepting or Giving Up? — Acceptance

Tier 1
Script: What is the difference between accepting a situation and giving up (or giving in) when life gets hard? In the next minute or two, try to think of a time when you gave up on something and a time when you accepted a feeling or situation. How are they different?

Tier 2
Discussion: When you accept a situation, you are willing to acknowledge that it is happening, are willing to make room for both negative and positive feelings, and understand that you have the ability to make your own choices. When you give up or give in, you're letting the bad feelings win, you're letting a tough situation bring you down, and giving up the chance to make choices. Giving up is like saying "I can't handle this, I won't deal with it anymore," while acceptance is like saying, "I know who I am, I am able to live with the difficult thoughts, and I am willing to go through this hard time until I can find peace and happiness in some way."

Experiential Activity: Draw a Venn diagram on the board. Write "Accepting" on one side and "Giving Up" on the other. As a group, brainstorm how acceptance and giving up are alike and different.

Tier 3
Discussion: What are some of the painful or upsetting parts of your life that you wish you could change? What is the difference between accepting these things and giving in to them? What effect does that have on your life?

Experiential Activity: Divide a piece of paper in half. Have each child draw what the situation that is challenging for him or her looks like when they give in to it on one side, and on the other side what it looks like when they are accepting of it. Which would they prefer their life look like?

| Day 42 | The Point of It All | Values |

Tier 1 — Script: Sometimes when we stick to our values, we have to do things or feel things that we do not like for a while. But we know that this is not permanent and that staying true to your values will pay off in the long run. What makes you stay true to your values?

Tier 2 — Discussion: When you're experiencing a difficult situation, focusing on the values you are moving toward can help you get through it. What are some things we "put up with" so that we can move toward our values? For example, you may be on the track team every year and run in the off season. Maybe you do track because your stamina grows and your muscles get stronger. This all relates to the value "health."

Tier 2 — Experiential Activity: Give each child a paper with a triangle on it, divided into three horizontal sections. What is something that you don't have to do, but you choose to do it anyway? Write or draw that activity in the bottom. Why do you do it? What about it is worth your time? Write your reason in the middle. Finally, boil that down to ONE WORD that explains why that activity is worthwhile to you. Write that word at the top of the triangle. That word is something that you value!

Tier 3 — Discussion: This works two ways. Once you know what you care about, can you still have a hard time knowing what to do to move you toward that value? Working backward can help you with this.

Tier 3 — Experiential Activity: Create another three-section triangle. This time, work from the top, identifying a value. In the middle, write down the reason why this matters. In the bottom, write or draw something than you can do to move toward this value.

| Day 43 | Chalk Thoughts | Defusion |

Tier 1 — Script: Have you ever gone outside and drawn with sidewalk chalk? Think about the art you've made out there; it's colorful, noticeable, and you spend a lot of time creating it, but once it rains, all of that chalk just washes away! Our thoughts are like chalk, they are real and we experience them, but just like that, they can be gone!

Tier 2 — Discussion: In what ways are our thoughts like sidewalk chalk? When we're having difficult thoughts how can it help us to remember that, just like chalk, our thoughts will wash away over time?

Tier 2 — Experiential Activity: Give each child a piece of chalk and have them all come up to a chalkboard (this can also be done outside on sidewalk). Tell everyone to start writing or drawing what they are thinking and feeling in that moment. After a minute, announce, "FREEZE." Everyone should stop and erase everything on the board. Repeat the process a few times and discuss how their thoughts changed each time.

Tier 3 — Discussion: What is one of the most difficult thoughts that you have a lot of the time? Does it feel permanent? Like it will never pass? When you have thoughts that feel this way, how does that effect your behavior? How would things be different if you remembered that these thoughts do not control you?

Tier 3 — Experiential Activity: Have each child write his or her difficult thought big and bold on the board. Remind them that you can erase chalk, but you can transform it to! Have them create a picture over the written thought. That thought is still there, under the pretty picture, but is it in your way anymore?

Day 44 — Water Droplet — Self-as-Context

Tier 1

Script: Today, try to spend some time noticing your self-as-context – that part of you that is always there – and try to think about ways that your content has changed over time. Maybe you got taller or started taking an art class or started getting in trouble at school. What part of you has stayed the same over time?

Tier 2

Discussion: Who knows the water cycle? Water falls from the sky in the rain and the snow, it pools up on the group in puddles, lakes, rivers, etc., and eventually it evaporates back into the air. Repeat, repeat, repeat! That one water droplet changes a whole lot throughout that cycle, but just like you, it always remains that same droplet.

Experiential Activity: Draw a droplet of water on the board. As a group, brainstorm all of the different forms that drop of water can take in a concept web. Some forms water may take include ice, snow, rain, a snow cone, a slip and slide, etc. No matter what shape the water takes, it is always water! How do you interact differently with the water in these different formats? Even though your behavior is different in each scenario, isn't that always the same you as well?

Tier 3

Discussion: In what ways can water be a good thing? (Great to drink, can swim in it, water plants, etc.) In what ways can water be a bad thing? (Hurricanes, drowning, slip on ice, etc.) Is the water itself good or bad, or does it just change in different situations? How does that relate to you and your behavior?

Experiential Activity: Repeat the activity above, however instead of brainstorming all of the different forms of a drop of water, brainstorm all of the different forms the children might take throughout their lives. Some of these will be good, and others bad…does that change who they are?

Day 45 — Come Back — Present Moment

Tier 1

Script: It can be easy to get lost in the hustle and bustle of the day. To lose sight of your values. To let your thoughts seem more permanent than they are. To forget about yourself as context and get caught up in your bad experiences. Today, when you notice these things happening, try to bring yourself back to the here and now.

Tier 2

Discussion: Have you ever noticed yourself getting caught up in thoughts, worries, frustrations that take you out of the present moment? Do you feel like you're moving into those feelings in the past or in the future, away from the here and now?

Experiential Activity: Sit in a comfortable position, with your spine straight and your shoulders relaxed. Sit with your thoughts for five minutes, taking regular, deep breaths noticing each time you inhale and exhale. Each time you feel your thoughts or feelings move away from the present moment, gently say to yourself "Come back."

Tier 3

Discussion: We can bring ourselves back to the present moment anytime during the day that we feel ourselves getting pulled into our thoughts and feelings. You don't need to be meditating to do it! How can you bring yourself back when you feel this happening?

Experiential Activity: Complete some other activity such as reading a book, completing a task, doing an art project. Encourage the children to remain in the present moment when completing the activity. When they feel themselves slipping away, have them tally each time they need to "come back" to the present moment.

Module 10: Bringing the Outside Inward

Module Description:
This week, children will explore the parts of the hexaflex as they relate to changes in nature and the weather.

Preparation Notes:
This week's weather/nature theme is easy to revisit on a regular basis, as the children will contact nature and weather changes on a daily basis. Try to relate these metaphors, concepts, and exercises to real life events regularly over the next few weeks!

Materials List:

Tier	Day 46	Day 47	Day 48	Day 49	Day 50
2	»WS D46T2 »Markers/ Crayons	»Paper »Markers/ Crayons	None	»WS D49T2 »Pen/Pencil	»Nature Sounds »Paper »Markers/ Crayons
3	»Black paper »Light color crayon	»WS D47T3 »Pen/Pencil	None	None	»Nature Sounds

Journal Prompt:
When people think of mindfulness and acceptance, a lot of the time it brings up images of nature (things like water, sky, fresh air). Why do you think this is? Can you relate to this idea?

Day 46 — **Let It Rain** — **Acceptance**

Tier 1 — Script: Don't you hate when you get caught in the rain with no umbrella? Would you let something like that ruin your day, or would you let it go and move on? How could practicing acceptance in a situation like that benefit you?

Tier 2 — Discussion: We all hate getting caught in the rain when we have somewhere we need to be. Wouldn't it be great if we could find a way to stop it from raining? Then we would never have to deal with those dark, gloomy days! What could be the problem with doing this? Maybe, the best thing you can do when it is raining is to let it rain.

Experiential Activity: Divide a sheet of paper into three sections. In the first, draw a picture of you getting caught in the rain outside in a park with no umbrella, soaking wet, and gloomy. In the middle, draw a dome above that blocks the rain. But what would happen to the trees, flowers, and ponds in the park with no rain? They would dry up and wilt. Draw the effect on the plant life in the middle panel. What if we learned to enjoy the rain, even if it means we get a little wet sometimes? In the last panel, draw what life would be like if you appreciate the rain in that park with the happy, healthy plants!

Tier 3 — Discussion: Sometimes people use the idea of a "black cloud" to talk about something bad or sad that they are feeling. What are some of the "black clouds" in your life? Should we try to hide from those clouds or let them hang over us while we go about our day?

Experiential Activity: Take a few sheets of black construction paper; using a light-colored crayon, have each child write down the "black clouds" in his or her life. Crumple them up to resemble clouds, and hang them from the ceiling. Do those black clouds need to be in the way, or can you let them stay with you?

Day 47	Weather Channel	Self-as-Context
Tier 1	**Script:** Do you or someone in your family check the weather each morning? Think about how much the weather changes where you live. Whether it's rainy, sunny, or snowy, it's always your home. Think about that today, and notice if it brings you a feeling of comfort.	
Tier 2	**Discussion:** Your hometown, no matter what kinds of weather comes its way, will always be your home; it is the context where all of your memories and experiences have happened. Do you have good memories in all sorts of different kinds of weather? How is this like yourself as context?	
Tier 2	**Experiential Activity:** Make a "memory" book of your home, with a page for each season. Be sure to show how different each season can look and feel, and include a memory you have during each of those seasons. If you hate winter, does that change how you feel about your home?	
Tier 3	**Discussion:** We know now that weather comes and goes, changing what your hometown looks and feels like, but never changing the fact that it is *your home*. Have you ever tried to watch the weather channel for predictions? Are those predictions about how the weather might act ever wrong? Has anyone ever made bad predictions about how you might act? How does that make you feel? Does it change who you are?	
Tier 3	**Experiential Activity:** Have each child create a 10-day "weather forecast" for their own behavior. On which days might they be sunny and happy, on which days might they feel a little dark or stormy? Does this forecast change who they are or control what they do?	

Day 48	Bird's Eye View	Defusion
Tier 1	**Script:** Have you ever thought about what it would be like to be a bird, flying high above the clouds during a rain shower or a storm? How is that different from your perspective down here on the ground?	
Tier 2	**Discussion:** Standing outside during a rainstorm, it might seem like you can feel, hear, or see each raindrop falling. Imagine that each of those drops is one of your thoughts. Good or bad, surrounding you, leaving you soaked. Sometimes we can get so caught up in the thoughts (or the raindrops around us), they can seem much bigger than they are.	
Tier 2	**Experiential Activity:** Close your eyes, imagine raindrops, each with a thought or feeling you are having. Notice how they surround you, how they make you feel. Now slowly zoom out, imagine you slowly floating above the clouds. From way up here can you even tell one raindrop from another? What happens to those thoughts?	
Tier 3	**Discussion:** Have you ever had a thought, and felt like you couldn't let it go? Like it was going to be stuck with you forever? If our thoughts are like raindrops, will they last forever? What happens to a raindrop when it hits the ground? What happens to your thoughts after you've had them?	
Tier 3	**Experiential Activity:** Guided visualization: Sit comfortably in your chair, with your shoulders relaxed, and your eyes gently closed. As you breathe steadily, imagine a rain shower start to fall around you. Notice those raindrops falling. Each time you have a thought, see it inside one of those drops. Watch it fall from the clouds, coming quickly down from the sky, crashing into the ground, where it disappears. Let yourself watch these thoughts come and go for the next few minutes.	

| Day 49 | Turbulence | Committed Action |

Tier 1
Script: This week, we have talked a lot about the weather, how it relates to our own experiences with thoughts and feelings. Sometimes, the weather can seem like it's trying to get us off track, like a plane flying through turbulence. What do we do when that happens?

Tier 2
Discussion: When people flying on an airplane experience turbulence, it means that the air around them is rocking or shaking the plane, making it harder for the pilot to stay on track, but he or she must get to the destination. In your life, the destination is your values; what can you do when you hit some turbulence along your way?

Experiential Activity: As a group, brainstorm things that could cause turbulence on a flight toward values. On paper, have each child write down a value at the top and list the committed actions they can take to keep their planes on course toward their values. Then, fold the paper into paper air planes, and see how far they can fly when they stay committed to those values.

Tier 3
Discussion: When a pilot encounters turbulence, he or she can choose to fly through it, go around it, or make an unplanned landing. You have choices every time you encounter a new obstacle on the way to your values. Whatever choice you make will have a different outcome. Have you ever thought of more than one way to handle a problem?

Experiential Activity: Have the children sit in a circle. Ask one of the children to suggest an obstacle someone could face on the way toward a value. Have the person next to him or her suggest a way to handle that obstacle (good or bad), and the person next to him or her name the effect that could have. Repeat until everyone has had a chance to identify all three parts for a different value.

| Day 50 | One with Nature | Present Moment |

Tier 1
Script: When practicing mindfulness, do you ever like to have something specific you are looking at or listening to? Think of a time when you were outside really in the present moment, and the kinds of sights, smells, and sounds that you noticed.

Tier 2
Discussion: If you listen carefully to something, without being able to see it, do you think you could figure out what you are hearing? What would you need to be able to do in order to notice all of the details?

Experiential Activity: Play a clip of a nature sound (a rainforest, storm, windy day, etc.), and tell the children to listen to it mindfully, silently paying attention to each and every moment of the sound clip, while taking deep, steady breaths. Then, have them draw a picture, trying to include every element of the nature sounds.

Tier 3
Discussion: Do you ever notice that you feel stressed, upset, or worked up during the day or at night when you're in bed? Some people play nature sounds to help them relax or even to fall asleep at night. Mindfully listening to these calming sounds could help you to live more in the present moment.

Experiential Activity: Play a white noise track that involves some nature-related sounds. Have the children sit and practice mindful breathing while listening to the track. Repeat this with a few other tracks, and have the children identify which tracks they felt most present listening to. Use these in these classroom during stressful times!

Module 11: Transformations

Module Description:
This week, children will relate the concept of transformations to mindfulness and willingness practices.

Preparation Notes:
As you become more familiar with the ACT language and concepts, try to build in your own metaphors or exercises that relate to current events such as holidays, school events, and others!

Materials List:

Tier	Day 51	Day 52	Day 53	Day 54	Day 55
2	»Clay	None	»Cups »Water »Food Coloring	»Ice Cubes	»WS D55T2 »Pencil »Brads
3	»Clay	»Paper »Pencil	»WS D53T3 »Crayon/Markers	»Ice Cubes »Cups	None

Journal Prompt:
How have you changed throughout your life in both good and not-so-good ways? In what ways do you want to continue to grow over time?

Day 51 — Shaping Your Future — Values

Tier 1
Script: Your values, those things that are most important to you in life, do not only help you make decisions about how to live today, but they help you make a plan for the future. How do you want your life to take shape?

Tier 2
Discussion: Values help you shape your choices so you feel fulfilled and get what you want out of life. How do you think that the things you value help you create the life that you want?

Experiential Activity: Take a piece of playdough or clay. Mold it into a shape or symbol that represents the value that is most important to each child. Let it dry and put it in an important place where it can remind the children that they are shaping their future with every choice they make.

Tier 3
Discussion: Do you think the values that you have today will be the same for the rest of your life? Or do you think they may change or evolve as you get older? How have the things you cared about when you were five years old changed? How have they remained similar?

Experiential Activity: Use a different piece of clay and ask each child to mold what would have been a value they held when they were four years old. How has that value change over time? Re-work the clay to represent the present values. Finally, ask the children to mold the clay into what they believe their values might be like in five or ten years.

| Day 52 | Redecorating | Self-as-Context |

Tier 1

Script: We all know that there is the part of us that is observing, the part of us who has always been there. Just because that core of who we are doesn't change, it doesn't mean that we don't evolve and change over time. Take a moment to reflect on how you have evolved in your life so far.

Tier 2

Discussion: Everyone has a bedroom where they sleep. That bedroom might change over time, but it has the same four walls. How does this relate to our self-as-context? Just like your bedroom, what people see and think about you may change, but you are always the same person.

Experiential Activity: Engage in the following guided meditation: Sit in a comfortable position. Close your eyes and practice taking steady, deep breaths. Picture yourself in your bedroom. Now, travel back to when you were a baby. How was it different? Notice the color on the wall, furniture, the stuff on the dresser, etc. Fast forward, how does it change? Note each and every change. Walk around your room exactly how you left it this morning. Imagine how you would like it to be in a year or two. How will it be different to reflect how you change? Each and every time you walk into that room you are able to recall all of your memories, no matter how it has changed.

Tier 3

Discussion: The way you decorate your room is one way of letting people know how you want them to think of you. It's a way to let them see who you are. How can you do the same thing with your behavior and how you act?

Experiential Activity: Provide each child with a piece of paper or pencil. Have them brainstorm (drawing or writing) how the way they behave might make people think of who they are. Is this the truth, does this behavior represent how they are deep down inside?

| Day 53 | Color Meld | Present Moment |

Tier 1

Script: It's amazing how things can change right before our eyes! Have you ever noticed something transform right there in front of you? How can things change over time? If you are not paying attention, how could you miss out on these amazing events?!

Tier 2

Discussion: Have you ever been cooking or watching someone else cook and someone gets distracted? Before you know it, the dish may have burned! It changed, and because you were out of the moment, you missed it. If we're not paying attention what else could we miss?

Experiential Activity: Give each child a small cup of water. Put one or two drops of two different colors in the cups. Encourage each child to mindfully observe the way the colors meld; while breathing deep, steady breaths, observe how the colors slowly meld, how they change as you simple observe.

Tier 3

Discussion: Have you ever heard of a gradient? It shows the increase or decrease from one end of a spectrum to another. Have everyone look at a gradient (perhaps from black to white). It shows how a color can transform, slowly but steadily. How can a gradient relate to your behavior?

Experiential Activity: Have each child make a "behavior gradient," which demonstrates how their actions and feelings change as they move from calm to angry or vice versa. Then take a few moments, while breathing mindfully, for each child to sit and imagine how their body changes as they move through that gradient.

Day 54	Melting	Defusion

Tier 1

Script: We talked about the water cycle before; how water can change its shape and form, but it always remains water. Just like that, your thoughts, which always occur in your own experience can change over time.

Tier 2

Discussion: When ice melts, it is transforming. It's moving from one form to another. Just like ice, your thoughts can change over time, they are always occurring in your experience, but the content of them is always shifting. Can you notice when your thoughts are changing?

Experiential Activity: Give each child a piece of ice to hold in their hand. Tell them to imagine that ice cube contains one of their painful thoughts. As they hold it in their palm, ask them to observe it melt, change into a new form. Have them imagine how that thought transforms into something new along with the ice.

Tier 3

Discussion: Good or bad, our thoughts all come together at some point, in order to form our experience. How can your good, bad, exciting, painful, embarrassing, funny, crazy thoughts all come together to form the life and experiences that you lead?

Experiential Activity: Give each child three-five ice cubes, one at a time. Have them label each ice cube with a different thought or feeling that they experience as they put it into a cup. Over the next hour or two, keep the cups nearby, encouraging the children to observe how the ice cubes melt into one cup of water, something they couldn't live without!

Day 55	Time Change	Acceptance

Tier 1

Script: Every year, we turn the clocks forward and backward; it's called daylight savings time. How can we do that? Where does that time go or come from? How can we hold on to that time…or should we?

Tier 2

Discussion: Time is relative. When do you want to go back in time? Can you move time backward? Can you move it forward? If you were to try, you would keep floating in a space that doesn't even exist! When would you miss out right here and NOW if you were always busy trying to change time?

Experiential Activity: Have each child draw a clock. Instead of where the numbers belong, have them write or draw moments in time of their life. Attach the hands of a clock using brads. Slowly move the hands of the clock, letting it touch each moment in time. What would you miss if you jumped forward or backward?

Tier 3

Discussion: Sometimes we all wish that we could go back in time and rewrite history, to fix some mistake that we made, or change something that happened to us. But that would change our whole lives. How could it benefit you to accept the way your life has happened, and focus on learning from those experiences?

Experiential Activity: Review a historical event. One in which things did not go smoothly, and may have had a bad outcome. Then, discuss how that event could have been avoided if we were able to go back and rewrite history. But, what would happen to us here today? Would we even be here? Could it be better to accept our histories and always focus on living life here, today, in this moment?

Module 12: Part of a Whole

Module Description:
This week, children will examine how thoughts, feelings, and actions fit together to form their life experiences.

Preparation Notes:
With these mindfulness and acceptance exercises, the more hands-on the children can be in the experience, the better! The experiential learning part of ACT is key!

Materials List:

Tier	Day 56	Day 57	Day 58	Day 59	Day 60
2	»Video	»WS D57T2 »Crayons/ Markers	»Multipurpose item (i.e. Q-tip)	»Popcorn	»Small cups »Small rocks »Markers
3	»WS D56T3 »Crayons/ Markers	»Pizza dough »Unusual toppings »Oven	»Building items	»WS D59T3 »Crayons/ Markers	»Rocks from above »Barrier

Journal Prompt:
You have had good, bad, and neutral experiences in your life. How have these, taken all together, helped shape you into you who are today? How would your life be different if you refused to accept anything you didn't like?

Day 56 — A Part of this World — **Present Moment**

Tier 1
Script: It can be really easy for us to get caught up in the world inside our heads, and to lose sight of the world we are a part of, right here and now. Throughout the day today, pause and reflect on how you fit into this earth. How are you part of this amazing, lively world?

Tier 2
Discussion: Have you ever stopped to think about how huge, complex, and majestic the world is? Raise your hand if you think about this on a daily basis. Most likely not. So many of us can get lost in focusing on our own experiences, and lost sight of the big picture. How can stay aware of the amazing world we are a part of?

Experiential Activity: Play a video of the wonders of earth (or maybe an ocean) with instrumental music overlaying it. Encourage the children to be mindful as they watch this video. As they focus on awareness of their breaths, remind them to reflect on how, right now, in this moment, they are a part of this world.

»Tier 3
Discussion: When we see ourselves as the center of the world, and lose sight of everything happening around us, we can let our thoughts and feelings overtake us. Have you ever noticed yourself seeing the world as "one-sided" from your own point of view?

Experiential Activity: Give each child a piece of paper. On one side, have them draw themselves in the middle, and surround themselves with words or images that represent the world they have create in their minds. On the other side, have them draw the world, and where they fit into it. What are you missing out on when you lose this perspective?

	Day 57	Pizza Mismatch	Defusion
Tier 1	**Script:** We've talked about how our language can be a good or a bad thing, depending on the situation. Today consider how the ideas we have about things before they happen—and about what they will be like—might be wrong. How is what we say about things sometimes different from how things really are?		
Tier 2	**Discussion:** Think of your favorite pizza. Now, think of your favorite food that doesn't belong on a pizza. How do we decide what does and doesn't go together? Just like words, we make decisions about what does and doesn't go together, but at the end of the day, food is just food and words are just words.		
Tier 2	**Experiential Activity:** Give each child a piece of paper and have them draw a pizza that has all the foods they like that "don't" belong on a pizza. Then, take a moment to sit and imagine eating that pizza. Can you re-imagine it in a way that makes that weird pizza totally delicious?		
Tier 3	**Discussion:** We sometimes make decisions about how things are going to be before we even give them a change—our language gets in the way and things we've never experienced can feel real. Do you think there's a chance that a mismatched pizza could actually be yummy?		
Tier 3	**Experiential Activity:** As a group, make a "mismatched" pizza with some foods that wouldn't normally be put on a pizza (but in the end might make a good combination). Have everyone taste the pizza, and then discuss how having pre-determined ideas can lead you to miss out on a whole lot of good things.		

	Day 58	Re-Build	Self-as-Context
Tier 1	**Script:** When things change over time, like as you get older, your interests change, or you start to act differently, we can forget that there is that steady, observing part of ourselves that is always a part of us. What are the "building blocks" of who you are?		
Tier 2	**Discussion:** Think of some multi-purpose item. It's function changes with every different task that it performs, but does the item ever change? How is that like you, how your self as context holds steady while your self as content changes?		
Tier 2	**Experiential Activity:** Give all of the children an item that they can use for multiple purposes (like Q-tips). Give them "challenges" for using the item in various ways (i.e. blending crayon colors together, cleaning out a keyboard). If this item can take on so many roles, how does it maintain its true identity?		
Tier 3	**Discussion:** Have you ever seen a video of an animal (such as an ant or a beaver) use materials in their environment to create something new? Have you ever made a mistake or gotten in trouble? How can you take the things about yourself and re-build them to adapt to new situations?		
Tier 3	**Experiential Activity:** Give each child a set of items to build a structure with (i.e. crayons, Q-tips, straws, etc.). Have them build a structure. Then, challenge them to use the same materials to build something entirely new. The form of the structure may change, but those building blocks remain the same.		

| Day 59 | Popcorn | Acceptance |

Tier 1 — Script: When you go through life trying to get rid of everything that you don't like or that challenges you, you may wind up missing out on a lot of other things around you. Could accepting these events let you live a happier life?

Tier 2 — Discussion: Who has ever made a bag of popcorn, and noticed that some of the seeds didn't pop. You get one in your mouth, and have to spit it out! Then, you take the time to sort through all of the rest. Sometimes, when we encounter a thought or feeling we don't like, we do the same thing. Is this helpful in our lives?

Experiential Activity: Give everyone a small bag of popcorn, that has some kernels in it. Tell them that those kernels are bad thoughts and they need to all be kicked out before they can enjoy the movie you are putting on. Start the movie and let them get rid of the kernels. Did the miss out on the movie when they were focused on something else? Now, just live with the kernels and enjoy your popcorn and movie. Is this better?

Tier 3 — Discussion: Another problem when you might have when you eat popcorn is getting a piece stuck in your tooth. Sometimes you really just need a toothpick or toothbrush to get it out. But what if you're at a movie, and have to wait until you get home; would it be better to spend the whole time trying to get it out or just live with it and enjoy the movie?

Experiential Activity: Pass out a piece of paper to each child. Have them draw two pictures: one of them living with the kernel and one of them trying to get it out. Make a list of ways to practice acceptance in uncomfortable or annoying situations.

| Day 60 | Gravel Pile | Committed Action |

Tier 1 — Script: Each one of the actions you take each day may not seem very important in the big picture of your life, but when you take them together they have a huge effect on your life. What small steps can you take to move you toward your values?

Tier 2 — Discussion: Gravel (old crushed up rocks) can be used for many things; you can fill holes in the ground, drain plants, and more. Each little piece of gravel doesn't mean much individually, but taken together they can do a lot. Think of the little behaviors you engage in daily, and how, when you put them all together, they move you toward your values. What are your committed action behaviors?

Experiential Activity: Give each child a small cup, and have them write one of their values on the cup. Provide each child with enough rocks to fill the cup; have them write committed actions they can take to move toward that value on each rock, placing them in the cup as they do. Discuss how impactful all of those rocks together are.

Tier 3 — Discussion: While you are acting in a way to move you toward your values, you are likely to find some barriers along the way. You will have to engage in even more committed actions to help you get past those obstacles. How can you stick with it when these things happen?

Experiential Activity: For the value they identified in the previous activity, have each child identify a related barrier that they may face. Have them create an actual barrier, and figure out how to arrange their committed action rocks so that they can overcome that obstacle, and continue on the path to their values.

Module 13: Not Alone

Module Description:
This week, children will focus on incorporating mindfulness into relationships with others – and themselves.

Preparation Notes:
If the children you are working with may struggle with activities that involve physical interaction with another child, consider revising the activity to reduce or eliminate the physical interaction, opting instead for discussion-based versions of the activity.

Materials List:

Tier	Day 61	Day 62	Day 63	Day 64	Day 65
2	None	None	»WS D63T2 »Crayons/Markers	»WS D64T2/3 »Crayons/Markers	»Task materials (May vary)
3	None	None	»Paper »Pen/Pencil	»WS D64T2/3 »Crayons/Markers	»Paper/Pencil

Journal Prompt:
Who are the people in your life that you have or want to have a relationship with? How can those strong, healthy relationships help you in developing your mindfulness and values-based practice?

Day 61	Lean on Me	Present Moment

Tier 1 — Script: While mindful practice can benefit you when you are alone, you can also be mindful with a friend, using your awareness of one another to come back into the present moment. Aren't a lot of things better when you're with someone who cares about you?

Discussion: Can anyone think of a time when you were having a hard time, but a friend or family member helped you through it? How can having someone to support you help bring you back to the present moment?

Tier 2 — Experiential Activity: Have each child find a partner, and stand back to back. Slightly lean back toward one another, bending knees into a squat or seated position, using one another for support. Once in position, tell the children, "Breathe mindfully, but rather than being aware of your own breath, see if you can feel your partner's breath as you lean on one another. Can you sense how his or her back moves as they inhale or exhale? See if you can be mindful together for 1 to 3 minutes."

Discussion: Practicing mindfulness with someone else can help you to feel the calm, and to help build your friendship. However, that doesn't mean that everyone's experience in the present moment is the same. Here in the same room at the same time, do you think you and your partner noticed anything different?

Tier 3 — Experiential Activity: After practicing partner mindful breathing, allow the children a few minutes to talk with their partners. Ask them to share what they noticed during their time being in the present moment together, and to compare and contrast what they felt, heard, and saw.

| Day 62 | Say It Out Loud | Defusion |

Tier 1
Script: We all know that we have thoughts and feelings that feel big and scary, but don't always reflect what is really going on! Has there ever been a time that you thought something terrible, but when you said it out loud to someone you realized it was just your mind playing tricks on you!

Tier 2
Discussion: Can you think of a time when you had a terrible, horrible, no good thought, but when you said it aloud to someone, they helped you realize it just plain silly?! Maybe you thought your new haircut made you look like a donkey, but when you got home and told your mom or dad, they thought that was nuts and started laughing…and you couldn't help but start laughing with them?

Experiential Activity: Give everyone a moment to think of a terrible, horrible, no good thought that they've kept in their mind. Have everyone take a turn saying it aloud to the class, and see if it's as terrible then – or if it just seems like some silly nonsense!

Tier 3
Discussion: Sometimes, the terrible, horrible, no good thoughts that you have don't sound so silly when they come out. Sometimes, they still hurt after you say them aloud. How could having someone else around to hear them help you out?

Experiential Activity: Give everyone a moment to think of a not-so-silly painful thought. Then, in partners, have them say it to one another. This time, instead of finding the humor in it, encourage the children to help each other take a different perspective and see if they can take the power away from the thought together.

| Day 63 | What's Inside? | Values |

Tier 1
Script: We all have people that we love – friends, family members, classmates – and whose relationship is something we value. But what is it about those people, those relationships that you care so much about?

Tier 2
Discussion: Take a moment to think of all the people you love. What is it about those people, and those relationships that you value? What are the characteristics in people and relationships that you value?

Experiential Activity: Give each child a piece of paper with the outline of a person on it. Tell them to draw a person that represents the characteristics and relationship qualities that they value, and label all of the parts that they include. Take some time to share them with one another.

Tier 3
Discussion: At times, you might find yourself angry at someone you care about because they did something that hurts your feelings, or is not in line with your values. What are the best ways to handle these situations, while still moving toward your values (even if you are really, really mad!)?

Experiential Activity: As a group, talk about the scenarios described in the discussion. Together, brainstorm a list of ways that they can behave when someone they care about does something they feel is wrong, but will not move them farther from their own values. Discuss how they can mend those friendship or family problems.

| Day 64 | Mirrors | Self-as-Context |

Tier 1

Script: When you look into a mirror, do you think you see the same things everyone else sees? Or do you think you may see something better, worse or somehow both? Today, let's consider how the way we view ourselves is not always the same as how others view us – and that it doesn't define who we are.

Tier 2

Discussion: Who has had a day when they've looked in the mirror and thought they looked terrible, but had someone compliment them that day? Perhaps what other people see doesn't always reflect what we see in ourselves. Do we want to let how others see us define who we are?

Experiential Activity: Give everyone the opportunity to look into a mirror. Then, have each child create a representation what they see in the mirror, but instead of drawing a picture of their face, have them write or draw the parts of themselves that they see every time they look in the mirror (maybe their kindness, courage, or pain).

Tier 3

Discussion: We all know that sometimes we behave in ways that do not align with who we believe we are, and that sometimes people see some things in us that are just content, not the parts of ourselves that stay with us forever. What might other people see sometimes that doesn't reflect who you are?

Experiential Activity: Give everyone back their mirror representations. This time, have them draw or write things that other people see that do not always represent who they are around the mirror. Reflect on how even with these things around the mirror, it does not change who they see when they look inside themselves.

| Day 65 | Help | Acceptance |

Tier 1

Script: This week we've talked a lot about how our relationships with other people can help us move toward mindfulness and our values, but how it is not always an easy thing. One of the hardest things we can do is to accept two things: 1) that sometimes we need help, and 2) we need to let someone help us sometimes.

Tier 2

Discussion: Does anyone here ever have a hard time saying they can't do something alone, or needs someone's help to get something done? What kinds of feelings come up when you think of not being able to do something on your own? Maybe weakness or failure? But how does accepting help when you need it represent strength and courage?

Experiential Activity: Have some kind of task to complete that will be much easier with two or more people working on it (i.e. building a house of cards). First, have the children try it on their own, then have them work in teams to complete it. How does accepting help make the task more manageable?

Tier 3

Discussion: These situations happen in real life all the time. Who can think of a time when they needed help, but felt ashamed or embarrassed and tried to fight help instead of accepting it? How can we notice those feelings, let them be, but continue to move forward anyway?

Experiential Activity: Have each person create a "choose your own adventure" story. In the beginning, they should have a problem arise that would be helpful to have someone around to help with. In one potential ending, they might deny the help, but in the second, they might be willing to accept it. Which ending do they prefer?

Module 14: Family, Good Times and Bad

Module Description:
This week, children will relate mindfulness and values to families, dealing with positive and negative thoughts.

Preparation Notes:
This week brings up a lot of discussion of building strong relationships, but also provides some discussion of self-care and self-compassion practices. It may be beneficial to supplement this discussion by talking to children about what self-compassion can look like for children.

Materials List:

Tier	Day 66	Day 67	Day 68	Day 69	Day 70
2	»WS D66T2 »Art supplies	»WS D67T2/3 »Construction paper/Scissors »Markers »Glue/Staples	»Journal or Paper »Pen/Pencil	»WS D69T2 »Pen/Pencil »Crayon/Markers	None
3	None	»WS D67T2/3 »Construction paper/Scissors »Glue/Staples	None	None	None

Journal Prompt:
How does it affect you when you have an argument or a problem with someone in your family? What kinds of thoughts or feelings do you experience in these situations?

Day 66	Family Dinner	Defusion

Tier 1
Script: Who has ever gone to a family member's house for dinner, maybe for a holiday, and when you get there, you find that they made your absolute LEAST favorite food? On one hand, you don't want to be rude, but on the other, you keep thinking how gross that food will be! What do you do?!

Tier 2
Discussion: Who has been in this family dinner situation? What do you do? There's a big plate of YUCK sitting in front of you that you don't want to eat. You keep thinking, "If I eat this, I'll throw it up!" How can we transform thoughts so you can enjoy your meal!?

Experiential Activity: Have each child draw a plate of the WORST meal they can imagine having to eat. Then, have them re-name all of the foods to something silly, but delicious and decorate the plate with color, glitter, paint – whatever they need to transform that meal into something they can't wait to eat.

Tier 3
Discussion: Sometimes, spending time with family or friends can bring up unpleasant thoughts that are a little more personal than a disgusting dinner. Does anyone here ever have some painful thoughts when they are around people they love? Maybe worries about them being disappointed in you or angry about something you did in the past?

Experiential Activity: Just like your thoughts about a gross meal, you can transform those more personal painful thoughts as well – sometimes it just takes some real effort on your part. This time, instead of decorating your thoughts, think of something to counter them. Maybe your grandma was angry last month when you broke one of her nice dishes. What's a time she was proud of you? Take turns sharing painful thoughts and expanding them with positive thoughts.

| Day 67 | Thankful | Values/Committed Action |

Tier 1

Script: Each year, people find time to come together with family and friends, and give thanks for everything we are a grateful for in our lives. What are those things you are thankful for? Why are you thankful for them? Is it because these represent the things you value?

Tier 2

Discussion: Do you take time each year to stop and think of the things you are grateful for? Before holiday dinners, do your mom or dad make everyone around the table say something they want to give thanks for? Why is it important that we take time to do these things?

Experiential Activity: Give each child construction paper in the colors needed to make an autumn tree. Cut out the trunk and branches of a tree and 10-15 leaves in varying colors. On each leaf, have the children write down something they are thankful for and on the other side, write down the value that aligns with it. Have them create a 3D "Values Tree" by gluing/stapling one end of each leaf to the branches of the tree so that both sides are visible.

Tier 3

Discussion: Although we all have things to be thankful for in our lives, sometimes during the holiday season we can be reminded of the things we feel we are missing in our lives or wish we could change. In addition to being grateful for what we do have, how can we focus on those values we want to move closer toward?

Experiential Activity: Provide additional construction paper in green and blue. Have the children cut out a seed and raindrops from the paper. On the seed, write down the value they wish they were closer to in their lives. Glue it to the base of the tree. On the rain drops, write down actions they can take to move towards that value. Glue or staple them throughout the tree, as if they were "watering" the seed.

| Day 68 | Grounded | Acceptance |

Tier 1

Script: Everyone has times where they might have arguments with their parents, or do not follow the rules at home and get into trouble. Think of a time you might have had a conflict with a parent or some other adult who is important in your life. How did you react in that situation?

Tier 2

Discussion: Who here has had an argument with their parent or other important adult in your life? What was that argument about? What were the consequences of that argument? Maybe you were grounded or sent to your room. Now, who here tried to fight that consequence? Did that help – or just make things worse?

Experiential Activity: Create a small journal. Ask children to write two pretend entries. First, have them write it after a big fight with a parent, where they are angry and against having been sent to their room. In the second, have them write it after the same fight, but sitting in their room, reflecting on how peaceful it is there and what they learned from that argument. Which version of their thoughts do they prefer – the avoider or the accepter?

Tier 3

Discussion: In the moment, it is not always easy to be accepting of the consequences of our actions. It's something we have to work toward and practice. What makes this so difficult? What kinds of thoughts and feelings get in the way of your acceptance?

Experiential Activity: Have the children get into pairs. Have one child say a thought that they have that gets in the way of practicing acceptance. Have the other child respond with an alternative thought or challenge to that thought that can help them with accepting the consequences. Have the partners switch roles and practice both acknowledging avoidant thoughts and developing ways to face those thoughts and practice acceptance.

| Day 69 | Bad Kid | Self-as-Context |

Tier 1

Script: We've talked about the difference between the real you and the evaluations you or other people may make about you. Sometimes the hardest time to see this difference is when you are dealing with your family or the people you love the most. Do you have a hard time dealing with it when you think you let a loved one down?

Tier 2

Discussion: When we let down someone we care a lot about, we can have a hard time dealing with it, and may start to think things that aren't true. Maybe things like, "They don't love me anymore," or "I'm just a bad kid." What kinds of thoughts have started creeping when you let someone down? What might THEY really be thinking?

Experiential Activity: Ask the children to draw a picture of themselves and someone they love after an argument with thought bubbles coming out their heads. In the bubble above the child, ask them to write the thoughts about themselves they may be having. Above the loved one, ask them to write the thoughts they are probably actually having. Were their thoughts the truth?

Tier 3

Discussion: Even though we know the difference between the evaluations we think people make of us, and the reality of who we are, it can be hard to see that in the moment. How can you, in the moment, learn to find out what is really going on in the other person's head?

Experiential Activity: Ask the children to participate in a role play situation. Give a situation for them to act out that might be a common argument they could have with a loved one. Have one child practice using different language to communicate with the loved one and find out what they are really thinking in the situation.

| Day 70 | Loving-kindness | Present Moment |

Tier 1

Script: Loving-kindness is an idea that is common in a lot of mindfulness practices. It is the idea of giving open, tenderness and consideration towards others. It's like having an open heart. Who is someone in your life that you may get angry with, and you think you could send more lovingkindness?

Tier 2

Discussion: Who is someone you love very much, but may have a lot of conflict with? Sometimes we can have problems with those people because we have a lot of angry thoughts about them, and we start to forget the things we love about them. What could happen as a result of that?

Experiential Activity: Complete the following guided meditation: "Sit in a comfortable position, and focus on your breathing. Imagine the face of a loved one in front of you, see them looking back at you. Allow your angry thoughts about them to come and to pass. Then, think of loving thoughts you want to send to this person. Think 'May they feel love. May they be happy.' And so on. Take the next few minutes to send them loving-kindness."

Tier 3

Discussion: After a difficult event with a loved one, you may feel down on yourself, and need to practice loving-kindness with yourself. You deserve caring too! When do you think you may need to practice loving-kindness with yourself?

Experiential Activity: Repeat the loving-kindness meditation above, but instead of envisioning a loved one, have the children envision themselves, and send caring thoughts to themselves. Why do they deserve loving-kindness as well?

Module 15: Space

Module Description:
This week, the children will interact with the metaphor of space to engage with their difficult thoughts and feelings.

Preparation Notes:
You may notice that when activities include an open-ended prompt for children to draw a picture related to a metaphor do not have an accompanying worksheet or organizer in the appendix. If your children need more scaffolding for the activity, create your own!

Materials List:

Tier	Day 71	Day 72	Day 73	Day 74	Day 75
2	»Paper »Crayons/Markers	»Paper »Index Cards »Pen/Pencil	»Paper »Crayons/Markers	»Paper »Crayons/Markers	»Paper »Paint »Pen/Pencil
3	»WS D71T3	»WS D72T3 »Pen/Pencil	»Small paper »Pen/Pencil	None	»Pen/Pencil »Crayons/Markers

Journal Prompt:
What is one big, scary asteroid thought coming your way lately? How have you learned to manage this thought so that it doesn't interfere with your journey toward values?

Day 71	Breathing Space	Present Moment

Tier 1

Script: Have you ever been upset, worried, or anxious, and someone gets a little too close to you in your personal space? How do you react? Throughout the day today, try to be mindful of your personal space. When do you notice someone is in your space? How does it feel? Why does it matter?

Tier 2

Discussion: We all have an area of personal space that we feel comfortable with, almost as if it is a force field protecting us from outside invaders. Why do you think we feel this way? How can it help you to be mindful of or aware of your own boundaries?

Experiential Activity: Practice mindful breathing for 5 minutes. Encourage the children to visualize their personal space force field grow as they exhale, and return to them as they inhale. Then, give each child a piece of paper and ask them to draw themselves and their need for personal space – how large is their force field?

Tier 3

Discussion: Sometimes, when you're feeling bad or on the defense, somebody getting in your space can feel like a really bad thing, and you may have a reaction to it. How might you react to someone invading your space? If you remain mindful of your needs, how can you handle those space invaders without anger or fear?

Experiential Activity: As a group, discuss the inappropriate behaviors you may exhibit if you feel someone is entering your space. If you become mindful of this need, you may be able to handle that better. Together, create a list of strategies to appropriately handle it when you need space and someone is invading it (both literally and emotionally).

Day 72	Distant Thoughts	Defusion

Tier 1

Script: When you have a painful or upsetting thought, it can seem like it is right there in front of your space, unavoidable! It can be hard to go about your day with thoughts like this blocking your view – but what if our thoughts and feelings weren't front and center? What if we had some space between ourselves and our thoughts?

Tier 2

Discussion: Our thoughts, especially the ones that make us feel bad, can feel like they are surrounding us, getting in the way of our daily activities, making our lives harder. Who has ever felt this way? What if we were able to extend those thoughts in order to create some distance between them and us? How would that change things?

Experiential Activity: Have each child think of 2-3 painful thoughts that are "in their face" and interrupt their life, writing each one on an index card. On a piece of paper, have them draw themselves on the far-left side of the page, and place the cards right in front. Then, explain that a "thought extender" can create distance between you and thoughts. For example, if you add, "I'm having the thought that…" before your negative thought, it creates space and that thought loses power. Have them move their index cards over, and write thought extenders stretching between themselves and their thoughts.

Tier 3

Discussion: When we do not see the space between ourselves and our thoughts, it can be hard to focus on anything else, and lead to inappropriate behaviors. When have your thoughts, right in front of your face, led you to some trouble? How can we change this?

Experiential Activity: Make a 3-column chart. Provide a scenario in which upsetting thoughts might get in the way. In one column, have the children identify how trouble could come if their thoughts are too close. On the other, have them explain how they might handle the situation differently with space between them and thoughts. How will they create space?

Day 73	Asteroids	Acceptance

Tier 1

Script: Bad events or thoughts can feel like they are speeding toward you, ready to hit, like an asteroid flying toward a rocket ship. When these things happen, you have two choices – avoid them or accept them? Today, if something you don't like is happening, pay attention to if you avoid or accept the situation.

Tier 2

Discussion: Have you ever felt like a negative situation or feeling was attacking you? Sometimes it can feel easier to hide from these situations, try to block them out, pretend they are not happening. Does this work? What if, instead of trying to ignore these events, we accepted them and adjusted our behavior to handle them?

Experiential Activity: Give each child a sheet of paper. On one side, have them draw a rocket ship flying in space, with an asteroid coming. What would happen if the ship stayed its course, acting like nothing was happening? On the other side, have them draw a ship that has accepted the asteroid is coming, is preparing to handle damages, and is working to change course to safety. Which way is better – avoidance or acceptance?

Tier 3

Discussion: We make choices on a daily basis whether to try to avoid situations or accept them and move on. This is not always the easy choice – in the moment trying to avoid hard events might seem better, but learning to accept the event and adjust your life will pay off in the long run. When do you need to make these kinds of choices?

Experiential Activity: On small pieces of paper, have the children write down their personal "asteroids," the situations in their lives that they would like to ignore. Then, have some fun. Crinkle the papers into balls, and have an "asteroid fight." If they didn't respond to the incoming asteroids, they got hit! How did accepting the incoming asteroid pay off?

Day 74	My Space	Self-as-Context

Tier 1

Script: Imagine an astronaut up in space, floating weightless through the stars. Within that suit is everything that astronaut needs – his or her self-as-context, observing the universe all around. Outside of that suit there are places to go, experiences to have, but it doesn't change what is inside. Today, be the observer within the space suit.

Tier 2

Discussion: Like an astronaut in space, you can find everything you need to define yourself within. All of the things floating around in your environment create the content of your life, but what is inside your space suit? What is your self-as-context?

Experiential Activity: Provide each child with a piece of paper to draw themselves as astronaut up in space. On their helmet, draw their self-as-context, the observer of the journey through space. Around them, have them draw the evaluations and content that they experience along the way. Should they let them in or observe them as they go by?

Tier 3

Discussion: None of us are perfect, and sometimes we all let those evaluations and content slip in to our idea of who we are. What happens when we let those evaluations into our space?

Experiential Activity: Have a group discussion about how you can stop yourself from letting those evaluations and content define who you are – how can you leave them floating in space, watching them as they go by, without letting them in?

Day 75	Galaxies	Committed Action

Tier 1

Script: Have you ever looked at a picture of a galaxy? It looks almost like a painting, one beautiful image. However, in reality, there are so many elements that make up a galaxy, so many moving parts that keep it together. How is your life like a galaxy?

Tier 2

Discussion: What makes up a galaxy? Just like a galaxy, your life can seem like one big event, but in reality, it is a collection of experiences, events, and actions that come together. In your life, what are all of the committed actions you do to help create the galaxy of your values?

Experiential Activity: Give each child some paper and paint to create a galaxy. Have them include all the parts that come together to form a beautiful picture. Then, once it's dry, have them name the galaxy after a value, and label all of its parts with a committed action that will help create that galaxy.

Tier 3

Discussion: A galaxy is massive; can you imagine trying to navigate around all of those stars and planets in space without a map? Life isn't too different from that. Sometimes we know our values, where we want to go, but the path to get there isn't easy to find. How do you avoid getting lost in the galaxy?

Experiential Activity: Have the children use the galaxy they created, turning it into a "map" to guide them toward their values. Have them connect the committed actions together in logical ways, create an order for them, almost as if they were a constellation. Will this make it easier to navigate through life?

Module 16: Multi-Sensory Mindfulness

Module Description:
This week, children will practice mindfulness and acceptance using all five of their senses.

Preparation Notes:
This week, the activities involve items the children interact with from all five senses. For each activity, it is better to have multiple exemplars of sense items (i.e. multiple smells, songs, etc.) so that the children have multiple opportunities to interact with that metaphor/experience.

Materials List:

Tier	Day 76	Day 77	Day 78	Day 79	Day 80
2	»WS D76T2 »Scented objects	»Brown paper bag »Tactile objects	»WS D78T2 »Song clips »Crayons/Markers	None	None
3	»Unpleasant scents	»Index cards »Pen/Pencil	»Paper »Pen/Pencil	None	»WS D80T3 »Crayons/Markers

Journal Prompt:
Imagine your senses had a "volume" button; you could turn down your senses to a 0 so you can't notice them or up to a 10 for being very aware of them. What volume do you keep your senses on a daily basis? Does that increase your potential for interacting with the world?

Day 76	Scent of the Moment	Present Moment

Tier 1

Script: You constantly encounter different smells during the day, from when you wake up and brush your teeth, to when you sit down for dinner. When was the last time you stopped to take note of the smells surrounding you at the moment? Try to do that today.

Tier 2

Discussion: Who ever stops to notice the scents around you during the day? Usually we only do this when there's something particularly good or bad for us to smell, right?! But we are surrounded by scents, which we might appreciate more in the moment.

Experiential Activity: Choose a scent, maybe a candle, food, or other fragrant object. Ask the children to sit with the scent right in front of them, not too far from their nose. Say, "Close your eyes and take ten deep breaths, taking in all of the characteristics of the smell. Pay attention to the different words, feelings, and images this smell brings to your mind. Does the scent bring up any specific memories or sensations? When you're done, make a list of these and/or share your experience with the group"

Tier 3

Discussion: Sometimes being in the present moment means we need to let some feelings we don't like hang out with us for a while, observing them and letting them fade away. What is something you absolutely hate the smell of? Have you ever stopped to notice how your body reacts to that smell, not just your mind?

Experiential Activity: Present the children with an unpleasant smell of some kind. Challenge them to practice mindful breathing for three minutes in the presence of that smell, and, instead of paying attention to their thoughts about it, to observe how their body reacts differently to the unpleasant smell.

| Day 77 | Feeling Perspectives | Defusion |

Tier 1
Script: All day long, we touch objects that feel all kinds of different ways – some smooth, hard, bumpy, and so on. Sometimes you accidentally put your hand on something that feels gross, like something slimy. We might react and pull away quickly from it, but maybe from a different perspective it wouldn't feel so bad.

Tier 2
Discussion: Who has accidentally touched something absolutely gross!? What did it feel like and what were your thoughts about it? Is there something about those items that is actually bad? Or do we just use words to describe it in a way that sounds awful?

Experiential Activity: Put an unpleasant tactile object into a bag (e.g. a ball of slime). Have each child in the group feel the item without looking at it, and say the unpleasant words they would use to describe it. Then, have them reconsider the description from the perspective of someone/things (e.g. a snail). How would the object be described from that other perspective?

Tier 3
Discussion: We can do this same sort of thing with the way we describe events in our lives. For example, what thoughts would you have if your friend cancelled your plans to hang out? Would that feel so great? But, from the perspective of a parent or sibling, that might mean that you spend more time with them. What thoughts might they have? Is there only one way to describe a situation?

Experiential Activity: Give each child a paper or index card. On one side, have them draw or write their perspective on an event that has caused them some unpleasant feelings. Then, have them choose someone else's perspective and draw or write it on the other side. Whose view is true? Or are they both? Or neither?

| Day 78 | Lyrics | Self-as-Context |

Tier 1
Script: Almost everyone has some song or lyrics from a song that they relate to, that they think helps describe who they are. If you stop and listen to a lot of songs, you might be able to relate to them – to their content. But do any of those songs represent your self as context?

Tier 2
Discussion: What songs does everyone here relate to? What about those songs connects you to them? What characteristics do they describe? How is this content different from your self-as-context? Who is that observing you?

Experiential Activity: Play several different song clips, and have the children discuss how they do or do not relate to the lyrics. Make a list of how these sounds are alike and different from who they are – what did they notice?

Tier 3
Discussion: Often times, we can become so attached to the idea that we are just like the lyrics from a song that we might even start acting differently – how we think we should act because of that. Can you think of a time when you might have done that? Did it change who you actually are?

Experiential Activity: We can do the same thing we do with lyrics with our own thoughts. We could think "I'm awful at basketball," and then not be able to make a shot! Does that thought actually change who you are? Write a song or poem that describes the thoughts that you get caught up on, and how you come back to find your true self.

| Day 79 | Make It Go Away | Acceptance |

Tier 1

Script: Visualization can be a great way to get present and to understand something that may be hard to grasp. For example, the idea of acceptance can be hard to explain, but easy to picture. If you're struggling with something today, think about how you can use imagery to understand it.

Tier 2

Discussion: What is your favorite food? What does it taste like? You're not even eating it, but I bet you can taste it! Isn't it amazing how that memory just stays with you, no matter how long it's been since you ate that food?

Experiential Activity: Say, "Close your eyes and picture your favorite food. Imagine how it looks, tastes, smells, and feels. It's like you're eating it now! Now, forget all of that. Completely erase it from your memory. Can you do that? No way! Try it again, but this time, picture a food that you hate. Repeat the imagery with this gross food item. Are you able to forget this one? No, but for some reason, when we don't like something we tend to try to forget it, which is impossible to do. Instead of spending time trying to make it go away, what can we do?"

Tier 3

Discussion: Yet again, we can apply this same idea to our painful thoughts and feelings! What kinds of painful, sad, or upsetting thoughts have you tried to erase from your memory? Did that really help you?

Experiential Activity: Repeat the visualization activity from Tier 2, but use a painful thought instead of a food. Ask the children to imagine how they feel, inside and out, when they have that thought, and then try to erase it. Discuss what the alternative to erasing those thoughts might be.

| Day 80 | Crystal Ball | Values/Committed Action |

Tier 1

Script: Have you ever wished you had a crystal ball that could help you see what your future would be like? When you imagine that future, what do you see? Is your life full of events that move you toward your values?

Tier 2

Discussion: If you had a crystal ball, what would you want to see? What parts of your life are you curious about? How do those relate to your values?

Experiential Activity: Say, "Close your eyes. Imagine a crystal ball right in front of you. You now have the ability to see into the future. Think of one of your values. How do you see your life taking meaning because of that value – how does it shape your future?" Have a class discussion regarding what the children "saw" in the ball.

Tier 3

Discussion: Not only do you now have the power to see into the future, you have the power to make those things happen! All it takes is some commitment to having the kinds of behavior that get you there. What can you do to make that future a reality?

Experiential Activity: Give each child a piece of paper and ask them to draw a crystal ball that shows what they see in their future. In the base of that ball, ask them to write down all of the ways that they will make sure that future becomes a reality. Discuss those committed actions together.

Module 17: Mindful Movement

Module Description:
This week, the children will think about the games and activities they participate in, and how they relate to or could benefit from mindful practice.

Preparation Notes:
Many of the activities this week encourage children to get up and MOVE to experience how they can incorporate mindfulness into their daily lives. Consider completing these activities outside, in a gym, or another large, open space that encourages movement.

Materials List:

Tier	Day 81	Day 82	Day 83	Day 84	Day 85
2	»WS D81T2 »Pen/Pencil	»Small papers »Pen/Pencil »Basket/Hoop	None	»WS D84T2 »Crayons/ Markers	None
3	»WS D81T3 »Crayons/ Markers	»Small papers »Pen/Pencil »Basket/Hoop	None	»Paper »Pen/Pencil	None

Journal Prompt:
What do you do to "get yourself in the zone" when you are preparing to play a sport or exercise? How can you apply these same practices to your everyday mindfulness practice?

Day 81	Tournament of Values	Values

Tier 1

Script: We've gotten familiar with all of our values over the past few months. Sometimes, though, we need to prioritize our values to help make a decision in the moment. Can you be constantly focusing on every value at every moment of the day? No way! Today, we will think about how we prioritize our values.

Tier 2

Discussion: What are some of your values? How many different values do you have? What kinds of challenges could you face if you don't think about how you prioritize your values?

Experiential Activity: Set up a bracket (like they do for college basketball) with 32 values (leave some open for the children to fill in). Give each child a copy of the bracket, and have them complete it to see which values come out on top for each pairing, and ultimately identify their most meaningful value!

Tier 3

Discussion: Now you've started thinking about how some values are more important to you than others, but they are all important to you to some degree. How do you decide when to make choices that move you toward which values? Does it depend on the situation you're in?

Experiential Activity: Have the children choose their top four values identified in the values bracket. Give them each a piece of paper divided into four sections, and have them write or draw a situation in which they would prioritize each value.

| Day 82 | Shooting Hoops | Committed Action |

Tier 1
Script: Have you played a game of basketball? Did you make every shot that you took, or did you miss some? Could you ever win a game if you gave up after you missed a few shots? Just like you need to stay in it to win in a game of ball, in life you need to stay committed to your values.

Tier 2
Discussion: Who has ever played a sport of any kind? Did you make errors, or were you perfect right off the bat? How did you get yourself to keep practicing, to keep your head in the game? What are the ways you can stay committed to your values, even if you've taken a few missteps?

Experiential Activity: On small pieces of paper, have the children write down a series of committed actions they can take to move toward one of your values. Then, have them crinkle the paper into balls, and "shoot" them into a basket (or bucket), not stopping until they've gotten all of their committed actions through the hoop.

Tier 3
Discussion: In a sport that you've played, how have you improved a skill? How can you apply similar strategies to improve your commitment that move you toward your values? How will you improve? It can be hard to keep going, even if you are disappointed, angry, or worn out.

Experiential Activity: As a group, brainstorm ways to practice staying committed, despite the feelings of giving up they may experience. Write these on pieces of paper, crumple them into balls, and practice making more and more difficult shots in the basket/hoop.

| Day 83 | Sometimes You Lose | Acceptance |

Tier 1
Script: Have you ever played a game and lost? How did you react? Were you angry, resentful, or a sore loser? We've all been there, but is that the best way to handle the situation? What if you took an acceptance point of view? Consider this as you go about your day today.

Tier 2
Discussion: Who here has ever played a game of any kind and lost? How did you feel afterward? Who here has ever felt cheated, resentful, or angry about a loss? Do those feelings change the outcome at all? What if we are accepting when things don't go our way?

Experiential Activity: Have the children role play situations in front of the class, such as situations in which someone loses a game and reacts in a variety of different ways. Ask other children in the class to make predictions about how the next game might work out for each situation.

Tier 3
Discussion: It's not always easy to be accepting when a game or other event doesn't go your way. It can be helpful to develop strategies to help you get through those situations. What are strategies that we can use to help practice acceptance in those situations?

Experiential Activity: Repeat the role play activity, except have the children each take turns demonstrating how he or she would use the strategies that were brainstormed with the group. Then, have the children predict how the next game might work out for each situation.

Day 84	The Field	Self-as-Context
Tier 1	**Script:** Have you ever heard a coach say to a team, "leave it on the field" after they've made a mistake? Take a few minutes to think about what that means. Why would the coach say that to their players?	
Tier 2	**Discussion:** What do you think the phrase "leave it on the field" means in the context of a sport? Do you think that the coach could be trying to let the players know that they shouldn't define themselves as players and/or people based on what happens in one game, one event? How does that relate to events in your life?	
	Experiential Activity: Have each child draw a picture of the "field of their lives" and the events, feelings, thoughts, and ideas that they need to "leave on the field" as they move forward in their lives. As a group, discuss how these are distinct from who they really are and who they want to become.	
Tier 3	**Discussion:** Sometimes it's easy to get caught up in the events on the field of your life. Who can think of a time when they couldn't leave something "on the field?" How does defining yourself in those events, feelings, and thoughts effect your life?	
	Experiential Activity: Ask each child to make a list of thoughts and feelings they often have about themselves – different ways that they define themselves. Then, go through that list and cross out everything that they should "leave on the field," leaving a list of things that are a fair representation of themselves.	

Day 85	Mindful Movement	Present Moment
Tier 1	**Script:** Athletes often talk about how they use different visualizations, breathing techniques, and other mindful practices to help them stay focused and do their best when they play. When you participate in different activities are you in the moment, or is your mind astray?	
Tier 2	**Discussion:** How could practicing mindfulness help you in different activities you participate in? What are different kinds of mindful practices you could incorporate into the sports or activities you are involved in?	
	Experiential Activity: Engage the whole class in a movement activity (i.e. stretching, going for a walk/jog, playing catch). During the activity, practice different kinds of present moment awareness (i.e. mindful breathing, noticing their thoughts as they pass by, being aware of how their body is moving, etc.).	
Tier 3	**Discussion:** You can also practice mindfulness before a sporting or other high-stress event, to help calm your nerves and help you prepare. Why might doing this be helpful? In what situations in your life might this be helpful?	
	Experiential Activity: Complete this guided meditation: "Imagine you are getting ready to perform in some way. Maybe on a test, game, play, or something else. Close your eyes and relax your body. As you breathe in, notice all of the feelings in your body that may be tense, and as you breathe out, let go of that tension, feeling the calm going through your body." Continue this meditation for 3-5 minutes.	

Module 18: Thoughts Can Be Puzzling

Module Description:
This week, children will consider the complexity of their thoughts, and how mindful practices can benefit them in living with this complexity, rather than succumbing to it.

Preparation Notes:
When activities are more abstract (such as developing a riddle), it may be more challenging for the children to complete independently. It is helpful to provide a series of examples for these tasks to provide a context for the children to understand the task at hand.

Materials List:

Tier	Day 86	Day 87	Day 88	Day 89	Day 90
2	»WS D86T2 »Tape/Glue »Crayons/Markers	»Values/Goals Cards	»Optical illusions	»WS D89T2 »Pen/Pencil	»Building materials
3	»Cardstock »Crayons/Markers »Scissors	»Index Cards »Pen/Pencil	None	None	»Block game (i.e. Jenga)

Journal Prompt:
You are a complex person! You have a lot of thoughts, feelings, memories, experiences, sensations, and actions that occur in your life! What parts of these can be confusing or puzzling to you? How can you stop that from getting off track?

Day 86	Puzzling Thoughts	Defusion

Tier 1

Script: Have you ever thought of your life as a beautiful work of art? Each experience is a part of that piece of art – if you removed any of those experiences, the artwork just wouldn't be the same! Today, spend some time thinking about how all of your experiences, good and bad, come together to create art!

Tier 2

Discussion: Have you ever thought about what life would be like if you could get rid of all your painful thoughts, memories, and feelings? Would that be all good, or would parts of your life be missing? Is it possible to appreciate all of your thoughts, for better or worse?

Experiential Activity: Give each child a set of puzzle pieces that fit together to make a flower or a tree. Ask everyone to write good and bad thoughts they experience on each piece. As a group, discuss how each thought can have a lot of control over you. Then, assemble the pieces together to see the image, glue, and decorate them. Think about how your thoughts help to create a beautiful life, but if you take any way, good or bad, the picture is incomplete.

Tier 3

Discussion: What would your life artwork look like? Would it be full of only your positive thoughts and experiences, or would you use the negatives to create your work of art? When we have painful thoughts, how can we transform them into a beautiful work of art?

Experiential Activity: Give each child a piece of cardstock. Have them create a piece of artwork that incorporates both their good and bad thoughts and experiences. Then, have them cut the artwork into a puzzle, and trade with one another to assemble, and share how their experiences have come together to create the work of art.

| Day 87 | Match It Up | Values |

Tier 1

Script: Do you remember the difference between values and goals? Values are ideas or feelings that help guide you through your life. Goals are something more concrete that you can achieve to help you live your values. It can be hard to see the difference between these sometimes! Today, practice telling the difference between these.

Tier 2

Discussion: What is the difference between values and goals? Why is it important to know how these are different? In what ways are values good...what about goals?

Experiential Activity: Create a game of memory by having two sets of cards. The first set of cards has an example of a value written on each, and the second set of cards has an example of a corresponding goal written on it. Divide the children into pairs, and tell the group, "You set goals to help you move toward your values, to help you feel fulfilled in your life. Let's play the game of memory, matching values to their corresponding goals."

Tier 3

Discussion: Let's make this a personalized game! What are YOUR values? What are the goals you have that move you toward your values?

Experiential Activity: Give each child a set of six to ten index cards. Have them write their values and corresponding goals on the cards. Then, shuffle all of the cards together, and play a game of memory as a group, challenging them to identify each other's value/goal combinations.

| Day 88 | Mind Illusions | Present Moment |

Tier 1

Script: Have you ever been distracted or mindless, and you see or hear something completely differently than it actually happened? Maybe you misheard someone talking or you saw something that wasn't really there. If you were living in the present moment, do you think these things would happen as often?!

Tier 2

Discussion: Has anyone ever heard of an optical illusion? It is almost like a mind puzzle; when you look at one, things are not always what they seem. How could being in the present moment help you solve these illusions?

Experiential Activity: Spend five minutes with the group engaging in mindful breathing techniques. Once everyone has encountered the present moment, show the group an optical illusion. While continuing to breathe mindfully, give the group the opportunity to figure out the optical illusion. Discuss how they were able to see the illusion.

Tier 3

Discussion: Sometimes, in your day to day life, you can experience some mind illusions of your own. Have you ever been mindlessly going through your day, and have your mind play a trick on you? How can this create challenges for you throughout the day?

Experiential Activity: Have each child share a time when their mind played a trick on them, but instead of telling the group what really happened, have them share the illusion, and see if the other children can guess what was really going on. Discuss the consequences of going mindlessly through life.

Day 89 — Riddle Me — Self-as-Context

Tier 1

Script: Sometimes, we can lose track of our three selves – the you that is your content, the you that is noticing, and the you that is always observing. Can you figure out which is which? It's kind of like a riddle! Today we will practice telling these three versions of ourselves apart.

Tier 2

Discussion: What is the difference between our self-as-content, self-as-process, and self-as-context? How can you tell these parts of you apart in your daily lives?

Experiential Activity: Have each child create a riddle about him or herself. The answer to the riddle should be one of the senses of selves discussed, and the clues should indicate how that sense of self experiences the world. Ask the children to share their riddles with one another and try to solve them.

Tier 3

Discussion: It can be hard to tell the difference between self-as-process and self-as-context. Why might we get these confused? Why should well tell them apart? Discuss the role each of these perspectives have in our lives.

Experiential Activity: Tell the group they are going to practice telling the difference between their selves as process and context. Ask each child to sit comfortably and say, "Notice how you're sitting for five seconds. Then, as you do, observe yourself noticing for five seconds." Repeat this activity for awareness of what they see, what they are thinking, what they hear, what they are feeling, etc.

Day 90 — Build It Up — Committed Action

Tier 1

Script: Every time you perform a committed action, it is like you are adding a brick to the building of your life. Each brick on its own doesn't mean a lot, but altogether they create something very special!

Tier 2

Discussion: Every time you identify a value and goals that will help move you toward your meaningful life, you need to create a plan of committed actions to get there. This can be big things like going to college, or small things like getting your homework done. Why is it important to plan how to stay committed to your values?

Experiential Activity: Divide the class into groups, and give each group a challenge of a structure to build (e.g. build a skyscraper using pick up sticks). Before they can begin, ask each group to identify a list of committed actions they will engage in to help achieve their challenge. Then, give each group a chance to build and discuss the outcomes in terms of their committed actions.

Tier 3

Discussion: Values and committed actions are like a two-way street. You need to be able to identify actions related to values and values related to actions. Which do you think is harder to do?

Experiential Activity: Obtain a block game (similar to the game Jenga). On each block, write a different value. Engage the children in the game. Each time they remove a block, they must name a committed action that aligns with that value.

Module 19: Your Way There

Module Description:
This week, children will develop their plan to move toward values and identify obstacles they may encounter, making plans revolving around committed action.

Preparation Notes:
Sometimes, ACT exercises done in a group setting require that children demonstrate some vulnerability around one another. Child may be nervous or uncomfortable about this sometimes. If you notice this, consider doing some team building or trust activities together.

Materials List:

Tier	Day 91	Day 92	Day 93	Day 94	Day 95
2	»WS D91T2/3 »Crayons/ Markers	None	None	»Whiteboard or large paper »Marker	»Song Clips
3	»WS D91T2/3 »Crayons/ Markers	»Whiteboard or large paper »Marker	»Large paper »Paint	»WS D94T3 »Scissors	»Paper »Pen/Pencil

Journal Prompt:
You've been on the journey of your life ever since you were born, but you still have a long, long way to go. Where do you want to be in five years, ten years, and twenty years?

| Day 91 | My Map | Committed Action |

Tier 1
Script: Have you ever been in the car with someone who didn't get directions for where you needed to go? It can really slow you down and make the journey there harder! Moving your life in the direction of your values is the same way; planning out how you will get there makes a difference!

Tier 2
Discussion: What are the important things you need to do to move toward your values? Why do you think it is important to plan for some of the committed actions that are important to you? What could happen if you don't focus on committed action?

Experiential Activity: Give each child a piece of paper and tell them that they are going to create their own values map. It doesn't need to look like a traditional map; they can design creatively so that it helps them see the values that they are striving for and the behaviors they will engage in to move in that direction.

Tier 3
Discussion: Sometimes when you're on a journey to go somewhere, you are forced to take a detour because there is some kind of obstacle in your way. You wind up going a different way, but it still gets you where you need to go. What are some of the barriers you may find on your way toward your values?

Experiential Activity: Ask the children to add to their maps. Now, the maps will include the likely barriers or setbacks they may encounter, as well as the detour (or change in behavior) they might need to go on so they can return to their course. Have the children share with one another, and brainstorm together to plan detours if necessary.

Day 92	Annoying Passenger	Acceptance

Tier 1

Script: Sometimes those sad or painful thoughts and feelings we all have really seem to stop us from being happy or acting the way we want, and so we work hard to get them out of our heads. Ask yourself, "Does fighting all of these ideas in my mind really help me out?" Today, think about this question whenever you have a painful thought.

Tier 2

Discussion: Who here has ever had to go for a long drive in a car with someone who was really getting on your nerves? Someone who wouldn't stop talking or crying or asking you to do things when you just wanted to enjoy the ride. Did you complain or focus on that person instead of enjoying the drive? What could you do in that situation?

Experiential Activity: Engage the group in a role play activity. Have children work in groups, pretending they are in a car on a long drive. One child will play the role of the annoying passenger. Ask them to play out two scenarios: one in which they focus on annoying person ruining the trip and one in which they accept that that person is there, and find ways to enjoy the ride. Ask them how this relates to their own thoughts.

Tier 3

Discussion: Sometimes, your painful thoughts and feelings might feel more like ten passengers filling up the car than just one annoying person. Wouldn't it be nice to just open the door and kick all of those passengers out?! What could be the problem with doing that? What would happen to all of your pleasant thoughts then?

Experiential Activity: On a large piece of paper, ask the group to draw a car. Inside of the car, have them each draw themselves and write/draw a thought they wish they wouldn't have. Then, ask everyone to include a pleasant or good feeling thought in the car. As a group, make a list of the ways they can practice acceptance of those negative thoughts, so they don't open the door and lose out on those pleasant thoughts.

Day 93	The Road	Self-as-Context

Tier 1

Script: There is a highway in the United States called I-90 that is over 3,000 miles long! That's just about the distance across the whole country! Imagine that. Imagine all of the different things you would see along that road. Even though the scenery might change along the way, that road is always the same road. How is your life like that long highway?

Tier 2

Discussion: Along a long highway, you will have lots of different scenery, cars, but just one long road. How does this relate to you, your experiences, and your thoughts? You aren't the scenery you experience, or the thoughts that come and go like cars on a highway, so what does that make you?

Experiential Activity: Ask the children to lie down on the floor and close their eyes. Ask them to imagine that they are the road, and from that point on to envision all of the different scenery created by their experiences along the road. Then, ask them to see all of the different cars on the road, coming on and off the highway, just like their thoughts do. How is taking the point of view of the road different from the view of each individual car?

Tier 3

Discussion: Self-as-context means thinking about your life as if you are the road. You are always there, as the thoughts and experiences you have change and move over time. Some of the scenery or cars on the road may not be so great, but the nice thing about a long road, is that there is always new content for you to experience along the way.

Experiential Activity: As a group, use a large piece of paper and paint a mural. On this mural, paint a long road across it, and on the road, have each child include a representation of him or herself. Then, along the sides of the road, have the children paint different experiences they've had (both good and bad) as the scenery. Finally, have the children paint cars coming on and off the road, writing or painting their thoughts on the cars.

Day 94	Past, Present, or Future?	Present Moment

Tier 1

Script: All of your thoughts are focused on one of three things: something in the past, something in present, or something in the future. Can you think of a time you've thought of each one? If you're always thinking past or future, what could you be missing out on in the present?

Tier 2

Discussion: It's normal to have thoughts that are about the past, present, and future, and it's actually important to think about all of them sometimes. However, sometimes getting caught up in the past or future can be a problem in the moment. When can it be good to have your thoughts in each of those times?

Experiential Activity: On the board or large piece of paper, draw a continuum. On either end of the line, write "past" and "future," and in the middle write "present." As a group, make a list of times it is appropriate to focus on each of the time periods above the line. Below the line, make a list of when focusing on those times could be a problem.

Tier 3

Discussion: It can be really hard to realize when you are caught up in the past or future, and losing out on your life in the present moment. There are some situations that you may always find yourself lost in your thoughts about another time. What situations might be hard to experience without getting lost in your head?

Experiential Activity: Give each child a similar continuum to the one described in T2 on a piece of paper, and have them cut out an outline of themselves from another piece of paper. Ask the child to place the person on the present moment part of the continuum. Present the children with various situations they may encounter, and have them slide the person to where they think their thoughts may be focused. For each, discuss how that position could help or hurt them.

Day 95	Car Radio	Defusion

Tier 1

Script: When you're in the car with your family or friends, do you ever sing along to the radio REALLY loud? It's pretty hard not to laugh when you do it, because the songs just start to sound so silly – even if the words of the song are sad or angry! How can we use this to help us with the sad or angry words we can't get out of our heads sometimes?

Tier 2

Discussion: What songs do you like to sing super silly in the car? Have you ever noticed how the words don't seem to matter anymore, and all of it just seems fun and silly? It's funny how just changing the way that you say things can change the power of those words. Can you do this with your thoughts in life?

Experiential Activity: Play different popular songs for the class, and encourage them to sing along in the loudest, silliest, craziest voices they can. Use songs with different emotional undertones. After each song, ask the children what the emotions they felt during the song were, and how defusing from the lyrics with silly voices played into that.

Tier 3

Discussion: You can use strategies like this to help you deal with your own painful thoughts and feelings. It might seem strange, but if you have a difficult thought stuck in your head, how do you think it might help you deal with those thoughts without letting them take over?

Experiential Activity: Ask each child to write a song/poem about something that they struggle with. Discuss the kinds of feelings they experience when writing/reading the song. Then, all at once, have the children sing their individual songs in a loud, silly voice. Talk about how the loud, silly mess of sound helped to take the power of those words away.

Module 20: Sharing Mindfully

Module Description:
This week, children will learn about using mindfulness techniques when they are in a situation in which they need to or would benefit from sharing items or thoughts.

Preparation Notes:
Depending on the age of your children and their abilities, you may want to focus more on sharing in terms of actual items or feelings. Some children may need to focus more on tangible sharing, while others may need to discuss more abstract sharing.

Materials List:

Tier	Day 96	Day 97	Day 98	Day 99	Day 100
2	»Blank booklet »Pen/Pencil »Crayons/Markers	None	»Whiteboard or large paper »Marker	»Blank card »Crayons/Markers	»Large paper »Crayons/Markers
3	»Booklet »Pen/Pencil »Crayons/Markers	»Index cards »Pen/Pencil	»WS D98T3 »Pen/Pencil »Crayons/Markers	»Card »Crayons/Markers	»WS D100T3 »Crayons/Markers

Journal Prompt:
What are sentimental or meaningful items in your life? Where did they come from, and how did they get that meaning for you? What values do they relate to?

Day 96	Why Did It Matter?	Values

Tier 1 — Script: We've all been in situations when we don't want to share something! It could be a favorite toy, book, or even to share what you think or feel. Think of a time when you had a hard time sharing – what were you being asked? Why did it matter so much to you?

Tier 2 — Discussion: A lot of the time, when we fight really hard to hold on to something, or not to share it, it's because it's something that means a lot. It may be something that reminds you of an important value. When have you had a hard time sharing?

Tier 2 — Experiential Activity: Give each child a blank booklet with 5-10 pages. On the cover, ask them to write or draw "My Book of Values." On the front side of each page, have them write or draw different items or ideas that are important to them, and the values they relate to. Then, ask them to share their values with one another, in a group or in pairs.

Tier 3 — Discussion: When something means so much to you, it can be hard to share it with others or let them see how much you care. Have you ever had a hard time sharing something? What kinds of thoughts or feelings did you have about it? When you think about it, does that one thing matter that much, or do you have other things in your life that remind you of the same value?

Tier 3 — Experiential Activity: Give each child the book of values they created in T2, which should have writing on the front of each page. Ask the children to brainstorm other items or experiences in their lives that go with the same value of each item in the book. On the back of each page, ask them to add in the other items/experiences they came up with for that value. Discuss how when we live a valued life, we realize that our values are what are important, not our things.

| Day 97 | Caught Up In Anger | Present Moment |

Tier 1
Script: Sometimes, sharing an emotion can feel like the hardest thing to do, especially when you are feeling sad, angry, or embarrassed. When you're feeling emotional, you may get caught up in your thoughts, and wind up saying something that is not your real feeling. Today, if you feel sad or upset, take time to stop and be mindful of your feelings.

Tier 2
Discussion: Who here has ever been in an argument or gotten in trouble, and felt really sad, angry, or embarrassed? How do you know when you're feeling that way? Sometimes, we try to hide what we are really feeling, and might say something to someone else that is mean or hurtful to them! Why do you think this might happen?

Experiential Activity: Engage the classroom in a role play activity. Create a situation when the children would likely argue with another person about something they have done wrong. In one scenario, ask the children to role play getting caught up in anger, and the kinds of things they might say because of it. In the other scenario, ask the children to demonstrate being mindful of their feelings of anger, and how they might be able to share their true feelings with the other person.

Tier 3
Discussion: When you get caught up in anger, it's not always so easy to stop, be mindful of your feelings, and share them with others. Who here has ever gotten so angry, they've wound up in more trouble? Mindfully sharing your feelings with others can be hard, and just like anything else, can take some practice!

Experiential Activity: Help each child create a 3-step "Mindfulness Strategy" on an index card to use when they are upset or angry to help get back in the present moment. This could be something like: 1) Notice my breathing. 2) Pay attention to the feelings from my head to my feet. 3) Take a deep breath before talking. Then, provide children with the opportunity to practice their strategies.

| Day 98 | Feedback | Acceptance |

Tier 1
Script: Everyone in this school has had a parent, teacher, or coach give them feedback. Maybe someone has said you need to work harder on your homework, talk less during class, practice your basketball skills more often, or something else. It can be hard to hear these things! Today we are going to be thinking about accepting this feedback.

Tier 2
Discussion: What are some examples of feedback you've gotten? It is nice to hear when you're doing great, but it's not easy to hear it when there's something you're doing wrong or could do better. Have you ever argued back when you hear these things? Why could practicing acceptance be helpful for you when someone shares feedback with you?

Experiential Activity: As a class, create a list of "constructive feedback" the children have been given in the past, the stuff that they were maybe upset about hearing. Then, go back to the beginning, and discuss how being accepting of each item of feedback, even though it is hard to hear, could be a good thing in life.

Tier 3
Discussion: When someone shares something with you that you don't want to hear, how might you act? What are the consequences of (or things that happen after) your actions? How could it be different if your actions are unwilling versus accepting?

Experiential Activity: Give each child a piece of paper with five squares drawn on it: one labelled "Feedback" on the left side, two stacked in the middle labelled "Unwilling" and "Accepting," and two on the right side labelled "Consequences." Ask the children to draw a time they received difficult feedback in the first box, and how their actions could be different in the two middle boxes, and the outcomes of the actions in the corresponding "Consequences" boxes.

Day 99	What You Share	Self-as-Context

Tier 1 — **Script:** Every day in our words and actions, we are sharing parts of ourselves with other people. Take a moment to think about what you share with others. Do you always share your true self with others?

Tier 2

Discussion: Take a minute to think about what you share with others through your words and actions. How would other people describe you? Have you seen a greeting card? On the outside, it may have something funny or silly, but on the inside, it gives the message the card is meant to share. Think about your behavior, does your "outside" match the "inside" message you want to share?

Experiential Activity: Give each child a blank card. Ask them to draw what they show people with their words and actions on the outside of the card, but on the inside, ask them to write or draw the message they want to share with people about the real them. Discuss whether or not the two match one another.

Tier 3

Discussion: Sometimes the words and actions we share with others do not match the thoughts and feelings we have inside. Why do you think that these are different sometimes? There may be things about yourself that you don't want to share with others, things you are trying to hide. Is it good to hide parts of you from others?

Experiential Activity: Give each child their card from T2. On the back side of the card, ask the children to write or draw their "secret messages," the things about themselves they have a hard time sharing with others. Share these with one another, and then discuss the idea that the front, inside, and back of the card are all parts of them – who they really are is the card as a whole.

Day 100	Giving It All Away	Defusion

Tier 1 — **Script:** We've talked about how silly language can be, and how words can get all sorts of different meanings that make us feel good and bad and everything in between. Today, we're going to be talking about how sometimes we can give meaning to things as well and how that is just another language game!

Tier 2

Discussion: Has anyone ever been to a garage or yard sale? To the person shopping, the items for sale are just things, but to the person selling them, those items could have a lot more meaning attached to them. Imagine a toy car at a yard sale – to you it might be just a toy, but what could it mean to the child who decided to give it away?

Experiential Activity: As a class, create a large picture of a yard sale – a picture containing at least a dozen items for sale. Then, ask the children to label each with the meaning that the owner might have attached to it. Have a discussion about why we attach meaning to items, and how that could make it difficult to give things away. Ask what is actually important – the item or the idea or memory it represents?

Tier 3

Discussion: We all have probably attached meaning to some items in our lives, or have things that are precious to us. Take some time to share some examples with one another. Is it truly those items that are important, or the feelings and emotions that you have when you see or hold those items?

Experiential Activity: Give each child a piece of paper to draw their own personal yard sale, with actual items they own that mean something to them. Then, have them label those items with their meanings. Share with one another and discuss the difference between the item itself and the meaning it holds.

Module 21: Setbacks

Module Description:
This week, children will learn about using mindfulness and acceptance techniques to handle setbacks while making values-based choices.

Preparation Notes:
This week, children are encouraged to open up about their own struggles with maintaining present moment awareness and values-based decision making. Being mindful isn't easy! Be open to having conversations about how challenging this can be.

Materials List:

Tier	Day 101	Day 102	Day 103	Day 104	Day 105
2	»Relay race supplies	»Paper »File folders »Pen/Pencil	»Paper »Crayons/Markers	None	»Box »Paper/Tape »Crayons/Markers
3	»Paper »Pen/Pencil	None	»WS D103T3 »Pen/Pencil	»WS D104T3 »Pen/Pencil	»WS D105T3 »Crayons/Markers

Journal Prompt:
What are the biggest setbacks you've encountered in your life? How did you respond to them? Would focusing on mindfulness and acceptance help in a situation like that?

Day 101	Relay Race	Committed Action

Tier 1

Script: Have you ever participated in a relay race? It's just like a regular race, except that there are challenges that a team must meet before they can reach the finish line. A relay team must stay focused, hardworking, and always get back on track when they mess up. Today we'll explore how life is like a relay race toward values.

Tier 2

Discussion: Who knows what a relay race is; how does it work? What kinds of things do you think a relay team must do in order to keep moving and reach the finish line? When they face obstacles or make mistakes, they never just give up, they get back on track and make it toward the end!

Experiential Activity: Set up a relay race for groups (carrying an egg on a spoon, a cup of water filled to the brim, etc.). Have each group identify a value to be their team name. Each time someone in that group makes a mistake, have them name a committed action for that value before they can move on. At the end, discuss the behaviors that allowed them to get back on track during the race.

Tier 3

Discussion: During a race like the one in T2, it can be easy to get discouraged or give up if you've made a few mistakes. Who here has ever wanted to give up on something important to them? What kinds of setbacks or challenges lead to those feelings? How can you be ready for those challenges?

Experiential Activity: As a group, identify the challenges that lead to setbacks for the group and the feeling that they want to give up. Try to find the characteristics of those events that are similar. Then, make a list of ways that they can overcome those setbacks without giving up.

| Day 102 | Thoughts Shield | Acceptance |

Tier 1

Script: Have you ever had a thought that made you feel bad, mad, or upset? What did you do in order to make that thought go away? Did you ever try to block it out or fight it like a knight fighting the enemy? Today, notice when you are fighting your thoughts and answer a simple question: "Is this fight good for me?"

Tier 2

Discussion: At the time, putting up a fight against thoughts and feelings you don't want in your life can feel good, but trying to protect yourself from them doesn't usually work out in the long run. What could be the outcomes of that fight that wind up making your life worse?

Experiential Activity: First, take a pile of small pieces of paper, and distribute them to the group. Then, have everyone write down good and bad thoughts or feelings on the paper. Next, give everyone a file folder to use as a shield. On the outside, have them write down or draw all of the thoughts or feelings that shield is designed to keep out. Once everyone has a shield that is ready to go, crumple up those sheets of paper, and have a thought battle, with each person trying to protect him or herself using the shields. Once the battle is complete, have a discussion about the benefits of those shields, did they survive with those thoughts around?

Tier 3

Discussion: During the last activity, did the shield help you block out the bad thoughts? Did they go away or were they always right there so you could never put your shield down? When you were focused on getting rid of bad thoughts, what happened to all of your good thoughts? Is that what you want in life?!

Experiential Activity: When we are focused on fighting bad thoughts, we lose out on the good ones too. Challenge the group to think of a painful thought, try to fight it out of their minds, while also thinking about something pleasant. Can you do both, or does that struggle get in the way?

| Day 103 | Critic | Defusion |

Tier 1

Script: Have you ever heard of or read a critic review a movie? That is someone who gives their opinion about how good or bad a movie is and why. They often point out all of the bad things about a movie. If you read that before watching, do you think you would be able to enjoy a movie without focusing on its flaws?

Tier 2

Discussion: Sometimes you can be the toughest critic in your own life. We might look at things we've done and decide whether we get a thumbs up or thumbs down, but those thumbs down might really bring you down and make you feel bad. When have you been your own worst critic?

Experiential Activity: Give each child a piece of paper, and ask them to draw a scene from the movie of their life that shows a time when they have had a setback or made a mistake. Take turns giving a review on these movies in front of the group. Are those reviews always fair or helpful to you?

Tier 3

Discussion: If one movie got really bad critic reviews, and then a sequel came out for it, do you think you would go see that movie? Why or why not? In our own lives, once we've decided we aren't good at something, we might avoid that situation in the future, but are those reviews we give always the truth?

Experiential Activity: Ask each child to share a situation they avoid because they think they will fail, such as getting called on during math to give an answer. For each situation, give a "one star" review (describing what avoiding that situation is like) and a "five star" review (describing what it is like to acknowledge those feelings, but do it anyway).

Day 104 — Terribly Mindless — Present Moment

Tier 1

Script: Here at school, we practice mindfulness a lot, to help you learn to experience the present moment. However, that is not always a fun or easy thing to do. Have you ever had the thought, "I hate mindfulness!?" Guess what, that's OK! It's normal to get frustrated with this stuff sometimes!

Tier 2

Discussion: Raise your hand if you've ever felt like you hated practicing mindfulness or were just terrible at doing it. Practicing mindfulness is not easy, and sometimes it can feel frustrating if you cannot get in the present moment. When you experience those setbacks, it's OK. You can even be mindful of those feelings, too.

Experiential Activity: Engage the group in a period of mindful breathing for five to ten minutes, but first, say, "Today, when you are practicing awareness of this moment, notice thoughts you may have about failing at mindfulness or being bad at it. Appreciate those thoughts, and let them go. Realize that by doing that you are succeeding."

»Tier 3

Discussion: When you are going through a hard time, trying to practice mindfulness can be a challenge. It can be hard to sit with your thoughts, because they feel overwhelming in the moment. Being in the present moment doesn't always mean the present moment is fun! Have you experienced difficult feelings or sensations when you are mindful?

Experiential Activity: Remind the group that practicing mindfulness can bring up some difficult feelings or sensations and their body might respond by feeling tense or tight. Lead the group through a progressive muscle relaxation activity: Ask them to lay on the floor, and starting with their toes, slowly tighten and relax each part of their body. Discuss how they can use this technique in their own life. Following, have them identify where they felt tense on their body during the exercise.

Day 105 — I Am...Good and Bad — Self-as-Context

Tier 1

Script: We've talked a lot about how what we show people on the outside doesn't define who we are deep down inside. In fact, sometimes, we might let our failures or the things we are bad at define who we think we are – but is that good or fair to ourselves?! Today, think about how you define yourself when you make mistakes.

Tier 2

Discussion: "Everybody makes mistakes." We hear that all the time, but it is a hard thing for us to really accept. Instead of seeing who we really are, and knowing that it's normal to mess up sometimes, we might be really hard on ourselves and let it define us. What kinds of things do you let define you?

Experiential Activity: Give each child a small box or something that is wrapped in paper. On the outside, have them write or draw "I AM" statements that focus on their shortcoming (i.e. "I am bad at math.") all over the outside. Share them with one another, then give the children permission to tear that paper off of the box! Inside, have them fill the box with drawings or writings about the experiences (good and bad) that make them who they really are.

»Tier 3

Discussion: It's important to remember that it is all right to acknowledge our mistakes or setbacks, without letting them define us. We don't want to pretend that we are perfect people, because no one is! What are some things about yourself that you accept, but do not let define you?

Experiential Activity: Give each child a piece of paper that has the following at the top, "Even though I _____ sometimes, that is not who I am. I am someone who will _____ when this challenge comes my way." Have them fill in those blanks, and draw a picture of themselves engaging those actions.

Module 22: The Role of Acceptance

Module Description:
This week, children will focus on the role of acceptance, and how it interacts with the other components of the hexaflex.

Preparation Notes:
This week is a good opportunity to revisit the overarching concept of "acceptance" with your children. At this point, children should understand the difference between accepting and giving up – and be able to explain what acceptance means to them.

Materials List:

Tier	Day 106	Day 107	Day 108	Day 109	Day 110
2	»WS D106T2/3 »Crayons/ Markers	»Tape	»Piece of paper »Pen/Pencil	»Several decks of cards	None
3	»WS D106T2/3 »Crayons/ Markers	None	»Coin »Marker	»WS D109T3 »Marker	None

Journal Prompt:
What thoughts, feelings, or events do you still struggle to accept? What is it about those experiences that you are trying to avoid? What is an exercise you could do to help?

Day 106 — My Tiny House — Acceptance/Values

Tier 1

Script: Have you seen or heard about tiny houses? Many people choose to give up most of what they own and live in a home that's not much larger than one room! Imagine making that choice-what would you have to leave behind to live in the tiny home? Could you do it?

Tier 2

Discussion: Who can describe what a tiny house is? How much space is in that house? What are the benefits of living there? When someone moves into a tiny home, they have to give up a lot of their possessions in order live that new lifestyle. Imagine that your mind is like a tiny house. You don't have room for every thought, feeling, memory, etc. Would you be willing to let go of some things to have the life you want?

Experiential Activity: Give each child a piece of paper with the outline of a head on it. Ask them to draw the tiny house in their mind and all of the things they would choose to keep inside of it. Around the head, ask them to draw all of the things they would accept leaving behind.

Tier 3

Discussion: If you're moving into that tiny home, once you have accepted that you need to let certain things go, you're left with a small collection of items that mean a lot to you. What might these items represent?! Your values! How can the thoughts and experiences you want to take with you represent your values?

Experiential Activity: Give the children back their tiny house in the mind drawings, and have them review the items in the house they drew. Talk about what values those thoughts/items stand for, and why they value those things. Then, have them add words or drawings of their values around the tiny house.

Day 107	Fingers	Acceptance
Tier 1	**Script:** Sometimes we take little things for granted. Even something as small as having five fingers we can use to do things throughout the day! When we face challenges that make it more difficult for us to accomplish our goals, we have two choices: be unwilling to work through them or accept them and move forward. Which will you choose?	
Tier 2	**Discussion:** What is something that you take for granted sometimes, but would be hard to accept if it were gone? We probably all have examples of these. What would be the result of unwillingness when we face those challenges? How about acceptance?	
	Experiential Activity: Tape two fingers together on both of each children's hands. Then, give them a task to complete that would normally need more fingers (i.e. tying their shoes). Give them time to try the task, then have a discussion about how unwillingness and acceptance played a role in their success or failure at the task.	
Tier 3	**Discussion:** Taping our fingers together was a fun example of the obstacles we may face when something goes wrong for us, but there are real examples of these in our lives. What are some things you have lost, and had a hard time accepting? What did you learn from those experiences?	
	Experiential Activity: Find a common experience for the group. Talk about what that obstacle or loss was like, the kinds of feelings and emotions that they experience during that time. As a group, identify the loss, the thoughts and feelings it caused, the ways they tried to escape it, how they could practice acceptance with it, and how they can move forward by doing so.	

Day 108	Hot and Cold	Acceptance
Tier 1	**Script:** Have you ever met a person who is ALWAYS either too hot or too cold!? It seems like it's never the right temperature for them, and they just keep complaining about it? What is the problem with putting all of your focus on this one tiny problem?	
Tier 2	**Discussion:** Who has heard the phrase "the grass is always greener on the other side?" What does that mean? How is the person who is always either too hot or too cold missing out on what is happening in the moment because of it? What are some things you might miss out on because you are waiting for things to be perfect before you can enjoy your life?	
	Experiential Activity: Choose a random word and write it on a piece of paper, where none of the children in the room can see. Then tell the children to work as a team to guess the word, and with each guess tell them they are getting warmer or colder. After a few tries, ask them if there is an easier way to find out the word without this back and forth game.	
Tier 3	**Discussion:** Who here has ever felt too hot or too cold? What did you do in that situation? If it were freezing outside, but your best friend wanted to play, would you say no because of a little cold? Or if it were really hot in the movie theater, would you leave before the movie ended? How do you decide?	
	Experiential Activity: Get a coin and present a scenario to the children (such as having a headache on the day of your field trip). Label one side of the coin "ACCEPT" and the other "AVOID." Flip the coin, and have the children describe how that situation would turn out, and vote it they would accept or avoid. Repeat with several different scenarios, then discuss which way they most often voted and why.	

| Day 109 | Go Fish | Acceptance/Committed Action |

Tier 1
Script: Think about someone who goes fishing a lot. Does that person always catch a big giant fish? If there's a day they don't catch anything, do they give up on fishing or do they go back the next day? Think about why those fishermen wouldn't give up after a bad day.

Tier 2
Discussion: Why do you think a fisherman keeps fishing even after he has a bad day, or week, or month? Every day he or she goes to the lake, they may not know what is coming next. But they show up, and keep trying. How does this demonstrate both acceptance and committed action? Is this a lesson you could use in your life?

Experiential Activity: Divide the class into groups of four to five children, and give each group a deck of cards. Tell them to play a game of "Go Fish" (teach them how, if needed). Each time they "go fish," that child needs to explain how he or she will demonstrate committed action that very day to move toward a value.

Tier 3
Discussion: If a fisherman has a stretch of not catching any fish, he or she doesn't give up, but they may make a plan to increase their success the next time they are out on a lake. Just like that, what kinds of plans could you make when you know something is not going your way?

Experiential Activity: Create cut outs of fish, and write down common obstacles or challenges the children face on a regular basis. Put them all face down in the middle of the table. Take turns "going fishing" and selecting one of the fish. For each turn, the child needs to describe how to move past that obstacle toward their values.

| Day 110 | Fly Like a Bird | Acceptance/Present Moment |

Tier 1
Script: We often think about how amazing it would be to be able to fly like a bird. Haven't you ever wished you could do it? But if you think about it, is a bird's life perfect?

Tier 2
Discussion: What could be the challenges a bird soaring through the sky might face? Does that take away from the beauty of soaring through the sky, seeing the world pass by below you? Do you think birds are caught up in the things they are worried might happen, or enjoy the flight and take things as they come?

Experiential Activity: Engage the class in a guided meditation as they practice mindful breathing. Tell them to close their eyes, relax their bodies, and take slow, steady breaths. Then walk them through a visualization of flying like a bird, bringing awareness to the feelings they would have while flying, and when encountering obstacles like rain, planes, etc.

Tier 3
Discussion: When you're going throughout your life, you know you will encounter obstacles and challenges along the way. You can choose to spend your time worrying about those things that might be coming, or you can choose to live in the moment, focusing on the here and now. What will you choose?

Experiential Activity: Take a mindful walk as a group. Encourage the children to focus on the moment, noticing everything that they see, hear, feel, and smell along the way. After, reflect as a group on the kinds of thoughts that came and went as they were walking.

Module 23: Sight

Module Description:
This week, children will reflect on how they "see" the world and how that influences their mindful or "mindless" behavior.

Preparation Notes:
This week the children interact with the metaphor of "sight." If you are interested in supplementing these activities with additional mindfulness, consider incorporating this theme on mindful walks, mindfully watching the clouds go by, etc.

Materials List:

Tier	Day 111	Day 112	Day 113	Day 114	Day 115
2	»Pieces of artwork	»Paper »Markers/ Crayons »Bucket/bowl of water	»Balloons »Paper/Tape »Markers	»Paper »Paint	»Paper »Markers/ Crayons
3	»Paper »Art supplies	»WS D112T3 »Markers/ Crayons	»Completed Materials form T2	»Ink Blot images »Paper/Pencil	»Pair of glasses

Journal Prompt:
Take a moment to think about the number of things you see each and every day: people, items, plants, cars, and so on. How many things can you remember seeing in the past day? Do you think you are mindful of what you see or going through life on autopilot? Why?

Day 111	What Do You See?	Present Moment

Tier 1 — Script: Have you ever been to a museum or art gallery? When you are there it's almost like there's so much to take in that it's hard to remember any individual art when you leave. Your day is kind of similar – there's often so much that happens that we lose track of individual moments! Today try to keep your attention to things in the moment.

Tier 2 — Discussion: Who here has been to a museum or somewhere where there are a lot of sculptures or paintings? Did you experience that overload that made it hard to remember the details? What if you went through that place mindfully, being in the moment for each work of art you see?

Experiential Activity: Gather or print out a number of posters/paintings/pieces of art and hang them around the room as if in a museum. Have the children go on a mindful "museum walk," spending 3-5 minutes at each piece of art and observing details in a mindful way. Repeat around the room. Then discuss their experience as a group.

Tier 3 — Discussion: How is your life like walking through a museum? There is so much to see and observe throughout the day – each person, thing, and event you encounter throughout the day has something to bring you in the present moment. How can we learn to slow down and see this artwork in our lives?

Experiential Activity: Ask each child to think of a different experience from their day. Give them each a piece of paper and some art supplies (i.e. colored pencils, paint, etc.) and ask them to create a piece of art from their day, including as many details from the event as they can recall, and challenge them to paint/color mindfully.

Day 112	Reflections	Self-as-Context
Tier 1	**Script:** We have talked about how what others see when they look at us is not always the same as what we see or we think we see – we looked into mirrors to reflect on this idea. However, the way other people see us isn't the only thing that can affect us…sometimes our own view of ourselves can be skewed!	
Tier 2	**Discussion:** Who has ever looked into a pool, lake, river, or other body of water and seen his or her reflection in the water? Was it a perfect reflection or were there ripples or swells in the water that skewed it a bit? Sometimes our own view of ourselves can be morphed in a similar way – does that change who you are?	
	Experiential Activity: Give each child a small piece of paper to draw a picture of his or her face on. Then, bring in a bucket or bowl of water, and ask the children to lay their papers face up on the surface. Then, one by one have them identify an experience that could change the way they see themselves and push their picture under water. After, discuss how their self-image can change, but they remain the same.	
Tier 3	**Discussion:** We all have an image of ourselves that we'd like to be like, one that we're afraid we might be like, and something that is probably closer to the real us! For example, you might wish you were a star athlete, but think you are the worst – even though you're actually pretty good! What three reflections do you see?	
	Experiential Activity: Ask each child to think of an area of his or her life that they think they have three distinct views of. Then, give them a piece of paper and ask them to draw a three-way mirror (like the ones in a dressing room) and draw, their "Wish," "Fear," and "Real" reflections related to that topic.	

Day 113	Fortune Teller	Values
Tier 1	**Script:** Fortune tellers say that they can see into your future to tell you what it will be like, however, you can be your own fortune teller! If you know your values and how to be committed to them, can you predict what you will be like in the future?!	
Tier 2	**Discussion:** Who here has ever been to a fortune teller or heard about one before? What kinds of things do they tell you? Are they exact events or ideas of what your life will be like? How can knowing your values help you see into the crystal ball of your future?	
	Experiential Activity: Give each child a balloon with a ring of paper attached around the bottom so that it can stand like a crystal ball. Give them each a marker, and tell them, using their values and their committed actions, to draw predictions of what their lives will be like in the next five or ten years. How can these predictions become reality?	
Tier 3	**Discussion:** Since we're all able to make predictions about our future using our values to guide us, we can probably also make predictions about what would happen if we do not live in accordance with our values. How would these predictions be different from our previous ones?	
	Experiential Activity: Ask the children to get into pairs and place their crystal balls between them. First, have one child look into the other's crystal ball and choose one of their predictions. However, instead of telling them that prediction, ask them to predict what would happen to the other if they didn't make the valued choices, then switch roles.	

Day 114 — Ink Blots — Defusion

Tier 1

Script: There's something called an ink blot test in which someone looks at the shape formed by the ink blot – some people think it can tell you about a person's personality, but the really interesting thing is that each person might see something different when they look at it! Those pictures are always changing meaning!

Tier 2

Discussion: We all know that sometimes we have upsetting or painful thoughts, and that certain words might make us feel really upset. How would we do something like the ink blot test to transform the meaning of the word? Could it mean something different when you or someone else looks at it?

Experiential Activity: Give each child a piece of paper folded in half and some paint; ask them to unfold it and use the paint to write down a word that makes them feel bad right along the crease. Then, have them fold and press it together, and open it up so that they can see the image. Pass them around and ask what everyone sees in the image.

Tier 3

Discussion: Just as much as words can give us certain feelings, when we have certain thoughts that bother us a lot we might notice that almost everything around us can remind us of those thoughts! What kinds of thoughts always seem to be at the front of your mind?

Experiential Activity: Print out or bring up ink blot images from a web search – show them to the group one at a time and ask them all to secretly write down the thoughts that they have when they see it. Then share the thoughts with the group and discuss if they are related to those thoughts everyone often has.

Day 115 — Glasses — Acceptance

Tier 1

Script: Do you or anyone you know wear glasses? A lot of people have a hard time wearing them because they do not want to accept that they need them to see better or don't think they'll like the way they look wearing them. Sometimes it's hard to accept something difficult in the moment, but in the long run it pays off.

Tier 2

Discussion: Practicing acceptance is kind of putting on a pair of glasses and seeing things clearly. When you're unwilling to accept a situation, you're pushing away from reality and from your life! But what happens when you put on your acceptance glasses? You may be able to see things more clearly and move in your valued direction! What situations have been difficult for you to wear your acceptance glasses?

Experiential Activity: Ask each child to identify a time when they had a hard time accepting a situation – maybe that they didn't do their homework and got a detention or something like that. Then give them a piece of paper and divide it in half – on one side draw what the situation looks like when you are avoiding reality, fighting against the situation (is it blurry? Dark?) and on the other, what it looks like when you practice acceptance (is it clearer?).

Tier 3

Discussion: Is how we interact with people in the moment is also different when we do not practice acceptance versus when we do? Do you notice a difference in your own words and behavior when you are or aren't wearing those glasses?

Experiential Activity: Invite two-three children to act out a role play for the group at a time. These role play activities should involve situations that may be hard for them to accept (i.e. a friend being angry at them for something they don't think is their fault). Ask each group to role play twice – one time without the "acceptance glasses" and one time with them. How are these different?

Module 24: Wild Metaphors

Module Description:
This week, children will examine metaphors that incorporate animals to examine elements of acceptance, mindfulness, and values-based living.

Preparation Notes:
Consider the possibility of arranging field trips that align with the themes of each mindfulness week! If your school has an annual zoo field trip, for example, coordinate it with this week of mindfulness, and try practicing some mindfulness at the zoo!

Materials List:

Tier	Day 116	Day 117	Day 118	Day 119	Day 120
2	»Video »Paper/Popsicle sticks »Markers/Glue/Tape	»Paper »Pen/Pencil »Crayons/Markers	»WS D118T2	»Paper »Art supplies	None
3	»Paper »Scissors »Markers	»WS D117T3 »Pen/Pencil	»Board/card game	None	None

Journal Prompt:
What do you think we can learn from animals in terms of being mindful, living in the present moment, and not letting language get in the way of our valued living?

Day 116	Beaver Dam	Committed Action

Tier 1 — Script: Have you ever seen the work of beavers building dams? They build something like an entire wall to help protect them and get food by moving branches and rocks, piece by piece, to complete the structure. They have even built walls almost 3,000 feet long! How do those beavers keep at it when it must take so long?!

Tier 2 — Discussion: Who knows how beavers build dams? (If possible, show a video clip of beavers building dams). What is so important to the beavers that they will put in so much effort? How can each rock or branch they move represent a committed action?

Tier 2 — Experiential Activity: On a large piece of paper, have the children work together to create a scene from a forest with a river. Provide a large quantity of strips of paper and popsicle sticks for them to build a "dam" in the mural. Before beginning, as a group identify a classroom value and give each child a set of strips/sticks that they must write committed actions for that value on. Then, have them glue or tape the pieces to represent the dam.

Tier 3 — Discussion: Part of why the beavers build the dams is in order to protect themselves from predators. These are the obstacles in their lives that they need to overcome to move toward their value of safety. What are the obstacles in our lives that we face as we work toward our classroom value (from T2)?

Tier 3 — Experiential Activity: Give the children paper, scissors, and markers in order to create animal predators that represent the obstacles they face. Then add them to the mural, and have a discussion about how the committed actions they identified will keep the class on track toward their chosen value.

Day 117	Stuck On Land	Acceptance

Tier 1 — Script: Did you know that penguins are one of the few types of birds that cannot fly?! They walk on two feet, just like you and me! Imagine if penguins could talk. Do you think they would be upset about their limitation or be willing to accept their differences from other birds?

Tier 2 — Discussion: If penguins could talk, what do you think they would have to say about being different from the other birds? How would you know if they were accepting of these differences? What are some ways you feel different from other kids or adults that you have a hard time accepting?

Tier 2 — Experiential Activity: Ask the children to write (or illustrate) a short story called, "The Odd Bird Out," in which a penguin is upset about being different from the other birds (for the reasons the children identified personally) but learns to accept and appreciate its difference as strength.

Tier 3 — Discussion: Did you know that penguins make a long journey across the frozen tundra each year in order to have a safe place to lay eggs? It is a long and dangerous journey, but if penguins could talk, they probably wouldn't complain! What are the hardships in your lives that you are willing to experience because of the good that it brings in the end?

Tier 3 — Experiential Activity: Ask the children to examine their hardships in the context of "If, Then" statements. Identify difficult situations they encounter (i.e. studying for a math test, cleaning their room, etc.) and put those situations in a context that identifies the positive outcome (i.e. earning good grades, an allowance, etc.) by placing them into "If, Then" sentences.

Day 118	Parrot	Defusion

Tier 1 — Script: Have you ever seen a parrot that can talk?! They repeat back pretty much anything they hear, but they sound so funny with their parrot voices! We've learned about how we can take the power of painful words away by making them silly – can we parrot our way out of our pain?!

Tier 2 — Discussion: When you teach a parrot to talk it repeats back words to you, it can backfire because the parrot repeats back things you may not want to hear! BUT, how could you use a parrot to help you defuse from words or phrases that bring you sadness or pain you don't need in your life?!

Tier 2 — Experiential Activity: Ask the children to divide up into pairs, and have each child identify a word or phrase that they think a lot and makes them feel bad. Then, have the partners take turns saying their words to one another, with the other saying the word/phrase back in a silly voice like the parrot. Repeat until the painful words have lost their powerful meaning.

Tier 3 — Discussion: It would be nice if we could always have someone with us to repeat back the thoughts and feelings we struggle with until they go away. But the worst thoughts and feelings often happen when we are alone! How can you defuse from those thoughts on your own? Like you had your own little parrot on your shoulder?

Tier 3 — Experiential Activity: Play a game of some kind – a board game or another game that involves talking. Tell the children to pay attention to their thoughts, and each time they have a negative thought, tell them to say it out in a silly parrot voice. Give them a point for each thought they share. At the end of the game, see who has the most points and discuss if those thoughts were so bad after all.

	Day 119 — Snakeskin — Self-as-Context
Tier 1	**Script:** Snakes shed their skin two to four times a year! Crazy! But guess what…you get all new skin every six weeks! And every seven years every single cell in your body is brand new! Is it the same snake when it sheds its skin? Is it the same you when you grow new cells? It must be.
Tier 2	**Discussion:** After a snake sheds its skin, is it still the same snake? After you shed yours are you the same you? Don't you have memories from throughout your life? There's some part of your that has always been there and will always be there. This is called your self-as-context. What is that part of you that is always you? **Experiential Activity:** Give each child art supplies and tell them to draw a representation of how they change over time by "shedding their skin," but always remain who they are.
Tier 3	**Discussion:** The snakeskin that disappears or the skin cells that you lose can represent a part of you too. This part of you is your self-as-content. This is the part of you that does change over time – the part that you outgrow and learn from as you grow up. What parts of you have you shed or you want to shed over time? **Experiential Activity:** Ask the children to identify the behaviors that often get them in trouble and to identify if that is part of their inner "snake" or "snakeskin." If they want to shed that part of their skin, what do they need to do? How can they get ready to let it go? Discuss these questions together as a group.

	Day 120 — Zen Zoo — Present Moment
Tier 1	**Script:** Have you ever been around an animal and felt a sense of calm or peacefulness? In the presence of an animal, we probably do not feel judged or worried what they think about us or what they might say about us. Today, think about how we can learn about living in the present moment from the animals we encounter.
Tier 2	**Discussion:** How do we know animals love us even though they can't tell us? How do you feel around them? In a lot of ways animals represent mindfulness; they are in the present moment, not worried about the past or future. They are simply there. How can we learn to be mindful from our pets and other animals? **Experiential Activity:** Engage the children in a visualization activity: Imagine the first time you ever pet an animal that you liked. If you haven't, imagine what it would feel like. Think of the way their fur felt in your hands, how warm they were, if you could feel their heart beating. Imagine the look of calm on the animal's face. Can you feel it too?
Tier 3	**Discussion:** You can use the mindfulness powers of an animal to help you in your own meditations! Have you ever been so caught up in your thoughts that you don't think you can even be mindful? Next time, maybe imagine that you are your favorite animal. Use their power to be mindful to bring yourself to the present moment! **Experiential Activity:** Tell each child to decide on an animal that represents their mindful being. Then, ask them to imagine they are that animal as they practice mindful breathing. Encourage them to notice the thoughts that come into their minds, but to let them go, because the animal can't talk and think like we do!

Module 25: Natural Disaster

Module Description:
This week, children will focus on continuing mindful practices, despite challenges that might arise throughout their lives.

Preparation Notes:
Activities this week bring up the distinction between trying to stop or change thoughts and taking the power away from thoughts (decreasing their influence). Take time to make sure children understand this difference and are able to provide examples of each!

Materials List:

Tier	Day 121	Day 122	Day 123	Day 124	Day 125
2	»Paper »Pen/Pencil »Markers/Crayons	»Large paper »Marker	None	»Paper »Pencil	»Storm soundtrack
3	None	»WS D122T3 »Markers/Crayons »Tape	»WS D123T3 »Paper »Art supplies	»Paper »Pencil »Art supplies	»WS D123T3 »Art supplies

Journal Prompt:
What is your favorite kind of weather? Imagine if you were always upset when it wasn't that climate outside…you would spend most of your time upset! How does this relate to feelings?

Day 121 — Shelter — Acceptance

Tier 1

Script: Have you heard ever sirens go off during a massive storm? Those sirens are telling you to stop what you are doing, go find cover, and protect yourself. This can be scary and hard to deal with. But it's one of those things that we just need to deal with! What are the sirens that go off in your life?

Tier 2

Discussion: What do sirens tell us during a storm or an alarm during a fire? What would happen if we ignored the alarms? It wouldn't go very well! We know things - like if you have a fire emergency you "Stop, drop, and roll!" When these emergencies occur, we have to accept that there is a problem, and get into action to stay safe! What might be a siren in your own life? Should we fight those warnings or accept them?

Experiential Activity: Have children develop their own method for responding to the "alarms" in their life (their own "Stop, Drop, and Roll") that demonstrates what they will do when they need to face a situation, accept it, and react. Give them a piece of paper and ask them to develop a flyer that explains and illustrates their acceptance method.

Tier 3

Discussion: Sometimes it feels easy to say what you will do when faced with an emergency or challenging situation, but it's not always so easy in real life when you're in the situation. What do we do in school to help us prepare for those emergencies? We have natural disaster drills to prepare! What kinds of real life situations might we need to use our own acceptance methods?

Experiential Activity: Ask each child to identify at least one situation in his or her life that he or she would need to utilize this method. Then, as a group, role play each situation so that child has an opportunity to practice his or her acceptance method.

| Day 122 | Rebuild | Committed Action |

Tier 1
Script: Have you ever watched the news while they were showing pictures of a town after a big storm, a tornado, a hurricane, or some other natural disaster? Sometimes, those places look so damaged they could never recover. But people rebuild. How do people do this in their own lives?

Tier 2
Discussion: What do you see when you watch the news or the weather channel after a big storm? There's a lot of damage, and people may have to repair their homes, businesses, parks, and other important things in their communities. Sometimes, people experience their own crises, and it feels like something important in their lives has been destroyed. What could be a difficult event for you to rebuild after? Would it be easy to recover from that and move on? What would you have to do to get your life back on track?

Experiential Activity: As a class, choose a difficult event that could threaten one of the classroom values. As a group, develop a "Crisis Plan" for how they would work together and stay committed to recovering from this difficult event. Post this on a large piece of paper in the classroom as a reminder of their commitment to maintaining their values.

Tier 3
Discussion: Everyone, whether it is a big deal or a small deal, has had something painful or challenging happen in their life that they had to recover from. What have you had to recover from in your own life? What was challenging about that event? What did you have to do to move past that crisis in your life?

Experiential Activity: Give each person a piece of paper with a home on it and a marker. Ask them to add words or pictures that represent their values. Because sometimes things challenge our values and make us feel "destroyed," ask the children to tear it up into many pieces. Then, give them the opportunity to work on rebuilding their paper, to put it back together like a puzzle, the best they can and tape it back together. While they may have been damaged, your values have not been destroyed.

| Day 123 | Changing Weather | Self-as-Context |

Tier 1
Script: Have you ever heard someone say, "The weather is hot today?" Or, "The weather is stormy today?" The weather is always changing - but there is ALWAYS weather! Spend some time today thinking about how the weather is like your self-as-context.

Tier 2
Discussion: Ask the children to quickly identify ten different kinds of weather they have experienced throughout their life. How can the weather be constantly changing - sometimes wonderful, sometimes dangerous - but always be just the weather? How does this relate to you and your self-as-context? Do you even behave differently in different weather conditions?

Experiential Activity: Play a game similar to "freeze." Tell the children a certain weather condition, and ask them to act how they would normally act in that weather, then yell "FREEZE" and provide them with a different weather condition to act out.

Tier 3
Discussion: We've talked about how we might act differently in different weather conditions, but do you even have your own "kinds" of weather? Is there a "stormy" you? A "sunny" you? Although you may act in many different ways, you are always there, experiencing it all.

Experiential Activity: Give children a piece of paper and art supplies. Ask them to identify at least two of their personal "weather conditions" and draw what they are like when they are feeling that way, using the list of weather conditions as a guide if needed.

Day 124 — Power's Out — Defusion

Tier 1

Script: When the weather is really bad, sometimes the power goes out! Whatever you are doing, all of a sudden it's just over because you can't see a thing! If you were watching T.V., it just disappears! Do you ever wish there was a power outage for your painful thoughts?!

Tier 2

Discussion: When you are having a rush of sad, upsetting, or painful thoughts, do you ever wish you could just take the power right out of them? While we know we can't stop thoughts and feelings from happening, we take away their power! How can we do that? Even though the thought is still there, taking its power away makes it easier to live with!

Experiential Activity: Give everyone a piece of paper, and ask them to write the most painful or upsetting thought they can think of on it. Have them hold the paper in front of them, with the thought staring them in the face. Talk about how it is hard to think of anything but that one thought. Then turn off the lights (make the room as dark as possible) and ask them if that thought is front and center in their minds still.

Tier 3

Discussion: Who can explain the difference between forcing a thought to go away and taking the power away from it? Which one of those strategies can help us handle our emotions and thoughts better? When we take the power away from thoughts, it can help us to focus our attention on what is going on in our lives in the here and now! We can let those thoughts hang out with us without letting them control us.

Experiential Activity: Ask the children to fill a piece of paper with many thoughts and feelings they have a lot - both good and bad. Then ask them to draw a picture of a real-life event they want to experience over the top of those thoughts. They are still there, but they are no long the most powerful thing on that paper.

Day 125 — The Calm During the Storm — Present Moment

Tier 1

Script: Some people really love the sound of storms in the distance - the rain falling, wind blowing, thunder clapping, while other people get scared just at the thought of a storm! Can you appreciate the beauty of a storm when you are safe and cozy in your own home?

Tier 2

Discussion: Raise your hand if you are scared of storms. Now, raise your hand if you love a good storm. When a storm is not dangerous, have you ever sat and enjoyed the sounds of it? Some people even play the sounds of rain or storms at night to help them fall asleep! Even if storms do make you nervous, like other situations in your life might, being present in the moment of the storm can help you find a sense of calm!

Experiential Activity: Ask the children to engage in some mindful breathing while listening to a storm soundtrack. While they are seated, with their eyes closed, taking steady, even breaths, prompt them to notice the sounds of the storm, the calm that that rainfall can bring them, and the peace they can find within themselves while there is a storm outside.

Tier 3

Discussion: We know that we can mindfully experience the sounds of a real-life storm, but what about the storms that happen with our lives? What could I mean by a "storm" in your life? What about when there's a situation that makes you angry or nervous, could you bring yourself to the present moment in those situations and find your sense of calm?

Experiential Activity: Give each child a piece of paper, and ask them to draw him or herself being mindful in the middle. Then, all around them have them draw "storms" they encounter in their lives, situations that make the angry or nervous. Just like in the picture, they can remain mindful, and find their calm during a storm.

Module 26: Quiet

Module Description:
This week, children will focus on mindfulness and acceptance of painful thoughts in the quiet of their minds.

Preparation Notes:
It can be so easy to get caught up in coaching/teaching the children through the lessons, that you can forget to engage with them yourself. Whenever you can, practice mindfulness with you children, as a model and for your own benefit!

Materials List:

Tier	Day 126	Day 127	Day 128	Day 129	Day 130
2	»Paper »Pencil/Pen »Highlighter	None	None	None	None
3	»Paper »Pencil/Pen »Markers/Crayons	»WS D127T3 »Pencil/Pen »Markers/Crayons	None	»Paper »Pen/Pencil	»WS D130T3 »Pen/Pencil

Journal Prompt:
When do you struggle most to be mindful? Does this have to do with the challenge of being alone with your thoughts – even the painful ones?

Day 126 — When No One is Watching — Values

Tier 1
Script: Even after learning a lot about values, it can still be hard to figure out what you REALLY value and what you THINK you are supposed to value! That's a problem a lot of people have! When you have time today, think about this – what is it that matters deep down to you? What values do you follow when no one else is watching?

Tier 2
Discussion: What are some examples of values that you know other people (you parents, friends, teachers, for example) might expect or want you to hold? Are these all the same as the values you have for yourself? Are there some that are different? How might you figure out which values are the ones that mean the most to you? Maybe these are the thing you do when no one else is watching!

Experiential Activity: Ask the children to make a list (together or individually) of values that they have and that they think other people might expect or want them to have. Then, give them highlighters, and ask them to identify which are truly their values, not ones they think they should have.

Tier 3
Discussion: If it is still confusing to you figure out if you are just listing values because you think they are what you are supposed to care about, that is OK! You can still figure it out! Have you ever done something that made you so proud or happy when you didn't think anyone else would know about it? Does that relate to a value you hold?

Experiential Activity: Ask each child – on a private "journal" piece of paper that no one else will read – to write or draw things they do privately in their life that represent their values. Then, ask them to fold them up and staple or tape them shut. Talk about how it is OK to live a valued life that is their own choice.

| Day 127 | Changing the Volume | Defusion |

Tier 1
Script: Have you ever been watching T.V. and a really annoying commercial comes on, and it seems like the volume is WAY louder than the show you are watching? Just like how those annoying thoughts you have sometimes seem so loud in your head? You can turn the volume down on those commercials, but what about those thoughts?

Tier 2
Discussion: Who here has turned the volume down on the T.V., radio, or iPod when there is something bad on? It doesn't make that thing disappear, but it certainly makes it easier to live with! Do you ever wish you could turn down the volume in your own mind sometimes?

Experiential Activity: Ask the children to identify annoying or irritating thoughts that come to mind that feel like they are on full volume in their minds. Then, have them all say them very loudly at the same time. Ask them to turn the volume down just a little bit and say them again. Repeat this until they are saying the thoughts so quietly you can hardly hear a sound in the room.

Tier 3
Discussion: Sometimes, when we fixate on the things that are annoying or irritating to us, it's like we're turning the volume up on those thoughts or feelings, when really, we want to be turning that volume down! What are the ways that you know when you've turned the volume up on a stressful thought or feeling?

Experiential Activity: Ask each child to identify a situation in which they are likely to feel very upset or irritated, and write that on the top of a piece of paper. On the left side of that paper, ask them to draw what it looks like when the volume is turned up on those thoughts, and on the right, what it would look like if the volume were turned down. Discuss how they can "turn down" the volume in real life when these events occur.

| Day 128 | Pause | Acceptance |

Tier 1
Script: Everyone here has probably heard the phrase ,"Think before you act." It helps us to handle situations without letting our emotions or thoughts take over. That isn't so easy to do though! That's because there's a step missing! Usually, before you can think something through, you need to take a second to pause first!

Tier 2
Discussion: Imagine that you are about to get very angry and start yelling. Maybe your parent is making you do something you don't like. If you stop and think before you speak, you might make a calmer response. How can you remember to stop and PAUSE so you can give yourself a moment to accept the situation before you think it through?

Experiential Activity: As a class, come up with a strategy to help them remember to pause before they respond to something that is upsetting to accept the situation, think it through, and then act. It can be a rhyme, a hand signal, or any other cue to "hit pause" on their behavior. Talk about how you can all help cue one another when someone is getting upset in class.

Tier 3
Discussion: Like always, these kinds of strategies are easier said than done! What are the real-life situations you might need to learn how to pause for acceptance before you think and respond? How can we practice this in a way that might make it easier when you are actually upset in the moment?

Experiential Activity: Engage the group in role play scenarios, in which all members of the event need to practice the pause before they think and react. These scenarios could be arguments or other confrontations in which they need to utilize the class' strategy to remember to pause.

| Day 129 | Watching You | Self-as-Context |

Tier 1

Script: Have you ever heard of someone saying they had an "out of body experience" in which they felt like they were watching him or herself doing something as if it were someone else? Think of how unusual that might feel. But could it be helpful in reminding yourself how to make the choices that move you toward your values?

Tier 2

Discussion: What would it be like if you were able to fly up above a situation and observe yourself interacting with people or completing an activity? Sometimes it would be cool, but other times it might be "cringe-worthy" to see yourself making choices that don't align with your values. What do you think you would tell yourself in those situations?

Experiential Activity: Ask the class to identify situations that might make them "cringe" if they had to watch it happen. Ask groups to come up to the front and act out these situations, with one person acting as the "out of body" version of the main character. Have that person narrate what they might say to him or herself during that situation.

Tier 3

Discussion: What kinds of things would you tell yourself if you could be there coaching yourself through difficult situations during which you might make choices that don't align with your values? If you could be your own "life coach," what advice would you most need to tell yourself?

Experiential Activity: Give each child a piece of paper and ask them to think of a time when they wished they would have acted differently. Ask them to write a letter to themselves as their own personal "life coach" giving them the advice that they think they need to live a life of choices that move them closer to their values.

| Day 130 | In the Stillness | Present Moment |

Tier 1

Script: We've practiced mindfulness in many different ways, and we've learned that you can be mindful in almost any situation. Sometimes, though, it can be helpful to find the stillness in your mind and meditate – practice mindful breathing – in absolute quiet.

Tier 2

Discussion: Do you ever find it hard to be in an absolutely quiet room? It can be hard to be with your thoughts and feelings with no distractions. But it's important to be mindful of that difficulty and learn to live with it. How can you learn to live with that stillness, with that quiet?

Experiential Activity: Ask the children to lay down on their backs on the floor. Remove as many distracting things from the room as possible, and make it as quiet as you can. Ask the children, for 5 minutes to practice mindful meditation laying on the floor as still as possible in absolute quiet.

Tier 3

Discussion: Many people who practice mindfulness have a regular schedule they use to practice their meditation. They might meditate every morning when the wake up, right when they get home from work or school, or at night before they go to be. They try to create a peaceful environment for a set time every day so they can practice mindfulness in the quiet of their own thoughts. How could you build mindfulness into your life?

Experiential Activity: Help the children develop their own meditation plan, in which they identify when they will practice mindfulness, for how long, and the kind of mindfulness they will practice. Ask them to formalize this plan by putting it on paper and to try, for just one week, to stick to this plan.

Module 27: Back to the Start

Module Description:
This week, the children will revisit some of the ideas and activities from previous weeks to "review" their progress and support their learning.

Preparation Notes:
The activities this week serve as a review of concepts and activities from previous weeks. If there are any other activities that you feel your children would benefit from revisiting, include them this week or any other!

Materials List:

Tier	Day 131	Day 132	Day 133	Day 134	Day 135
2	»Board/Large Paper »Marker	»Tape »Sticky notes »Pen/Pencil	»Board/Large Paper »Marker	»WS D134T2 »Crayons/Markers	»WS D135T2 »Crayons/Markers
3	»WS D131T3 »Pen/Pencil	»WS D132T3 »Pen/Pencil	»WS D133T3	None	None

Journal Prompt:
What have you learned about mindfulness since the beginning of the year?

Day 131	Value Review	Values

Tier 1 — Script: For many weeks now, you have been learning to realize your values and how to make your life meaningful by living these values. It's been so long, that it's important to check back in and see how you've changed!

Tier 2 — Discussion: Who remembers the kinds of things they said they valued at the beginning of the year? How are those things/ideas different from how we talk about values now? How are they the same? Do you think your values are something that stay constant or change as you grow and learn?

Experiential Activity: Create a "t-chart" on the board or a large piece of paper, with two columns labelled "Then" and "Now." As a class, make a list of values that the children held "Then" at the beginning of the school year, and those that they hold "Now." Discuss the similarities and differences. Are they able to "go deeper" now?

Tier 3 — Discussion: The year is not yet over! How do you think you can continue to develop your values? Do you think you could still "go deeper" about what you really care about? Maybe at the beginning of the year your cared about "video games," but then realized you really value "fun." Could you pinpoint you value even more?

Experiential Activity: Ask each child to choose one value that has developed over the past year. Give them each a paper with a triangle divided into three sections. In the top section, have them draw or what their initial value was (a more tangible value e.g. video games), in the middle a more precise description (e.g. fun), and in the bottom challenge them to think even more deeply about the value (e.g. friendship or alone time).

| Day 132 | How Am I Doing? | Committed Action |

Tier 1

Script: Just like you have been working on identifying values all year, you have been practicing ways to stay committed to those values. You've thought of ways to live your life to move it in the direction of those values. Today, think about how far you've come – how much progress you've made! Say, "Congratulations ME!"

Tier 2

Discussion: Can you remember where you stood with your values a few months ago? How were you doing then? How committed are you to them now? It's amazing how much you can improve your life by focusing on committed actions toward your values!

Experiential Activity: (Repeat activity from Day 21) Place a long piece of tape vertically on the wall for each person and give them 5 of two different colored sticky notes. On each set, have them write five values. Ask them to show how important each value is by sticking it somewhere along of the tape (the bottom is not important at all and the top is the most important). Repeat the activity with the other set, but this time, place the notes to show how good you are at sticking to this value. Now, the bottom is 'never follow this value' and the top is 'always follow this value.'

Tier 3

Discussion: Now that you've completed the same activity twice, how have you changed? What values are you sticking to more? What are the values you're still having troubles with? How could you stick to those more?

Experiential Activity: Ask each child to select one value that he or she thinks they could be sticking to more closely. Challenge each child to make a list of at least three committed actions toward that value they could make in the next week. In addition, create a plan to celebrate it when they complete the actions!

| Day 133 | Yes, AND | Acceptance |

Tier 1

Script: You are all experts on the idea of acceptance – you know that it is not worth fighting the thoughts and difficult experiences that you come across in life. But you also know the key to living a values-based life…when you need to accept something difficult in life, that doesn't mean you are giving in or giving up!

Tier 2

Discussion: Do you remember what you can say when a challenging or painful thought or experience occurs in your life? "YES!" We can always say yes to our thoughts, feelings, and experiences. However, so those events do not get you down, you can add something that to statement. We can say, "Yes, AND…" For example, if you are stuck on the thought that you're going to fail a test, you can think "Yes, I'm afraid of failing, AND I'm going to study hard and do my best!"

Experiential Activity: Take turns coming up with painful/challenging thoughts, feelings, or events that come in the children' lives. For each, develop a "Yes…AND…" statement for each, demonstrating how they are accepting of the events, but committed to moving forward.

Tier 3

Discussion: The alternative to saying "Yes…AND…" is saying "YES…BUT…" If you say that it might lead you to get stuck focused on those bad or painful thoughts, emotions, and events, and stop you from moving forward. What are times in your life when you say "Yes…but…?" How can you make that "but" an "and?"

Experiential Activity: Ask each child to identify something in their life that they still say, "Yes..but…" about. Maybe it's something like, "Yes, I'm doing badly in math, but there's nothing I can do about it." Then, ask each to turn it around and make it into a "Yes…and…" statement. Discuss how this view can help them out in life.

| Day 134 | Another Day, Another Thought | Defusion |

Tier 1
Script: For many weeks, we have been practicing becoming aware of our thoughts and feelings and letting them go – defusing from them so they do not have power in our lives! Think about this: are you ever going to be "done" letting go of painful or unhelpful thoughts?

Tier 2
Discussion: At the beginning of the year, you all had painful thoughts and feelings that you were dealing with, and you have practiced letting go or taking the power away from them. Are those thoughts the same today, or are they different? Will you ever be "done" letting go of painful thoughts?

Experiential Activity: Give each child a piece of paper divided into thirds. Label the columns: "Old Thoughts," "New Thoughts," "Same Thoughts," and as the children to write or draw representations of different thoughts they've been defusing from throughout the year. What is different today than the past – what thoughts are you still learning to let go?"

Tier 3
Discussion: It's not a bad thing if you have a thought you are still learning to let go of, something that you are still learning to deal with! We all have those thoughts or feelings that stick with us for a while. What are some thoughts you have been dealing with for a while?

Experiential Activity: Ask each child to select one thought that is persistent in his or her life. Then, choose a defusion technique that has been previously used (i.e. Thought Bubbles) and focus on defusing from that one thought. Discuss how defusion is an ongoing process that it's OK if some things take longer to let go of!

| Day 135 | Where Is Your Mind? | Present Moment |

Tier 1
Script: As you get better and better at living in the present moment, you might notice that you spend less time worrying about the past or future and more time enjoying your life as it happens right now! Today, try to take notice of how much you are changing in terms living in the moment.

Tier 2
Discussion: The goal of mindfulness is to help you live your live in the present moment, without judging your thoughts or feelings as they happen. Part of that means recognizing when you are living in the past or future. How can you practice becoming aware of those moments?

Experiential Activity: Give each child a piece of paper with three boxes on it, labeled "past," "future," and "NOW." Ask them to draw or write things that they think of in each time. Then, on a scale from 1-10 (never - all the time), have them rate how much time they spend "living" in that box.

Tier 3
Discussion: Like we talked about before, if you still get caught up in worrying about things in the past or the future, that is OK! We are just here to learn to notice those thoughts and feelings, thank our mind for those thoughts, and move back to the present moment. How can we do that?

Experiential Activity: Ask the children to practice five minutes of mindful breathing, always coming back to the NOW when they notice their minds drift off to the past or future. Challenge them to be aware of when they are drawn to the past or the future. After practicing mindfulness, discuss "where" their minds went, and how they came back to the NOW.

Module 28: Reading into It

Module Description:
This week, children will examine mindfulness and acceptance concepts through the metaphor of reading and stories.

Preparation Notes:
Part of the goal of this curriculum is to help infuse mindfulness practice into the school day, to make it a normal part of the children's days. Consider how else you could build "mindful moments" throughout the school day to supplement mindfulness practice.

Materials List:

Tier	Day 136	Day 137	Day 138	Day 139	Day 140
2	»Story to read aloud	»Passage from a book	»Story to read aloud	»WS D139T2 »Pen/Pencils »Crayons/Markers	»Paper »Pen/Pencil
3	»Books	»Paper »Pen/Pencil	»Paper »Pen/Pencil »Crayons/Markers	None	»WS D140T3 »Pen/Pencil

Journal Prompt:
How mindful are you when you read? Do you find yourself more mindful of the experience when you are reading for fun or for school? Which is more fun? How could you make both more fun?

Day 136 — Mindful Reading — Present Moment

Tier 1
Script: Over the past several weeks and months we've been exploring different ways to include mindfulness and present moment awareness into our everyday lives. Today, think about how you can be mindful throughout the school day, particularly when doing something you do the most – reading.

Tier 2
Discussion: When you've listened to someone read you a story, have you ever felt like you've gotten lost in the story – caught up in everything going on? You can turn this experience into a mindful moment! When you are listening, you can be aware of what you are hearing, seeing, feeling, and thinking!

Experiential Activity: Select a story to read to the class. Before reading, create a quiet, dim environment in the classroom, with the children seated comfortably. Prompt the children to be mindful of their breathing, and to be aware of all of the feelings, thoughts, images, and sensations they experience during the story.

Tier 3
Discussion: Who has ever had a hard time staying focused or paying attention to the book during silent reading time? What kinds of things distract you? Practicing mindfulness while you read to yourself can not only help you stay present, but can help you stay focused on your reading as well!

Experiential Activity: Ask each child to select a book for silent reading. Encourage each child to find a comfortable place in the room to read, and encourage them to be mindful of all of their experiences while reading, noticing their distractions, but bringing their attention back to the book. Silent read for 10-15 minutes.

Day 137	ReRead	Defusion

Tier 1
Script: Have you ever written your name a bunch of times on something and thought, "Is that even how you spell my name?! It looks so weird?! That doesn't sound right!" Sometimes when you read something over and over you start to defuse from it!

Tier 2
Discussion: Who has ever experienced reading something over and over again and all of a sudden it stops making sense and you feel like you're reading a different language?! Why do you think that happens? How can language play a trick like that on us?

Experiential Activity: Select a short passage from a book to read to the class. Sit in a circle and read it aloud to them several times, then pass it around for each child to read aloud to the group quickly. As the children start to jumble the words and laugh, discuss how they have become defused from the meaning of it.

Tier 3
Discussion: While we can experience that defusion from the feelings and meanings we attach to words with anything we read or write, how can we use this strategy to help us with our own painful thoughts or feelings?

Experiential Activity: Ask each child to write down a painful thought or memory they struggle with on a piece of paper. Then, ask all the children in the group to read the passage out loud (at the same time) over and over and over again for a couple of minutes. Discuss how the power of those words changed over time.

Day 138	Moral of the Story	Values

Tier 1
Script: When we read books, we often learn some sort of lesson from the story – we discover its moral. That moral is related to the value the author of that book wants to share with the reader. Today, think of your favorite books – what were the morals and the values in those stories?

Tier 2
Discussion: How could we figure out what values the author of a story wants us to think about because of the moral of that story? What clues could we look for within the story to help us figure it out? Why do you think it is important to look for the values in the stories we love…could it teach us about ourselves?

Experiential Activity: Select a story to read to the class that has a clear moral that can be linked to a value. Read the story aloud to the group, challenging the children to look for clues to the values included in that story. At the end, work together as a group to put the clues together and name the moral and the value(s) in the story.

Tier 3
Discussion: What is the moral of your life story? If your life was a book, what values would the readers find within it? Think about your life and your values. What is the lesson to be learned from your experiences?

Experiential Activity: Give each child time to write/illustrate his or her own life story, making sure to embed "clues" about the moral and values they want others to see. Then, exchange stories within the group, and see if the children can identify the moral of each other's' stories.

| Day 139 | Characters | Self-as-Context |

Tier 1

Script: Have you ever read a series of books? One that has the same main character or characters, but follows them around in different adventures and experiences? Even though those characters are the same people – their setting, behaviors, way of talking, even the way they look might change. How do you get to know those characters if their content is always changing?

Tier 2

Discussion: The story of your life is kind of a like a series of books; you experience different adventures, challenges, and events, and the only thing that ties them together is that YOU are there living that life. How do you change throughout these stories, and, more importantly, how do you know it is always YOU there?

Experiential Activity: Ask each child to identify three different books in the series of their lives (three different contexts or experiences), and give them a three circle Venn Diagram. In each ring, ask them to write or draw what makes their character different in that story, and in the overlapping sections, how they relate.

Tier 3

Discussion: Sometimes, we might even "play a character" when we think it is expected of us. In certain situations, you might behave a certain way, not because it is who you really are, but because it is who you think you are supposed to be in that moment. How can this have a negative effect on your life?

Experiential Activity: Give the group different "stock characters" that are common in stories (i.e. the villain, the victim, the damsel in distress, the hero, etc.), and ask them to recall times in their lives that they've played that character. Discuss how "playing that role" impacted their lives – for the worse.

| Day 140 | Turn a New Page | Committed Action |

Tier 1

Script: One of the best things about reading books is that every time you turn the page, the story changes. When things seem hopeless, they get turned around. When you think the bad guy won, the hero comes and saves the day. In your own life story, your committed actions help you turn the pages, they help move your life forward toward your values!

Tier 2

Discussion: Throughout a story, we learn about characters, events, obstacles, and other things, but the only thing that moves the story along is the actions of the characters, the things they do to move the story forward. How do you move your life story forward? How do you turn the page in your life?

Experiential Activity: On slips of paper, have words like "setting," "feelings," "characters," "obstacles," and "actions" written on them. Sit in a circle, and have each child select a slip of paper. As a group tell a story, moving in the circle and each person saying one sentence that lines up with their word. Discuss the importance of the "actions" to move the story forward.

Tier 3

Discussion: You have thought about your life story, and how it might be like a series of books. Think of this school year like one of those books. Each day or week or month is like a chapter of that book. How do you turn the pages in your own life? What actions do you do to move your life toward the value and the end of the book?

Experiential Activity: Ask the children to identify the "chapters" of their life this school year and put them into a list, and to identify the committed actions they have engaged in to move forward in their lives this year, moving from chapter to chapter. Write these committed actions down, and plan for the next action they need to do to move forward.

Module 29: Mind's Full

Module Description:
This week, children will learn to practice acceptance and mindfulness when they are feeling overwhelmed or burned out from the process.

Preparation Notes:
These activities are designed to be used to teach children about mindfulness and acceptance and to practice these skills, but it is up to you to bring them to life in the classroom! If you notice the class is distracted or "mind full," stop and incorporate mindfulness in the moment!

Materials List:

Tier	Day 141	Day 142	Day 143	Day 144	Day 145
2	»WS D141T2 »Marker »Scissors	None	»Paper »Crayons/Markers	None	»Paper »Art supplies
3	»Paper »Pen/Pencil	None	»Paper »Pen/Pencil	»WS D144T3	»Paper »Art supplies

Journal Prompt:
When do you feel most "mind full?" Can you see it coming, or does it get you by surprise? What can you do when these moments come up?

Day 141	Brain Strain	Defusion

Tier 1

Script: Have you ever been in a moment that your feel like you brain is at capacity, like you have so many thoughts and feelings going on that your head just might burst?! In those moments, it can be easy to give in to those feelings and get lost in the thoughts, but today we will focus on how to give yourself a little space when that happens.

Tier 2

Discussion: Who has ever felt like their brain was totally full? What does it feel like to you? How do you normally react? Those are easy times to give in and let your thoughts control you – but those are the times your brain needs you the most!

Experiential Activity: Give each child a piece of paper. Using a marker, ask them to write or draw all of the thoughts that come and go in their mind all over the paper, until it is absolutely covered. Then, ask them to cut the paper into the shape of a brain. Take a moment to look at their brains and all that they are able to accomplish. Can you appreciate that this happens in your brain?

Tier 3

Discussion: Sometimes, your brain gives you some pretty silly or "out there" thoughts. These thoughts can be good or bad. Instead of focusing on how those bad thoughts can bother you, what if you took a different approach? What if you used appreciation for your brain being able to think something that crazy?!

Experiential Activity: On a piece of paper, ask each child to add the header, "Thanks Brainiac…" Then, add a list of the thoughts that they just cannot believe they even have – the thoughts that are really "out there" (e.g. "All my friends will hate me if I wear this shirt."). Then discuss the absurdity of these thoughts as a group.

| Day 142 | Mind Rush | Present Moment |

Tier 1 — Script: Yesterday we talked about how full your brain can feel sometimes – today we're going to be thinking about when your mind is moving at a mile a minute. Have you ever felt like your mind was in fast forward? Today, pay attention to any feelings of "mind rush" that you might have.

Tier 2 — Discussion: We often talk about noticing your thoughts while practicing mindfulness, but is it ever hard for you to notice those thoughts when you feel like your mind is rushing? Sometimes, it is enough just to be aware of how many thoughts you are having when you are mindful, not just what those thoughts are!

Tier 2 — Experiential Activity: Engage the class in five minutes of mindful breathing. Prompt them to notice their thoughts as they arise, but today, instead of noticing what that thought is, to count that thought, and then let it go. After the breathing exercise, debrief about how many thoughts each child had during the five minutes.

Tier 3 — Discussion: Sometimes, during a mind rush, you can get so worked up that it throws you off, and you might even be able to feel it physically! What kinds of feelings do you have in your body when your mind is rushing? What can you do to help slow things down when they are moving so fast?

Tier 3 — Experiential Activity: Engage in a second breathing activity. This time, however, rather than counting thoughts, the children will focus on slowing down their thoughts. Prompt them to imagine their thoughts scrolling past them or playing like a movie; when a new thought comes up, imagine it moving in slow motion until it disappears.

| Day 143 | Roles | Self-as-Context |

Tier 1 — Script: Each one of you plays more than one role in life: you are a child, a friend, a sibling, a teammate, and so many other possible things! You know that these activities do not define who you are, but how do you manage it without losing yourself?

Tier 2 — Discussion: What are all of these roles in your lives? What kinds of expectations come along with those roles? How do you feel about those expectations, is it ever too much for you? Instead of being caught up in what other people expect you to be doing, how can you remain true to yourself?

Tier 2 — Experiential Activity: Take a piece of paper, blank on both sides. On one side, ask the children to draw a picture of "My Me" that represents who they are and on the other "Supposed-to-be-Me" that represents what other people expect them to be. Have them show one another their drawings and guess which is which.

Tier 3 — Discussion: Do you ever work hard to be "what you're supposed to be," but you're not even really sure what that means? It's hard to understand sometimes all of these expectations people have of us. However, at the end of the day, what matters is the expectations you hold for yourself. Those things related to your values that help you get to experience the "real you."

Tier 3 — Experiential Activity: Ask each child to generate a list or drawing representing the expectations they have of themselves. Then, take turns sharing these expectations with one another and explaining how they relate to their values and self-as-context.

Day 144 — Acceptance, Kindness, Compassion — Acceptance

Tier 1

Script: A while ago, we talked about lovingkindness, which is the idea of giving open, tenderness and consideration towards others. It's like having an open heart. When you are experiencing a lot of mind rushes or those feelings of a full brain, it's the perfect time to give some kindness to yourself! Give it a shot today!

Tier 2

Discussion: Acceptance is more than just accepting our thoughts as they are. It also means accepting our own limits and needs, and being OK with them! How do you know that you've reached your limit and are in need of a little lovingkindness?

Experiential Activity: Complete the lovingkindness meditation: "Sit in a comfortable position, and focus on your breathing. Imagine yourself in front of you, looking back at you. Allow your angry thoughts to come and to pass. Then, think of loving thoughts you want to send yourself. Think 'May I feel love. May I be happy.' And so on. Take the next few minutes to send yourself loving-kindness."

Tier 3

Discussion: The word compassion means to show caring for the misfortune or suffering of someone. Self-compassion means doing that for yourself. When do you deserve some self-compassion? What are the times in your life you wish you had a little more caring?

Experiential Activity: Ask each child to identify a time that they deserve some compassion and/or self-compassion. Then practice the following strategy for those moments: 1) Notice the need for compassion (Why do they need it?), 2) Accept that it is a part of life, and 3) Plan for compassion (What can I do right now to show myself compassion?).

Day 145 — Lost — Values

Tier 1

Script: Have you ever had so much going on in your life that you completely lost track of your values? It's something that happens to everyone! What matters is that you can tell when it happens and bring yourself back to your path! Today, we will think about what those times we get off track are like.

Tier 2

Discussion: Have you ever had so much going on, that you just wanted to do nothing? Or experienced times when you completely lost track of your goals and your values? What did those times feel like? What kinds of emotions did you experience?

Experiential Activity: Using paints or some other kind of art medium, ask the children to create an image of what it is like when they feel lost without their values (it can be literal or abstract). Discuss those feelings, and what they can do to get back on track when they feel that way.

Tier 3

Discussion: When you feel so trapped in a pile of stuff going on, how do you get back on track? How do you find your way back toward your values? How do you get unstuck? What are the feelings you have when you feel that you are living in line with your values?

Experiential Activity: Using paints or some other kind of art medium, ask the children to repeat the previous activity, but to create an image of what it is like when they feel like they are on the path toward their values. Then, compare and contrast the two images together.

Module 30: Spring has Sprung

Module Description:
This week, children will relate mindfulness and acceptance processes to the metaphor of "rebirth" in spring.

Preparation Notes:
With ACT, mindfulness and acceptance are never things that you "finish doing." They are ongoing processes, which may be difficult for children to understand. Emphasize process over end-goals to help children with this concept!

Materials List:

Tier	Day 146	Day 147	Day 148	Day 149	Day 150
2	»WS D146T2 »Whiteboard »Marker	»Sidewalk chalk »Water	»WS D148T2 »Crayons/ Markers	»Index cards »Pens/Pencils	»Whiteboard »Marker
3	»Paper »Crayons/ Markers	»Sidewalk chalk	None	»Paper »Art supplies	None

Journal Prompt:
What actions have you been engaging in recently that you could "clean out" out of your life? What kinds of actions would benefit you more in life?

Day 146	In Like a Lion, Out Like a Lamb	Acceptance

Tier 1 — Script: Have you ever heard anyone describe the month of March using the phrase, "in like a lion, out like a lamb?" Think about what this might mean in terms of the weather in spring. In the spring, we often need to remember that without some stormy skies and muddy days, we wouldn't have green grass and flowers in bloom!

Tier 2 — Discussion: What do you think the phrase "in like a lion, out like a lamb" means about the weather in March? March often starts out cold and rainy, but by April, it's sunny days and warmer weather. How does the weather in March relate to the idea of acceptance? If we're willing to put up with a little rain, we get to experience the spring!

Experiential Activity: Create a large "T-chart" on the board. Label one side "lion" and the other, "lamb." Brainstorm and discuss the different elements of the weather in March that nobody likes, and list them in the "lion section." Then, for each, state the way it "pays off" come springtime in the "lamb" column.

Tier 3 — Discussion: The idea that IF we are willing to experience some harder times, THEN we will experience a "payoff" later is not only related to weather! Think about how IF you are willing to spend a Sunday studying for a math test, THEN you get to experience a good grade! What other examples of this can you think of in your life?

Experiential Activity: Give each child a piece of paper. On one side, write "IF," and on the other, write "THEN." Ask each to write or draw something difficult they endure on the front side, and the benefit that acceptance brings them on the back side. Then, show one another the "IF" sides and see who can guess what the "THEN" side includes.

Day 147	Spring Showers	Defusion

Tier 1 — Script: Have you ever played outside with sidewalk chalk? What happens to your artwork outside on the pavement when a spring brings a sudden downpour?! How does this relate to what happens in your mind?

Tier 2 — Discussion: Who has ever used sidewalk chalk outside on a nice day?! What kinds of things can you create? What happens when it rains? Yes, all the chalk disappears! On one hand, it can be a bummer when your artwork disappears, but what does that make room for? If you really hated your drawing, how might you feel about the rain?

Tier 2 — Experiential Activity: Give everyone a piece of sidewalk chalk, then go outside where they can draw on the pavement. Ask the children to write or draw images of their thoughts, both good and bad. Then, using a hose or a bucket of water, wash it all away. Those thoughts are gone, but now there's room for more! Talk about how, just like the chalk, their thoughts are in a constant cycle of coming and going.

Tier 3 — Discussion: Sometimes, it feels like there are weeks and weeks with no rain. Do you ever feel like you have thoughts that are trapped in your head like chalk words that don't get washed away? What are those thoughts that stick? What happens when people walk over chalk again and again, even if it doesn't rain?

Tier 3 — Experiential Activity: Give each child another piece of chalk, and go outside somewhere where they can (anonymously) write or draw a painful thought on the ground. Talk about how it's hard to leave it there, knowing people might see it. In a few days, return to that spot to see if that thought faded over time, and if it bothers them so much to see it after a few days of having it out there.

Day 148	Spring Cleaning	Committed Action

Tier 1 — Script: Have your parents or someone else at home ever made you help them with spring cleaning? In the springtime, a lot of people want to go through their houses, get rid of things they don't need anymore, and make room for new things that they want now! How can you "spring clean" your actions?

Tier 2 — Discussion: During the spring, a lot of people like to clean out their houses to get rid of things they don't need anymore. For example, if someone used to play hockey, but don't anymore, they may get rid of that equipment, or clear out clothes they don't need anymore! How can you relate this to your values and committed actions?

Tier 2 — Experiential Activity: Ask each child to create an "actions closet" on a piece of paper. In the "closet," ask them to draw the actions they engage in a lot (both good ones and bad ones). Then, practice spring cleaning: cross out the actions that don't move them toward their values, and make a list of committed actions that can replace those.

Tier 3 — Discussion: Sometimes, people have a really hard time letting go of things that they do not need or aren't good for them anymore. Maybe a favorite shirt that shrunk in the wash or a toy that is broken. What are some behaviors you hold on to that don't help you in life, but are hard to stop? For example, arguing with mom or dad when they say it's time for bed?

Tier 3 — Experiential Activity: Ask each child to think of one behavior they keep doing, even though it doesn't move them toward their values. Talk about how it may be easier to get rid of this nonfunctional "item" if they have a plan for a functional replacement. Then, ask each one of them to choose an alternate action to engage in to replace it. What will that new behavior look like, feel like, and move them towards?

| Day 149 | Butterfly | Self-as-Context |

Tier 1
Script: Have you ever seen a butterfly in all the different stages of its growth? They are all so different from one another! There's almost nothing that seems the same about a caterpillar and a butterfly, but they are! How does this relate to you? Have you changed over time, but remained who you are?

Tier 2
Discussion: What are the different stages of a butterfly? Is there any way of looking a picture of 3 different caterpillars, then a picture of 3 different butterflies, and match up them? Why not, if they are really the same creature?! In what ways have you changed as drastically as a butterfly in your life? How do you know you're still you?

Experiential Activity: Give each child two index cards. On one, have them write or draw one thing describing how they were as a baby or young child. On the other, have them write or draw one thing about them now that is totally different. In groups, shuffle up the cards, and see if they children are able to match up the descriptions.

Tier 3
Discussion: Who here has a hard time with behavior or keeping out of trouble sometimes? Maybe you just want to hide away, like a butterfly in a cocoon! What changes can you make in your content (the stuff you do) to grow in the future? How will you know you are still you?

Experiential Activity: Draw the world from the perspective of the butterfly coming out of its cocoon: after all that time spent in the cocoon, what does it see when it finally becomes a butterfly, what are the values out in the world that it can finally encounter? Could it see those things as a caterpillar?

| Day 150 | Nature Walk | Present Moment |

Tier 1
Script: Over the winter, we may start to forget all of the fun little details of nature in spring! For instance, the patches of little purple or yellow flowers that appear in the grass, the way buds look on branches before they bloom, or the way you can see every blade of grass starting to grow back after the winter. Take some time today to notice these little things about springtime!

Tier 2
Discussion: What kinds of things might we notice about the spring that we haven't seen in a while? What sights, sounds, or smells might be around on a walk outside?

Experiential Activity: As a class, make a list of the smells, sights, and sounds they might notice on a springtime walk. Then, take a mindful walk outside as a group, paying attention to all of those little details. Then, upon return to the room, check the list to see if they noticed it all, or if there were things they hadn't even thought of!

Tier 3
Discussion: We've practiced a lot of different mindful breathing and meditation skills. Most of the time, we practice these things inside, in quiet places, but sometimes it can be nice to experience nature as you meditate, being aware of how we are a part of nature? What are the benefits of meditating outside?

Experiential Activity: Walk to a nearby courtyard, park, or playground, where each child can find a peaceful spot outside to sit. Practice mindful breathing in a seated position for five to ten minutes. Remind the children to let their thoughts pass, and for today, to imagine them as petals falling off of a flower as they come and go.

Module 31: Mandalas and Mindfulness

Module Description:
This week, children will interact with processes of acceptance and mindfulness using mandalas as a metaphor.

Preparation Notes:
There is a long and extensive history of mandalas and mindfulness practice. It may benefit the children to spend some time researching and learning about these practices.

Materials List:

Tier	Day 151	Day 152	Day 153	Day 154	Day 155
2	»Images of mandalas »Blank mandalas »Colored Pencils	»WS D152T2 »Art supplies	»Images of mandalas »Paper »Pen/Pencil	»Outline of circle »Art supplies »Scissors/tape »Large paper	None
3	None	None	»Mandala from Day 152	»Construction paper »Scissors/tape	»WS D155T3 »Pen/Pencil

Journal Prompt:
What does self-acceptance mean to you? In what areas of your life do you need to development more self-acceptance?

Day 151	Mindful Mandalas	Present Moment

Tier 1 — **Script:** Have you ever heard of or seen a mandala? They are circular designs with patterns and colors that represent the whole of a person or experience. They are often created and interpreted to help people through challenging situations. Today, take a little time to appreciate their beauty!

Tier 2 — **Discussion:** [Show the class several different mandalas online or in print.] What do you notice about how these mandalas look? Are there certain patterns that you notice or ways that they are all unique? How could you see someone using a mandala to help them get into the present moment?

Experiential Activity: Give each child a printed blank mandala (many free resources are available online, try to use more than one!) and colored pencils. Put on some music, and ask the children to mindfully color the mandalas, noticing, as they color, the thoughts and feelings that come and go, and how they affect their mandala colors and designs.

Tier 3 — **Discussion:** Often, people will interpret the designs and colors used in mandalas to figure out what people were thinking or feeling when they created them. What do you think different colors might represent? How could this activity help people become more aware of their experiences?

Experiential Activity: Take turns presenting each person's mandalas to the group. Ask each child to think back to what they were feeling when they chose each color in the mandala, and to share what it represents to them, linking it back to their feelings at the time.

Day 152 — Circles and Self — Self-as-Context

Tier 1

Script: Scientists have found that babies start to notice circles before other shapes – their parents' faces, bottles, and more all have a circular shape. In a big, new, confusing world, babies start to make sense out of circles before anything else. Think back through your life, how have circles shaped your view?

Tier 2

Discussion: Circles are so important to how we see, even our eyeballs are circular! Everything you see in your life, enters your world through two round holes, your pupils, and from there you start to understand the world and realize who you are! How can a mandala represent this sense of self?

Experiential Activity: Give each child a blank circle to create their "Self" mandala. In the center, tell them to make a representation of "YOU" as context, who you really are, and the farther out from center they get, add more content of what others see. Remind them that there are no rules for creating their mandala – only that it must remain in the circle.

Tier 3

Discussion: The mandalas that you made (in T2), represent who you are, from deep within yourself to the view others see. But that circle itself is just a picture! How does your real-life behavior translate into this mandala?

Experiential Activity: Have a conversation with the group about how the images they made in the mandalas translates into their behavior. Discuss whether or not they are acting from their self-as-context (their "center") or from the ways other people see them.

Day 153 — But What Does It Mean? — Defusion

Tier 1

Script: We've talked a lot about mandalas this week, and how they are interpreted in many different ways. However, just like everything else we read and say, these interpretations are JUST WORDS. Everyone's interpretation of meaning with different images can be completely different, but are they all true?

Tier 2

Discussion: What kinds of things do you think people interpret or analyze in a mandala (i.e. color, shapes, etc.)? How do these things come to mean something to the people interpreting them? If you showed the same design to two different people, would they think it means the same thing?

Experiential Activity: Show the group examples of various mandalas online or in print. As you show each image, ask the children to write down their interpretations of what it means on a piece of paper – secretly! Once everyone has explanations, take turns sharing them to see how similar or different they are!

Tier 3

Discussion: Could this same thing be true for our actions and what we say!? Is it possible that when we do or say things, people could completely misunderstand what you meant? Can anyone think of times you've done or said something and someone thought you meant something completely different?

Experiential Activity: Ask each child to take out their "Self" mandala from Day 152. Shuffle them up, and show the group one at a time. Have the group say what they think the mandala means, and then ask the child who created it to explain how they were right or wrong. Talk about how language and meaning can be confusing!

| Day 154 | Mandala Quilts | Values |

Tier 1 — Script: People create "mandala quilts" to represent how individuals are all unique, but that we are all unified and connected to one another. For example, you and your friends might have different values, but you all have values! Today, think about how this idea can help bring people together.

Tier 2 — Discussion: How could you create a mandala to represent your values? What kinds of images, shapes, or colors could you include to represent them? As a class, we will make a values mandala quilt; how will this represent our unity as a classroom? What do we all "bring to the table" that is unique, but valuable?

Tier 2 — Experiential Activity: Give each child a blank mandala, and ask them to create a mandala that represents his or her values. Then, ask them to cut the mandalas in half, and on a large sheet of paper, organize them like a patchwork quilt into a new design. Relate the final product back to the discussion earlier.

Tier 3 — Discussion: As a unified group, we can not only understand the value each one brings to the group, but we can work together to move toward our values! How can we support one another in moving toward our values? What committed actions can we make as a group to help each other live a valued life?

Tier 3 — Experiential Activity: As a group, cut construction paper into strips. Together, develop committed actions the group can take to support one another in moving toward their values, and write those on the strips. Then, attach the strips to the classroom quilt as a border.

| Day 155 | Meditation on Self-Acceptance | Acceptance |

Tier 1 — Script: This week we've focused on mandalas – how they represent our "self," and this might have brought to mind thoughts and feelings about yourself. Take a little time to think about those thoughts and feelings, how do they affect you?

Tier 2 — Discussion: What does self-acceptance mean? How does it relate to the acceptance we have been learning about the past few months? Think about some of the negative things you think about yourself sometimes – how do those thoughts limit you? Do you ever feel caught up in them like they are mesmerizing you?

Tier 2 — Experiential Activity: Ask the children to sit silently, close their eyes, and reflect on the questions that follow as you read them slowly aloud to the group, noticing when they are accepting and when they are judging: "Do I accept my body as it is? Do I accept my mind as it is? Do I accept my mood as it is? Do I feel I'm a bad person because of the way I behave?" (More questions can be added to reflect on self-acceptance.)

Tier 3 — Discussion: When we get caught up in those judgmental thoughts about ourselves, like some of the ones we thought during T2, it's almost like you are caught in a "trance of unworthiness." What can you do to transform those thoughts into statements of self-acceptance? Is it the thought that needs to change, or how we handle them?

Tier 3 — Experiential Activity: Ask each member of the group to make a list of areas in their lives that they could be more self-accepting. Then, for each of those areas, ask them to develop an affirmation, something they can meditate on to remember to practice acceptance. For example, if they often think, "I'm not good enough," they can use the statement, "I may not feel good enough sometimes, but that doesn't change my value!"

Module 32: The Long Run

Module Description:
This week, children will navigate mindfully through their committed actions, despite challenging thoughts and feelings that may distract them.

Preparation Notes:
Whenever children encounter a trial in school, try to challenge them to relate it back to acceptance and mindfulness and come to a resolution using this terminology.

Materials List:

Tier	Day 156	Day 157	Day 158	Day 159	Day 160
2	»T-Chart	None	None	»Trail Mix ingredients »Plastic bags »Markers	None
3	»WS D156T3 »Crayons/Markers	None	»Paper »Pen/Pencil	»Construction paper »Markers »Plastic bags	»WS D160T3 »Art supplies

Journal Prompt:
Life is a long journey. What can you do to take care of yourself so that you can continue to mindfully navigate through your life?

Day 156 — Fried Foods — Committed Action

Tier 1
Script: Who doesn't like eating fried food? It seems like we can fry just about anything these days, from chicken to cookies, and even alligator! The funny thing is it almost all tastes the same. Many people say it all tastes like chicken! We all know this food isn't good for us, why do we eat it anyway?

Tier 2
Discussion: Fast food tastes pretty good at first, but is bad for our health in the long run – from how our skin looks to how healthy our hearts are. Many of the choices we make every day that have nothing to do with eating are just like this – feeling good now and bad for us later. What are some examples of "fast-food choices" people make in their lives?

Experiential Activity: Create a t-chart on a whiteboard or large piece of paper, with the columns titled "Now" and "Later." As a group, come up with a list of behaviors or activities that feel good or pay off now, but then have negative outcomes later on. Discuss why people have the tendency to make these choices if they aren't the best for their lives.

Tier 3
Discussion: I bet we could all think of examples of when we choose the "good now" things over the "good later" things. Do these choices ever get us in trouble when we are at home or at school? How does it feel when we make these choices?

Experiential Activity: Ask each child to identify a choice that they made that felt good in the moment, but had a negative consequence in the long term. Then identify a different choice that would have positive long-term consequence. Draw these in diagram demonstrating the choice point the children have in these situations.

| Day 157 | Mindful Tortoise Wins the Race | Present Moment |

Tier 1 — Script: We've all heard the story of the tortoise and the hare. Who wins in the end of that story – the tortoise who went slow and steady or the hare who speeded along without paying attention to his body or the tortoise? Think about the lesson about mindfulness this story has to teach us.

Tier 2 — Discussion: Who can tell the story of the tortoise and the hare? Which one of the characters were practicing mindful awareness more than the other? What does this fable teach us about the value of living mindfully?

Tier 2 — Experiential Activity: Set up a "mindful race" for the children. Challenge them to move from one side of the classroom to another, but the winner is the person who finishes LAST, after taking each step across the room mindfully, patiently, and with full awareness

Tier 3 — Discussion: In your life, do you think you are most often the tortoise or the hare? How has either position benefitted you in your life? Are there times when you find yourself acting more like one than the other over and over again?

Tier 3 — Experiential Activity: Role play different situations that the children identify acting like one of the two characters. Practice each scenario from both the "tortoise" and the "hare" perspectives.

| Day 158 | I Can't | Acceptance |

Tier 1 — Script: Do you ever find yourself telling yourself you can't do things you really can do? Like when your mind tells you "I can't do my homework, I'm too tired" or "I can't clean my room, it's too boring" or "I can't get an A on that test, it's too hard." Most of the time, is your mind right about that?

Tier 2 — Discussion: Too often, our minds are busy trying to convince us we can't do the things we need and want to do to live a valued life! Sometimes, it succeeds, and we give up on something. How does that feel? Sometimes we do those things anyway, how does that feel?

Tier 2 — Experiential Activity: Generate an activity idea, such as "jumping up and down." Tell everyone in the class to say out loud, "I cannot jump up and down (or insert your own idea)," over and over again, while they stand up and do the activity. Talk about how amazing it is that they can do one thing while their mind says another!

Tier 3 — Discussion: Sometimes those I "can't" messages our mind tries to tell us takes other forms. For example, "I'm not good enough" or "It doesn't matter what I do, I'll always get in trouble." Who has had thoughts like that before in their life? We all have at some point or another! What are some of the "can't" messages your brain has sent you?

Tier 3 — Experiential Activity: Ask each child to select one of his or her "can't" messages and write it on a piece of paper. Then, draw a picture of themselves doing the opposite of what the message says. Ask each child to make a plan of how they will handle that message the next time it arrives in their mind.

Day 159	Values Variation	Values

Tier 1

Script: We've talked a lot about values, and have worked to clarify them a lot the past few months. The amazing thing about values is that, when something is really important to you, it will grow and change with you in your life. How have the way your values "looked" in your life changed over time?

Tier 2

Discussion: What are some ways your values, although they are the same, have changed the way they look over time? For example, if you value friendship, how does that seem different now than it did when you were younger? How will it be different when you are older? It's kind of like a trail mix – you add in a bunch of individual ingredients (committed actions) and depending on what you add, it will be different each time you make it, but it will still be trail mix!

Experiential Activity: Bring in a variety of trail mix ingredients (i.e. raisins, chocolate chips, seeds, etc.). Give each child a small plastic bag, and ask each child to write a value on it. Then, ask each child to add in whichever ingredients they want into their trail mix. Then, as they eat it, pay attention to the number of each item that was added. If they made it again, would it be the same mix, or would there be some variation?

Tier 3

Discussion: Think of one of your most important values. What does it look like today? What are the committed actions you are "adding" to your values mix most often today? Is that how you want it, or would you like to change it? How will that mix be different in five years from now?

Experiential Activity: Cut or tear colored construction paper in to small pieces, and give each child a plastic bag to make a "symbolic trail mix." Ask the children to make each color a different kind of committed action, label them, and then add the appropriate amount of each into your trail mix. How does it look today?

Day 160	Cut It Out	Defusion

Tier 1

Script: When things get hard in life, we all have the tendency to want to give up at some point or another. It's something every single one of us has felt! The problem is, if that something is important to you, giving up is not the best option for you, no matter what your mind says. What will we do about the "give up" story your mind tells you this time?

Tier 2

Discussion: Have you ever heard of someone telling a joke to make people laugh during a tough situation, to make it just a little less difficult? You can do that with your own mind! Think of something you've wanted to give up on in your life. What was it? What was your mind saying to you? Could you use humor to help realize that you don't need to take your mind so seriously?

Experiential Activity: In pairs, ask the children to come up with jokes about "giving up" they could tell their minds when they need to. For example, Mind says, "Give up on that homework!" You can tell your mind a joke: "Knock knock. Who's there? Mind. Mind who? Mind your own business!" Then, take turns telling each other the jokes.

Tier 3

Discussion: When you're having a really tough time with your mind and a thought, a joke isn't meant to make fun of you for having those thoughts, it's just to remind you that your thoughts are just thoughts, and don't need to control you. What are some thoughts you need to learn to lighten up about?

Experiential Activity: Clowns exist just to make people laugh! Ask each child to draw a picture of a funny looking clown, with a speech bubble showing what that thought would be. Talk about how it's harder to take those thoughts seriously when they are coming out of a clown's mouth!

Module 33: Listening Carefully

Module Description:
This week, the children will engage with exercises and activities related to 'listening,' both literally and metaphorically.

Preparation Notes:
Developing a sense of "intentionality" or "purpose" in mindfulness practice is important, even for children! Helping them to determine why mindfulness matters to them will help it become a more personal activity, rather than another school "task."

Materials List:

Tier	Day 161	Day 162	Day 163	Day 164	Day 165
2	None	»WS D162T2 »Paper/Pen	»Scenarios	»Large Paper »Markers	»Mindfulness bell
3	»Paper »Pen/Pencil »Timer »2 highlighters	»Completed WS D162T2	»WS D163T3 »Pen/Pencil	»WS D164T3 »Pen/Pencil »Brads	»WS D165T3 »Pen/Pencil

Journal Prompt:
Do you always listen to what your mind tells you? How can you learn to know the difference between when you should and shouldn't listen to what your mind says?

Day 161	Listen Carefully!	Acceptance

Tier 1 — Script: How many times have you heard someone say, "Pay attention!" or "Listen Carefully!" Probably, most of the time, this is a signal that you are doing something wrong…but today, be very gentle with yourself and try to "listen carefully" to your mind.

Tier 2 — Discussion: What does it mean to "listen carefully?" We all know how to do that when it comes to following directions or completing an assignment, but what does that mean in terms of your mind – how can you be careful when listening to your own thoughts?

Experiential Activity: Play a game of telephone with the group; sit in a circle, and whisper quietly to the first person a neutral thought, and have it passed along the group. Afterward, discuss if it traveled correctly, and how the way you interpret what you hear (and think) affects how you act.

Tier 3 — Discussion: In the context of your own mind, how can you "listen carefully?" Does that mean to make sure you hear each and every thought you have, or to be mindful of your thoughts, accepting them all, but choosing which ones will have an influence over you?

Experiential Activity: Give each child a piece of paper and a pen or pencil. Set a timer for five minutes. For those five minutes, ask the children to sit mindful of their thoughts, and write down every thought that comes in and out of their mind during that time – not missing one! Then, with a highlighter, go back and highlight in one color thoughts they need to act on, and in another, thoughts they can defuse from.

| Day 162 | Listen Honestly | Values/Committed Action |

Tier 1 — Script: Over time, we have reflected on values from many different perspectives. Today, reflect on this question: "Am I being honest with myself about my true values? Deep down inside, are these the things or feelings that give meaning to my life?"

Tier 2 — Discussion: We have talked about the difference between your own values and the values others might expect you to have. How is that different from being really honest with yourself about the values that are true to you?

Tier 2 — Experiential Activity: Ask the children to complete a "Truth AND Dare" activity. In one section of a paper, ask them to identify three "truths" about their values, to really dig deep and be honest about what they want. In another section, ask them to commit to three "dares" related to these value truths: three actions they will take that will not be easy, but reveal how much those values matter to them.

Tier 3 — Discussion: Sometimes we have to "trust our gut" and go with what we know "feels right." How do you know when something is the right or wrong action to take in a situation? What signals does your mind or your body give you?

Tier 3 — Experiential Activity: Give each child their truths and dares from T2, ask them to sit mindfully for 3-5 minutes, "listening" to these in their minds over and over, noticing the feelings in their bodies as they hear these things in their own mind. Then, discuss how they felt – did they feel right, or was something off about them?

| Day 163 | Listen with a Grain of Salt | Defusion |

Tier 1 — Script: Have you ever heard the phrase "take it with a grain of salt?" That line is meant to signal that there may not be 100% truth to what someone is saying or doing. Today, try to treat what your mind tells you with a grain of salt. Should you believe everything you hear?

Tier 2 — Discussion: What does "take it with a grain of salt" mean? Does that mean that the source is untrustworthy or just that you need to be aware that not everything you hear is true all the time? What kinds of things should you "take with a grain of salt?"

Tier 2 — Experiential Activity: Provide a set of scenarios to the group, each depicting a scenario that makes it seem like they should either take what is being said at face value or be cautious at accepting what they hear as the truth. After this detective work, discuss whether their minds should be taken at face value or with "a grain of salt."

Tier 3 — Discussion: Should you believe everything your mind tells you? Why or why not? What are some of the thoughts your mind tells you that you know you shouldn't just accept as true? How do you know?

Tier 3 — Experiential Activity: Give each child a piece of paper, and ask them to identify five thoughts that they have that they know they shouldn't take at face value – some mind tricks they know their minds try to play on them. Then, discuss how they can defuse from these thoughts and see them for what they really are!

| Day 164 | Don't Listen! | Self-as-Context |

Tier 1 — **Script:** There is one time you may not need to listen carefully: that is when other people try to tell you who you are! Think about how it feels when someone else tries to define you. How can they know the person at your core?

Tier 2
- **Discussion:** How does it feel when other people try to tell you who you are or act like they know you better than you know yourself? How can you know when not to listen to people saying things like this? How can you stop it from becoming part of who you think you are?
- **Experiential Activity:** On a large sheet of paper, draw a large "don't" or "X" symbol. Give each child a marker, and ask everyone to write down things others have said about them that do not represent who they really are. As a group, discuss how it feels to separate those ideas from who they really are.

Tier 3
- **Discussion:** Sometimes, if you hear something about yourself enough times, even you may start to believe it is true, and even start acting that way! What if people called you "class clown" all the time? You might start to feel like you have to act that way! Do you?
- **Experiential Activity:** Give each child the pieces to make a puppet and some brads. Cut out the pieces, and assemble them. One each part of the body, write down an action the children have made that is because of what other people said. Discuss how even though others may have things to say about you, you are still your own puppet master!

| Day 165 | Just Listen | Present Moment |

Tier 1 — **Script:** You hear things all around you, all day long. Sometimes it's very important to pay attention to particular sounds, other times to just take in all the sounds around you. However, do you ever just stop and listen – without thinking about what you hear?

Tier 2
- **Discussion:** Have you ever tried to just stop and listen? Some traditional mindfulness practices include ringing a bell sound to signal your intention to stop, be mindful, and take time to just listen to the sound of the bell. It's not as easy as you'd think!
- **Experiential Activity:** Obtain a mindfulness bell sound (purchase one, find one online, or use a different bell). Engage the children in a task of some kind, but every few minutes, ring the bell, asking them to stop what they are doing and only be mindful of the sound of the bell.

Tier 3
- **Discussion:** One of the keys of the mindfulness bell is that it sets an "intention" for mindful practice. It makes it a directed effort, it's like you're saying, "right now, I will be mindful, despite whatever else is going on." What do you need to set intentions for in your life?
- **Experiential Activity:** Show the class a list of questions that can help them develop their own intentions, such as "find balance," "connect with others," "stay calm." Remind them that an intention is meant to bring clarity: it can be a wish, or a phrase they would like to be connected to. After completing the list of questions, ask the children to develop one intention.

Module 34: Mindfulness, Defined

Module Description:
This week, the children will examine the parts of the hexaflex one last time, developing their own definitions of each core process.

Preparation Notes:
As important as it is for children to understand acceptance, present moment awareness, defusion, self-as-context, values, and committed action in the way we have presented them, it is equally important they can articulate their own understanding of these processes!

Materials List:

Tier	Day 166	Day 167	Day 168	Day 169	Day 170
2	»WS D166-70T2 »Paper »Art supplies	»WS D166-70T2 »Paper »Art supplies	»WS D166-70T2 »Paper »Art supplies	»WS D166-70T2 »Paper »Art supplies	»WS D166-70T2 »Paper »Art supplies
3	»WS D166-170T3 »Pen/Pencil	»WS D166-170T3 »Pen/Pencil	»WS D166-170T3 »Pen/Pencil	»WS D166-170T3 »Pen/Pencil	»WS D166-170T3 »Pen/Pencil

Journal Prompt:
What does it mean to be mindful and accepting in your own life, and no one else's?

Day 166 — Present Moment

Tier 1

Script: Present moment awareness means to focus on the here and now, to live your life in this moment, not lost in thoughts of other times. Today, reflect on the words "Present Moment." What do they mean to you?

Tier 2

Discussion: What does "present moment awareness" mean to all of you? What does it look like in your life? How is that different from one another?

Experiential Activity: Give each child a blank "personal hexaflex." Ask each child to spend some time filling in a definition for "present moment" on the diagram. Then, give them each a piece of paper, ask them to write this definition on it, then use art supplies to create a piece of art that IS present moment awareness. Share with one another.

Tier 3

Discussion: You have all come so far this year in developing your present moment awareness. That doesn't mean you are "done" being in the present. What challenges do you still face in this area?

Experiential Activity: Give each child a piece of paper with a section for each part of the hexaflex labelled. Ask them to reflect on their present moment awareness and the "hills" they still have to climb in this area, and record them on the paper.

Day 167	Acceptance	Acceptance
Tier 1	**Script:** Acceptance means to be willing to experience thoughts, feelings, events, and sensations as they are, without trying to change them. Today, reflect on the word "Acceptance." What does it mean to you?	
	Discussion: What does "acceptance" mean to all of you? What does it look like in your life? How is that different from one another?	
»Tier 2	**Experiential Activity:** Give each child their partially completed "My Hexaflex" paper from the previous day. Ask each child to spend some time filling in a definition for "acceptance" on the diagram. Then, give them each a piece of paper, ask them to write this definition on it, then use art supplies to create a piece of art that IS acceptance. Share with one another.	
»Tier 3	**Discussion:** You have made many strides this year in developing acceptance. That doesn't mean you are "done" learning how to accept. What challenges do you still face in this area?	
	Experiential Activity: Give each child their mountains diagram from the previous day. Ask them to reflect on their acceptance practices and the "mountains" they still have to climb in this area, and record them on the paper.	

Day 168	Defusion	Defusion
Tier 1	**Script:** Defusion means to observe your thoughts objectively, without letting them rule or have power over you and your life. Today, reflect on the word "Defusion." What does it mean to you?	
	Discussion: What does "defusion" mean to all of you? What does it look like in your life? How is that different from one another?	
»Tier 2	**Experiential Activity:** Give each child their partially completed "My Hexaflex" paper from the previous day. Ask each child to spend some time filling in a definition for "defusion" on the diagram. Then, give them each a piece of paper, ask them to write this definition on it, then use art supplies to create a piece of art that IS defusion. Share with one another.	
»Tier 3	**Discussion:** You have spent a lot of time this year learning how to defuse from your thoughts when they are interfering in your life. That doesn't mean you are "done" learning how to defuse. What challenges do you still face in this area?	
	Experiential Activity: Give each child their mountains diagram from the previous day. Ask them to reflect on their defusion practices and the "mountains" they still have to climb in this area, and record them on the paper.	

Day 169 — Self-as-Context — Self-as-Context

Tier 1
Script: Self-as-context you see the part of you that is unchanged by time and experiences, the part of you that is constant throughout your life. Today, reflect on the words "Self-as-Context." What do they mean to you?

Tier 2
Discussion: What does "self-as-context" mean to all of you? What does it look like in your life? How is that different from one another?

Experiential Activity: Give each child their partially completed "My Hexaflex" paper from the previous day. Ask each child to spend some time filling in a definition for "self-as-context" on the diagram. Then, give them each a piece of paper, ask them to write this definition on it, then use art supplies to create a piece of art that IS self-as-context. Share with one another.

Tier 3
Discussion: You come so far in learning how to see the difference between you as content and you as context. That doesn't mean you will never have a hard time identifying the difference again in your life. What challenges do you still face in this area?

Experiential Activity: Give each child their mountains diagram from the previous day. Ask them to reflect on their self-as-context awareness and the "mountains" they still have to climb in this area, and record them on the paper.

Day 170 — Values and Committed Action — Values/Committed Action

Tier 1
Script: Values represent the parts of life that are really, truly, deeply important to you. Committed actions are the behaviors you engage in to help move your life in the directions of those values. Today, reflect on the words "Values and Committed Action." What do they mean to you?

Tier 2
Discussion: What does "Values" mean to all of you? What does "Committed Action" mean to all of you? What do they look like in your life? How is that different from one another?

Experiential Activity: Give each child their partially completed "My Hexaflex" paper from the previous day. Ask each child to spend some time filling in definitions for "values" and "committed action" on the diagram. As well, ask them to fill in the center "me" section in whatever way feels right to them. Then, give them each a piece of paper, ask them to write these definition on it, then use art supplies to create a piece of art that IS values and committed action. Share with one another.

Tier 3
Discussion: This year you have found lot of clarity regarding what you value and what it takes to get you there. However, in life, you will continue to need to reexamine your values and refocus yourself on committed actions that will move you in that direction. What challenges do you still face in these areas?

Experiential Activity: Give each child their mountains diagram from the previous day. Ask them to reflect on their values and committed actions and the "mountains" they still have to climb in these areas, and record them on the paper.

Module 35: Staying Present, Looking Forward

Module Description:
This week, the children will summarize the mindfulness, acceptance, and values work they have engaged in throughout the school year.

Preparation Notes:
As the year comes to an end, do your best to help your children develop ways to continue their mindful practices throughout the summer. It may help to provide some information to their parents and guardians to support them in this!

Materials List:

Tier	Day 171	Day 172	Day 173	Day 174	Day 175
2	»Construction paper »Art supplies	»Cups »Dirt / Water »Paper/Pen	»Paper »Pencil	»Paper »Pencil	»WS D175T2 »Art Supplies »Pen/Pencil
3	»Strips of paper »Marker »Tape/stapler	»Mud »Various supplies	»Paper »Pencil »Plastic bag	»Paper »Pencil »Jar	»"Yearbooks" »Markers/Pens

Journal Prompt:
How will you carry your mindfulness, acceptance, and values-based practices into your summer vacation?

Day 171	Flag Pole	Values

Tier 1 — Script: Today, look outside at some point and notice the flagpole in front of the building. All schools and other community buildings have a flag pole at their entrance, with one or more flags flying high each day. What do these flags represent? What does it mean to you to look up at those flags?

Tier 2 — Discussion: What do the flags in front of the building represent? Why do they fly each and every day, even though there is a lot of effort involved? A flag is meant to represent a group or institution, what it's mission is, and act as a reminder for all those who look at it. What would your flag look like? How would it represent you and your values?

Experiential Activity: Give each child a blank piece of construction paper and art supplies they can use to design their own values flag. Allow them to make the flag as literal or abstract as they want, as long as it represents what is meaningful to them in their lives. Then, present the flags to one another, summarizing their values.

Tier 3 — Discussion: Flags fly way up in the sky – you need to look up to see them! Most flags we will never touch or look at close up. How is this similar to values? What are the challenges of focusing on goals when they are not something we can see or touch? How do you know when you are living your valued life; what are the feelings you experience?

Experiential Activity: Give each child a long strip of paper (that will later be attached as the flag pole) and a marker. Ask them to breathe mindfully, remembering the feelings they have when they are moving toward their values. Write these feelings on the flag pole and attach it to the flag. These poles are what connect us to our values.

| Day 172 | Muddled | Committed Action |

Tier 1
Script: Have you ever tried to run through a huge puddle of mud? It's not easy, is it?! It can really slow you down when you're trying to get somewhere. That mud can be a symbol of the challenges you have and will face in being committed to your values. What do you need to do to make it through the mud?

Tier 2
Discussion: Mud can be so hard to get through, that they even make special tires for cars to drive better in it! Knowing how much of a challenge mud can be, what will you do to get through it? What is the mud in your life? Will it stop you or just slow you down?

Experiential Activity: Give each child a cup with some dirt in it. Then, on small pieces of paper, write a value, and put them in the cup. Add water to each cup and mix it all together, turning the dirt into mud. Then, using a tool of some kind (like a spoon), dig out the values. It may not be easy, but those values are still there!

Tier 3
Discussion: Sometimes you get stuck in the mud. You've done the best you can to avoid it, but there you are, standing in a puddle of mud. You have two choices: 1) Get upset you were thrown off or 2) Have some fun in the mud! Which will you choose?

Experiential Activity: Have some "fun" with the mud from T2. Give the children paintbrushes to use it as paint, or try to build sculptures with it, or even take it outside to throw at a target. Whatever you do, remind the children that life will have challenges, but it is up to them how they face those challenges.

| Day 173 | To Whom It May Concern | Present Moment |

Tier 1
Script: You have learned to practice present moment awareness, and probably have realized that being mindful isn't always easy! Sometimes it helps to reflect on your experiences to remember how and why you try to stay present in your life.

Tier 2
Discussion: What advice would you give yourself if you could go back in time to the first day of school? What have you learned this year about yourself, life, and mindfulness? Now think of yourself on the first day of school next year. What would you say to yourself then?

Experiential Activity: Ask the children to imagine themselves, at the start of next school year, walking into the school building, present and aware of the moment. Give them each paper and a pencil, and ask that they write a letter to this future present self. What would they say? Seal it in an envelope to pass along to their next teacher.

Tier 3
Discussion: You can practice mindfulness whether or not you are in school, with your class. What have been your favorite methods of engaging with the present moment? When do you know it's time to practice mindfulness?

Experiential Activity: Give each child five pieces of paper and a plastic bag. Ask them to think of five ways they could practice mindfulness at home on their own, and write one on each slip. Then, put them into the bag to take home, to keep somewhere safe in their room to use whenever they need a mindful moment.

| Day 174 | Pay It Forward | Self-as-Context |

Tier 1 — Script: You have learned to experience your self-as-context, the part of you there experiencing every moment of your life. This part of you has seen and encountered a lot in your life. This part of you holds some wisdom. How can you pay it forward, sharing what you know with someone else?

Tier 2 — Discussion: What are some things you have learned that you think other people would benefit from knowing? Perhaps they are general things, or related to specific topics like friendship or schoolwork or values. How can you take what you have experienced and use that knowledge to help someone else?

Tier 2 — Experiential Activity: Ask each child to write a letter to a new child coming to the school next year. Their goal is to both teach the child about mindfulness and acceptance and pass along the wisdom they have gathered from experiences this year, accessing their self-as-context.

Tier 3 — Discussion: Have you ever gotten Chinese food and opened a fortune cookie? What kinds of things do they say? A lot of time they provide a piece of advice for the reader. What kinds of "ACT" fortunes could you come up with?

Tier 3 — Experiential Activity: On strips of paper, ask the children to write ACT fortunes to save for the class next year. Have them fold up the strips of paper in interesting ways, and put them in a jar. Let them know that the next groups of children will pull one of their fortunes every day of the next school year until they are gone.

| Day 175 | Yearbook | All Components |

Tier 1 — Script: This year, you have learned about the ACT hexaflex; how you can engage in present moment awareness, acceptance, defusion, self-as-context, values, and committed action to help you live your own meaningful life. Take a couple minutes to reflect on these components and your feelings about them.

Tier 2 — Discussion: What is the point of a yearbook? To store all of the memories and events from a school year. If you were to make a yearbook for ACT this year, what would be included? What were your best, worst, and never will be forgotten parts of ACT this year?

Tier 2 — Experiential Activity: Give each child a piece of paper to write and/or draw his or her "best," "worst" and "never will be forgotten" ACT moments from this year. Put them together in a book, and read it together as a class. Reflect on the year, and how they will carry these lessons with them throughout their lives.

Tier 3 — Discussion: It's a yearbook tradition to sign the yearbook with something special. Why do you think that is a tradition? What is the meaning? If you were going to sum up ACT this year in one sentence, what would it be? Why?

Tier 3 — Experiential Activity: Taking the class yearbook made by the group in T2, make a copy for each child. Then, sign each other's yearbooks. Ask the children to include their one-sentence summary of the year as well as a special message to each person.

Chapter 5:
Data Collection &
Progress Monitoring Forms

AIM Point Calculator A

Name: Date: Starting Points:

Time Period	Classroom Behavior Points			ACT Behavior Points			
	Points Earned	Points Lost	Target Positive Behaviors	Points Earned	Points Lost	Challenging Behaviors	Function
	0 5 10	0 5 10		0 5 10	0 5 10		A E T S
	0 5 10	0 5 10		0 5 10	0 5 10		A E T S
	0 5 10	0 5 10		0 5 10	0 5 10		A E T S
	0 5 10	0 5 10		0 5 10	0 5 10		A E T S
	0 5 10	0 5 10		0 5 10	0 5 10		A E T S
	0 5 10	0 5 10		0 5 10	0 5 10		A E T S
	0 5 10	0 5 10		0 5 10	0 5 10		A E T S
	0 5 10	0 5 10		0 5 10	0 5 10		A E T S
	0 5 10	0 5 10		0 5 10	0 5 10		A E T S
TOTAL:	POSSIBLE =			EARNED =			

10 pts for >1 instances of appropriate/targeted positive behavior OR violations of rules/negative behavior
5 pts for 1 instance of appropriate/targeted positive behavior OR violation of rules/negative behavior
0 pts for 0 instances of appropriate/targeted positive behavior OR violations of rules/negative behavior

	Bank Balance:			ACT Reflection	
AM	Earned Points:	+	Student Ex.	Present Moment:	
	Lost Points:	-		Acceptance:	
	Sub-Total:	=		Defusion:	
	Cash Out:	-		Self-as-Context:	
	Total:	=		Committed Action:	
	Purchase Function: A E T S			Values:	
PM	Earned Points:	+	Teacher Ex.	Present Moment:	
	Lost Points:	-		Acceptance:	
	Sub-Total:	=		Defusion:	
	Cash Out:	-		Self-as-Context:	
	Total:	=		Committed Action:	
	Purchase Function: A E T S			Values:	

Notes:

End of Day Balance: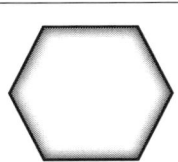

AIM Point Calculator B

Name: Date: Therapist:

Store

$ Point Range =	$$ Point Range =	$$$ Point Range =

Session Behavior | ACT Behavior

Expectations: **Target Behaviors:**

Time/Activity	Points Earned	Points Lost	Behavior	Points Earned	Points Lost	Behavior	Function:
	0 5 10	0 5 10		0 5 10	0 5 10		A E T S
	0 5 10	0 5 10		0 5 10	0 5 10		A E T S
	0 5 10	0 5 10		0 5 10	0 5 10		A E T S
	0 5 10	0 5 10		0 5 10	0 5 10		A E T S
	0 5 10	0 5 10		0 5 10	0 5 10		A E T S
TOTAL:	POSSIBLE:			EARNED:			

10 pts for >1 instances of appropriate/targeted positive behavior OR violations of rules/negative behavior
5 pts for 1 instance of appropriate/targeted positive behavior OR violation of rules/negative behavior
0 pts for 0 instances of appropriate/targeted positive behavior OR violations of rules/negative behavior

Cash Out Center

Total
- Earned Points: _____
- Lost Points: _____ −
- **Total:** _____ =

Purchases
- Low: _____
- Medium: _____
- High: _____

Purchase Function: A E T S

ACT Reflection

Examples
- Present Moment:
- Acceptance:
- Defusion:
- Self-as-Context:
- Committed Action:
- Values:

Notes:

End of Session Total: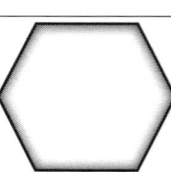

AIM Point Calculator C

Name: _____ Date: _____ Starting Points: _____

Time/ Activity	Session Behavior Points			ACT Behavior Points				
	Points Earned	Points Lost	Target Positive Behaviors	Points Earned	Points Lost	Challenging Behaviors	Function
	0 5 10	0 5 10		0 5 10	0 5 10		A E T S
	0 5 10	0 5 10		0 5 10	0 5 10		A E T S
	0 5 10	0 5 10		0 5 10	0 5 10		A E T S
	0 5 10	0 5 10		0 5 10	0 5 10		A E T S
	0 5 10	0 5 10		0 5 10	0 5 10		A E T S
	0 5 10	0 5 10		0 5 10	0 5 10		A E T S
	0 5 10	0 5 10		0 5 10	0 5 10		A E T S
	0 5 10	0 5 10		0 5 10	0 5 10		A E T S
	0 5 10	0 5 10		0 5 10	0 5 10		A E T S
TOTAL:	POSSIBLE =			EARNED =				

10 pts for >1 instances of appropriate/targeted positive behavior OR violations of rules/negative behavior
5 pts for 1 instance of appropriate/targeted positive behavior OR violation of rules/negative behavior
0 pts for 0 instances of appropriate/targeted positive behavior OR violations of rules/negative behavior

Bank Balance:

AM
- Earned Points: +
- Lost Points: −
- Sub-Total: =
- *Cash Out:* −
- **Total:** =
- Purchase Function: A E T S

PM
- Earned Points: +
- Lost Points: −
- Sub-Total: =
- *Cash Out:* −
- **Total:** =
- Purchase Function: A E T S

ACT Reflection

Student Ex.
- Present Moment:
- Acceptance:
- Defusion:
- Self-as-Context:
- Committed Action:
- Values:

Teacher Ex.
- Present Moment:
- Acceptance:
- Defusion:
- Self-as-Context:
- Committed Action:
- Values:

Notes:

End of Day Balance: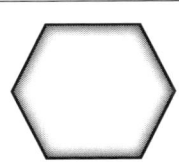

AIM Point Calculator D

Name:　　　　　　　　　　　Date:　　　　　　　　　　Therapist(s):

Classroom Behavior

Session	Points Earned	Behavior	Points Lost	Comments
1	0 10 20		0 10 20	
2	0 10 20		0 10 20	
3	0 10 20		0 10 20	
4	0 10 20		0 10 20	
5	0 10 20		0 10 20	

ACT Behavior

Targeted Positive Behavior
1)
2)
3)

Targeted Negative Behavior
1)
2)
3)

Function:
A = Attn.
E = Esc.
T = Tang.
S = Sens.

Session	Points Earned	Points Lost	Function
1	0 10 20	0 10 20	A E T S
2	0 10 20	0 10 20	A E T S
3	0 10 20	0 10 20	A E T S
4	0 10 20	0 10 20	A E T S
5	0 10 20	0 10 20	A E T S

10 pts for >1 instances of appropriate/targeted positive behavior OR violations of rules/negative behavior
5 pts for 1 instance of appropriate/targeted positive behavior OR violation of rules/negative behavior
0 pts for 0 instances of appropriate/targeted positive behavior OR violations of rules/negative behavior

Bank Balance:

Session 1
Earned Points: +
Lost Points: -
　　Sub-Total: =
Cash Out:
　　Total: =
Purchase Function: A E T S

Session 2
Earned Points: +
Lost Points: -
　　Sub-Total: =
Cash Out:
　　Total: =
Purchase Function: A E T S

Session 3
Earned Points: +
Lost Points: -
　　Sub-Total: =
Cash Out:
　　Total: =
Purchase Function: A E T S

Session 4
Earned Points: +
Lost Points: -
　　Sub-Total: =
Cash Out:
　　Total: =
Purchase Function: A E T S

Session 5
Earned Points: +
Lost Points: -
　　Sub-Total: =
Cash Out:
　　Total: =
Purchase Function: A E T S

ACT Reflection

Child Ex.
Present Moment:
Acceptance:
Defusion:
Self-as-Context:
Committed Action:
Values:

Therapist Ex.
Present Moment:
Acceptance:
Defusion:
Self-as-Context:
Committed Action:
Values:

Start　　End

AIM Point Calculator E

Name: Date: Family Member:

Store

$ Point Range =	$$ Point Range =	$$$ Point Range =

Home Behavior				ACT Behavior			
Expectations:				**Target Behaviors:**			
Time/Activity	Points Earned	Points Lost	Behavior	Points Earned	Points Lost	Behavior	
	0 5 10	0 5 10		0 5 10	0 5 10		
	0 5 10	0 5 10		0 5 10	0 5 10		
	0 5 10	0 5 10		0 5 10	0 5 10		
	0 5 10	0 5 10		0 5 10	0 5 10		
	0 5 10	0 5 10		0 5 10	0 5 10		
TOTAL:	**POSSIBLE:**			**EARNED:**			

10 pts for >1 instances of appropriate/targeted positive behavior OR violations of rules/negative behavior
5 pts for 1 instance of appropriate/targeted positive behavior OR violation of rules/negative behavior
0 pts for 0 instances of appropriate/targeted positive behavior OR violations of rules/negative behavior

Cash Out Center

Total
- Earned Points: ____
- Lost Points: ____ −
- **Total:** ____ =

Purchases
- Low: ____
- Medium: ____
- High: ____

Purchase Function: A E T S

ACT Reflection

Examples
- Present Moment:
- Acceptance:
- Defusion:
- Self-as-Context:
- Committed Action:
- Values:

Notes:

End of Day Total: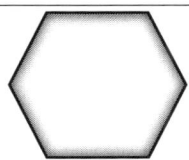

AIM Point Calculator F

Name: Date: Starting Points:

Classroom Behavior Points

Time Period	Points Earned	Points Lost	Target Positive Behaviors	Function
	0 5 10	0 5 10		A E T S
	0 5 10	0 5 10		A E T S
	0 5 10	0 5 10		A E T S
	0 5 10	0 5 10		A E T S
	0 5 10	0 5 10		A E T S
	0 5 10	0 5 10		A E T S
	0 5 10	0 5 10		A E T S
	0 5 10	0 5 10		A E T S
	0 5 10	0 5 10		A E T S
TOTAL:	POSSIBLE =		EARNED =	

10 pts for >1 instances of appropriate/targeted positive behavior OR violations of rules/negative behavior
5 pts for 1 instance of appropriate/targeted positive behavior OR violation of rules/negative behavior
0 pts for 0 instances of appropriate/targeted positive behavior OR violations of rules/negative behavior

Bank Balance:

AM
- Earned Points: +
- Lost Points: −
- Sub-Total: =
- *Cash Out:* −
- **Total:** =
- Purchase Function: A E T S

PM
- Earned Points: +
- Lost Points: −
- Sub-Total: =
- *Cash Out:* −
- **Total:** =
- Purchase Function: A E T S

My Reflection

Student Ex.
Successes:

Challenges:

Teacher Ex.
Successes:

Challenges:

Notes:

End of Day Balance:

AIM: My ACT Monitor

Name: Date:

Each day, keep a log of moments that you demonstrated flexibility by recording the component of the ACT hexaflex like a tally! Include moments of inflexibility by recording an X.

Tally Key:

P	A	D	S	V	C	X
Present Moment	Acceptance	Defusion	Self-as-Context	Values	Committed Action	Inflexibility

My ACT Monitor

Monday	
Tuesday	
Wednesday	
Thursday	
Friday	

Totals:

Present Moment	Acceptance	Defusion	Self-as-Context	Values	Committed Action	Inflexibility

Last Week's Total FLEXIBLE Moments:

This Week's Total FLEXIBLE Moment:

AIM ABC Record Log   Name:

ID #: Date: Time: Setting: Initials:	**Antecedent:** ☐ Present task ☐ Asked to wait ☐ End activity ☐ Activity Denied ☐ Item Denied ☐ Transition ☐ Alone ☐ Item Removed ☐ Loud setting ☐ Given attention ☐ Other:	**Behavior:** ☐ Refusal ☐ Physical aggression ☐ Verbal aggression ☐ Self-Injury ☐ Elopement ☐ Disruption ☐ Other:	**Consequence:** ☐ Verbal redirect ☐ Physical prompt ☐ Ignored ☐ Continue task ☐ Verbal reprimand ☐ Removed from activity/location ☐ Alternative task ☐ Time out ☐ Other:	**Duration:** ☐ <1 m ☐ 1-5 m ☐ 5-15 m ☐ 15-30 m ☐ .5-1 h ☐ 1-2 h ☐ 2+ h **Intensity:** ☐ Low ☐ Medium ☐ High	**Possible Function:** ☐ Attention ☐ Escape ☐ Tangible ☐ Sensory ☐ Unclear **Possible Inflexibility:** ☐ Lack of contact with moment ☐ Experiential avoidance ☐ Fusion ☐ View self-as-content ☐ Unclear values ☐ Inaction/Impulsive action ☐ Unclear

Notes:

| ID #:
Date:
Time:
Setting:
Initials: | **Antecedent:**
☐ Present task
☐ Asked to wait
☐ End activity
☐ Activity Denied
☐ Item Denied
☐ Transition
☐ Alone
☐ Item Removed
☐ Loud setting
☐ Given attention

☐ Other: | **Behavior:**
☐ Refusal
☐ Physical aggression
☐ Verbal aggression
☐ Self-Injury
☐ Elopement
☐ Disruption

☐ Other: | **Consequence:**
☐ Verbal redirect
☐ Physical prompt
☐ Ignored
☐ Continue task
☐ Verbal reprimand
☐ Removed from activity/location
☐ Alternative task
☐ Time out

☐ Other: | **Duration:**
☐ <1 m
☐ 1-5 m
☐ 5-15 m
☐ 15-30 m
☐ .5-1 h
☐ 1-2 h
☐ 2+ h

Intensity:
☐ Low
☐ Medium
☐ High | **Possible Function:**
☐ Attention ☐ Escape
☐ Tangible ☐ Sensory
☐ Unclear

Possible Inflexibility:
☐ Lack of contact with moment
☐ Experiential avoidance
☐ Fusion
☐ View self-as-content
☐ Unclear values
☐ Inaction/Impulsive action
☐ Unclear |

Notes:

| ID #:
Date:
Time:
Setting:
Initials: | **Antecedent:**
☐ Present task
☐ Asked to wait
☐ End activity
☐ Activity Denied
☐ Item Denied
☐ Transition
☐ Alone
☐ Item Removed
☐ Loud setting
☐ Given attention

☐ Other: | **Behavior:**
☐ Refusal
☐ Physical aggression
☐ Verbal aggression
☐ Self-Injury
☐ Elopement
☐ Disruption

☐ Other: | **Consequence:**
☐ Verbal redirect
☐ Physical prompt
☐ Ignored
☐ Continue task
☐ Verbal reprimand
☐ Removed from activity/location
☐ Alternative task
☐ Time out

☐ Other: | **Duration:**
☐ <1 m
☐ 1-5 m
☐ 5-15 m
☐ 15-30 m
☐ .5-1 h
☐ 1-2 h
☐ 2+ h

Intensity:
☐ Low
☐ Medium
☐ High | **Possible Function:**
☐ Attention ☐ Escape
☐ Tangible ☐ Sensory
☐ Unclear

Possible Inflexibility:
☐ Lack of contact with moment
☐ Experiential avoidance
☐ Fusion
☐ View self-as-content
☐ Unclear values
☐ Inaction/Impulsive action
☐ Unclear |

Notes:

| ID #:
Date:
Time:
Setting:
Initials: | **Antecedent:**
☐ Present task
☐ Asked to wait
☐ End activity
☐ Activity Denied
☐ Item Denied
☐ Transition
☐ Alone
☐ Item Removed
☐ Loud setting
☐ Given attention

☐ Other: | **Behavior:**
☐ Refusal
☐ Physical aggression
☐ Verbal aggression
☐ Self-Injury
☐ Elopement
☐ Disruption

☐ Other: | **Consequence:**
☐ Verbal redirect
☐ Physical prompt
☐ Ignored
☐ Continue task
☐ Verbal reprimand
☐ Removed from activity/location
☐ Alternative task
☐ Time out

☐ Other: | **Duration:**
☐ <1 m
☐ 1-5 m
☐ 5-15 m
☐ 15-30 m
☐ .5-1 h
☐ 1-2 h
☐ 2+ h

Intensity:
☐ Low
☐ Medium
☐ High | **Possible Function:**
☐ Attention ☐ Escape
☐ Tangible ☐ Sensory
☐ Unclear

Possible Inflexibility:
☐ Lack of contact with moment
☐ Experiential avoidance
☐ Fusion
☐ View self-as-content
☐ Unclear values
☐ Inaction/Impulsive action
☐ Unclear |

Notes:

AIM ACT Record Log   Name:

ID #:	Awareness:	Communicate:	Treat:
Date: Time: Setting: Initials:	☐ Not in the current moment ☐ Fused to thoughts ☐ Chasing non-values ☐ Losing commitment ☐ Wrong self ☐ Difficulty with acceptance	☐ Let's get back in the present moment. ☐ It's ok that did not work out. We need to accept things, even stuff we don't like. ☐ Is this the real you that is here right now? ☐ Did this get your closer to your values? ☐ Tell me what your values are today. ☐ Stop, pause, and come back to the present. ☐ Let's commit to doing better moving forward. ☐ I like the real you I see right now.	☐ Acknowledge current environment ☐ Stepping back from current verbalizations ☐ Reminding of stated values ☐ Encouraging commitment ☐ Refocus to self-as context ☐ Acceptance of the entire event

Notes:

ID #:	Awareness:	Communicate:	Treat:
Date: Time: Setting: Initials:	☐ Not in the current moment ☐ Fused to thoughts ☐ Chasing non-values ☐ Losing commitment ☐ Wrong self ☐ Difficulty with acceptance	☐ Let's get back in the present moment. ☐ It's ok that did not work out. We need to accept things, even stuff we don't like. ☐ Is this the real you that is here right now? ☐ Did this get your closer to your values? ☐ Tell me what your values are today. ☐ Stop, pause, and come back to the present. ☐ Let's commit to doing better moving forward. ☐ I like the real you I see right now.	☐ Acknowledge current environment ☐ Stepping back from current verbalizations ☐ Reminding of stated values ☐ Encouraging commitment ☐ Refocus to self-as context ☐ Acceptance of the entire event

Notes:

ID #:	Awareness:	Communicate:	Treat:
Date: Time: Setting: Initials:	☐ Not in the current moment ☐ Fused to thoughts ☐ Chasing non-values ☐ Losing commitment ☐ Wrong self ☐ Difficulty with acceptance	☐ Let's get back in the present moment. ☐ It's ok that did not work out. We need to accept things, even stuff we don't like. ☐ Is this the real you that is here right now? ☐ Did this get your closer to your values? ☐ Tell me what your values are today. ☐ Stop, pause, and come back to the present. ☐ Let's commit to doing better moving forward. ☐ I like the real you I see right now.	☐ Acknowledge current environment ☐ Stepping back from current verbalizations ☐ Reminding of stated values ☐ Encouraging commitment ☐ Refocus to self-as context ☐ Acceptance of the entire event

Notes:

ID #:	Awareness:	Communicate:	Treat:
Date: Time: Setting: Initials:	☐ Not in the current moment ☐ Fused to thoughts ☐ Chasing non-values ☐ Losing commitment ☐ Wrong self ☐ Difficulty with acceptance	☐ Let's get back in the present moment. ☐ It's ok that did not work out. We need to accept things, even stuff we don't like. ☐ Is this the real you that is here right now? ☐ Did this get your closer to your values? ☐ Tell me what your values are today. ☐ Stop, pause, and come back to the present. ☐ Let's commit to doing better moving forward. ☐ I like the real you I see right now.	☐ Acknowledge current environment ☐ Stepping back from current verbalizations ☐ Reminding of stated values ☐ Encouraging commitment ☐ Refocus to self-as context ☐ Acceptance of the entire event

Notes:

AIM: ACT Phrases to Go

Acceptance:

(P) Accepting that you had to do work now was awesome. I know it can be hard to do sometimes.

(P) I see you are accepting that's time for work.

(P) I see you accepted that free time is over.

(P) I know you want me to help you now, so thanks for accepting I will be there soon.

(N) You have to accept that everything is not going to be perfect. And that's ok.

(N) I know you really wanted X to happen. Accepting we have to do work is part of the day.

(N) Your points are not high enough to buy X. Let's buy something else and accept it's a bummer. Let's get ready for next time.

Defusion:

(P) Letting go of that thought was rough to do. Good job remembering what's really important.

(P) You let go of your disappointment and did not lose points. Way to go!

(P) Great job not responding to those comments/thoughts. Good defusion!

(N) You don't need to be fused to that thought now. We have other things to do.

(N) Are you letting those thoughts control you? Why don't you defuse them?

(N) Cut the fuse off this mess, and let's get back to earning points.

Self-as-Context:

(P) I like how are being the real (STUDENT NAME) right now!

(P) I noticed that you seem ok right now being who you really are.

(P) I like how you put that mess in the back of your mind for now, and are focused on right now.

(N) Are you acting like the real you right now or is this behavior just the thoughts you have?

(N) Are these thoughts just what other people say, or is this TRUE?

(N) Are these thoughts descriptions or evaluations?

(N) Where is the real (STUDENT NAME) right now?

Values:

(P) I really like the way you are doing X. You must be working towards getting stuff you value from the store later today.

(P) You are letting me know you value (learning/friendship/graduation/etc.) by doing (work/participating, etc.).

(P) You are getting really close to getting your X. Keep chasing those values.

(N) (Remember) what you are working for?

(N) Do you value buying (bad behavior point removal), or buying (stuff in the store)?

(N) You told me earlier that you wanted to buy X. Have you changed your values now that you are doing (bad behavior) instead?

Present Moment:

(P) I really like how you are staying in the present now and not letting other stuff bug you.

(P) I like how you are focusing on X. You are in the present moment! Way to go.

(P) Way to block out those distractions right now. Hold on to the present.

(N) Worrying about the future or what you think is happening is not part of the present.

(N) That's all fine I guess, but I am staying in the present. Are you?

(N) Are you right here right now, or have you drifted into the past to worry about x?

Committed Action:

(P) You are doing a great job staying committed to your values. It's hard sometimes but you are keeping on track.

(P) You are not letting of anything get in your way of completing your work today. Awesome! Stay committed!

(P) I love how you came back and did X after you fell off the path towards your values.

(N) I think you wanted to buy X later at cash out. Are you moving towards or away from the thing you value? Let's get back on track!

(N) Doing X is not being committed to your values. Those are still your values, right?

(N) Can you jump over this mess and stay committed to your value?

AIM Point System Matrix

Use this grid to develop rules for point exchange and cash outs.

Age	Exchange	Points	Positives	Negatives

Use this grid to ensure that functional reinforcers are available at various price points.

Function	Low Cost	Medium Cost	High Cost
Attention			
Escape			
Tangible			
Sensory			
Notes:			

AIM Point Loss Matrix

Use this grid to develop rules for loss of points contingent on certain behaviors.

Response	Cost

Notes:

AIM Weekly Point Exchange Log (5 Days)

Name: Dates:

Day	Starting Balance	Earned Points	Possible Points	Items Purchased	Purchase Price	Primary Function
MONDAY						A E T S
TUESDAY						A E T S
WEDNESDAY						A E T S
THURSDAY						A E T S
FRIDAY						A E T S
Weekly Total:				Weekly Points Percentage:		

AIM Weekly Point Exchange Log (7 Days)

Name: Dates:

Day	Starting Balance	Earned Points	Possible Points	Items Purchased	Purchase Price	Primary Function
MONDAY						A E T S
TUESDAY						A E T S
WEDNESDAY						A E T S
THURSDAY						A E T S
FRIDAY						A E T S
SATURDAY						A E T S
SUNDAY						A E T S
Weekly Total:				Weekly Points Percentage:		

AIM Program Design Checklist

Component	✓	Notes
Daily ACT Lessons		
Schedule		
# of Lessons/Week		
Tier Divisions Outlined		
Implementers Selected		
Groups Created (if needed)		
ACT Communication Planned		
Point System & Reinforcement		
Point Calculator Selected		
Time Intervals Selected		
Implementers Selected		
Self-Management Considered		
Reinforcer Store Organized		
Frequency of Cash Outs Determined		
Price Points Outlined		
Reinforcers Selected		
Reinforcer Menu Created		
Variability Established (ie Sales)		
Response Cost Outlined		
Bank Management Planned		
Physical Space		
Points Posted		
Menu / Store Info Posted		
Hexaflex Posted		
Lessons Posted		
Values/Actions Posted		

Additional Notes:

AIM: ACT Evaluator (5 Day)

Individual Name: Week of:

Day of Week	Awareness Individual was aware of opportunities to deliver ACT.	Communicate Verbal responses to child problem behavior were consistent with the ACT model.	Treat ACT language was delivered to increase probability of psychological flexibility in the future.
Monday	1 2 3 4 5	1 2 3 4 5	1 2 3 4 5
Tuesday	1 2 3 4 5	1 2 3 4 5	1 2 3 4 5
Wednesday	1 2 3 4 5	1 2 3 4 5	1 2 3 4 5
Thursday	1 2 3 4 5	1 2 3 4 5	1 2 3 4 5
Friday	1 2 3 4 5	1 2 3 4 5	1 2 3 4 5

Total Score: _____ / _____ (max) = _____ %   *Scale: 1 = never..........5 = always*

Exceptional Moment of the Week:	
Teachable Moment of the Week:	

AIM: ACT Evaluator (7 Day)

Individual Name: Week of:

Day of Week	Awareness Individual was aware of opportunities to deliver ACT.	Communicate Verbal responses to child problem behavior were consistent with the ACT model.	Treat ACT language was delivered to increase probability of psychological flexibility in the future.
Monday	1　2　3　4　5	1　2　3　4　5	1　2　3　4　5
Tuesday	1　2　3　4　5	1　2　3　4　5	1　2　3　4　5
Wednesday	1　2　3　4　5	1　2　3　4　5	1　2　3　4　5
Thursday	1　2　3　4　5	1　2　3　4　5	1　2　3　4　5
Friday	1　2　3　4　5	1　2　3　4　5	1　2　3　4　5
Saturday	1　2　3　4　5	1　2　3　4　5	1　2　3　4　5
Sunday	1　2　3　4　5	1　2　3　4　5	1　2　3　4　5

Total Score: _____ / _____ (max) = _____ %   *Scale: 1 = never……….5 = always*

Exceptional Moment of the Week:

Teachable Moment of the Week:

AIM: ACT Treatment Fidelity Checklist

Location: _____ Date of Evaluation: _____

Implementer: _____ Observer: _____

Treatment Component	Absent	Needs Improvement	Acceptable	Not Observed	Comments
1. Visible hexaflex in the room					
2. Completed ACT experiential activities displayed in room					
3. Completion of ACT lesson each day					
4. Earned points displayed in room					
5. Points delivered on schedule					
6. Variety of items in store across behavior functions					
7. Store items for sale across range of values					
8. Cashing out occurs at pre-set intervals					
9. Using ACT during crisis/problem behavior episodes					
10. Adult use of ACT language					
11. Organization of ACT materials					
12. Data management system updated regularly					

Overall Appraisal Rating (circle one):   Needs Improvement   Average   Above Average   Excellent

Definitions of items are as follows:

1. Visible hexaflex in room
   - *Absent*: No hexaflex
   - *Needs Improvement*: Hexaflex without text/component labels, difficult to see
   - *Acceptable*: Hexaflex is in clear site, appropriate component labels in visible/readable text
2. Completed ACT experiential activities displayed in room
   - *Absent*: No hexaflex
   - *Needs Improvement*: Some lessons displayed; no current lessons displayed,; displayed but not visible
   - *Acceptable*: Updated lessons displayed in visible areas
3. Completion of ACT lesson each day
   - *Absent*: No ACT lesson completed at all
   - *Needs Improvement*: ACT lessons completed less than days per week
   - *Acceptable*: ACT lessons completed 5 days per week
4. Earned points displayed in room
   - *Absent*: No points displayed in classroom
   - *Needs Improvement*: Displayed points are not visible; interval differences in points are displayed
   - *Acceptable*: Points displayed in a visible part of room
5. Points delivered on schedule
   - *Absent*: No points delivered on schedule
   - *Needs Improvement*: Points delivered, but not on schedule
   - *Acceptable*: Points delivered on schedule
6. Variety of items in store across behavior functions
   - *Absent*: No items presented across functions
   - *Needs Improvement*: Items provided across some functions; no student-specific items offered
   - *Acceptable*: Items provided across four common functions
7. Store items for sale across range of values
   - *Absent*: Items have same values
   - *Needs Improvement*: 25%+ of items have similar values
   - *Acceptable*: <10% of items have similar values
8. Cashing out occurs at pre-set intervals
   - *Absent*: No cash out at set intervals in place
   - *Needs Improvement*: Variable cash out intervals in place
   - *Acceptable*: Cash out intervals in place with 90% adherence to schedule
9. Using ACT during crisis/behavior episodes
   - *Absent*: No ACT language emitted during behavior event
   - *Needs Improvement*: Minimal or low rates of ACT language emitted during behavior event; inconsistent use of ACT language
   - *Acceptable*: Consistent and frequent use of ACT language during behavior event
10. Adult use of ACT language
    - *Absent*: No use of ACT language
    - *Needs Improvement*: Inconsistent use of ACT language
    - *Acceptable*: Consistent use of ACT language
11. Organization of ACT materials
    - *Absent*: No ACT materials
    - *Needs Improvement*: Unorganized ACT materials; no student worksheets present
    - *Acceptable*: Organized ACT materials; student worksheets present
12. Data management system updated regularly
    - *Absent*: Data system is not current
    - *Needs Improvement*: <85% of data current to-date
    - *Acceptable*: 85%+ of data current to-date

AIM: ACT Quantitative Analysis Scale (AQAS)

Name: _____   Date: _____

Use the rubric below to rate the individual's responses to ACT lesson experiential activities, both written and verbal. Sum the scores for precision, scope, and depth to obtain a total score.

Score	Precision	Scope	Depth
0	Not applicable/no answer	Not applicable/no answer	Not applicable/no answer
1	Answer is broad and generic, could apply in many settings, not just the current setting/question	Answer applies to the current activity/discussion ONLY	Gave minimal details/elaborations OR gave details/elaborations that did not satisfy requirements of current activity
2	Answer is logically sound and meets requirement of the activity, but is broad	Applies to the current activity; with the help of researcher/therapist can be elaborated to fit other scenarios	Gave enough detail/elaboration for the researcher to understand, but not enough to fully complete the activity
3	Answer is detailed and concise, meets requirement of activity, and fully answers the question	Response fulfills requirement of the current activity and translates easily into novel areas which are related to the original prompt/question	Gave elaboration/details which were fully understood by the researcher and fulfilled the requirements of the activity
Sub-scores:			
Total Score:			

Developed by Kelsey Kryszak, MS, BCBA, Jordan Belisle, MS, BCBA, and Dr. Mark R. Dixon, BCBA-D (2017)

AIM Weekly ACT Report

Name: Date:

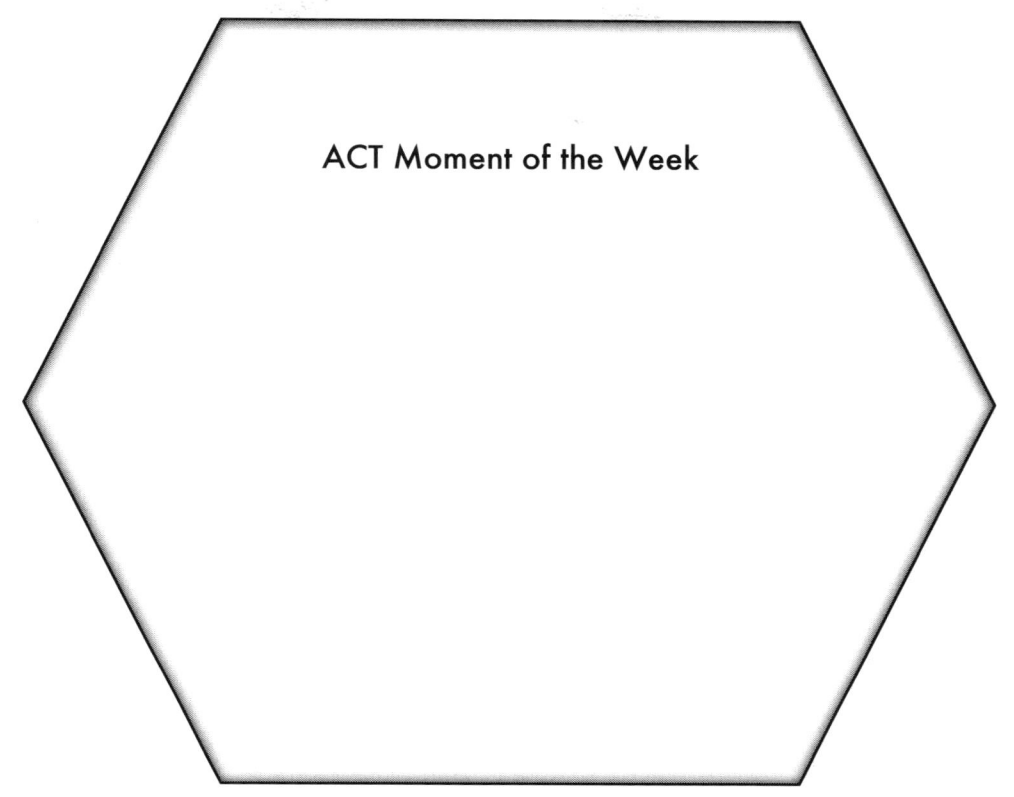

Component	Child Example	Adult Example
Present Moment		
Acceptance		
Defusion		
Self-as-Context		
Committed Action		
Values		

Page left blank

CPFQ Children's Psychological Flexibility Questionnaire: CHILD REPORT

Name: _____ **Date:** _____ **Assessor:** _____ **Modality:** ☐ Written ☐ Oral

Directions: Read or listen to the following questions. For each one, say how much you feel that way by choosing a circle.

Item	Question	NEVER	A LITTLE BIT	SOME-TIMES	A LOT	ALL THE TIME
1	I always notice things around me and what people say.	0	1	2	3	4
2	If I think something, that doesn't mean it's true.	0	1	2	3	4
3	There are things that I really care about.	0	1	2	3	4
4	If I do something bad, then I am a bad person.	0	1	2	3	4
5	I notice when my body feels different.	0	1	2	3	4
6	When I mess up, I get mad at myself.	0	1	2	3	4
7	Nothing matters that much to me.	0	1	2	3	4
8	If I cry it means that I'm wrong or bad.	0	1	2	3	4
9	It's OK to be scared.	0	1	2	3	4
10	I notice my thoughts and feelings, but that is not me.	0	1	2	3	4
11	I miss seeing stuff happen or hearing what people say.	0	1	2	3	4
12	My thoughts don't make me do what I do.	0	1	2	3	4
13	Everything I think and feel must be real.	0	1	2	3	4
14	It's OK to feel mad.	0	1	2	3	4
15	I know what I want to work for today.	0	1	2	3	4
16	If I lose I try again right away to do better.	0	1	2	3	4
17	I give up when things are too hard.	0	1	2	3	4
18	I worry a lot about stuff I did or need to do.	0	1	2	3	4
19	If I get angry, it means I messed up.	0	1	2	3	4
20	My thoughts and feelings tell me what to do.	0	1	2	3	4
21	I am what other people say about me.	0	1	2	3	4
22	If I did something wrong, that doesn't make me bad.	0	1	2	3	4
23	Grown-ups tell me what is important to me.	0	1	2	3	4
24	I try really hard every day.	0	1	2	3	4

© 2017 Mark R. Dixon, PhD, BCBA-D & Dana Paliliunas, MS, BCBA

CPFQ Children's Psychological Flexibility Questionnaire: Child's Score Report

Name: **Date:**   **Assessor:**   **Modality:** ☐ Written ☐ Oral

Directions: Record the child's scores for each item next to the corresponding item number in the tables below. Items are grouped by ACT core process. Items in grey boxes are to be reverse scored using the metric below. Sum the items within each category to obtain the Core Process Subtotal. Sum all items to obtain a Psychological Flexibility Total Score. Higher scores indicate greater psychological flexibility, while lower scores suggest greater inflexibility.

Reverse Scoring Metric: 0 = 4   1 = 3   2 = 2   3 = 1   4 = 0

[CHILD'S SELECTION] = [SCORE RECORDED]

PRESENT MOMENT		SELF-AS-CONTEXT	
1		4	
5		10	
11		21	
18		22	
ACCEPTANCE		**VALUES**	
8		3	
9		7	
14		15	
19		23	
DEFUSION		**COMMITTED ACTION**	
2		6	
12		16	
13		17	
20		24	

CORE PROCESS SUBTOTALS:	
PRESENT MOMENT	
ACCEPTANCE	
DEFUSION	
SELF-AS-CONTEXT	
VALUES	
COMMITTED ACTION	

PSYCHOLOGICAL FLEXIBILITY TOTAL SCORE:

NOTES:

© 2017 Mark R. Dixon, PhD, BCBA-D & Dana Paliliunas, MS, BCBA

CPFQ VISUAL SCALE

When reading the questions aloud to the child, present the visual scale to aid his/her responding.

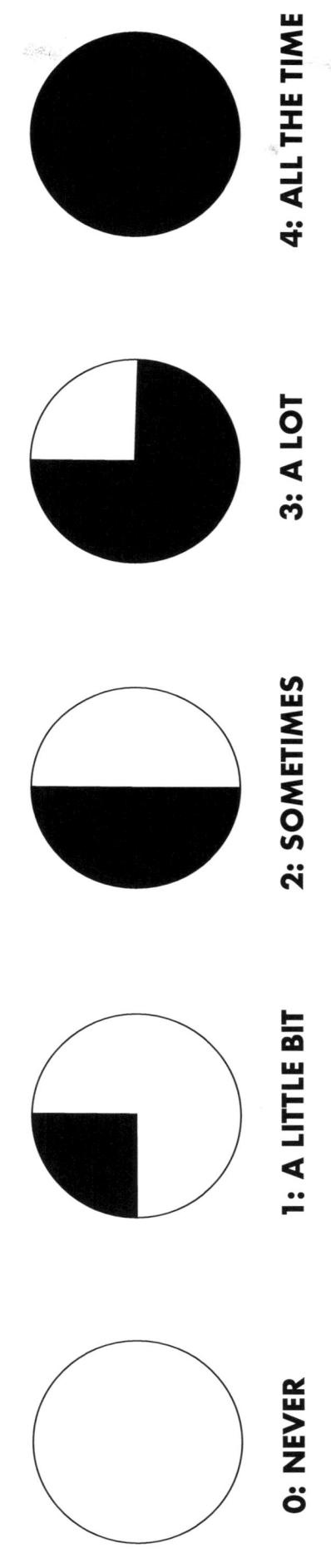

© 2017 Mark R. Dixon, PhD, BCBA-D & Dana Paliliunas, MS, BCBA

Page left blank

CPFQ Children's Psychological Flexibility Questionnaire: CAREGIVER REPORT

Name: **Date:**   **Assessor:**   **Relationship:** ☐ Family ☐ Provider

Directions: Read the follow statements. For each, indicate how frequently the child exhibits these behaviors using the following scale:

0 = *Never*;   1 = *Rarely*;   2 = *Sometimes*;   3 = *Often*;   4 = *Always*

Item	Question	NEVER	RARELY	SOMETIMES	OFTEN	ALWAYS
1	The child is aware of and listening to what is happening around them.	0	1	2	3	4
2	The child does not tend to believe the content of thoughts is literally true.	0	1	2	3	4
3	The child reports having clearly identified values (i.e. family, athletics, toys, school, etc.)	0	1	2	3	4
4	The child tends to define him or herself as "bad" when they engage in inappropriate behavior.	0	1	2	3	4
5	The child reports changes in body feeling at appropriate times (change of temperature, pressure placed).	0	1	2	3	4
6	When the child makes a mistake, they exhibit anger and blame him or herself for the event.	0	1	2	3	4
7	The child does not appear to have items, events, people, or activities that are important to them.	0	1	2	3	4
8	When the child cries or becomes upset, they appear concerned with what others think about them.	0	1	2	3	4
9	When the child gets scared, they appear to understand that it is an emotion everyone experiences.	0	1	2	3	4
10	The child uses phrases like "I am lonely, upset, etc." but does not believe that is who they are.	0	1	2	3	4
11	The child appears not to notice events in the environment or when they are being spoken to.	0	1	2	3	4
12	The child appears to understand that their behavior is not controlled by their thoughts and emotions.	0	1	2	3	4
13	The child reports that their thoughts and feelings are literally true, despite contrary evidence.	0	1	2	3	4
14	When the child gets mad, it appears that he or she accepts that emotions without attachment to it.	0	1	2	3	4
15	The child is able to identify specific items or events that are motivating to him/her in the moment.	0	1	2	3	4
16	When the child makes an error or loses, he or she tries again right away.	0	1	2	3	4
17	When a situation is challenging, the child appears to give up or stop trying quickly.	0	1	2	3	4
18	The child reports worrying about things that have already happened or that may occur in the future.	0	1	2	3	4
19	When the child exhibits anger, he or she reports having "messed up" or being at fault.	0	1	2	3	4
20	The child tends to be under the power of his / her thoughts and unable to control them.	0	1	2	3	4
21	The child tends to define him/herself based on what others say (i.e. "I am dumb," "I am ugly," etc.).	0	1	2	3	4
22	When the child does something wrong, he or she acknowledges that it is normal to make mistakes.	0	1	2	3	4
23	The child appears to rely on adults to tell him/her what is important or of value in their life.	0	1	2	3	4
24	The child appears to put forth his/her best effort to behave each day.	0	1	2	3	4

© 2017 Mark R. Dixon, PhD, BCBA-D & Dana Paliliunas, MS, BCBA

CPFQ Children's Psychological Flexibility Questionnaire: Caregiver's Score Report

Name: **Date:**   **Assessor:**   **Relationship:** ☐ Family ☐ Provider

Directions: Record the responders' scores for each item next to the corresponding item number in the tables below. Items are grouped by ACT core process. Items in grey boxes are to be reverse scored using the metric below. Sum the items within each category to obtain the Core Process Subtotal. Sum all items to obtain a Psychological Flexibility Total Score. Higher scores indicate greater psychological flexibility, while lower scores suggest greater inflexibility.

Reverse Scoring Metric:	0 = 4	1 = 3	2 = 2	3 = 1	4 = 0

[RESPONDER'S SELECTION] = [SCORE RECORDED]

PRESENT MOMENT		SELF-AS-CONTEXT		CORE PROCESS SUBTOTALS:	
1		4		PRESENT MOMENT	
5		10		ACCEPTANCE	
11		21		DEFUSION	
18		22		SELF-AS-CONTEXT	
ACCEPTANCE		VALUES		VALUES	
8		3		COMMITTED ACTION	
9		7			
14		15		PSYCHOLOGICAL FLEXIBILITY TOTAL SCORE:	
19		23			
DEFUSION		COMMITTED ACTION		NOTES:	
2		6			
12		16			
13		17			
20		24			

Chapter 6:
ACT Worksheets

D1T2: Past, Future, NOW

PAST

FUTURE

NOW

D6T2: Life Chameleon

D6T3: Hiding the Real Me

How I Hide Myself	The Real Me

D12T3: Chaotic Mind

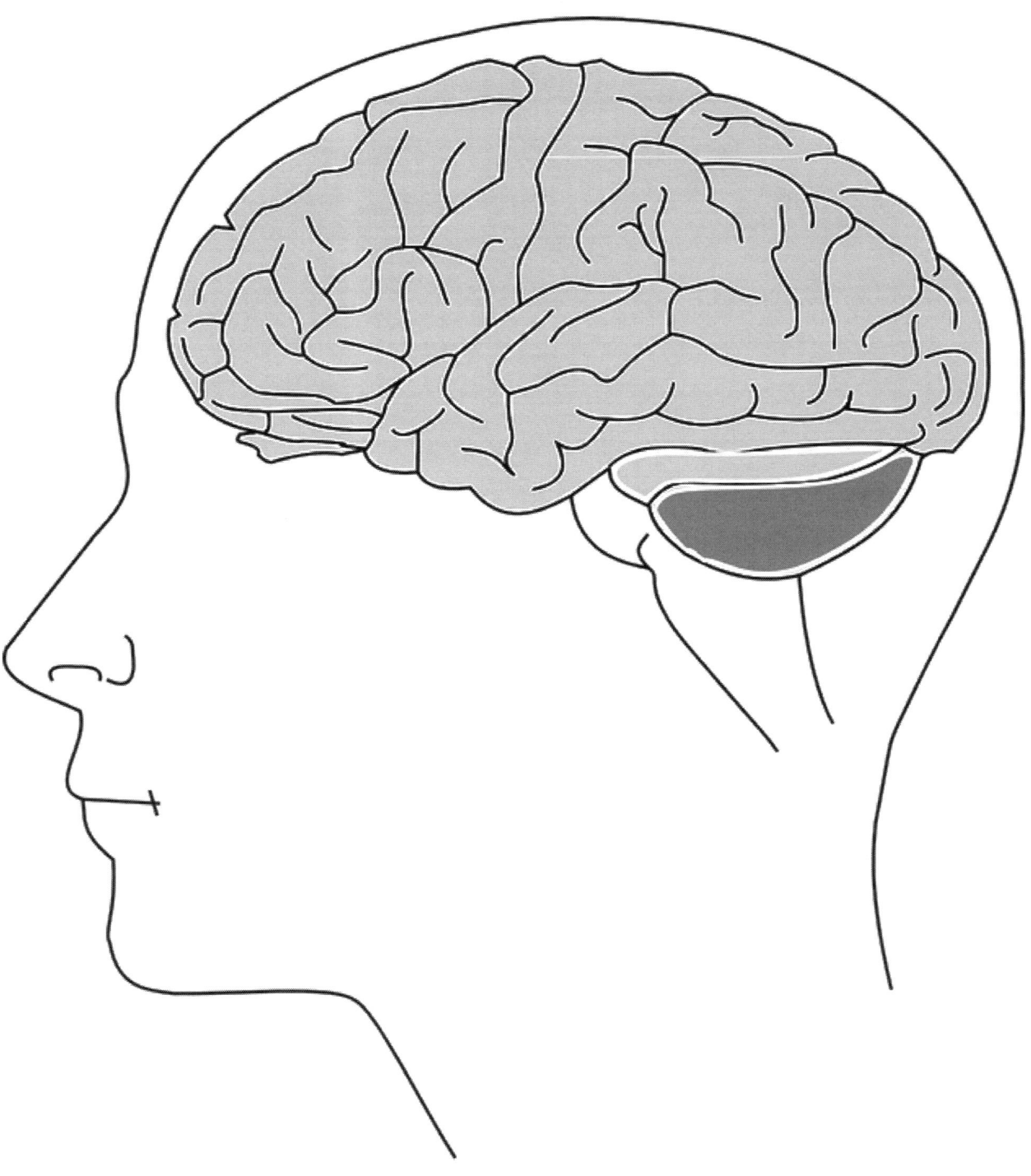

D15T2: Values List

Example Values List:

Being Athletic
Gratitude
Understanding
Being Compassionate
Trusting
Companionship
Truthfulness
Creativity
Learning
Feeling Free
Independence
Fairness
Relaxation
Experiencing Adventure
Friendship
Family
Being Wealthy
Achievement in School
Feeling Peaceful
Courage
Love
Being Genuine
Being Determined
Having Fun

D15T3: Prioritization Pyramid

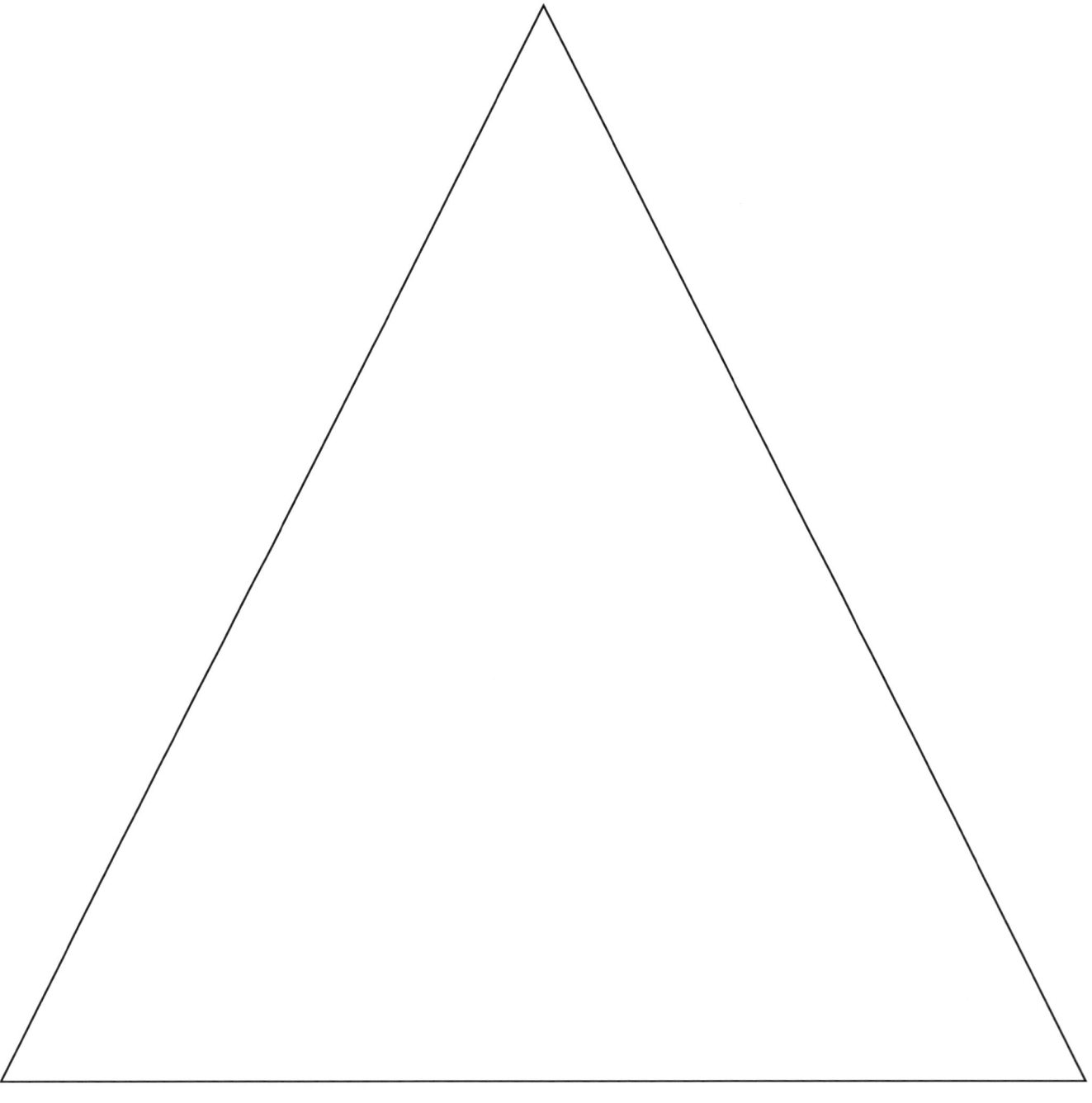

D17T2: Mad Lib

My name is _____.

I am the world's best _____.

Whenever I meet anyone new, they always tell me they think I'm _____.

I disagree, there's no way I'm _____, I'm ALWAYS, _____!

On the other hand, I am the world's worst _____.

Every single time I _____, I mess it up!"

D19T2/3: Lotus Model

D21T2/3: Values List

Example Values List:

Being Athletic
Gratitude
Understanding
Being Compassionate
Trusting
Companionship
Truthfulness
Creativity
Learning
Feeling Free
Independence
Fairness
Relaxation
Experiencing Adventure
Friendship
Family
Being Wealthy
Achievement in School
Feeling Peaceful
Courage
Love
Being Genuine
Being Determined
Having Fun

D22T2: Storyboard

D24T3: Connections

In the boxes, write two words that you have related together in a way that is troublesome for you. Along the web line, write how they are connected in your mind.

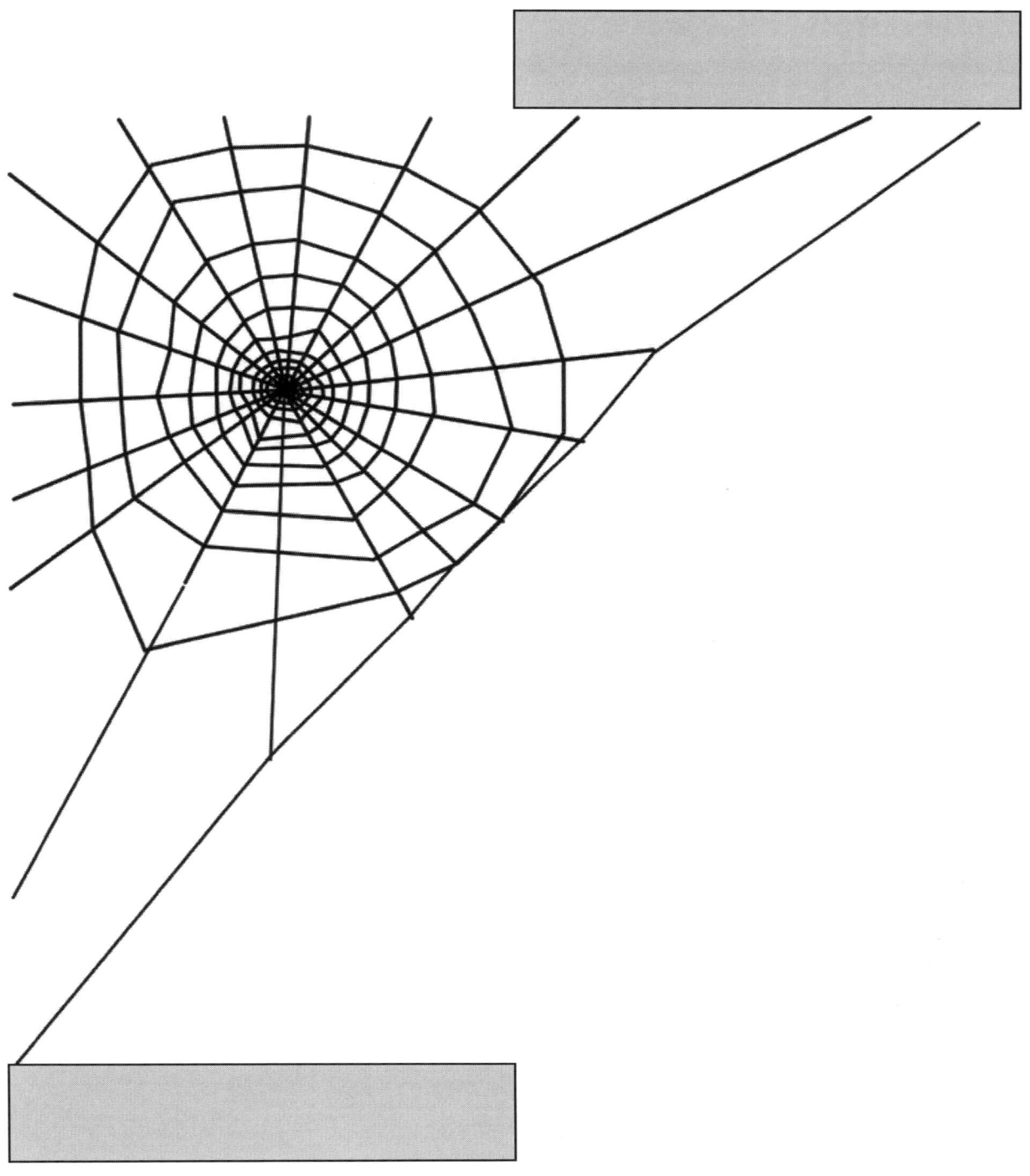

D26T3: Values Clouds

Foggy Day Cloud

Clear Day Cloud

D27T3: One Committed Action Plan

My Value:

☐	Monday	
☐	Tuesday	
☐	Wednesday	
☐	Thursday	
☐	Friday	
☐	Saturday	
☐	Sunday	

D29T2: Stupid Transformed

T30T3: Mindfulness Glasses

Event:

<u>**Blurry Vision**</u>

<u>**Mindfulness Specs**</u>

D31T3: What Willingness Looks Like

WILLING

UNWILLING

D33T2: Thought Circles

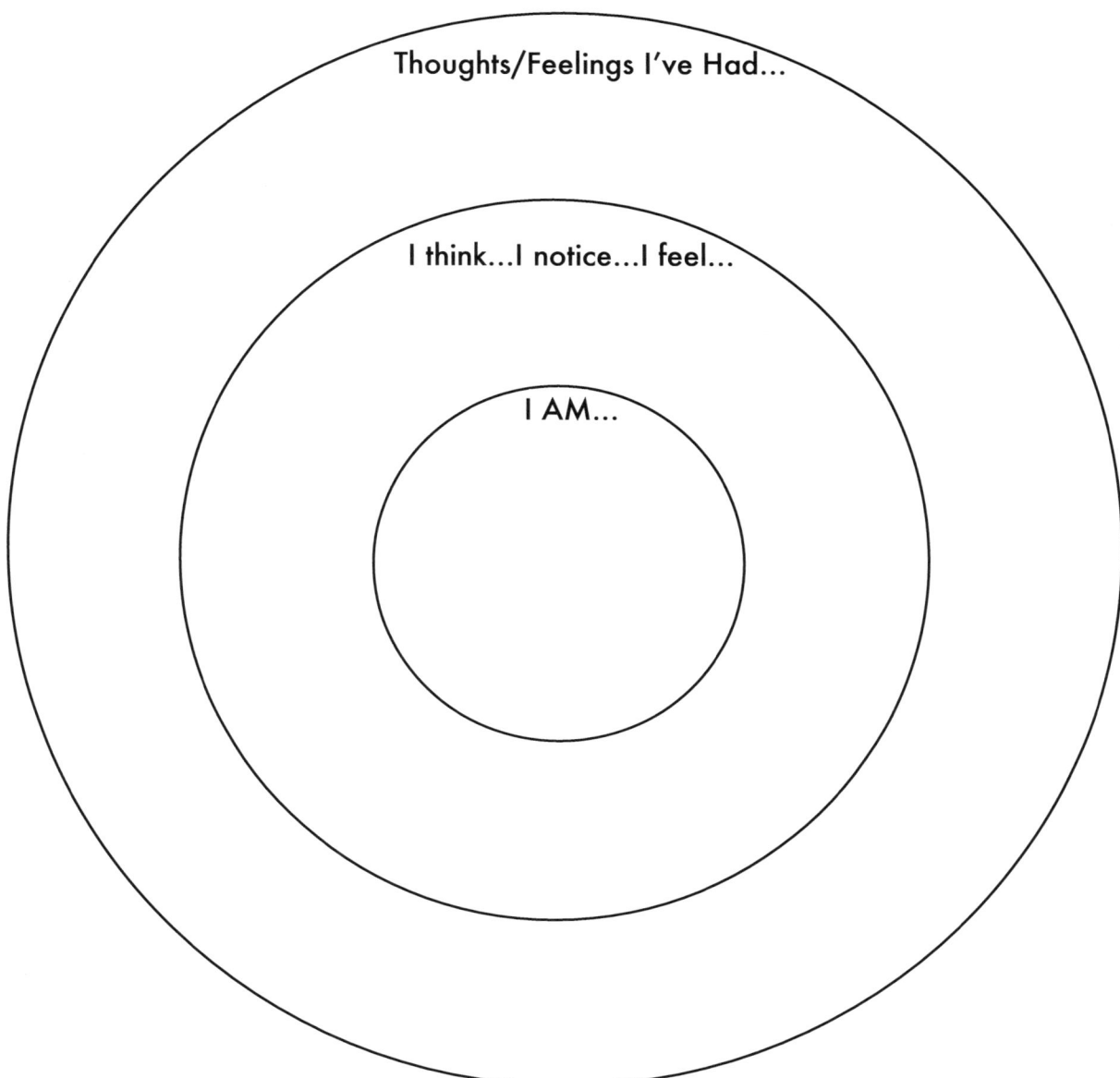

D35T3: Thought Billboard

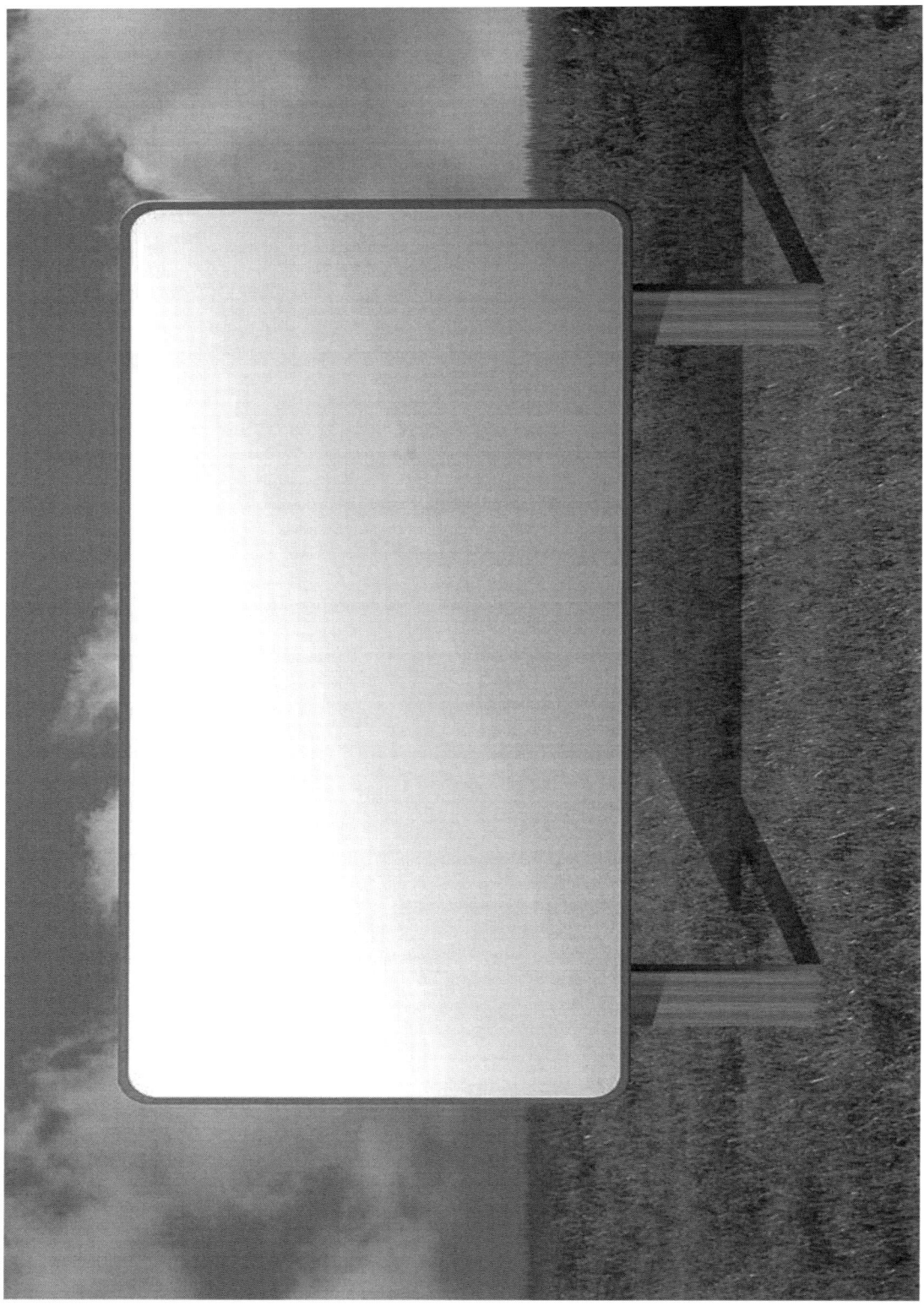

D37T3: Acceptance Toolbox

D38T3: Web of Relations

D39T3: Opposites

SMART	DUMB
FUNNY	SERIOUS
POLITE	RUDE
KIND	MEAN

D40T2: Heroes and Villains

Villain Values:

Hero Values:

D41T3: Accepting vs. Giving Up

ACCEPTING

GIVING UP

D42T2/3: Values Triangle

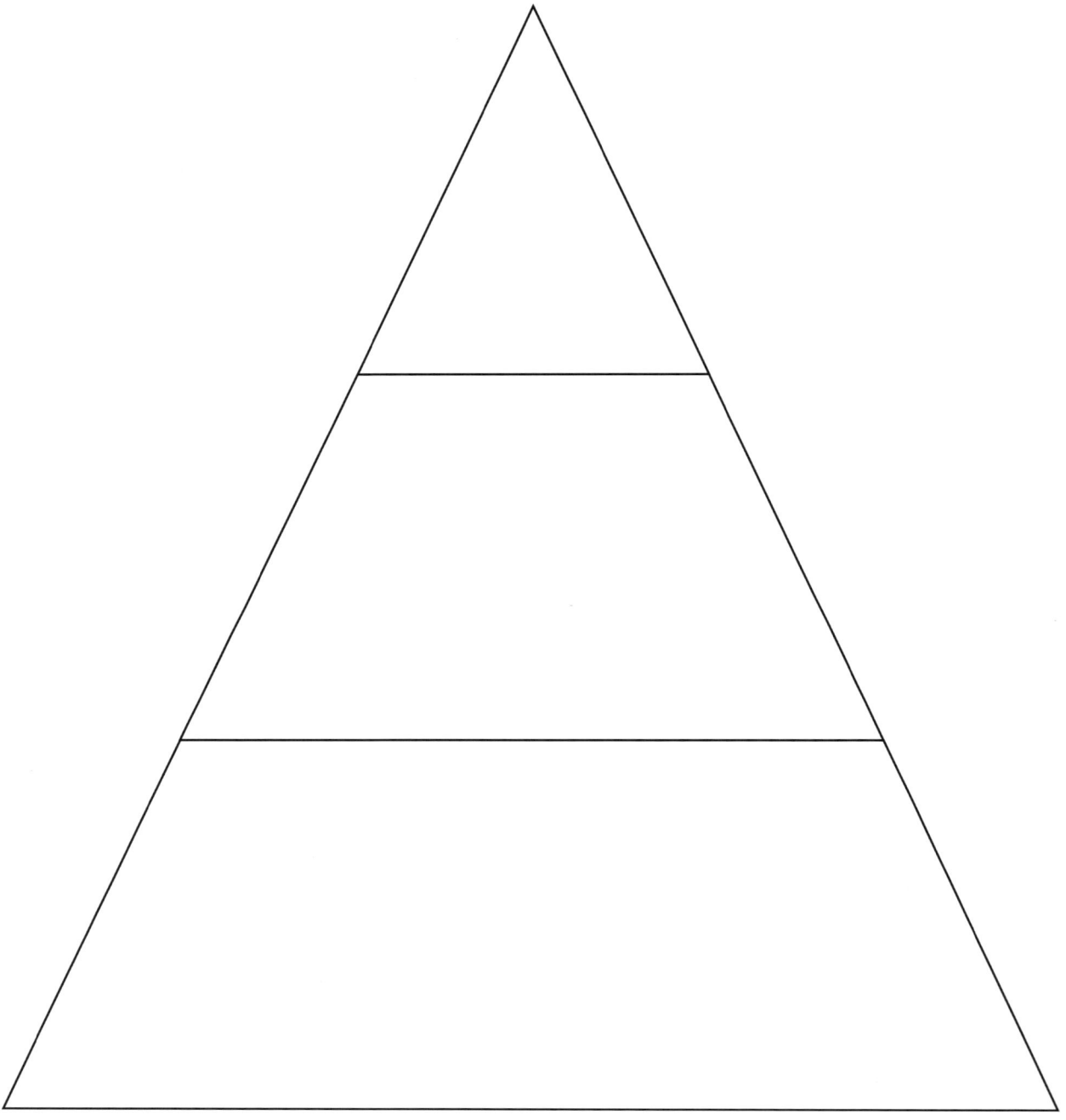

D46T2: A Little Rain

Caught in the Rain

Protective Dome

Accepting Rain

D47T3: 10-Day Forecast

Day 1	Day 2
Day 3	Day 4
Day 5	Day 6
Day 7	Day 8
Day 9	Day 10

D49T2: Airplane Turbulance

Obstacles:

Committed Actions:

D53T3: Behavior Gradient

ANGRY ↑
↓ CALM

D55T2: Life Time

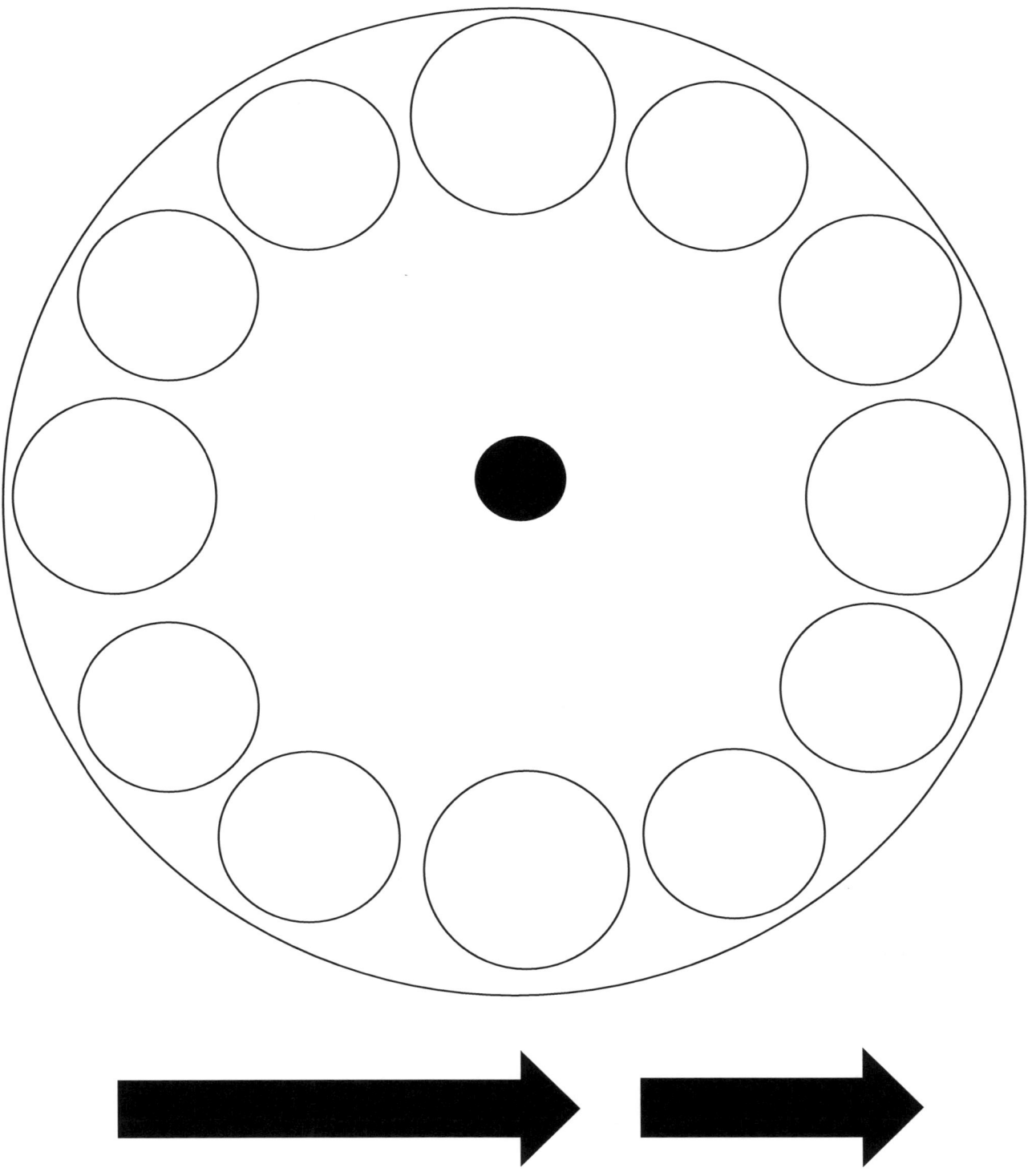

D56T3: One Sided World (Fold in Half)

D57T2: Word Pizza

D59T3: Kernels

Get it Out!	Let it Be!

I can practice acceptance by...

D63T2: A Good Friend

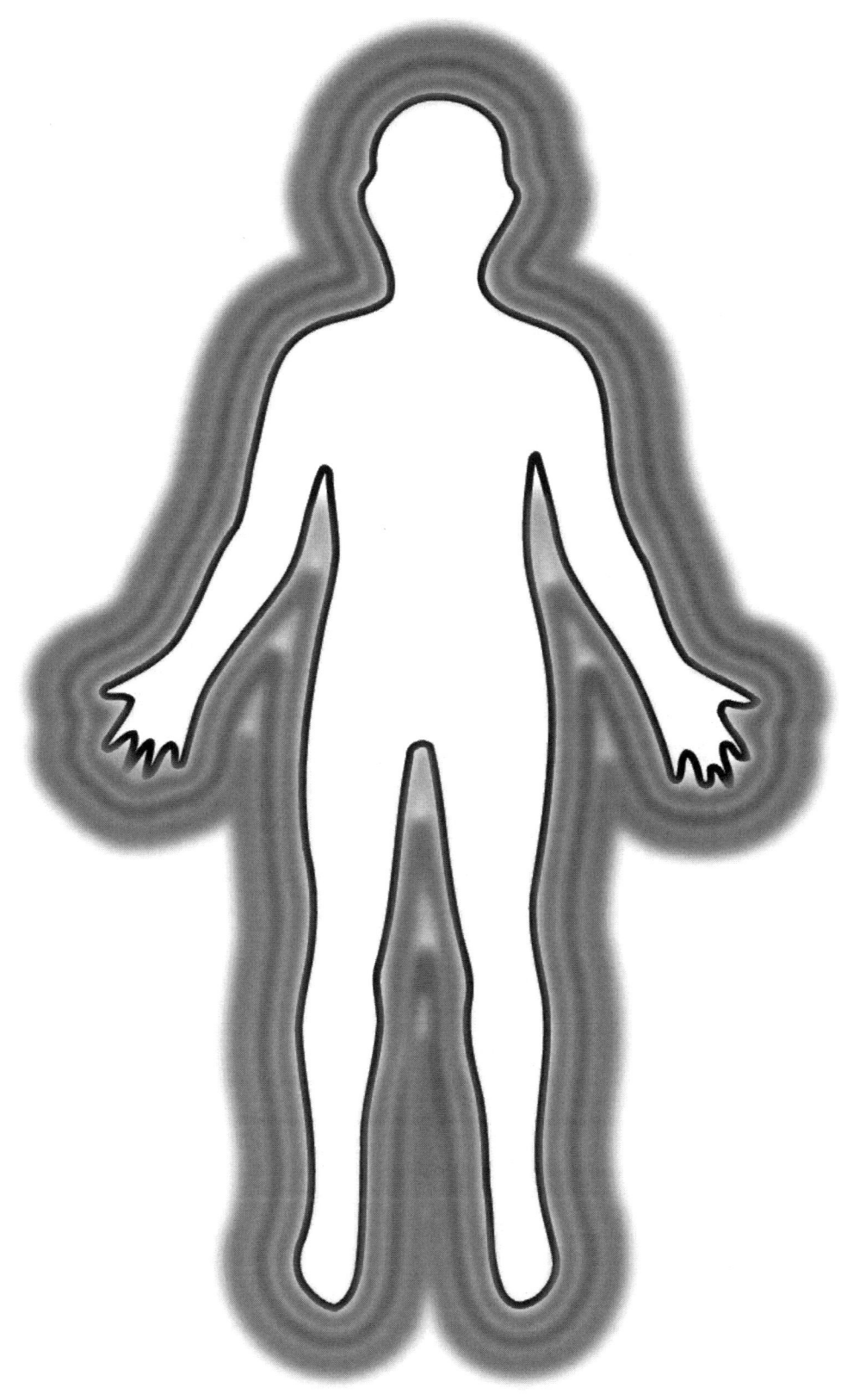

D64T2/3: Reflection

D66T2: Disgusting Dinner

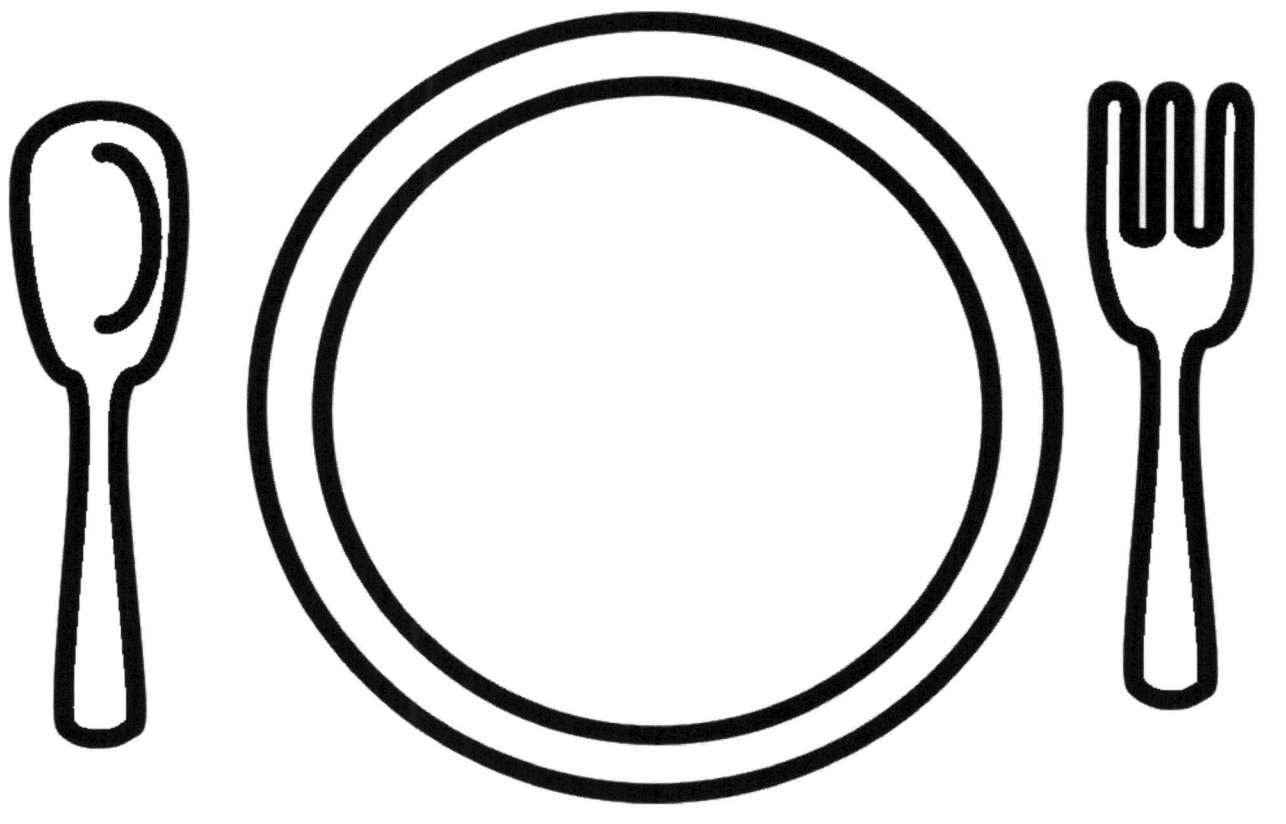

D67T2/3: Gratitude Tree

D69T2: What Were You Thinking?

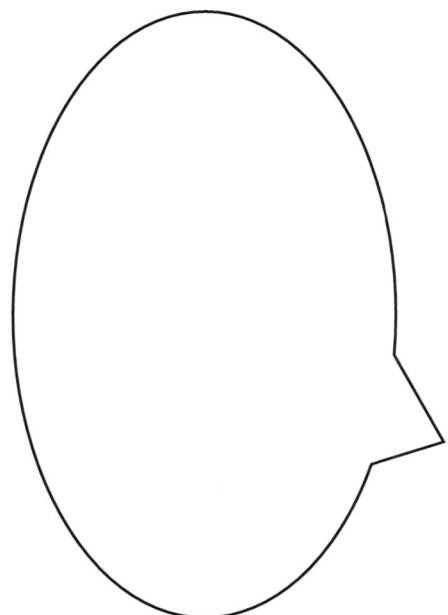

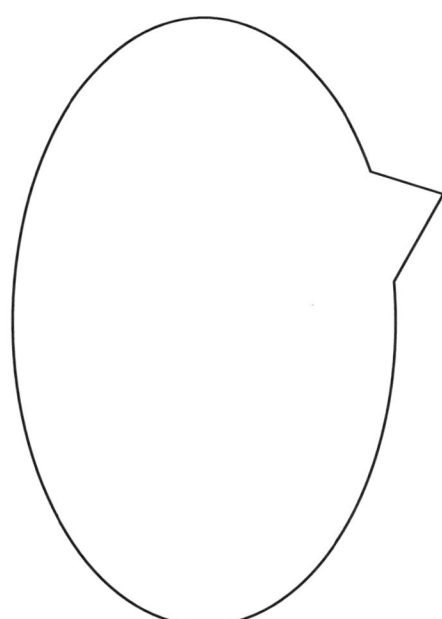

D71T3: Breathing Room

Inappropriate Reactions to Space Invaders	Mindful Reactions to Space Invaders

D72T3: Creating Space

Creating Space:

Trouble:

Upsetting Thoughts:

D76T2: Did you smell that?

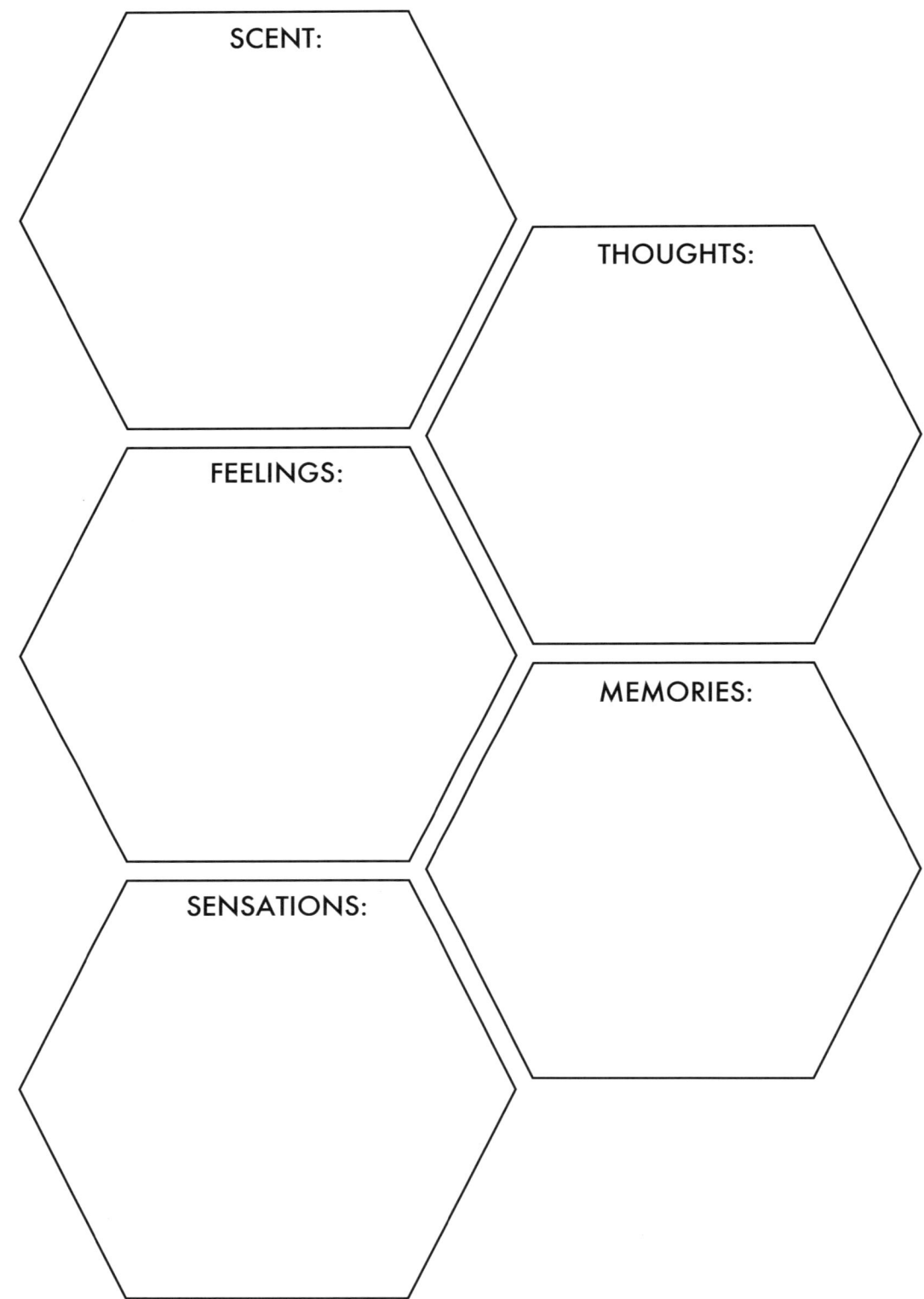

D78T2: Lyrically Speaking

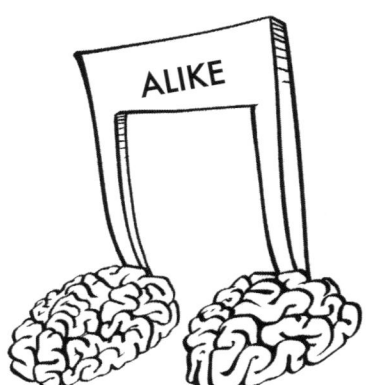

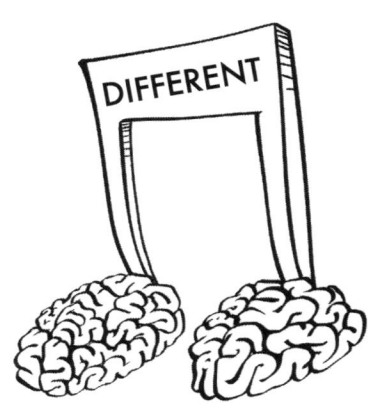

D80T3: Crystal Ball

D81T2: Values Bracket

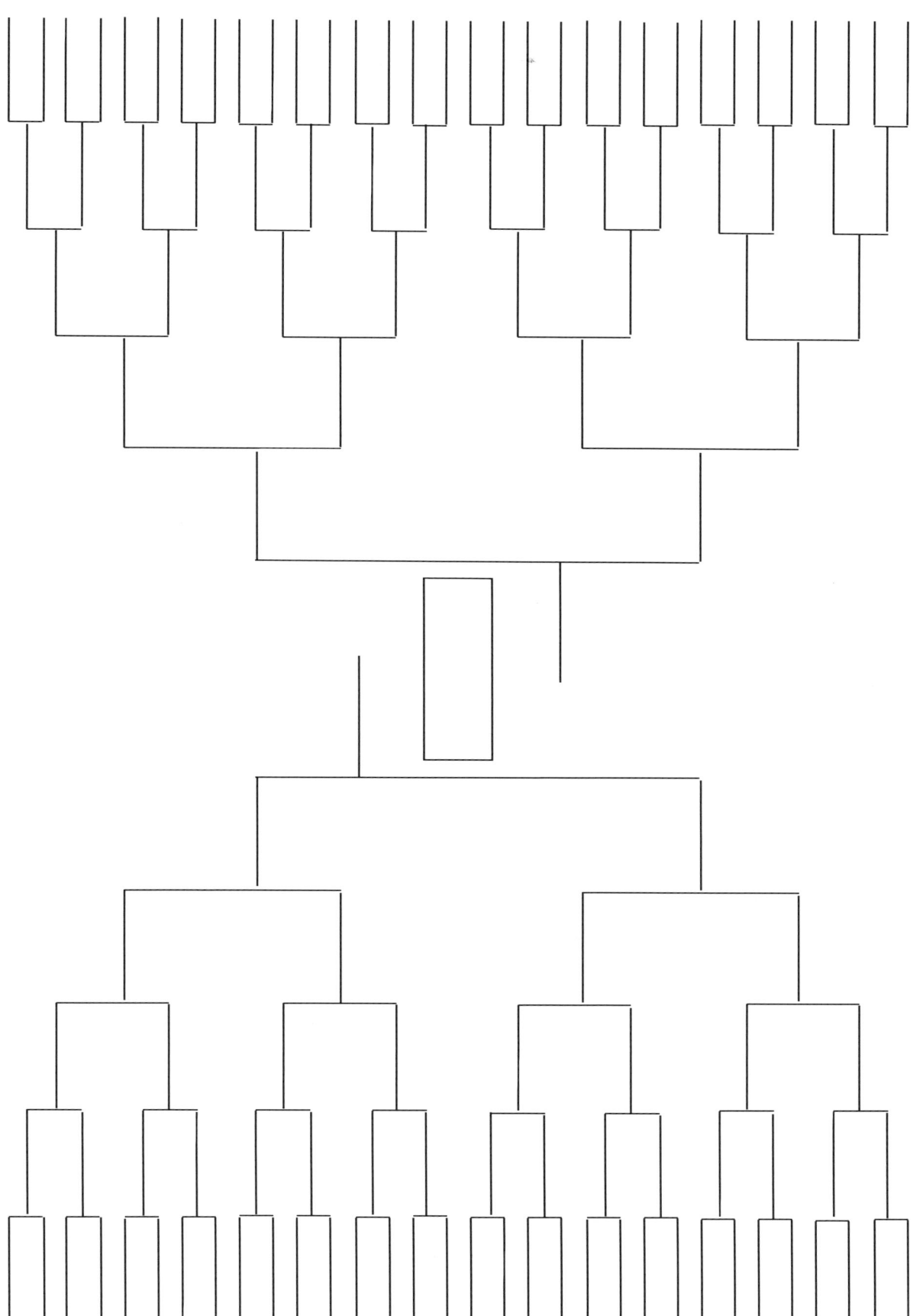

313

D81T3: Prioritizing Values

Value:

Value:

Value:

Value:

D84T2: Leave It on the Field

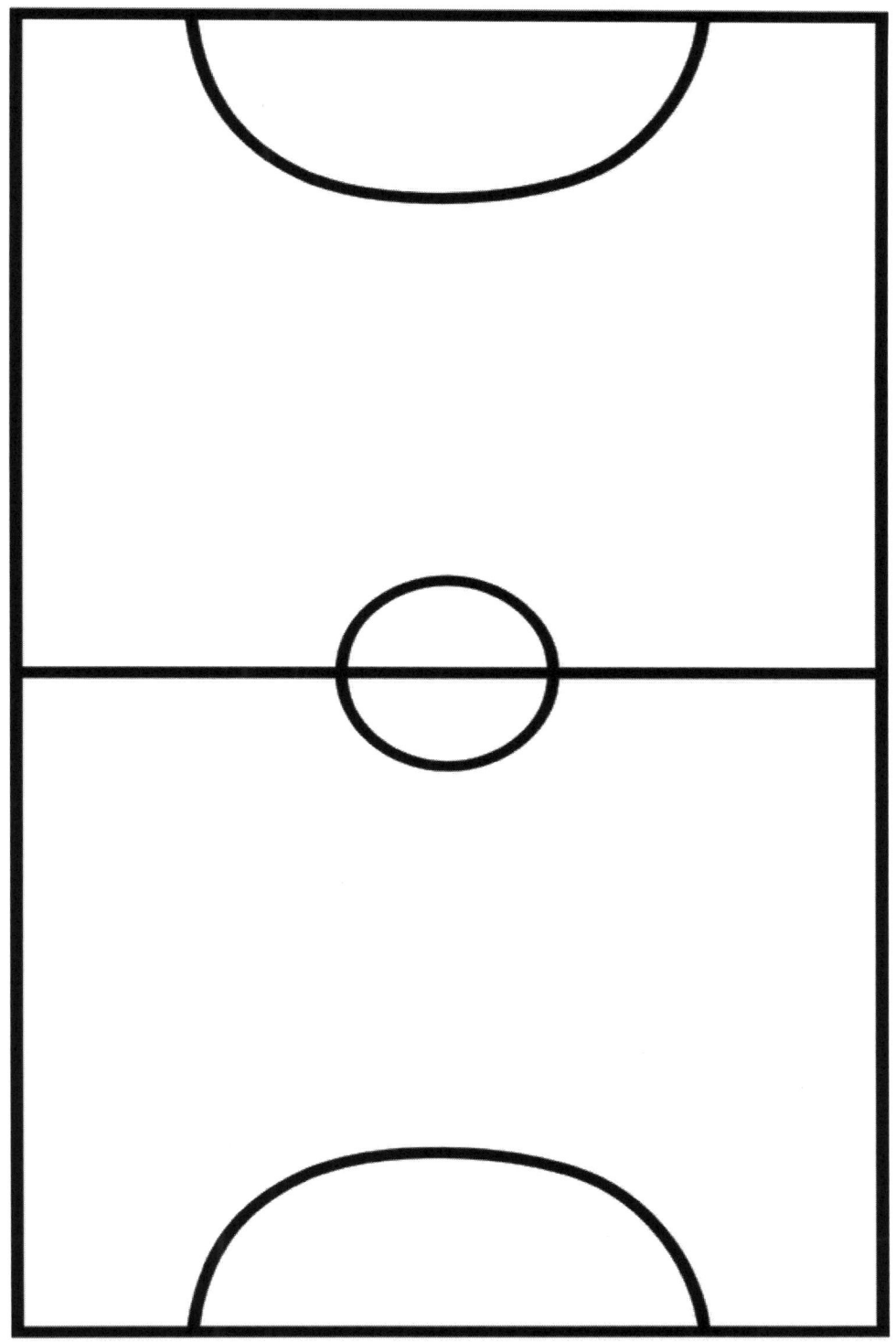

D86T2: Thought Puzzle

D89T2: Riddles

Self as Content Riddle (Labels)

Self as Process (Experiences Right Now)

Self as Context (Constant Facts)

D91T2/3: My Map

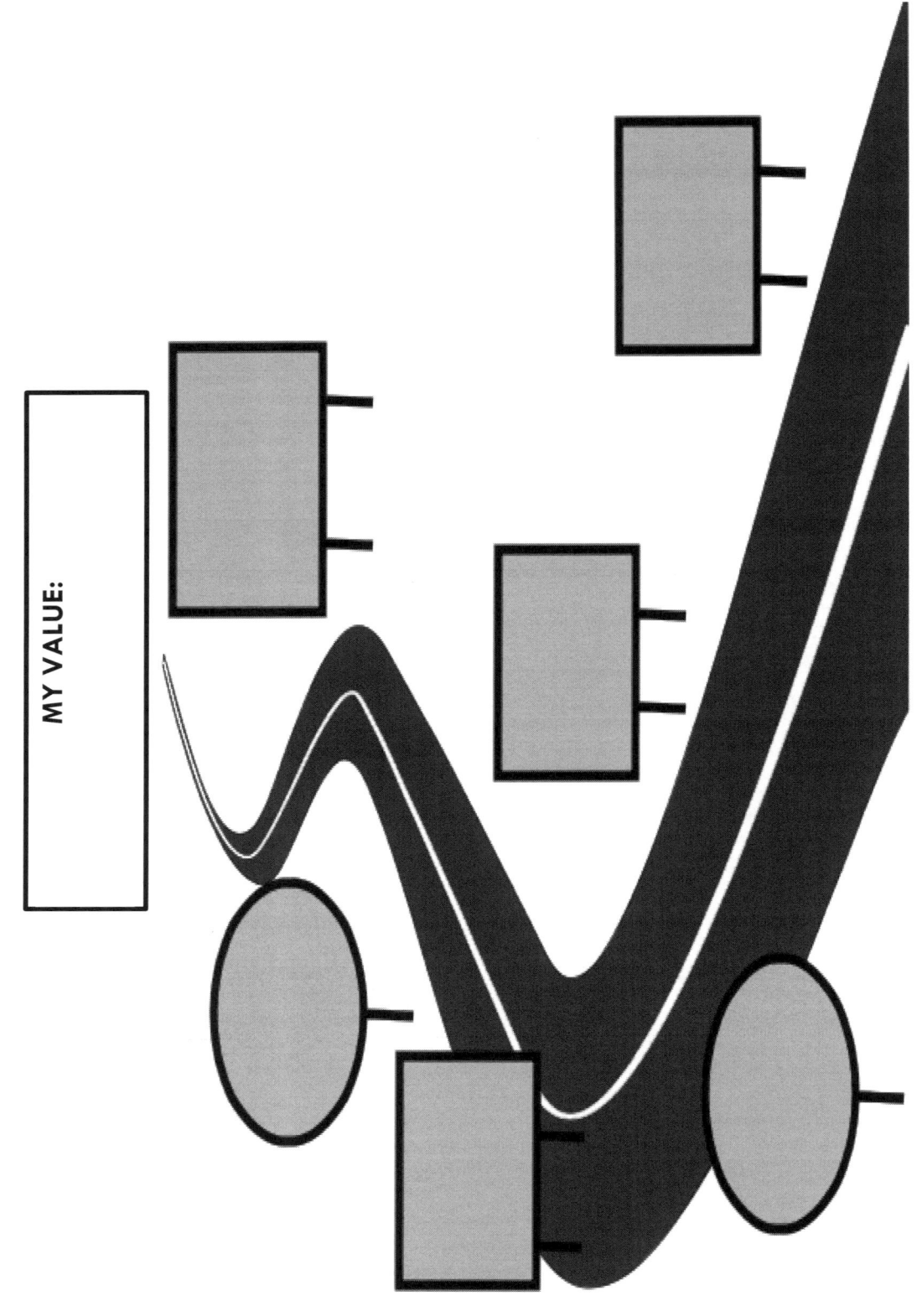

D94T3: Along the Road

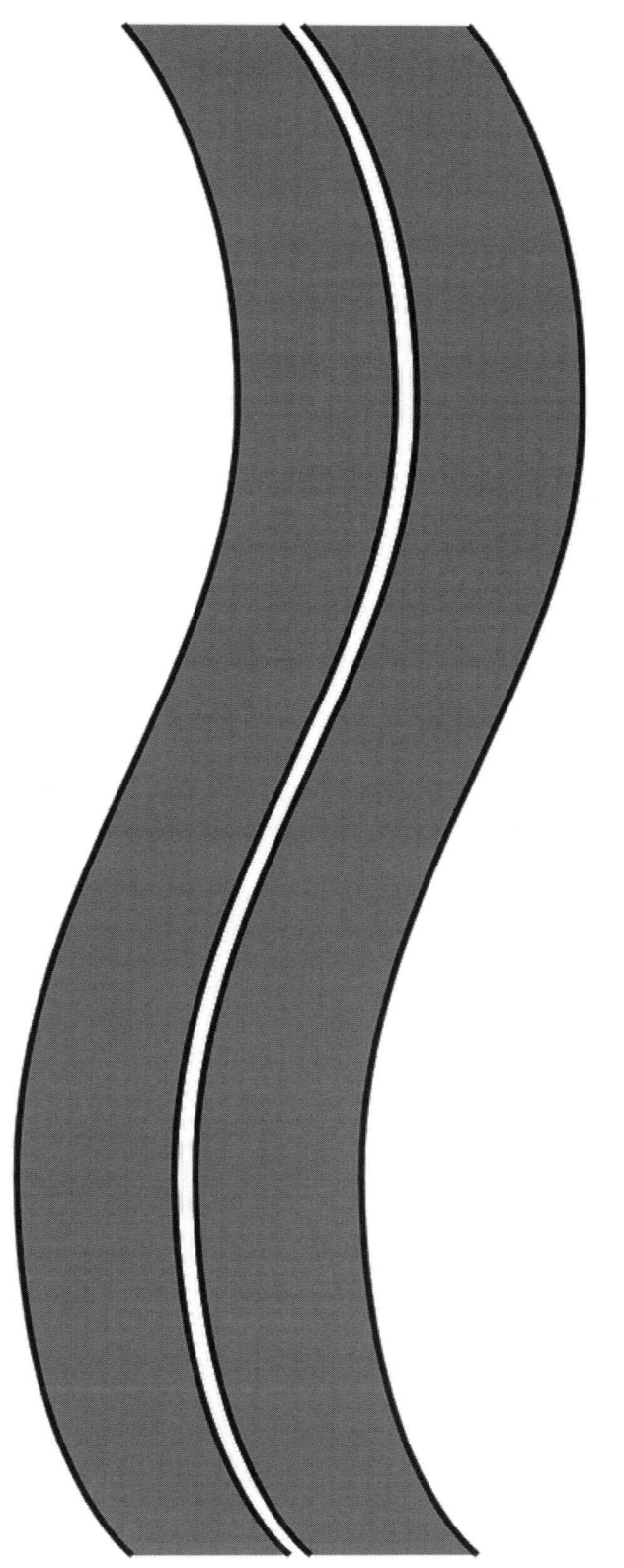

D98T3: Feedback Responses

D100T3: Yard Sale

D103T3: Movie Reviews

D104T3: Where Does It Hurt?

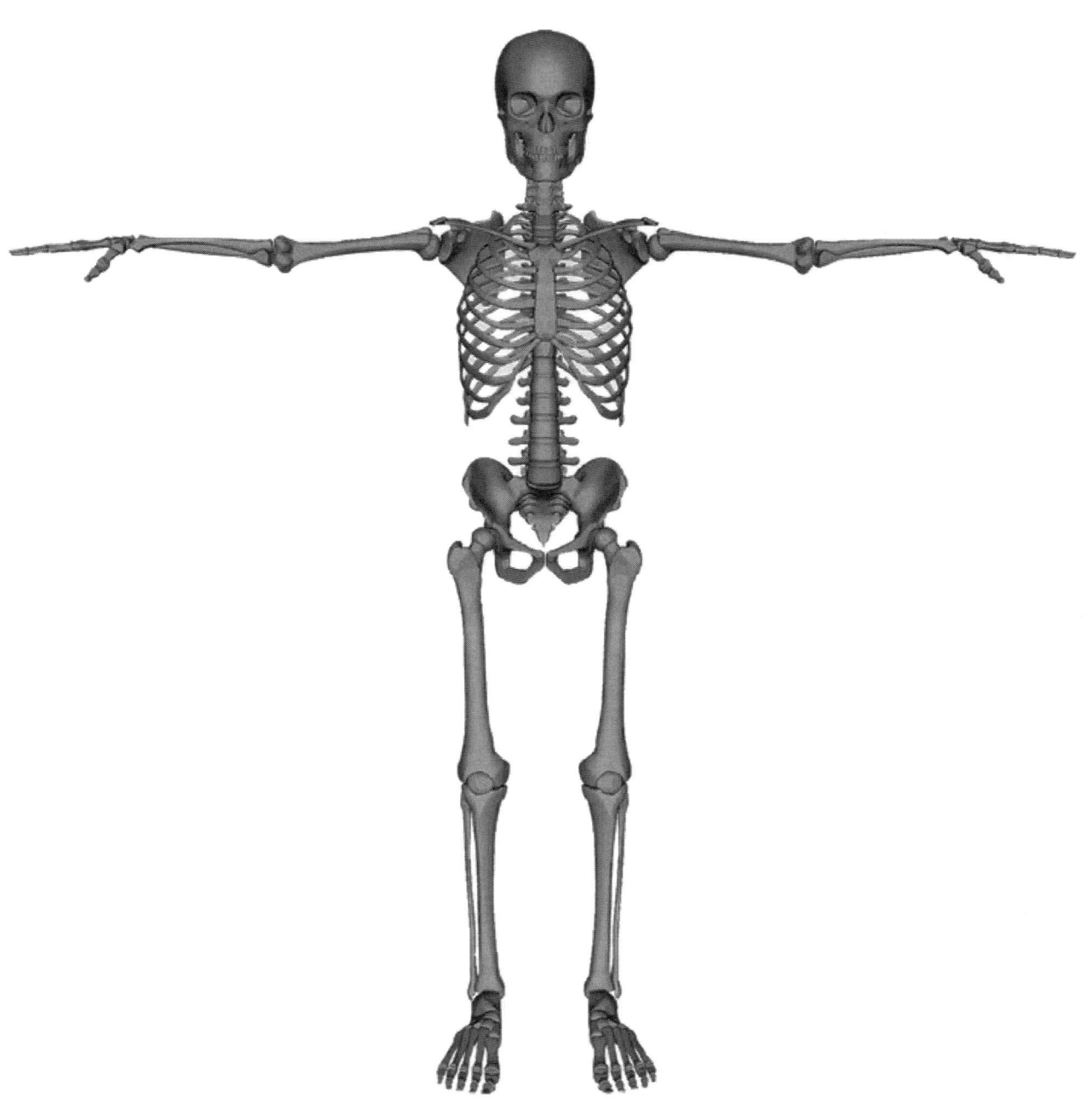

D105T3: I Am…

Even though I

_____ sometimes,

that is NOT who I am. I am someone who will

_____

when this challenge comes my way!

D106T2/3: Tiny Home in My Mind

D109T3: Fishing

D112T3: Wish, Fear, Real

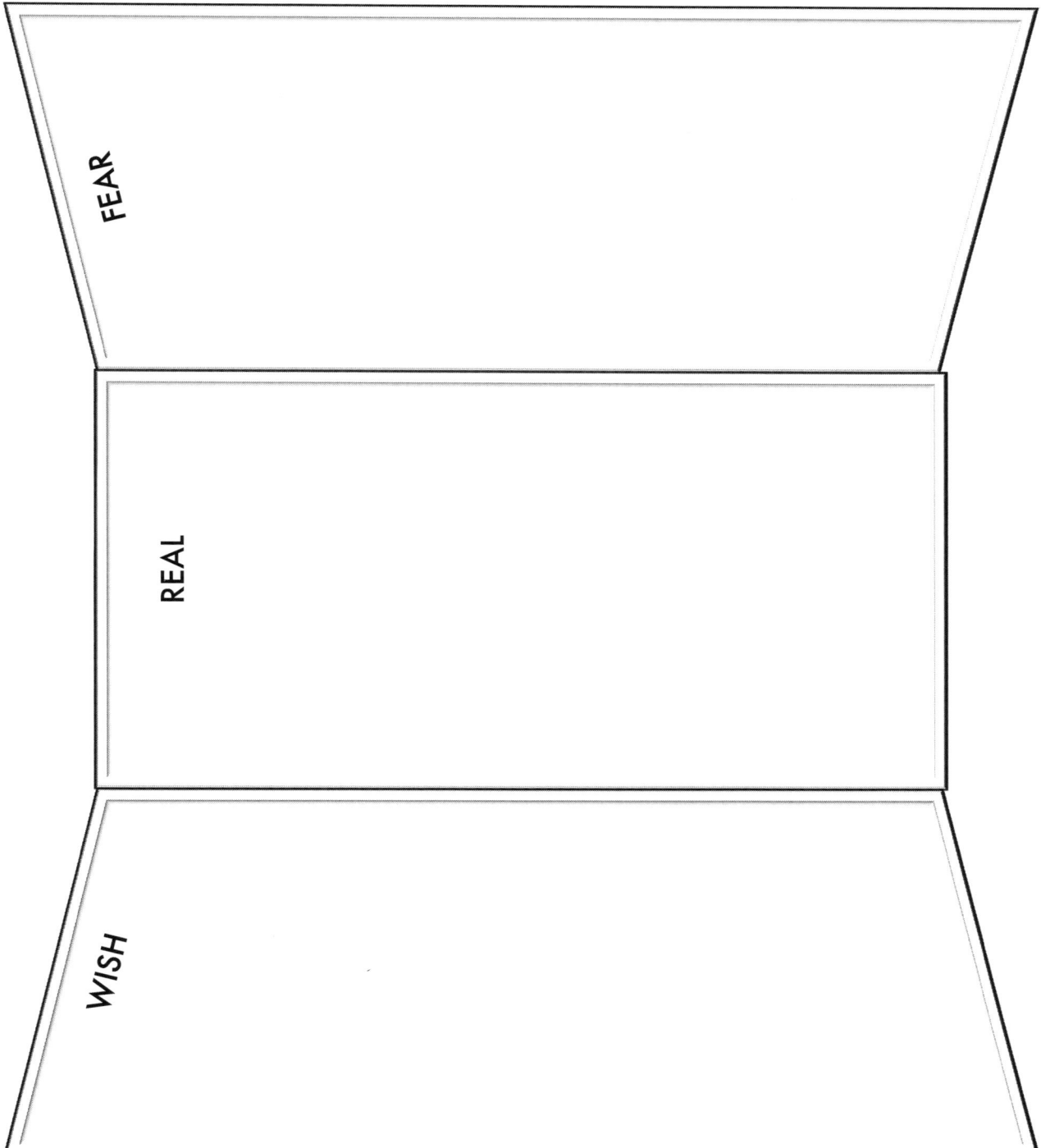

D117T3: If, Then

IF...	THEN...

D118T2: Parrot

REPEATING THOUGHTS:

-
-
-

D122T3: Rebuilding Home

D123T3: Weather Conditions List

Weather Conditions:

Rainy
Stormy
Sunny
Cloudy
Hot
Cold
Dry
Wet
Windy
Hurricane
Typhoon
Tornado
Humid
Foggy
Snowy
Hailing
Dry
Thundering
Breezy
Damp
Cool
Frigid
Still
Overcast

D125T3: Calm in the Storm

D127T3: Volume Control

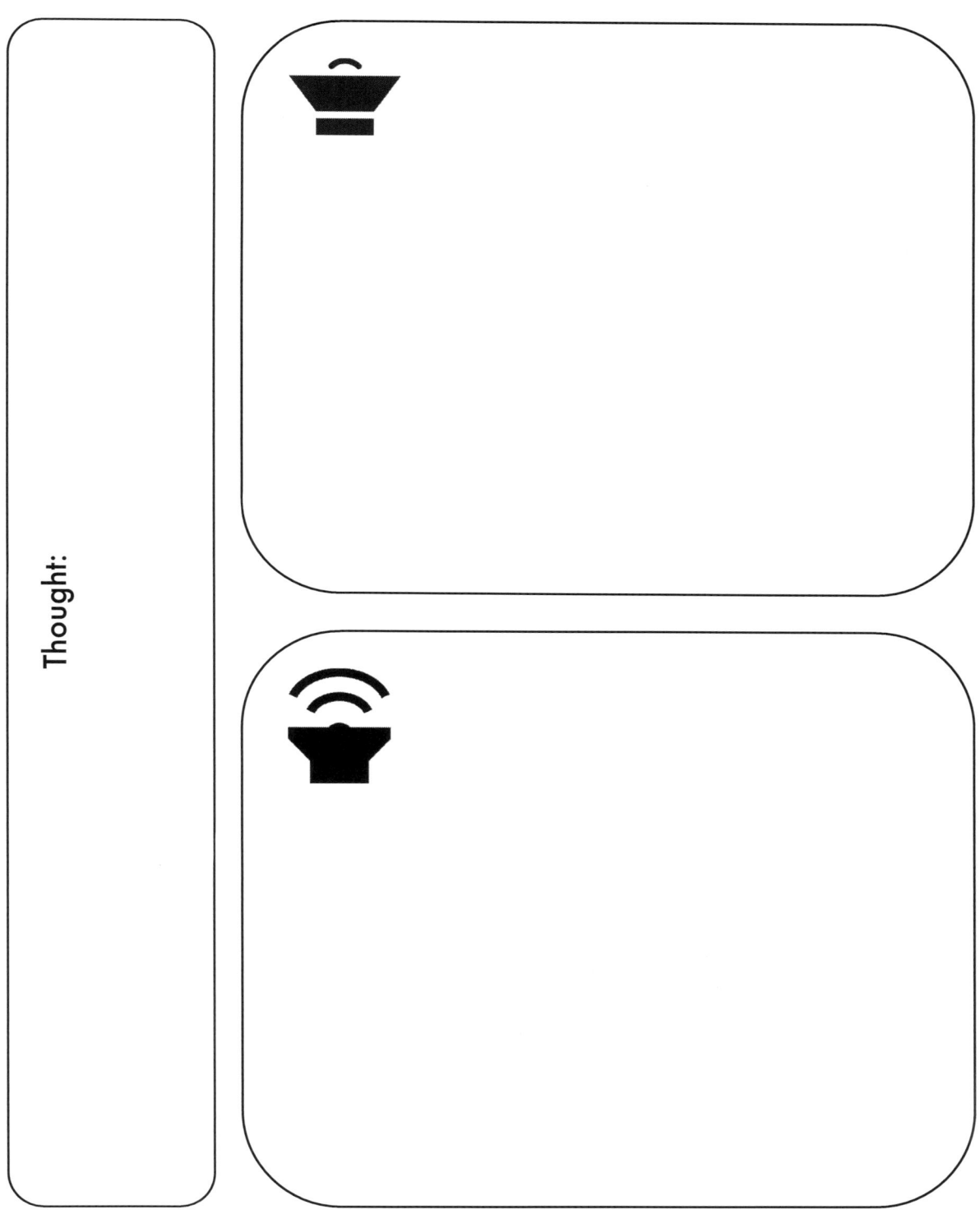

D130T3: Mindful Plan

Plan for Mindfulness

When?	
How long?	
In what way?	
How will this benefit me?	

D131T3: Deep Values

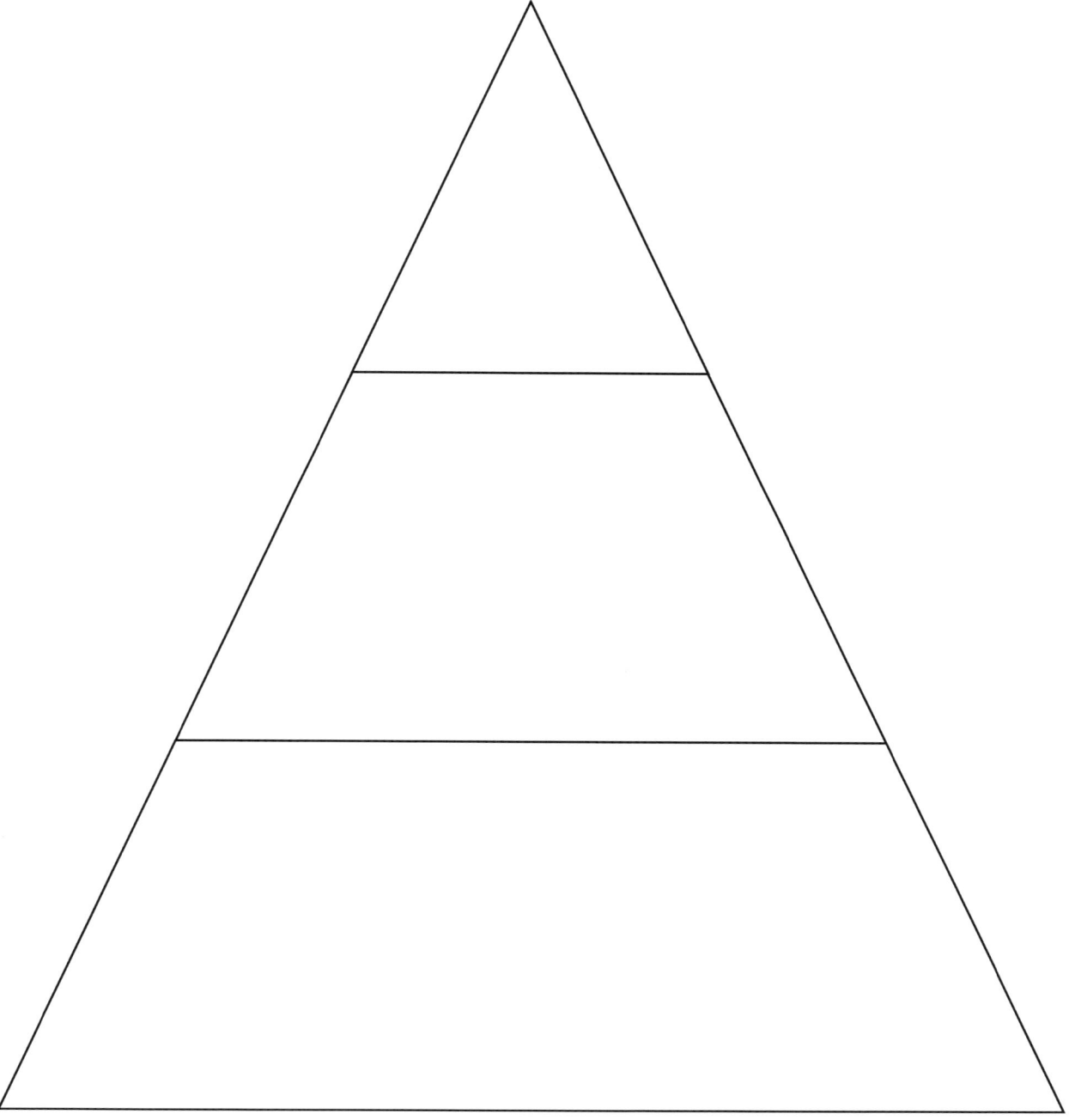

D132T3: Committed Action Plan

Plan for Committed Action

VALUE:

COMMITTED ACTION 1	
COMMITTED ACTION 2	
COMMITTED ACTION 3	

MY CELEBRATION!

D133T3: Turning BUT into AND

YES, BUT...	↑ YES, AND...
YES, BUT...	↑ YES, AND...
YES, BUT...	↑ YES, AND...
YES, BUT...	↑ YES, AND...
YES, BUT...	↑ YES, AND...

D134T2: Changing Thoughts

OLD THOUGHTS

NEW THOUGHTS

SAME THOUGHTS

D135T2: Where Are Your Thoughts?

Past

Rating: _____

Future

Rating: _____

NOW

Rating: _____

D139T2: Character Comparison

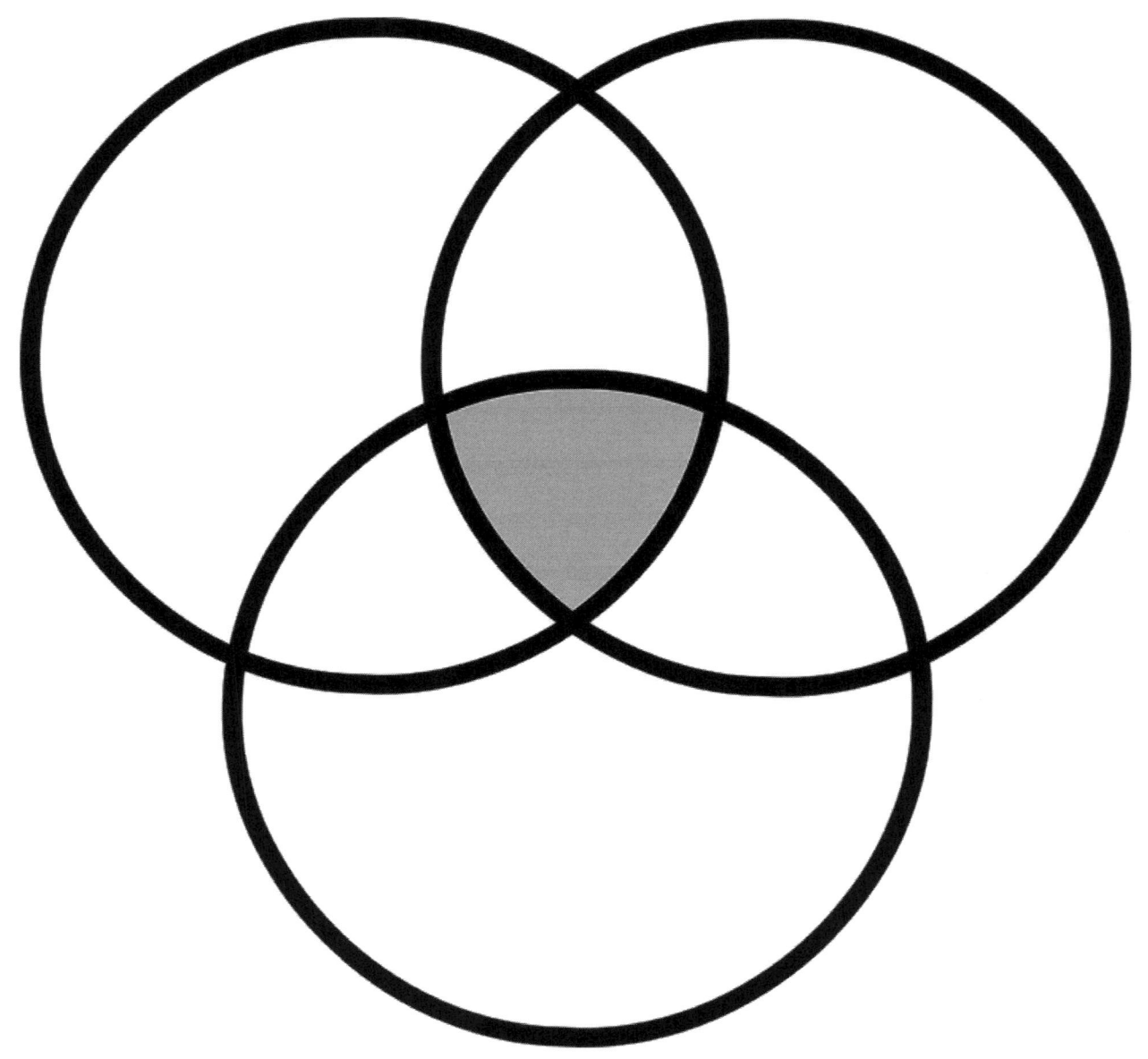

D140T3: Chapters of Your Life

Chapter 1	Action
Chapter 2	Action
Chapter 3	Action
Chapter 4	Action
Chapter 5	Action

D141T2: Brain's Full

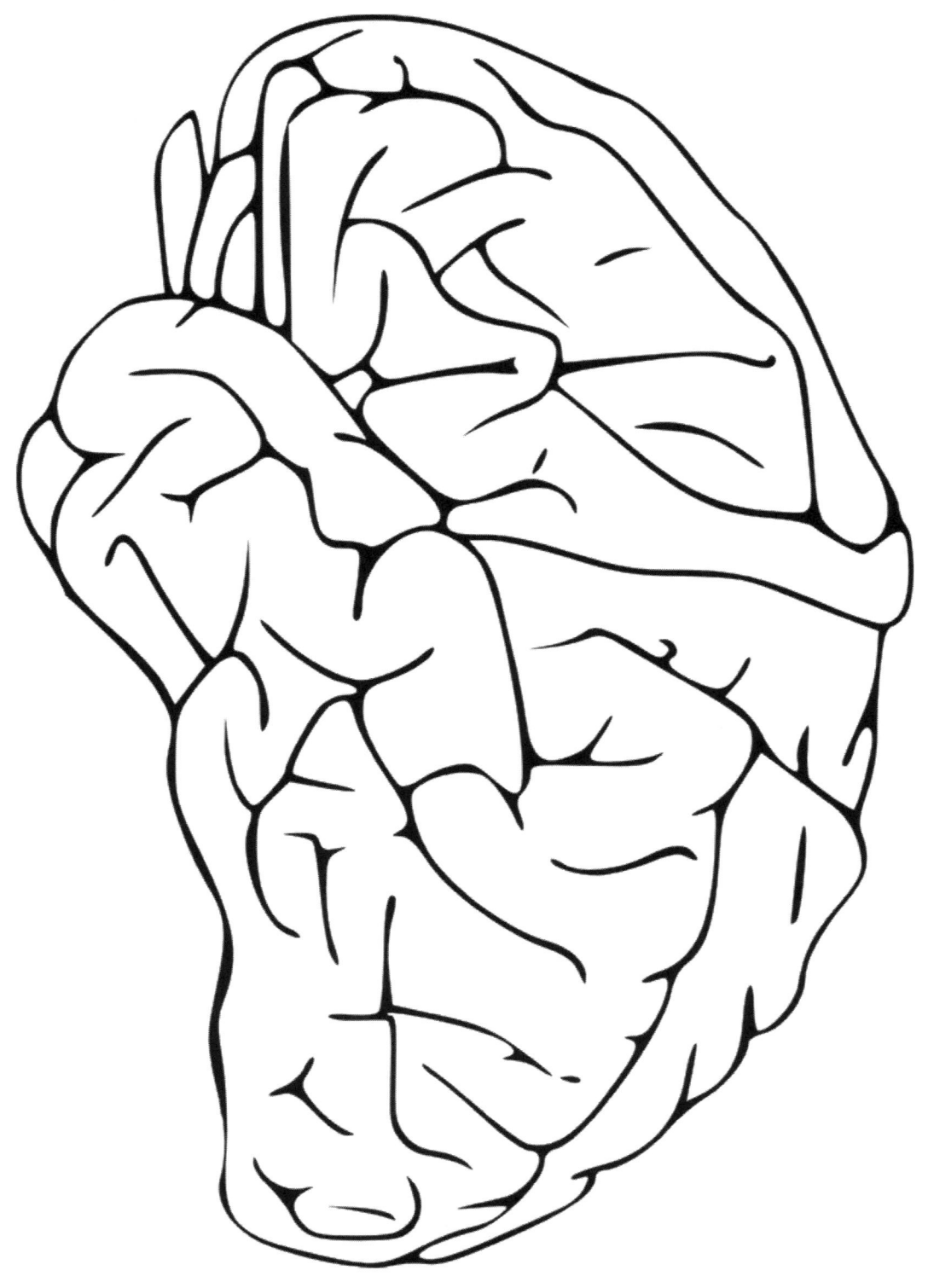

D144T3: Self-Compassion

I need compassion when...

D146T2: Lion/Lamb

D148T2: Action's Closet

D152T2: Blank Mandala

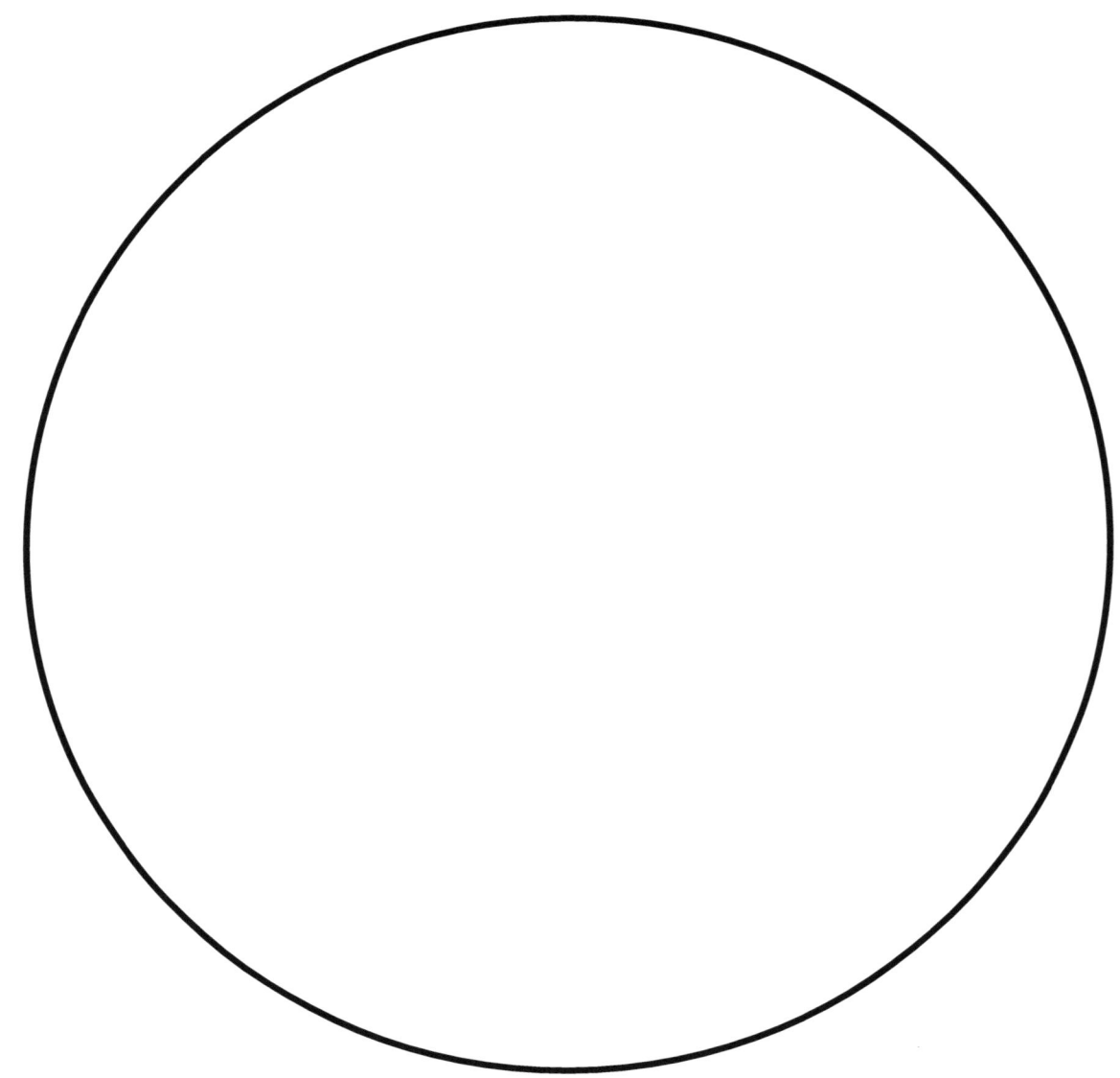

D155T3: Self-Acceptance

I need more self-acceptance... ⬆ My Affirmation:

I need more self-acceptance... ⬆ My Affirmation:

I need more self-acceptance... ⬆ My Affirmation:

D156T3: Choice Points

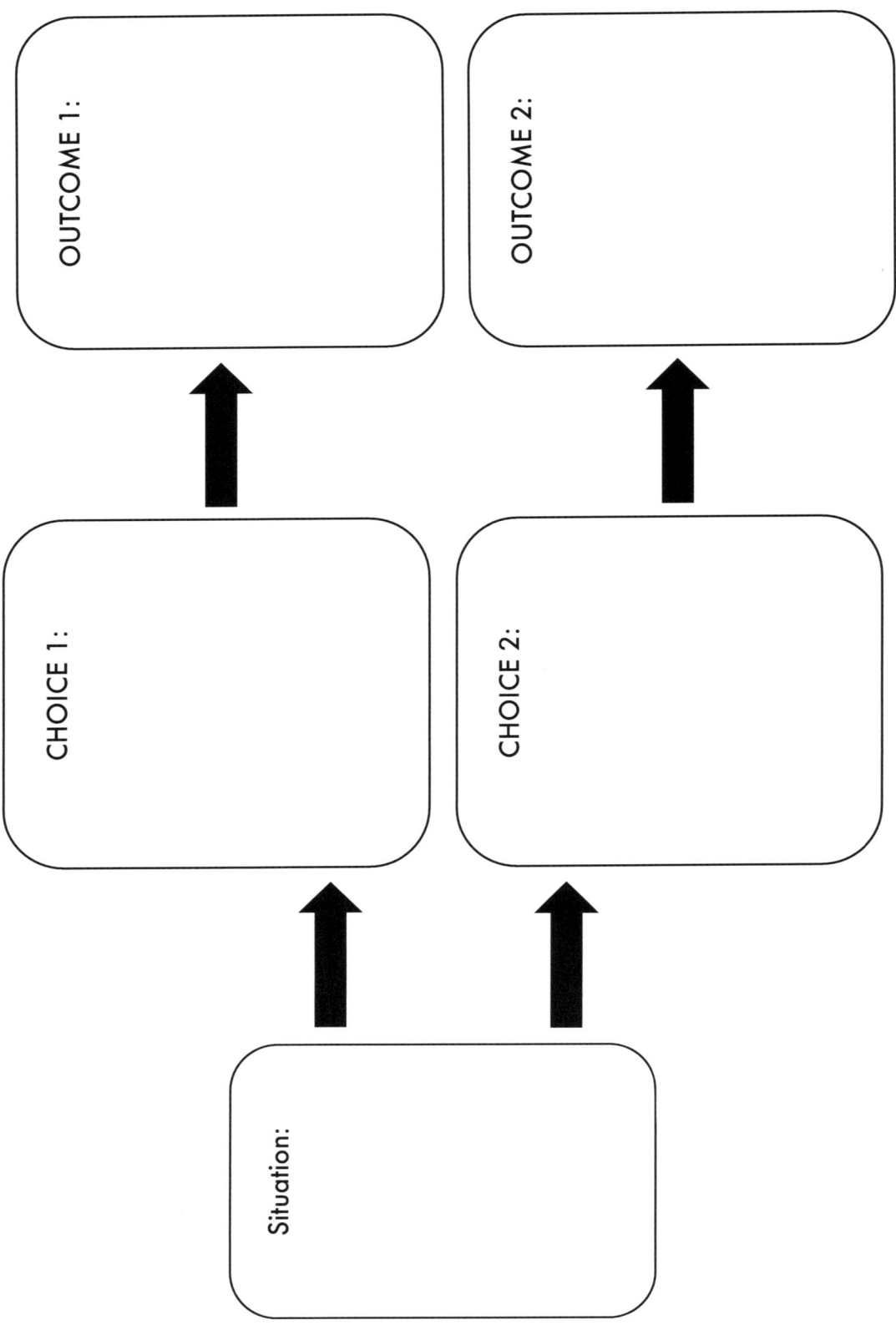

D160T3: A Clown's Thoughts

D162T2: Truth AND Dare

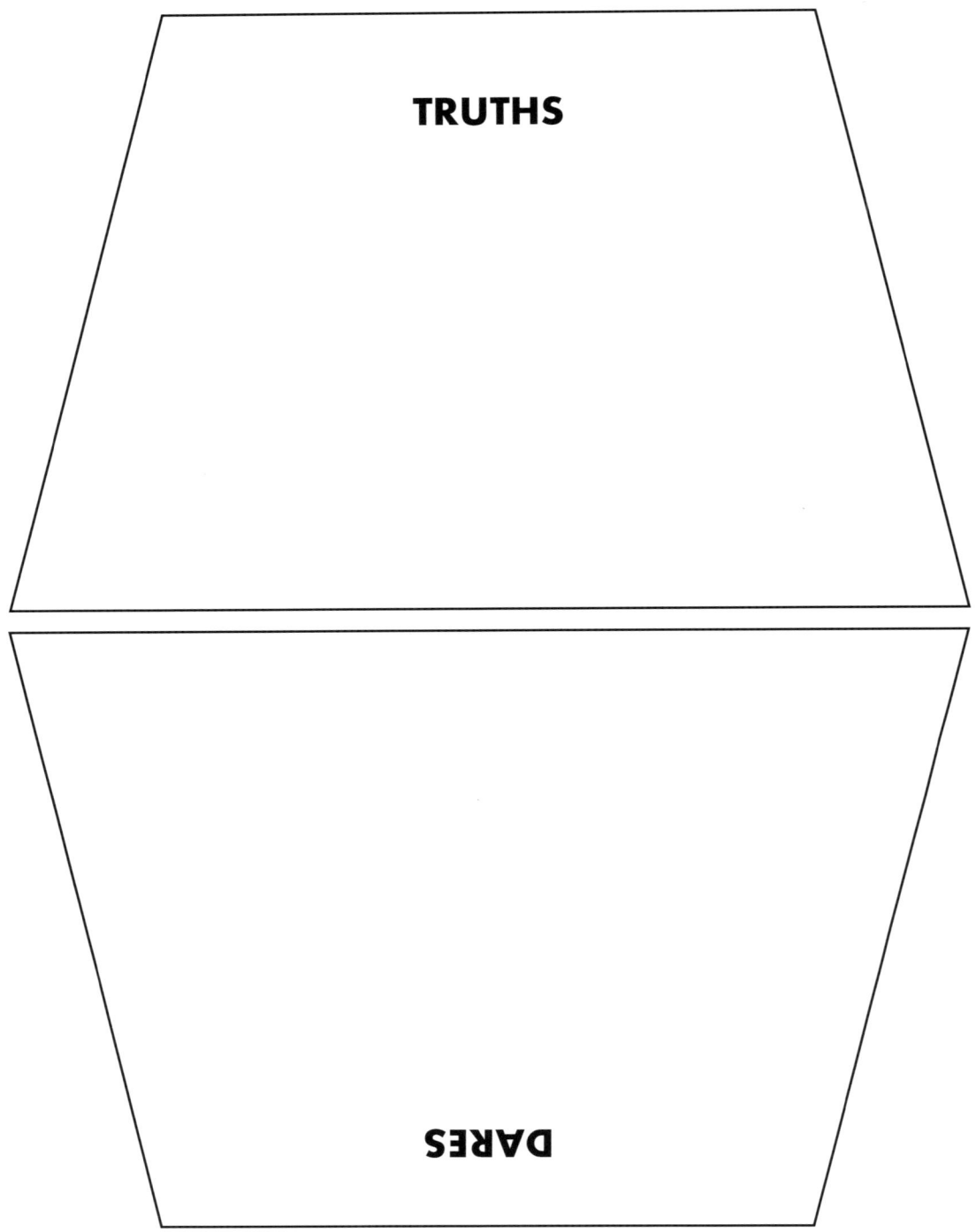

D163T3: Salt Shaker

D164T3: Puppets

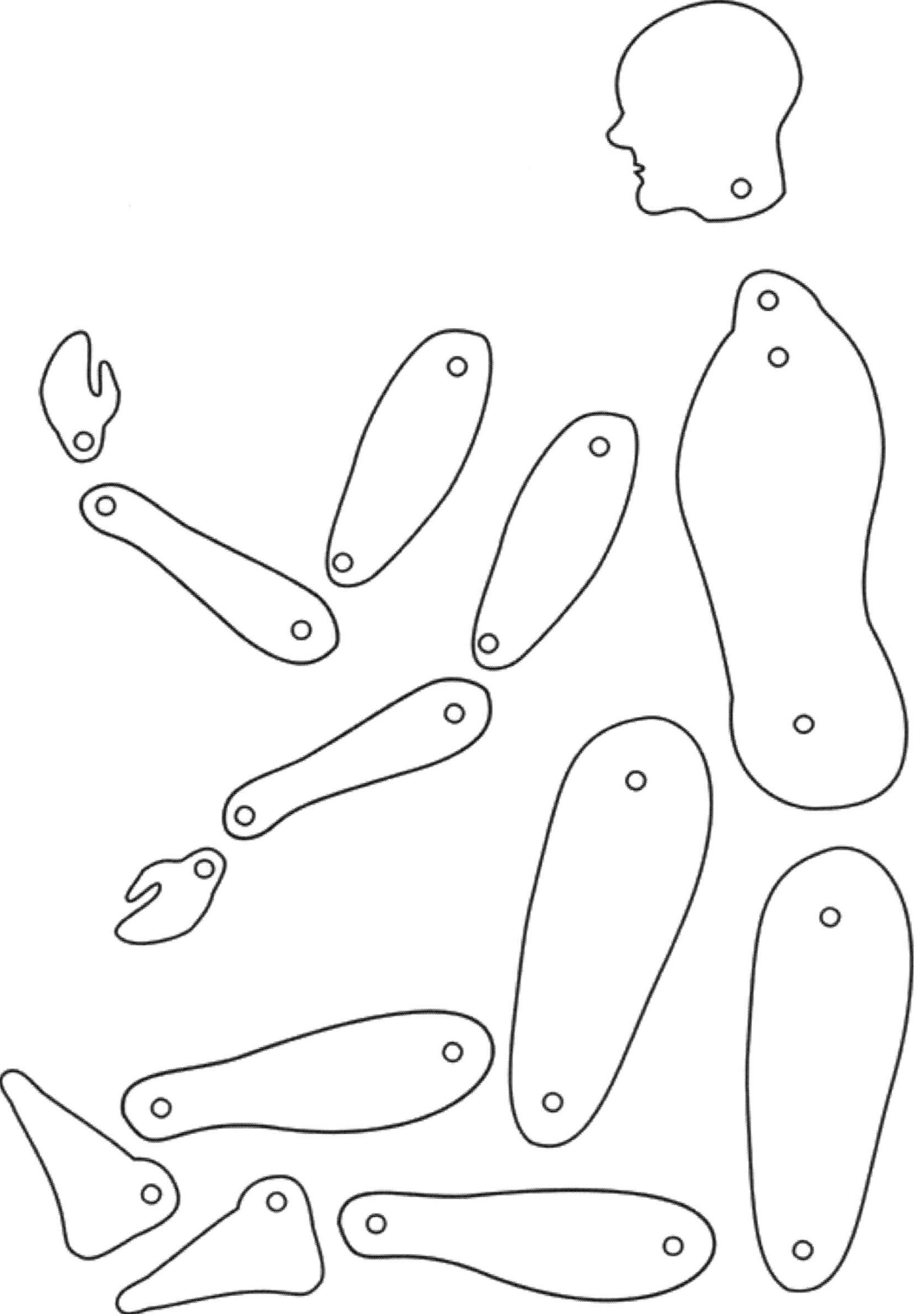

D165T3: Intentions

Intention

What do you value?	
What in life matters most to you?	
How do you want to feel?	
What are you grateful for?	
What words or quotes do you connect with?	

My Intention:

D166-70T2: My Hexaflex, My Way

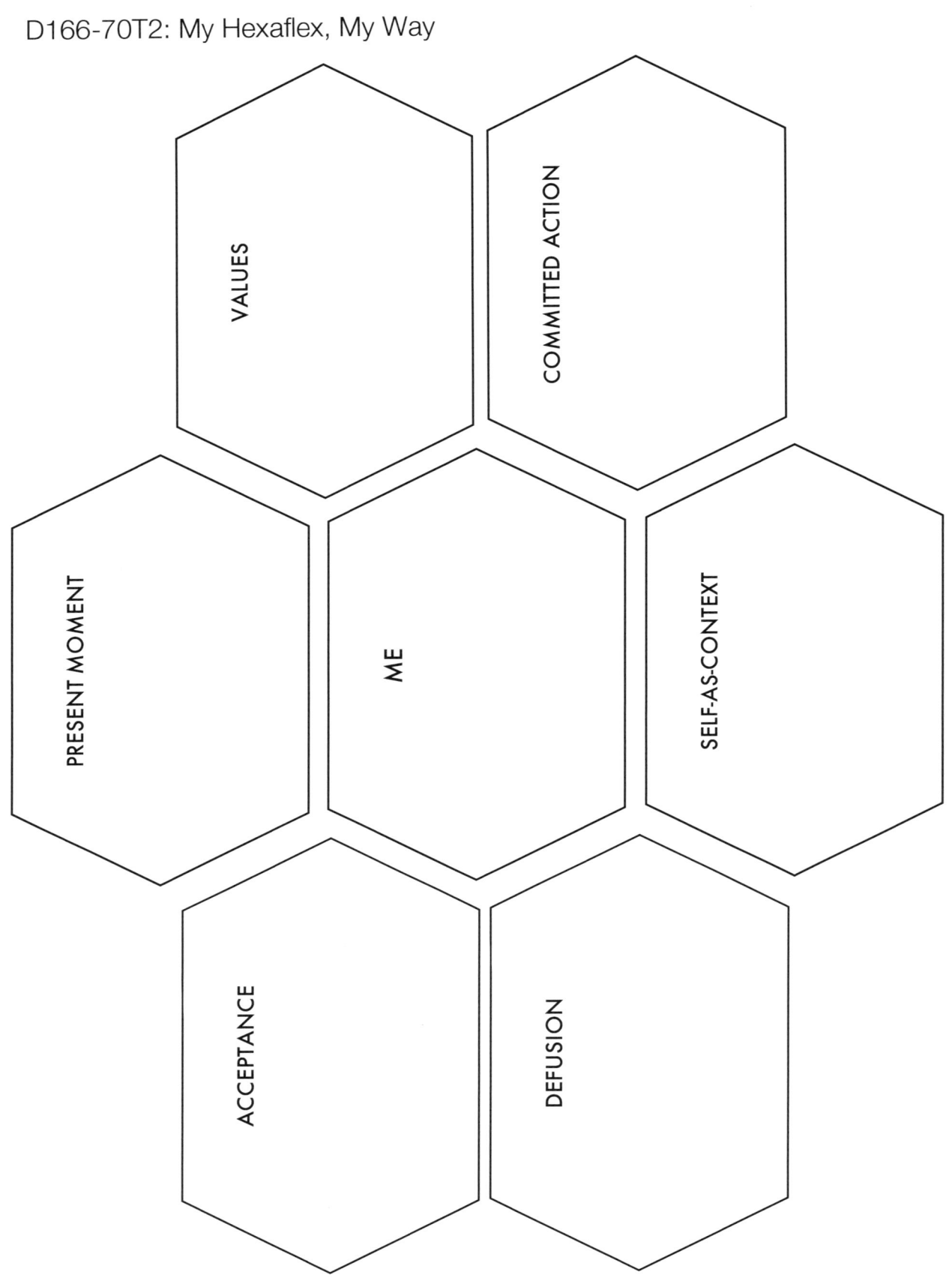

D166-70T3: My Mountains to Climb

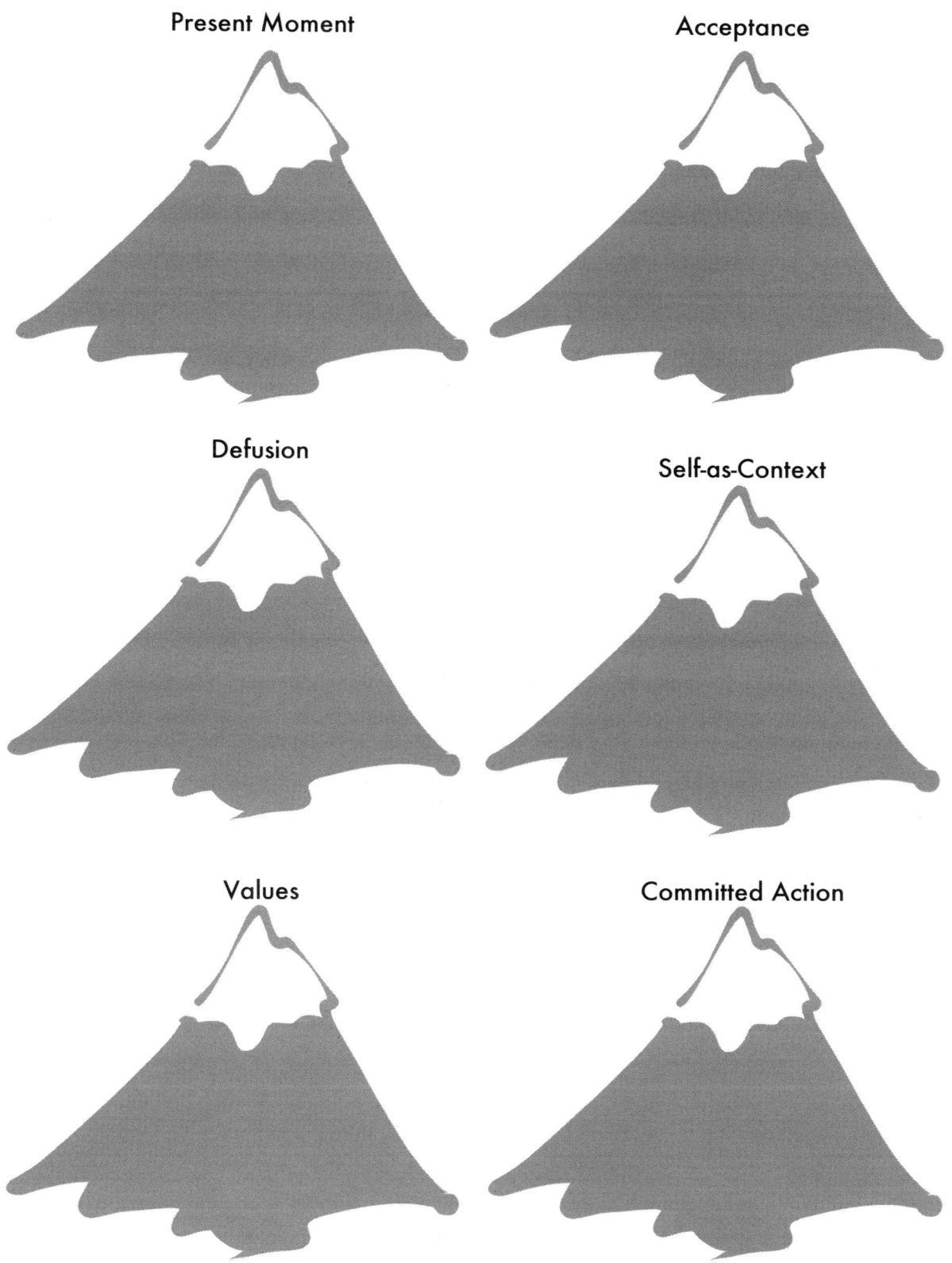

D175T2: Yearbook

Chapter 7:
Further Reading

Mindfulness

Burke, C. A. (2010). Mindfulness-based approaches with children and adolescents: A preliminary review of current research in an emergent field. *Journal of Child and Family Studies*, 19(2), 133-144.

Germer, C. K., Siegel, R. D., & Fulton, P. R. (Eds.). (2016). *Mindfulness and psychotherapy*. Guilford Publications.

Greco, L. A., & Hayes, S. C. (Eds.). (2008). *Acceptance & mindfulness treatments for children & adolescents: A practitioner's guide*. New Harbinger Publications.

Greenberg, M. T., & Harris, A. R. (2012). Nurturing mindfulness in children and youth: Current state of research. *Child Development Perspectives*, 6(2), 161-166.

Greenland, S. K. (2010). *The mindful child: How to help your kid manage stress and become happier, kinder, and more compassionate.* Simon and Schuster.Some

John Kabat-Zinn, J. (2009). *Wherever you go, there you are: Mindfulness meditation in everyday life.* Hachette UK.

Kallapiran, K., Koo, S., Kirubakaran, R., & Hancock, K. (2015). Effectiveness of mindfulness in improving mental health symptoms of children and adolescents: a meta-analysis. *Child and Adolescent Mental Health*, 20(4), 182-194.

Khoury, B., Lecomte, T., Fortin, G., Masse, M., Therien, P., Bouchard, V., ... & Hofmann, S. G. (2013). Mindfulness-based therapy: a comprehensive meta-analysis. *Clinical Psychology Review*, 33(6), 763-771.

Zenner, C., Herrnleben-Kurz, S., & Walach, H. (2014). Mindfulness-based interventions in schools—a systematic review and meta-analysis. *Frontiers in Psychology*, 5.

Zoogman, S., Goldberg, S. B., Hoyt, W. T., & Miller, L. (2015). Mindfulness interventions with youth: A meta-analysis. *Mindfulness*, 6(2), 290-302.

Acceptance and Commitment Therapy

A-tjak, J. G., Davis, M. L., Morina, N., Powers, M. B., Smits, J. A., & Emmelkamp, P. M. (2015). A meta-analysis of the efficacy of acceptance and commitment therapy for clinically relevant mental and physical health problems. *Psychotherapy and Psychosomatics*, 84(1), 30-36.

Bailey, A., Ciarrochi, J., & Hayes, L. (2012). *Get out of your mind and into your life for teens: A guide to living an extraordinary life*. New Harbinger Publications.

Biglan, A., Hayes, S. C., & Pistorello, J. (2008). Acceptance and commitment: Implications for prevention science. *Prevention Science*, 9(3), 139-152.

Coyne, L. W., McHugh, L., & Martinez, E. R. (2011). Acceptance and commitment therapy (ACT): Advances and applications with children, adolescents, and families. *Child and Adolescent Psychiatric Clinics of North America*, 20(2), 379-399.

Dixon, M.R. (2014). *ACT for children with autism and emotional challenges*. Carbondale, IL: Shawnee Scientific Press.

Harris, R. (2013). *The happiness trap: Stop struggling, start living*. Exisle Publishing.

Hayes, S. C. (2005). *Get out of your mind and into your life: The new acceptance and commitment therapy*. Oakland, CA: New Harbinger Publications.

Hayes, S. C., Levin, M. E., Plumb-Vilardaga, J., Villatte, J. L., & Pistorello, J. (2013). Acceptance and commitment therapy and contextual behavioral science: Examining the progress of a distinctive model of behavioral and cognitive therapy. *Behavior Therapy*, 44(2), 180-198.

Hayes, S. C., Strosahl, K. D., & Wilson, K. G. (1999). *Acceptance and commitment therapy*. New York: Guilford Press.

Luoma, J. B., Hayes, S. C., & Walser, R. D. (2007). *Learning ACT: An acceptance & commitment therapy skills-training manual for therapists*. Oakland, CA: New Harbinger Publications.

Murrell, A. R., & Scherbarth, A. J. (2006). State of the research & literature address: ACT with children, adolescents and parents. *International Journal of Behavioral Consultation and Therapy*, 2(4), 531.

Applied Behavior Analysis

Biglan, A. (2015). *The nurture effect: How the science of human behavior can improve our lives and our world*. New Harbinger Publications.

Cooper, J.O., Heron, T.E., & Heward, W.L. (2007) *Applied behavior analysis*. Upper Saddle River, N.J.: Pearson/Merrill-Prentice Hall.

Hanley, G. P., Iwata, B. A., & McCord, B. E. (2003). Functional analysis of problem behavior: A review. *Journal of Applied Behavior Analysis*, 36(2), 147-185.

McConnell, S. R., Sisson, L. A., Cort, C. A., & Strain, P. S. (1991). Effects of social skills training and contingency management on reciprocal interaction of preschool children with behavioral handicaps. *The Journal of Special Education*, 24(4), 473-495.

Miller, D. L., & Kelley, M. L. (1994). The use of goal setting and contingency contracting for improving children's homework performance. *Journal of Applied Behavior Analysis*, 27(1), 73–84.

Miltenberger, R. G. (2011). *Behavior modification: Principles and procedures*. Cengage Learning.

Ring, B. M., Sigurdsson, S. O., Eubanks, S. L., & Silverman, K. (2014). Reduction of classroom noise levels using group contingencies. *Journal of Applied Behavior Analysis*, 47(4), 840–844.

Scott, T. M., Bucalos, A., Liaupsin, C., Nelson, C. M., Jolivette, K., & DeShea, L. (2004). Using functional behavior assessment in general education settings: Making a case for effectiveness and efficiency. *Behavioral Disorders*, 29(2), 189-204.

Zettle, R. D., Hayes, S. C., Barnes-Holmes, D., & Biglan, A. (2016). *The Wiley handbook of contextual behavioral science*. John Wiley & Sons.